International Economics
A Microeconomic Approach

International Economics

A Microeconomic Approach

Henry Thompson

Auburn University

Longman
New York & London

International Economics: A Microeconomic Approach

Longman, 10 Bank Street, White Plains, N.Y. 10606

Associated companies:
Longman Group Ltd., London
Longman Cheshire Pty., Melbourne
Longman Paul Pty., Auckland
Copp Clark Pitman, Toronto

Sponsoring editor: David J. Estrin
Development editor: Susan Alkana
Production editors: Cracom Corporation, Ann P. Kearns
Cover photo: Comstock Inc./Billy Brown
Text art: Cracom Corporation
Production supervisor: Anne P. Armeny

Library of Congress Cataloging-in-Publication Data

Thompson, Henry.
　　International economics : a microeconomic approach / Henry
　Thompson.
　　　　p.　　cm.
　　Includes index.
　　ISBN 0-8013-0860-7
　　1. International economic relations.　2. Microeconomics.
　I. Title.
　HF1359.T46　　1992
　337—dc20

92-34705
CIP

1 2 3 4 5 6 7 8 9 10-HA-9695949392

Brief Contents

Contents

CHAPTER 2   **CONSTANT COST PRODUCTION AND TRADE   37**

PART TWO   NEOCLASSICAL TRADE THEORY   73

CHAPTER 5   THE TERMS OF TRADE   140

CHAPTER 9   INTERNATIONAL ECONOMIC INTEGRATION   295

PART FIVE   INTERNATIONAL FINANCIAL ECONOMICS   329

CHAPTER 10   BALANCE OF PAYMENTS, DEFICITS, AND POLICY   331

CHAPTER 11   **FOREIGN EXCHANGE**   **365**

Note to Instructors

This text is unique in several ways. It is designed for a one-term course in international economics for students who have studied principles of economics. This text stresses the positive principles of microeconomics and price theory applied to the central issues in international economics.

THEMES OF THE TEXT

- Excess supply and excess demand
- Constant cost (Ricardian) production and trade
- The production possibility frontier: goods and services
- Offer curves
- Gains from trade
- Protectionism versus free trade
- Specific factors and factor proportions models
- Industrial organization and trade
- Trade policy and income redistribution
- International migration and capital movement
- The foreign exchange rate and trade
- Monetary policy and the exchange rate

Broadly interpreted, international economics covers the entire realm of economics, with national boundaries in the way. This text narrows its scope to microeconomic techniques, using general equilibrium analysis to study the entire economy. Unemployment is seen as arising from wage rigidities in the labor market.

The foreign exchange rate and concepts from the balance of payments are integrated throughout the text. International investment is approached conceptually through the market for loanable funds. The crucial role of the money supply in influencing the price level and the exchange rate is stressed.

AUDIENCE FOR THE TEXT

Macroeconomics of the 1950s and 1960s, income determination in a closed economy, is evolving into open economy macroeconomics. Certainly, the use of IS–LM and aggregate supply and demand analyses in the study of open economies is an important part of international economics. This macroeconomic material, however, belongs in a different course. The mid-term transition from microeconomics to macroeconomics is confusing and unfocused. Either a microeconomic or a macroeconomic approach clearly covers enough material for a complete undergraduate course in international economics. Macroeconomics and income determination are best left to specialists.

This text is designed for students who have not had intermediate theory and are not typically economics majors. Many colleges and universities require a "service" course in international economics for different majors in business and the liberal arts, and for the M.B.A. This text is aimed at students in such a course. A wealth of tools and ideas in international economics is within the grasp of the typical college student who has completed the principles of economics course.

PEDAGOGY

Graphs and Numerical Examples

Technical points in this text are made with graphs and numerical examples. Few algebraic symbols are used to carry out algebraic manipulation. A course in international economics is not the place to teach algebra to students who have not mastered the basics. Nor is it wise to spend time trying to teach the concepts of intermediate microeconomics to students who have not had that course. This text generally avoids use of first-order conditions from intermediate microeconomics and does not assume students have had the course. Students who have had intermediate theory will benefit from the thorough and careful development of theory.

Boxed Examples

The text includes 122 numbered examples. These examples are boxed material intended to give the student real-life illustrations of how to apply the theory being discussed.

Organization

Teaching with examples, this text takes students from partial equilibrium supply and demand analysis through the general equilibrium factor proportions model of production and trade and on to various models of industrial organization. The course is rounded off with studies of international factor movements, economic integration, and financial economics. The approach is simple, thorough, and rigorous.

Problems

Each chapter section is followed by a problem set that induces the student to use the tools and ideas just introduced. At the end of each chapter are Review Problems. These problems are central to the text, often introducing important ideas. Working problems encourages the student to progress through a relatively difficult subject in small steps. My teaching method involves calling on a number of students (at once) every class period to work problems at the board for credit. Going to the board keeps students actively learning throughout the term. Challenging problems can be assigned for credit. An *Instructor's Manual* is available.

You will enjoy teaching international economics from this text and be surprised at how much your students learn through this consistent, straightforward approach. Remember that international economics is the most difficult and challenging subject many of your students will take. It is up to you (and this text) to make it the most rewarding.

International Economics: A Microeconomic Approach is aimed at making the essentials of international economics accessible to the typical college student. As the U.S. economy opens itself increasingly to international markets, a broad understanding of the forces at work is essential to the success of your students and the nation.

ACKNOWLEDGMENTS

The author would like to thank the following reviewers for their helpful suggestions:

Adil Abdalla—Illinois State University
Kaz Miyagiwa—University of Washington
Richard Ault—Auburn University
James Hartigan—University of Oklahoma
Eden S. H. Yu—Louisiana State University
Richard E. Gift—University of Kentucky
E. Kwan Choi—Iowa State University

Others have offered suggestions and ideas that have wound up in this text. I cannot begin to credit everyone who deserves it. Teachers, colleagues, and students have contributed. Roy Ruffin, Joel Sailors, and Ron Jones provided inspirational examples of teachers and international economists at work. The Economics Department at Auburn University is full of excellent colleagues, every one. International economists at the Midwest and Southeastern Economic Theory Meetings are irreplaceable. The excellent manuscript staff at Auburn and the professional staff at Longman made the chore of writing the text possible. Students at Auburn have suffered through early drafts without too many complaints. My family (Madeline, Alexi, and Stacy) have put up with my working too much on the book, which is dedicated to them.

Writing a textbook is a humbling experience. The science of economics progresses bit by bit as we slowly build on the sweat of those before us. These pages reflect the efforts of all those who have gone into making international economics the exciting field it is today.

Note to Students

The goal of this text is to prepare you to understand the forces of international economics that will influence your private and business lives. International economics is intriguing because of its relevance and elegance. For many students, it is the most exciting sort of economics.

Nations are becoming more interdependent through increased international trade and investment. The world is effectively shrinking. Events in the Middle East may seem remote, but OPEC is an economic force affecting everyone. International migration and foreign investment contribute to the economic development of every nation, even the rich industrialized countries. The foreign exchange market is the largest and the single most important market in the world. Industries wax and wane in the face of global competition.

There are continual calls for government policy to cope with pressures on an economy open to international trade and investment. Industries seek tariffs and quotas to protect themselves from foreign competition. Protectionism distorts the pattern of international trade and ultimately lowers the overall standard of living. Tax policy handicaps domestic multinational firms trying to compete worldwide. Central banks attempt to fix the foreign exchange rate and pursue inconsistent monetary policies.

This text presents the microeconomic foundation of international trade and investment in a simple and rigorous fashion. Microeconomics is based on the study of markets, visualizing the economy as a vast collection of interdependent markets. International trade involves the foreign exchange market, where importers buy the foreign currency required to pay foreign exporters. The estimated balance of payments summarizes the nation's international commercial transactions. The role of government policy in international economics can be vital. The crucial issue of income redistribution that occurs as the result of trade and the array of government policies is studied with microeconomic tools.

International economics begins with the study of the production and exchange of goods and services between nations. Comparative advantage and the gains that come from specialization and trade are important concepts in economics. International economics doubly emphasizes this point. It would be difficult to estimate how much standards of living would fall if international specialization and trade were to decrease by even as little as 10%.

Why then do some groups lobby for tariffs and other restrictions on international trade? The answer is simply that these groups stand to gain from the particular restriction they favor. Their gain unfortunately comes at the expense of others. While there are theoretical situations in which a tariff can create overall gains, the costs of protection invariably outweigh the benefits.

The typical impetus to international trade is that the price of something is lower in one nation than in another. International arbitrage occurs when traders buy goods and services at a cheap foreign price and sell at a higher domestic price.

What causes prices of certain goods and services to be lower in some nations than in others? What determines the goods a nation exports and imports? What determines the level of trade?

What happens if a country's international trade is not balanced, if the value of its exports and the value of its imports do not match? What role does the foreign exchange rate play in international trade?

Which groups in a nation gain and which lose through tariffs and other forms of protection? Do the effects of protection vary depending on whether the foreign exporter is a monopolist, and oligopolist, or a competitive industry?

Why do domestic firms want to establish foreign branch plants, and why do foreign firms set up domestic operations? Why do some exporting firms sell their product to foreign importers, while other firms set up foreign distribution and marketing systems?

What is the effect of the foreign exchange rate on the pattern and volume of trade? How are trade deficits financed? How does a government's monetary policy affect the nation's pattern of international trade and investment?

These are the types of questions this text answers. International trade spans a wide variety of production and economic activity.

Minerals such as oil, gold, and copper can be produced and exported only if the resources are deposited inside the nation. The climate and soil of some nations are not suited to grow certain agricultural goods. The United States cannot readily grow bananas or coffee, while Panama and Colombia are not well suited for growing wheat. International trade in primary and agricultural products is best understood as arising from the physical geography and climate of particular regions.

For manufactured goods and services, an international difference in price is summarized through a comparison of the market supply and demand in each nation. Supply, based on the resources used in production, varies from nation to nation. Demand, based on tastes and income of local consumers, can vary as well.

Each of the thousands of international markets for particular goods and services is composed of hundreds of thousands of participants. These economic agents, both firms and consumers, make optimizing decisions based on their particular information, situation, and outlook. How can general statements or conclusions be made when the reality of international economics is so complex?

Like other sciences, economics builds simple models to capture the essence of what is being studied. The models are then tested, applied, and refined. International economists have been doing this scientific research for more than two hundred years. The classical model of comparative advantage and trade was one of the first scientific models and illuminates the pattern of trade today. The price–specie–flow mechanism is another successful economic model whose origins date back over two hundred years. This text develops and applies the fundamental scientific models of international economics that have developed as international economists search for understanding based on sound theory.

Through a consistent microeconomic approach to international economics, you will begin to understand the causes and effects of international trade and finance. All you need for background are the principles of economics. Numerous graphs, examples, applications, and problems are the tools of learning. Graphs summarize complex mechanisms and reinforce concepts. Examples and applications provide background and depth to illustrate and go beyond theory. Working the problems at the end of each section and chapter is essential for learning. Hints and answers for the even-numbered questions are provided at the end of the text.

I think you will enjoy *International Economics: A Microeconomic Approach.*

PART ONE

Introduction

CHAPTER 1

International Markets

CHAPTER PREVIEW

This chapter introduces the fundamental concepts of international trade. Among these are:

(a) *International markets,* where supply and demand from different countries interact
(b) *Excess supply and demand,* the basic tools used to study international markets
(c) *Comparative advantage,* which underlies observed international trade
(d) *The balance of trade,* which reports the net value of an economy's observed international trade in goods

INTRODUCTION

The most fundamental and important tools of economics are market supply and demand. A market is any place or mechanism in which buying and selling of goods and services takes place. Markets determine the value of goods and services, both in nominal or currency terms and relative to one another. Markets include everything from the corner convenience store to the stock market to the market for brain surgeons to the foreign exchange market to a neighborhood lemonade stand to the international market for steel. In market transactions, money changes hands between buyer and seller according to an agreed price.

An international transaction arises when the buyer and seller of a good or a service reside in different nations. International markets involve economic agents (consumers and firms) of different nations and cultures, which may make transaction costs higher than in domestic markets. Two currencies are involved in an international transaction, so the buyer's and the seller's currency must be exchanged.

Another fact that distinguishes international economics is that governments easily and selectively tax and limit transactions at the international border through tariffs, quotas, nontariff barriers, and financial restrictions. International economics is also different because of the lack of labor mobility between nations. Workers can move within a nation with relative ease, but international migration is more difficult and typically restricted by law. Investment is also more inhibited across national boundaries than within a nation.

An important concept introduced in this chapter is the balance of trade. The balance of trade regularly makes headlines, but exactly what it attempts to measure, how well it does so, and in what ways its level is important are rarely made clear. A crucial concept in international economics is comparative advantage, one of the cornerstones of economics. Comparative advantage, a relative edge in efficiency, is the fundamental cause of international trade. The principle of comparative advantage rests on the important idea of opportunity costs.

The opportunity cost of an action is the value of the next best alternative. When a nation turns its resources to producing a particular good or service, it is giving up producing alternative goods and services. Since productive resources or inputs are limited, it is important to employ them in the most efficient pattern internationally.

A.   INTERNATIONAL SUPPLY AND DEMAND

We are all involved in international markets every day. Almost everything we buy has some foreign element or component in it. Virtually every job provides something to our country's exports and uses imports. International markets provide a beginning toward understanding the complex world of international economics. This section presents the picture of an international market.

1.   Demand Curves

The law of demand states that as the price of a good rises, the quantity demanded falls. Examples of the law of demand are everywhere. If a clothing retailer wants to clear the shelves, lower prices will do the trick. Car dealers offer discounts and rebates when their inventories build too high. Fast food restaurants introduce specials with low prices to increase their volume of sales.

Figure 1.1 shows a domestic market demand curve *D* for new rugs. This demand curve represents the quantity of a particular quality of rug that would be demanded at various prices by domestic consumers. If the price of a rug is $15, 100 units (a unit could be 1,000) will be demanded per month. If the price is $10, 200 units will be demanded. If price falls to $5, consumers will want 300 units. Demand curves show how much consumers would want to buy at various prices.

Demand curves slope downward for two reasons:

(a) The *substitution effect*—a higher price for a good induces con- sumers to look for substitutes

(b) The *income effect*—a higher price of a good, especially one that makes up a large share of consumers' budgets, will lower real in- come and force consumption of all goods to fall.

A lower price for a good induces consumers to switch toward consuming it (the substitution effect) and raises real income to increase consumption of all goods (the income effect).

Some goods have readily available substitutes. If the price of beef rises with a quota on imported beef, consumers quickly switch to pork, chicken, lamb, or fish. If the price of electricity rises by 50% because of more expen- sive imported oil, people trade in their old electric appliances for new gas ones. If the price of Japanese autos rises with a new quota or voluntary export restraint, consumers switch to European or U.S. cars. If the price of Dutch cheese rises with a tariff, consumers switch to Wisconsin cheese.

Many other goods do not have such readily available substitutes. Inter- national telephone service has no good substitutes; international mail is slow, telegraph is impersonal, and so on. There is no good substitute for original artwork, since each artist produces a limited amount of work. Teak

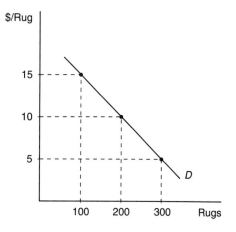

Figure 1.1. The Domestic Demand (D) for Rugs The quan- tity demanded is inversely related to price. When price goes up, the quantity demanded falls. When price goes down, the quantity demanded rises.

is a hard, durable wood from East India with no good substitutes. When fewer substitutes exist, demand is less responsive to price changes.

Embargoes of the Organization of Petroleum Exporting Countries (OPEC) during the 1970s significantly raised the price of crude oil. This meant that the price of gasoline rose relative to other goods. Consumers began to substitute away from gasoline consumption, but real incomes fell in the process. The higher relative price of gas lowered consumers' purchasing power. This income effect significantly lowered consumption of all goods. Another example of the income effect comes from the entry of Japanese autos into the U.S. market in the late 1960s. Japanese imports were much cheaper than cars made in the United States. Consumers who bought Japanese cars noticed their real incomes rising. The purchasing power of their income rose because they were spending less on transportation. They could consume more of all goods.

Many types of manufactured goods, from big screen television sets to shirts to refrigerators are traded internationally. The world of international economics is extremely complicated. It must be simplified by abstraction to permit an understanding of what is going on. The process of abstracting from the real world and simplifying is a crucial step in the scientific method. Scientists build and test simple models that reflect what goes on in the real world. If a theoretical model performs well by predicting what will happen in the real world, it becomes accepted theory. The demand curve in Figure 1.1 presents the first step of model building.

Demand curves slope downward because of the substitution effect and the income effect.

Demand curves will probably be much different across nations. Various factors determine the position of a demand curve:

(a) Tastes of consumers
(b) The number of potential consumers
(c) The price expectation of consumers
(d) Income of consumers
(e) Prices of related goods

Tastes affect demand in an obvious way. As consumer tastes for a good become stronger, demand for the good grows and the demand curve shifts to the right. This means that consumers will be willing to pay a higher price for the same quantity of the good. Put another way, consumers will demand more of the good at any price.

Tastes change and are difficult to analyze. Only 25 years ago, consumers in the United States had little taste for Japanese cars and did not trust Japanese electronics. Imported beer, beverages, food, bicycles, and clothes were rare. Advertising is one way to change tastes. Foreign firms spend resources advertising their products in the United States. Advertising can inform consumers of product quality and of new products. In the same way, U.S. firms advertise abroad.

An increase in the number of potential consumers in a market increases demand. As nations grow in population, the demand for goods and services grows. When a nation enters into international trade, the number of potential buyers of its products expands, increasing demand. The U.S.-Canadian free trade pact increases the demand for the goods of both nations by eliminating protection between the two nations. When the U.S. government outlaws trade with Cuba, potential consumers are taken away and the demand for U.S. exports falls. When Europe opens its protected agricultural industry to free trade, the demand for U.S. agricultural products increases.

Expectations of higher prices induce consumers to buy now in order to avoid higher prices later, increasing the current demand. When approval of the U.S. free trade agreement with Canada was pending, U.S. buyers of Canadian lumber waited when possible for the tariff to be eliminated. In this case the expectation of lower prices in the future lowered present demand. With news that the Ukranian wheat harvest is expected to be poor, buyers of wheat expect higher prices in the future, increasing their demand in the present.

Higher income raises demand for *normal* goods but lowers demand for *inferior* goods. Income limits what consumers can spend on all goods and services. As income rises, consumers increase spending and save some of their income for future consumption. The Japanese save a larger share of their personal income than most people. As incomes rise in newly industrializing nations such as South Korea, Mexico, and Brazil, their demand for normal goods rises. This increases the demand for U.S. exports of business services. Demand for public transport, a typical inferior good, may decline in these countries as more people switch to private cars.

Many goods are related in consumption. Coffee and tea, broadly speaking, are *substitute* beverages. One can be used in place of the other. When the price of coffee rose in the early 1970s as the international coffee cartels restricted output, demand for tea increased. Demand for a good is positively related to the price of its substitutes. Other examples of substitutes are new versus used cars, public versus private transport, and junior college education versus university education. Coffee and sugar are *complements*. The two are used together. If the price of sugar tripled, demand for coffee would fall. Demand for a good is negatively related to the price of its complements. Other examples of complements are gas and tires, cereal and milk, and tuition and textbooks.

When the demand curve in Figure 1.1 increases because of any of these nonprice influences, it shifts to the right. At a price of $15, consumers will want to buy more than 100 units. To consume 200 units, consumers will be willing to pay more than $10 per unit. A decrease in demand would be represented as a shift of D to the left. Consumers will buy less at the same price or pay less for the same quantity when demand decreases.

Demand curves shift to the right (increase) or left (decrease) because of nonprice influences, some of which can be international in origin.

2. Supply Curves

Supply curves are based on the costs of production of the firms in an industry. *Marginal cost* is the additional or extra cost of producing one more unit of output. Marginal cost slopes upward for two reasons:

(a) *Diminishing marginal productivity* of the inputs (land, labor, and capital)
(b) Increasing output, which may bid up the prices of the inputs it hires

Evidence for the law of diminishing marginal productivity is overwhelming. The law says that the additional output per unit of an added input declines as the input is increased, holding other inputs constant. For any given physical plant or productive facility, the marginal product of additional workers declines after some point. For some large industries, increasing output will also mean higher demand for inputs and higher input prices.

The marginal cost curve of a typical firm thus slopes upward. When output in an industry rises, firms within the industry are producing more or new firms are entering the industry. Output in an industry will generally rise only when the price of output in the industry rises. Thus there is a positive association between price and output.

Figure 1.2 shows the upward sloping domestic supply of a manufac-

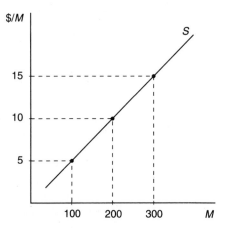

Figure 1.2. The Domestic Supply (S) of Manufactures (M)
The quantity supplied is positively associated with price. When price goes up, the quantity supplied rises. When price goes down, the quantity supplied falls.

tured good. Supply curves are likely to differ across nations. The following influence the position of the supply curve:

(a) Technology
(b) The number of firms
(c) Price expectations of firms
(d) Prices of productive inputs

Improved technology means that firms can produce more output with the same amount of inputs. Fuel efficient jet engines have enabled the cost of international air travel to fall. With the same amount of labor, fuel, and other inputs, airline companies can supply more passenger miles at the same price, or lower the price for the same quantity of travel. This improved technology is represented as a shift of the supply of air travel to the right, an increase in supply. An increase in the supply of international telecommunication occurs as satellite transmission improves.

An increase in the number of firms in an industry also increases supply. A good example of this occurred in the personal computer (PC) market. The original PCs were made by a few companies, which consequently enjoyed high prices and profits. Other firms began to enter the industry, many of them foreign firms or domestic firms using foreign components. As firms entered the market, supply rose and price fell. PCs that might have sold for $5,000 were soon selling for $2,000.

Lower input prices also increase supply. Many U.S. manufacturing firms import intermediate inputs. Consider a tariff on imported television components. A tariff is a tax on an imported good that must be paid at the border. Suppose the tariff is lowered. This decreases the price of inputs used in making televisions inside the United States. Firms would be willing to produce more televisions at the same price, or they would be willing to lower price for the same output.

Labor, natural resources, and capital equipment are productive inputs or factors used to produce goods and services. A change in the price or wage for labor, for instance, shifts the supply of manufactures. For example, the immigration of Latin Americans lowers wages in the labor markets they enter. Lower wages in turn increase the supply of manufactured goods.

If firms expect higher prices in the future, they will hoard their products, decreasing current supply. If firms expect lower prices in the future, they will want to sell off their inventories, increasing current supply.

The international oil market provides a classic example of how expectations of prices affect current supply. International oil dealers and brokers stockpile oil, buying it from oil producers and selling it to refineries or other dealers and brokers. If an OPEC meeting breaks up in disagreement, dealers expect oil prices to fall. An OPEC agreement keeps oil prices high by restricting output among the member countries. Falling oil prices mean the stockpiles held by brokers and dealers will be worth less in the future.

Now is the time to sell, so supply increases immediately and price falls right away. When OPEC is able to keep peace among its members, dealers expect high prices in the future and build up their inventories, decreasing current supply and increasing price right away.

> Supply curves slope upward, reflecting the higher marginal cost typically associated with increasing output. Supply curves shift because of nonprice influences, which can be international in origin.

3. Changes in Supply and Demand versus Changes in Quantity Supplied and Demanded

Shifts in supply or demand curves must be distinguished from movements along the curves. A change in price causes a change in the quantity supplied or demanded along the curve. A change in a nonprice influence shifts the entire supply or demand curve. Students are invariably confused about this distinction and often miss the point on an exam or in a newspaper article. In fact, journalists are often confused themselves and fail to explain correctly the underlying economics.

4. Markets and Market Clearing

The domestic market for manufactures is pictured in Figure 1.3. It is composed of domestic demand and supply. The domestic *equilibrium price* is determined where the quantity buyers are willing to consume just equals the quantity suppliers are willing to produce. In this example the equilibrium price is $10/unit. Firms produce 200 units, which are exactly consumed at the equilibrium price.

At any other price the quantities supplied and demanded would not be equal. At a price of $15, production at 300 is greater than consumption at 100 and inventories increase by 200 units per time period. Suppliers

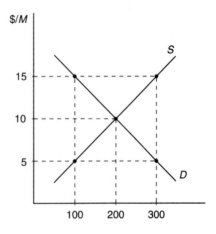

Figure 1.3. The Domestic Market for Manufactures (M) Domestic supply (S) and demand (D) interact to determine the domestic equilibrium price of $10 and the domestic equilibrium quantity of 200. The equilibrium price equates the quantity supplied with the quantity demanded.

naturally want to lower the price to keep their inventories from accumulating. At a price of $5, desired consumption at 300 is greater than production at 100. Consumers naturally bid up the price in competition for the underpriced good. The excess demand of 200 units is eliminated through a rising price.

This market clearing mechanism is fundamental in economics. It explains why government policymakers cannot arbitrarily set prices and expect the economy to respond with desired production and consumption. Suppose a government official thinks a $5 price of manufactures is desirable. A price ceiling is put into effect, a law that will not allow the price to go above $5. Buyers will want 300 units, but suppliers will produce only 100. They have no incentive, given the costs of production, to make more than 100 units. Somehow the 100 units that are produced must be allocated among the consumers clamoring for 300 units. A black market may arise, with the good quietly changing hands at $15, the price that allocates the good to those willing to pay the high price. The government may allocate coupons or other devices to determine who gets the goods at the artificially low price.

At the other extreme, a government policymaker may decide that a $15 price floor or support would benefit the manufacturing industry. Firms respond to the high price by expanding output, but consumers will not buy the 300 units produced. The government may buy up the surplus, as happens with U.S. agriculture. Otherwise the goods will begin to overflow in the warehouses. The only price that matches the quantity suppliers produce with the quantity buyers demand is the market clearing equilibrium price of $10.

A market clears at the equilibrium price, which equates quantity demanded with quantity supplied.

5. International Markets

In the international market for a particular good, there are buyers at home as well as buyers in other nations. Imagine there are only two nations. Figure 1.4 shows the markets for manufactured goods M in two nations, home and foreign. In the figure, asterisks are used for the foreign nation. Since supply and demand are different between nations, price is almost always different. In this example the equilibrium price in the home market is $10 and the equilibrium price in the foreign market is 250 yen.

When comparing price in the foreign country with the prices at home, traders must convert to a common currency. This conversion is necessary first to determine where the good is cheaper and then to carry out the transaction. This is the role of the foreign exchange market. The *exchange rate* is expressed as the dollar value of the yen ($/yen) or the yen value of the dollar (yen/$). The exchange rate is the price of one currency in terms

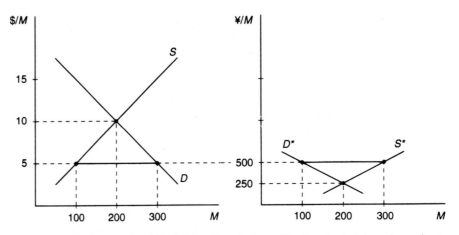

Figure 1.4. The International Market for Manufactures (M) Free trade takes place where the excess demand from one country equals the excess supply from the other country. At a price of $5/M, excess demand of 200 from the home country equals excess supply of 200 from the foreign country. The foreign country will export 200 units of manufactures to the home country. S = supply; D = demand; asterisks are used for the foreign country.

of another. In the example in Figure 1.4, the exchange rate is assumed to be $/yen = 0.01 or yen/$ = 100. Each yen buys one cent, and it takes 100 yen to buy $1.

This international market offers an opportunity for trade or *arbitrage*. Traders can begin buying manufactured goods in the foreign nation at a price of 250 yen or $2.50 = 250 × 0.01. This is less than the $10 domestic price. Traders want to buy goods where they are cheap and transport them to where they are more expensive. In Figure 1.4, manufactured goods are cheap before trade in the foreign nation. It is profitable to buy the goods in the foreign nation and sell them in the home nation. This arbitrage across national markets is the foundation for all international transactions.

International trade occurs at a price where quantity demanded outweighs quantity supplied in one nation by the same amount as quantity supplied outweighs quantity demanded in the other. At any other price the amount one country is willing to export will not equal the amount another country wants to import.

An international price of $5 clears the market in Figure 1.4. The home country imports 200 = 300 − 100 units of M at a price of $5 or 500 yen. This is an import market for the home nation. Domestic firms produce 100 units of output at the international price. Domestic production falls from 200 to 100 with the opening of international trade and falling price. Domestic consumers enjoy lower prices with international trade and increase the quantity they demand from 200 to 300 units.

On the foreign side, production rises from 200 to 300 with the increase in price from 250 yen to 500 yen. Foreign consumers suffer higher prices, cutting their level of consumption from 200 down to 100.

International trade creates winners and losers. In an export market, domestic firms are made better off while consumers suffer. In an import market, the domestic industry suffers while consumers benefit. Since efficiency is improved through international trade, global benefits outweigh costs. There are overall gains from trade. Sound arguments and overwhelming evidence favor free trade.

> International markets arise where domestic market prices vary across nations. International markets clear at a price where the excess of demand over supply in an importing nation matches the excess of supply over demand from the exporting nation.

In practice, international traders are also concerned with *transport costs,* which include shipping, storage, insurance, delivery, and so on. If each unit of M in Figure 1.4 cost $6 to transport from the foreign country, imported goods would cost $5 + $6 = $11 above the domestic market price. An importer who disregards transport costs would soon be out of business! For simplicity, transport costs are assumed to be zero in Figure 1.4 and through most of the text, unless mentioned explicitly.

The model of international markets has been repeatedly tested using data and experience from actual international markets. This fundamental model of international markets has become widely accepted theory. International economists rely on the scientific method to build, test, and revise the theory of international trade.

EXAMPLE 1.1   Growing International Trade

International Trade, published by the General Agreement on Tariffs and Trade (GATT), presents a picture of steadily increasing international trade in manufactures, minerals, and agriculture. World commodity output has increased dramatically since 1950, and international commodity trade has increased at an even faster rate. There is also increased international trade in business and other services, which are not included in these figures. Even more impressive is the growth of international financial transactions. International markets are extremely busy places. With free international trade and finance, gains are enjoyed all around. The odds are good that the firm you work for will be involved in international transactions. From 1950 to 1970 the world's capacity to produce output nearly tripled, growing by 186%. The yearly level of trade in commodities (raw materials and manufactured goods) grew 355% (four-and-a-half times). Growth in world production and trade has been more modest since 1970, but the total level of world trade has still nearly doubled since then.

Growth	*1950 to 1969*	*1970 to 1986*
In world output	186%	55%
In commodity trade	355%	85%

EXAMPLE 1.2   The Weight of U.S. Exports and Imports

According to data from *International Financial Statistics,* published by the International Monetary Fund (IMF), the United States produces about 40% of the gross national product (GNP) of all industrial nations, making it the world's largest economy. It leads all nations in the share of international trade. These percentages of exports in total world exports are reported in the first column of the accompanying tabulation. Even though trade in the United States is big relative to world trade, trade in the United States is small relative to the size of the economy. Ratios of exports to GNP for these same nations are presented in the second column.

	Exports/World Exports	*Exports/GNP*
United States	15%	7%
West Germany (former)	11%	32%
Japan	9%	13%
United Kingdom	6%	26%
France	5%	18%
Canada	4%	27%
Italy	4%	18%
The rest	60%	——

The U.S. economy is very large and productive, involved much less than other economies in international trade. The U.S. economy is described as a closed giant. The percentage of exports plus imports relative to GNP is 21% for the United States and ranges from 40% to 50% for Europe and Japan. The United States has become much more open over the past 20 years. Its volume of trade relative to GNP continues to rise.

Problems for Section A

A1.   Draw the shift in the demand curve for manufactured goods in the home country if the quantity demanded at every price in Figure 1.1 increases by 200. Find the new domestic market equilibrium price and quantity in a market diagram similar to Figure 1.3.

A2.   Predict what will happen to the international price and quantity traded of manufactured goods in Figure 1.4 with an improvement in technology in the domestic market.

A3.   Suppose the domestic wage of manufacturing labor rises because of a new labor contract. Diagram a new domestic supply curve, and show what happens in the international market of Figure 1.4.

A4.   Create a diagram similar to Figure 1.4 in which demand in both nations is identical and trade arises because of differences in supply. Create another diagram in which supply is identical across nations but differences in demand give rise to trade.

B.   INTERNATIONAL EXCESS SUPPLY AND DEMAND

This section introduces the important tools of excess supply and demand, tools that simplify the picture of international markets. The difference between the quantity demanded and the quantity supplied at any price is called the market's *excess demand*. The difference between the quantity supplied and the quantity demanded at any price in a market is called *excess supply*. When these concepts are used, the model of an international market in Figure 1.4 can be reduced to a simpler diagram with only two curves.

1.   International Excess Demand

At the domestic market clearing price of $10, excess demand *XD* at home is zero, as pictured by the *XD* curve in Figure 1.5. At lower prices, excess demand becomes positive. At $5, *XD* is 200, since home firms would produce 100 units and home consumers would buy 300 units. The home nation is willing to import 200 units at an international price of $5. The *XD* curve in Figure 1.5 is derived from the supply and demand curves of the home country in Figure 1.4.

An increase in domestic demand will shift the home country's *XD* curve. Suppose an increase in demand drives the domestic equilibrium price up to $12.50. Excess demand increases as in Figure 1.6. *XD* has become zero at $12.50. This increase in *XD* makes the home nation more willing to import manufactures. At any international price the nation will want to import more. At $10 the quantity imported jumps from zero to 100. At $5, imports jump from 200 to 300. Decreased supply resulting from ris-

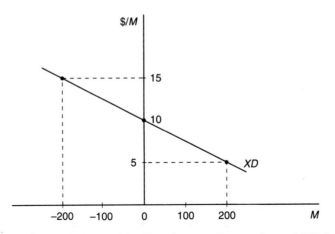

Figure 1.5. Home Excess Demand for Manufactures Excess demand (XD) is inversely related to price. When price rises, XD falls. At P (price) = $10, XD = 0. When P < $10, the quantity demanded is greater than the quantity supplied, and XD > 0. At prices above $10, there is negative excess demand or positive excess supply.

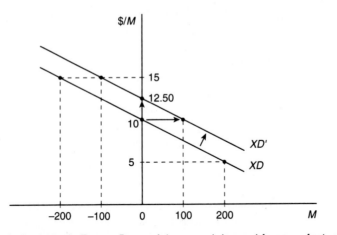

Figure 1.6. An Increase in Excess Demand Increased demand for manufactures in the home country has the effect of shifting the excess demand (XD) for manufactures (M) to the right. Decreased supply of manufactures in the home country has the same effect. The difference between the quantity demanded and quantity supplied rises at every price.

ing costs in a particular market will also cause the nation to become more of an importer of the good associated with the rise in cost.

An increase in domestic supply has the opposite effect on home *XD* for manufactures. The home nation becomes less willing to import manufactures. At any price, *XD* falls. This can be visualized by a shift from *XD'* to *XD* in Figure 1.6. At $5, home imports would drop from 200 to 100. The increased domestic supply and falling *XD* switch the economy away from importing manufactures. Decreased demand or increased supply causes *XD* to fall.

> Excess demand shows the quantity of a good a country wants to import at every price. International excess demand shifts whenever the nation's underlying supply or demand shifts.

2. International Excess Supply

Excess supply from the foreign country can be derived from the foreign demand and supply curves in Figure 1.4. Foreign excess supply of manufactures is labelled *XS** in Figure 1.7. At the foreign market clearing price of 250 yen ($2.50 by the exchange rate), *XS** is zero. As price increases, *XS** rises. At 500 yen ($5), *XS** equals 200 *M*. Changes in foreign supply and demand shift foreign excess supply, similar to the shifts discussed previously for excess demand. A good exercise at this point is to diagram shifts in *XS** resulting from increases and decreases in foreign supply and demand.

> International excess supply shows the quantity of a good a country wants to export at every price. Excess supply shifts whenever the nation's underlying supply or demand shifts.

3. International Markets Again

In a viable international market at the current exchange rate, excess demand from one nation equals excess supply from the other at a certain price. If not, the market will have no international trade. The interaction

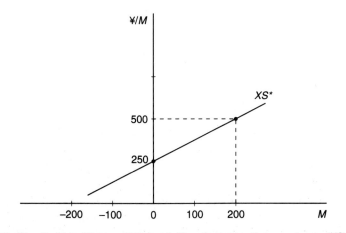

Figure 1.7. The Foreign Excess Supply of Manufactures Excess supply (*XS*) is positively related to price (*P*). As price rises, the quantity supplied by the foreign country rises and the quantity demanded by the foreign country falls. When *P* > 250 yen, *XS** > 0. At prices below 250 yen, there is negative excess supply or positive excess demand from the foreign country.

of international excess supply and excess demand determines the quantity traded and the *international equilibrium price* of the traded good. In the international market of Figure 1.8, the international price of manufactured goods is $5 (500 yen). The excess supply that is left after consumption in the foreign country is just matched by the excess demand at home when the common international price is $5. The market for these manufactured goods clears internationally.

At an international price below $5, $XD > XS^*$ and there is a shortage of manufactures on the international market. Exporters in the foreign nation will notice they cannot meet the high production level, and their inventories start declining. Importers want to buy more than exporters are willing to produce. This is a clear signal for foreign producers and exporters to raise the price.

If the international price is above $5, $XS^* > XD$ and there is an international excess supply. Producers are making more than they can sell, and inventories accumulate. The best way to move merchandise is to lower the price, which is exactly what happens. The international equilibrium price balances the forces of supply and demand across nations. An automatic adjustment process pushes the international market toward the international equilibrium price of $5 with the quantity of goods traded at 200.

> International markets clear at a price at which excess demand from importing countries equals excess supply from exporting countries.

For simplicity, transport costs, which include shipping, handling, and insurance, are assumed to be zero. These costs can of course be crucial in

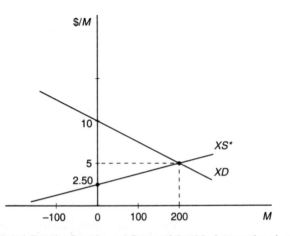

Figure 1.8. International Excess Supply and Demand In this international market for manufactures, the foreign country exports 200 units of *M* to the home country. The international equilibrium price of $5 equates excess demand (*XD*) from the home country with excess supply (*XS**) from the foreign country. In this example, there is an exchange rate of yen/$ = 100.

determining whether a good is traded internationally. Gravel, cement, and similar goods are heavy relative to their value and cost too much to ship internationally. At the other extreme, the ratio of weight to value is low for electronic components and drugs, goods that are traded heavily.

4.   Shifting Excess Supply and Excess Demand

A point worth emphasizing is the importance of the exchange rate in determining international prices and the level of trade. An exchange rate of $/yen = 0.01 results in the international price of $5 and trade level of 200 units of M in Figure 1.8. If the dollar depreciates in the foreign exchange market, its value falls and the value of the yen rises. This *currency depreciation* means the exchange rate $/yen rises; the same dollar price of manufactures from Japan translates into a lower yen price.

Since the foreign manufacturers do business in yen, they are concerned with the yen price they receive for their goods. With XS^* a function of the dollar price, the foreign nation supplies less at every dollar price when the dollar depreciates. The yen appreciation creates a reduction of XS^* as pictured in Figure 1.9. The international price (in dollars) rises, and the volume of trade falls. The price of imports in the home nation rises, and the quantity imported falls.

A reduction in foreign supply of manufactures, resulting perhaps from higher costs or declining technology, will also cause XS^* to fall as in Figure 1.9. An increase in foreign demand for manufactures, perhaps because of higher income or changing tastes, will cause the same decline in XS^*. On the other hand, a depreciating yen, an increase in foreign supply, or a de-

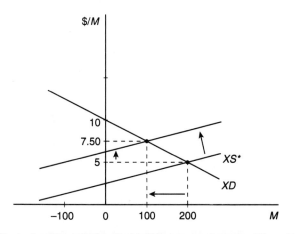

Figure 1.9. The Effect of a Depreciating Home Currency on Imports When $/yen rises, foreign excess supply (XS^*) falls. Dollar prices translate into lower yen prices for foreign producers. The decline in foreign excess supply pushes up the international dollar price of manufactures and lowers the level of trade. A depreciation raises the price of imports and lowers the level of imports. XD is excess demand in the home country.

crease in foreign demand will cause an increase in *XS**. The international dollar price of manufactures will then fall as the quantity traded increases.

Other international changes can be illustrated with an excess supply and demand diagram. Suppose the home nation is specializing away from manufactured goods, producing more services and agricultural goods for international trade. As the number of domestic manufacturing firms declines, domestic supply falls, resulting in an increase in excess demand as pictured in Figure 1.10. In this situation a higher international price comes with a higher volume of trade. In Figure 1.10 the international price rises to $6.25 and the quantity traded rises to 300. An increase in *XD* could be caused by an increase in domestic demand, perhaps resulting from an increase in income or the number of consumers.

As another application, suppose the trading partners are involved in negotiations to lower protection against imports. Tariffs (taxes on imports) are one form of protection. Quotas (quantitative limits on imports) are another popular form of protection. Current examples of trade negotiations are those between the United States and both Canada and Mexico, as well as those among the European nations. Domestic producers competing with foreign exporters expect lower prices and falling profits when trade is liberalized. This anticipation of falling prices causes some domestic producers, the most inefficient, to exit the industry. Domestic supply falls and *XD* rises. A higher international price and more trade occur, as in Figure 1.10.

Anything that affects the underlying supply or demand in a trading country shifts its excess demand or excess supply, changing the international price and quantity traded.

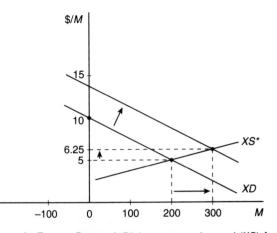

Figure 1.10. An Increase in Excess Demand Rising excess demand (*XD*) for manufactures (*M*) from the home country increases the international price of manufactures from $5 to $6.25 and raises the level of trade from 200 to 300. *XS** is excess supply in the foreign country.

EXAMPLE 1.3   International Trade in Manufactured Goods

The broadest division of what is produced is between goods and services. Goods (cars, stereos, sweatshirts, food, and so on) are thought of as having a physical existence. Services (of the mechanic, plumber, barber, accountant, economist, and so on) are embodied more in the direct labor. The old saying is that you cannot drop a service on your foot. World trade in manufactured goods is summarized in these figures from the *International Financial Statistics* of the IMF. Most manufactured goods (65%) come from industrial nations such as the United States, Japan, and Europe. Most of these exports (72%) from industrial nations are shipped to other industrial nations. Eastern Bloc nations (the former Soviet republics, Yugoslavia, East Germany, etc.) account for only 10% of the world trade in manufactures, and trade mostly among themselves. Developing nations in Africa, South America, and Asia produce 25% of the world's exports of manufactures. Most of their exported manufactures (65%) are shipped to the industrial nations.

From Industrial Nations			*From Developing Nations*		
to:	Industrial	72%	*to:*	Industrial	65%
	Developing	23%		Developing	26%
	East	5%		East	8%

EXAMPLE 1.4   The World's Largest Industrial Firms

Rank	Company	Headquarters	Product	Sales ($billions)
1	General Motors	Detroit	Motor vehicles	$102
2	Shell	The Hague	Oil refining	78
3	Exxon	New York	Oil refining	76
4	Ford	Dearborn, MI	Motor vehicles	72
5	IBM	Arnouk, NY	Computers	54
6	Mobil	New York	Oil refining	51
7	British Petroleum	London	Oil refining	45
8	Toyota	Japan	Motor vehicles	41
9	IRI	Rome	Metals	41

10	General Electric	Fairfield, CT	Electronics	39
14	Du Pont	Wilmington, DE	Chemicals	30
20	Unilever	London	Food	27

SOURCE: *Fortune* (1 August 1988).

Problems for Section B

B1. If the exchange rate rises above yen/\$ = 100 (the dollar appreciates), show what happens in the international market for manufactures in Figure 1.8.

B2. Illustrate the effects of a simultaneous decrease in domestic demand and increase in domestic supply on the country's international excess demand diagram. Predict what will happen to the international price and quantity traded.

B3. Suppose Japan imports wood and the domestic Japanese supply of lumber rises when a planted forest matures. Show the effect on the international market for lumber, assuming excess supply comes from the United States.

C. THE BALANCE OF TRADE

Can the home country simply import manufactured goods, or is there more to trade? Trade implies exchanging one thing for something else: my marbles for your pocketknife, manufactured goods for ... ? Imports are goods that we are able to enjoy consuming without having to spend valuable resources producing. Exports are goods that we have to go to the trouble of producing and cannot enjoy consuming. Importing firms and ultimately consumers in the home country must pay firms in the foreign country for the goods that they import. When thousands of goods are traded internationally among hundreds of nations, how is a balance struck? This section begins to examine this question by introducing the balance of trade.

1. International Transactions

Considered as a whole, the nation pays for some or all of its imports with the foreign currency it collects through exports. The foreign exchange earned on exports is spent on imports. In any economy, thousands or millions of individual transactions take place every day. Each individual firm or consumer makes the best choice given available information, prices, budgets, and so on. A wheat broker looks for the best place to sell wheat. If the broker sells to the Russians, it is because they offer the best price. Car buyers look for the best deal for their money. If they decide to buy Japanese cars, it is because they perceive Japanese cars to be better bargains.

When an exported good is sold from the United States, the foreign importer must convert local currency into dollars to pay the U.S. exporter. This involves a bank or foreign exchange dealer who is willing to trade one currency for the other. The foreign importer trades the local currency for dollars. The dollars are then paid to the U.S. exporter or transferred into the exporter's bank account. When an importer in the United States buys foreign goods, dollars must be traded for foreign currency to pay the foreign exporter. The U.S. importer has to find a bank or foreign exchange dealer willing to trade dollars for the foreign currency. Traders can keep bank accounts in foreign currency to avoid frequent foreign exchange transactions.

2. Finding the Balance of Trade

The *balance of trade* (BOT) is the difference between *export revenue* and *import expenditure* for the nation:

$$\text{BOT} = X - M = (P_{\text{exp}} \times Q_{\text{exp}}) - (P_{\text{imp}} \times Q_{\text{imp}})$$

The BOT regularly makes the headlines and the evening news. It is called a trade deficit when negative and a trade surplus when positive.

A typical nation exports many types of goods. For simplicity, however, suppose that agricultural goods are the one type that is exported. The United States is a net exporter of agricultural goods and will probably continue to specialize in their production. The international market for agricultural goods, with domestic excess supply and foreign excess demand, is pictured in Figure 1.11. The exchange rate is taken to be yen/$ = 100. In the foreign country the price would be 1,500 yen ($15) per unit of agricultural good if there were no trade. The price without trade is called the foreign *autarky price. Autarkeia* is an ancient Greek word meaning self-sufficient.

Excess supply comes from the home country, where the autarky price would be $5. The international market clears at $10 (1,000 yen) with 100 units of agricultural goods exported from the home to the foreign country. Export revenue for the home country is $10 × 100 = $1,000. Suppose import expenditure on manufactures for the home country is also $1,000, as in Figure 1.8. The balance of trade for the home country in this situation is zero. Trade is balanced.

Balanced trade almost never occurs in the real world, where international markets for thousands of different goods are working simultaneously. Suppose, for instance, a bumper crop of agricultural goods is enjoyed in the importing country pictured in Figure 1.8. Foreign supply increases, lowering foreign excess demand (*XD**). This causes the world price of agricultural goods to fall below $10 and the level of home country exports to fall below 100. Import revenue for the home country clearly falls

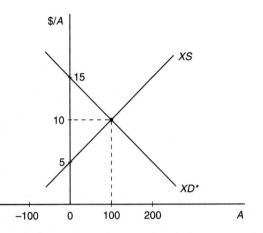

Figure 1.11. The International Market for Agricultural Goods Excess supply (*XS*) from the home country and excess demand (*XD**) from the foreign country meet at an international equilibrium price of $10, with 100 units of agricultural goods (*A*) exported from the home country to the foreign country.

below $1,000, creating a BOT deficit. There are, however, forces that create a tendency for an economy to move toward balanced trade in the long run.

> The balance of trade reports the difference between revenue from exports and spending on imports. It is the international net flow of cash resulting from trade in goods.

Table 1.1 shows the merchandise balance of trade for the United States in dollars per household, given the estimated 90 million households. Manufacturing firms in the United States like to suggest that a trade deficit is the cause of many economic ills. Their suggested remedy is protection, which allows their relatively inefficient manufacturing production to continue. When viewed on a household basis, the dollar amounts of the merchandise trade deficit have not been overwhelming. Both exports and imports are growing as the U.S. economy becomes more open. Before 1970 the United States had chronic BOT surpluses. The BOT deficits in recent years are offset in part by surpluses in service trade. Furthermore, most experts agree that the quantity of exports is significantly underestimated.

3. Trade Deficits

What happens if a country spends more on imports than it receives from exports? A deficit in one nation will be mirrored by trade surpluses in other nations. Essentially, a country with a deficit may:

(a)   Borrow internationally (go into debt), or
(b)   Spend its stock of savings (sell equity)

TABLE 1.1. U.S. Merchandise Balance of Trade ($/household)

Year	Exports	Imports	Net
1975	$1190	−$1091	$99
1976	$1275	−$1380	−$105
1977	$1342	−$1688	−$346
1978	$1578	−$1956	−$378
1979	$2050	−$2356	−$306
1980	$2492	−$2775	−$283
1981	$2634	−$2945	−$311
1982	$2347	−$2752	−$405
1983	$2241	−$2988	−$747
1984	$2444	−$3694	−$1250
1985	$2399	−$3756	−$1357
1986	$2493	−$4097	−$1604
1987	$2781	−$4553	−$1772
1988	$3559	−$4970	−$1411
1989	$4005	−$5281	−$1276

SOURCE: From *Economic Report of the President*, p. 414, U.S. Department of Commerce, 1990, Washington, DC: U.S. Government Printing Office.

Debt is often essential for economic growth. Firms borrow to invest in capital equipment they need to increase future productivity. Consumers assume the debt of a mortgage to buy a place to live, borrow to buy a car, or borrow to go to college. Debt creates the means to enjoy growth and future increased productivity. Nations likewise often must go into debt if they want to grow.

A deficit in the balance of trade arises when the nation spends more on buying imports than it receives from selling exports.

Mercantilism is an ancient and mistaken belief that deficits should be avoided. Scrooge was a devout mercantilist, bent on hoarding wealth (gold). As Adam Smith preached 200 years ago in *The Wealth of Nations,* wealth is not measured by the amount of gold or money that is amassed. Productivity is the true measure of wealth. It is perfectly rational to go into debt or sell assets to acquire capital that will increase productivity in the future. As a college student, you are doing just that, acquiring human capital. Growing nations must typically experience BOT deficits, importing the capital machinery and equipment that increase productivity.

There is another good reason not to become too excited over the BOT figures reported on the evening news. They are not very reliable. Figures reported in the United States are accumulated through surveys done by the Department of Commerce. Margins of error are large, and revisions of earlier estimates never make the news. Nations keep better records on imports that are subject to tariffs and quotas. The United States underestimates its merchandise exports, as other nations' data on imports from the United States clearly indicate. Using Canadian data on imports from the United States, recent studies question whether the United States has had a trade deficit at all during the 1980s.

Another mistake to avoid when thinking about trade deficits is to concentrate on bilateral trade with one nation. The United States has recently had BOT deficits with Japan. Figure 1.12 shows how their trade with the rest of the world (ROW) might be arranged. The United States has a trade deficit with Japan; Japan has a deficit with ROW; and ROW has a deficit with the United States. These bilateral deficits can be totally offset, however, by the bilateral surpluses in the opposite direction. The United States has a trade surplus with Europe; Europe has a surplus with Japan; and Japan has a surplus with the United States. When more than two countries are trading, trade may be persistently imbalanced between any pair, yet remain balanced overall.

Even in the face of a trade deficit, it is not clear that any government policy should be undertaken to remedy it. Automatic adjustment processes lead to international balance over time. Economists can be classified according to those who believe markets work as efficiently as anything could, and those who do not. The latter favor active government policy to remedy economic imbalances or ills. To be successful, a policymaker must recognize an economic illness and act in a timely fashion.

If economics teaches us anything, it is that government policy is not an automatic cure. The analogy between economics and medicine can be extended. Every policy (medicine) has side effects, which may make the economy (the patient) worse off than allowing the economy's (the body's) own automatic adjustment to work. In some cases medicine can save lives, but in other cases the cure is worse than the illness.

EXAMPLE 1.5   Regional Trade Flows Relative to Total World Trade

This diagram summarized from data in the *Direction of Trade Yearbook* (1990), published by the IMF, presents the volume of flows between re-

Figure 1.12. Multilateral Trade Balance Trade in this example can be balanced for each nation—the United States (U.S.), Japan, and the rest of the world (ROW)—while bilateral deficits persist. The United States has a bilateral deficit with Japan; Japan has a bilateral deficit with the rest of the world; and the rest of the world has a bilateral deficit with the United States. Still, multilateral or global trade is balanced.

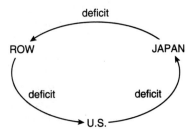

gions of the world as percentages of total world trade. In 1989, merchandise trade totaled $3.1 trillion in the world. The listed trade flows add up to only 17% of total world trade. Other flows among these regions are each less than 1% of total world trade. There is also international trade within the regions of the diagram.

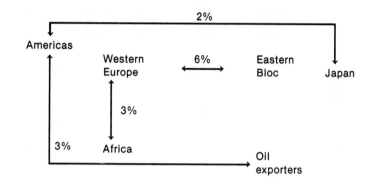

These percentages of total world trade from the IMF emphasize that the bulk of international trade originates in the industrially developed nations:

Industrialized nations	67%
Oil exporters	18%
Developing nations	15%

Data from GATT's *International Trade* (1989–90) indicate that Asia is gaining importance in world trade. Trade among Asian countries amounted to 10% of world merchandise trade in 1989, after growing a phenomenal 12% annually over a decade. Trade between Asia and North America amounted to 12% of total world trade, after growing at a 13% annual rate over a decade.

EXAMPLE 1.6   Largest Trading Partners of the United States

Canada and Japan rank as the largest trading partners of the United States, as reported by *International Economic Conditions* (Federal Reserve Bank of St. Louis, January 1990). The United States, Canada, and Mexico have entered into a reciprocal free trade agreement, which will eliminate protection on trade. The same policy has been suggested for Japan. During the 1980s, Japan overtook Canada as the largest single source of U.S. imports. The rest of the world (ROW) has decreased in importance relative to these five major trading partners, which account for about half of U.S. total trade. These are percentages of total U.S. trade.

	U.S. Exports					
	Canada	Japan	Mexico	U.K.	W. Germany	ROW
1983	19%	11%	5%	5%	4%	56%
1988	22%	12%	6%	6%	4%	50%

	U.S. Imports					
1983	20%	16%	6%	5%	5%	48%
1988	18%	20%	5%	4%	6%	47%

Problems for Section C

C1. Find the revised import expenditure given the increased demand for manufactures in Figure 1.10. Using the export revenue in Figure 1.11, find the BOT.

C2. Predict what will happen to the BOT if excess supply of agricultural goods in Figure 1.11 increases with improved technology in the exporting home country.

D. COMPARATIVE ADVANTAGE AND SPECIALIZATION

If there is a single slogan that international economists live by, it is "specialize and trade." International economics is constantly sharpened on the arguments put forth by domestic industries seeking protection from foreign competitors through government tariffs, quotas, and other nontariff barriers. The purpose of protection is to isolate parts of the economy from international competition. Free trade leads to increased international specialization, with relatively inefficient domestic firms failing in the face of more efficient foreign competition. This section introduces the principles of opportunity cost and comparative advantage. The gains from specialization and trade come through comparative advantage.

1. Opportunity Cost and Comparative Advantage

When you sit down to read this text, you are giving up alternative activity. The value of your best alternative is your opportunity cost studying international economics.

Opportunity cost is the value of the best alternative an economic agent has when a choice is made.

Consider the example of you and your roommate and the two tasks of cooking and washing dishes. Your roommate might be better at both, taking less time than you to finish either task. But suppose you are a relatively quicker cook. The *opportunity cost* of your cooking is lower than your roommate's. If you cook while your roommate cleans house, you both will gain. The two of you could specialize and trade and each spend less time on these routine tasks.

As another example, suppose you and your roommate open a sideline business of delivering local packages in the afternoon. Both of you wait by the phone for an order. When a call comes in, one of you jumps on your bike, picks up the package, delivers it, and comes back home to wait for another call. If one of you instead waits by the phone, takes orders, and routes the other from place to place over the phone, your firm's output will increase. Specialization increases efficiency. Of the two of you, the biker with the lower opportunity cost of organizing potential should be on the road. You might be the better biker and the better telephone organizer. But the difference between you is relatively greater in biking than it is in answering the phone. You have a comparative advantage in biking, and your partner has a comparative advantage in organizing by phone.

2. Absolute Advantage versus Comparative Advantage

Absolute advantage in producing a particular good simply means a lower unit labor input. In the example of cooking and washing dishes, your roommate took less time to finish either task and had an absolute advantage in each activity. In the example of a local delivery service, you were a better biker and telephone organizer and had an absolute advantage in both activities.

With an absolute advantage in a good, less of resources such as labor and energy is used to produce a unit of the good. Suppose the United States has an absolute advantage relative to other nations in producing both manufactured goods (such as cars, appliances, and clothing) and services (such as banking, telecommunications, education, and entertainment). Perhaps the United States has more capital machinery and equipment or more highly trained labor than Mexico. Does this mean the United States should be totally self-sufficient, consuming only the goods it produces and not trading at all?

Mexico might still have lower opportunity costs or a comparative advantage in producing manufactured goods. *Comparative advantage* is based on a lower opportunity cost that one economic agent has compared with another in a particular productive activity. When comparing labor inputs across goods, Mexico uses *relatively* less labor in manufacturing than does the United States. The opportunity cost of lost service output when the

United States produces manufactures is higher. Mexico gives up more manufactures output when it produces services. Both nations can end up consuming more of both goods if each specializes in producing the type of good in which it has a comparative advantage and trades with the other. In this example the United States will specialize in services and export them to Mexico in exchange for manufactured goods.

No trickery is at work. Each country is simply spending its time and resources on the activity in which it has the lower opportunity cost. Total output for the world will clearly increase when each nation specializes. Countries may have absolute advantages in most goods, some goods, or even very few goods. Still, each nation will want to specialize according to its comparative advantage.

International economists study the process of organizing production the best way globally or worldwide. The terms of trade between two nations will be determined by the interaction of the supply and demand of each country. Both nations can potentially consume more of both types of goods when they specialize and trade because the world's ability to produce goods is increased.

> Looking for comparative advantage means looking for activities with low opportunity costs. This relative efficiency advantage explains why specialization and trade are beneficial.

3. Labor Inputs and Comparative Advantage

For a concrete example, suppose the hours of labor it takes to produce a unit of manufactures (M) or services (S) in the United States and Mexico (MEX) are given by this array:

	U.S.	MEX
S	2	3
M	3	4

The United States has an absolute advantage in producing both M and S, since less time is required to produce a unit of either good compared with Mexico.

Nevertheless, the relative value of services will be less in the United States than in Mexico. In the time it takes to produce a unit of S, only 2/3 of an M could be produced in the United States. Since it requires 3 hours to produce an M in the United States, 2/3 of an M would be produced in 2 hours. In Mexico, 3/4 M could be produced in the time it takes to produce a unit of S. The opportunity cost of producing S is higher in Mexico than in the United States. In other words, Mexico gives up more M when its resources produce a unit of S. The United States has the comparative advantage in producing services.

In the time it takes to produce one M, 3/2 units of S could be produced in the United States but only 4/3 units of S could be produced in Mexico. The opportunity cost of producing M is higher in the United States than in Mexico because the United States gives up more S when it produces a unit of M. Mexico has the comparative advantage in producing manufactures.

Comparative advantage can be found by comparing the opportunity costs or relative prices across nations.

Nations naturally tend to specialize according to their comparative advantage. Global resources are used more efficiently, and total world output increases through specialization according to comparative advantage. Competitive forces lead nations toward specialization according to comparative advantage. This idea is one of the oldest in economics and remains one of the most vital. With specialization and trade, the values of consumption and welfare increase in every country.

Comparative advantage is abstracted from all the details of market supply and demand and international equilibrium for the goods involved. It is a simpler yet more sophisticated way of explaining the pattern of trade. Prices of goods in the domestic and foreign markets and the exchange rate take on secondary importance when it is understood that comparative advantage offers a more fundamental explanation of trade and a foundation for the free trade argument. Domestic industries constantly appeal to their government for protection from the forces of international competition. The major lesson of comparative advantage is that a nation should specialize and trade.

The original example of comparative advantage created by David Ricardo more than 200 years ago involves the production of wine (W) and cloth (C) by Portugal (PORT) and England (ENG):

	PORT	ENG
W	80	120
C	90	100

Note that Portugal has the absolute advantage in both goods. In the time it takes to produce one W, $80/90 = 8/9$ of a C can be produced in Portugal and $120/100 = 6/5$ units of C can be produced in England. The opportunity cost or relative price of wine is lower in Portugal. Portugal gives up less C to produce a W and will do well specializing in W. Portugal has the comparative advantage in wine. England must have the comparative advantage in cloth.

4. The Power of Comparative Advantage

Comparative advantage is the basic principle in international economics explaining why nations have the tendency to specialize. Economists use comparative advantage to predict trends in the pattern of trade between countries and to improve trade policy.

The economic agents involved (producers, exporters, importers, consumers, and so on) do not have to worry about comparative advantage. Firms are looking for profit opportunities, and consumers are seeking better and cheaper goods and services. International trade and finance arise naturally when agents happen to find cheaper or better economic goods abroad than at home. You do not need to learn the principle of comparative advantage to run a successful business involved in international markets. Rather, the principle of comparative advantage underlies a great deal of economic activity and organization. It offers a simple and unifying principle for understanding how people, firms, and nations make choices.

Comparative advantage is a powerful tool of explanation and understanding. It is perhaps the one true principle in the social sciences that has no exception. No matter how inefficient a country might be in an absolute sense, it must have a comparative advantage in some activities.

Comparative advantage works just as well when comparing regions, states, cities, neighborhoods, or individual firms as it does when comparing nations. Specialization between people can also be understood through comparative advantage. Architects do not do their own typing, no matter how good their typing is, because their comparative advantage lies in planning buildings.

EXAMPLE 1.7   U.S. Revealed Comparative Advantage

These figures from the U.S. Department of Commerce *Survey of Current Business* report net trade for the United States during 1980 in various goods. When a good is exported, money is paid into the nation and a positive number is recorded. These are broad categories of goods, so the United States both imports and exports some of each type. Positive signs indicate goods in which the United States is a net exporter, revealing its comparative advantage. The United States must have relatively low labor inputs in agriculture, high-tech goods, and services. Negative signs indicate goods in which the United States is a net importer. The United States must have relatively high labor inputs in low-tech goods, consumer goods, and autos.

Surplus Goods

High technology	$39 billion
Services	$36 billion
Agriculture	$24 billion

Deficit Goods

Petroleum	− $76 billion
Low technology	− $35 billion
Consumer goods	− $18 billion
Automobiles	− $11 billion

Explaining the pattern of trade and revealed comparative advantage is part of the job of international economics. High-tech goods and services use relatively large amounts of skilled labor in their production. The United States has relatively more skilled labor than its trading partners. Trade in both agriculture and petroleum is based on the natural resource inputs available in the country. These relative inputs and the availability of inputs go a long way toward explaining comparative advantage and the pattern of international specialization and trade. ·

Problems for Section D

D1. You are a whiz and can vacuum the floor in 15 minutes and clean the kitchen in 30, while your roommate takes 20 and 45 minutes respectively for the two tasks. Find who has the absolute and comparative advantages in each activity.

D2. Determine the absolute and comparative advantage in this hypothetical situation of labor inputs between the United States (U.S.) and Canada (CAN):

	U.S.	CAN
S	2	3
M	3	2

Does one nation have the absolute advantage in both goods? Find the opportunity costs and relative prices of M and S in each country. Which country is likely to specialize in which good?

CONCLUSION

The overall picture of international trade that should be beginning to develop in your mind is one of many international markets, constantly adjusting to grind out the relative prices of traded goods. The fundamentals of every market are the same, which means that with practice you can recognize and predict patterns of change and adjustment. You are a consumer and will ultimately (when you graduate and find a job) be involved in the production of goods and services. Probably your firm and industry will be exporting or facing import competition. It is important to become familiar with the fundamentals determining adjustments in international prices and levels of trade.

KEY TERMS

Absolute and comparative advantage	Export revenue
Arbitrage	Import expenditure
Autarky price	International equilibrium price
BOT surplus and deficit	Mercantilism
Currency depreciation	Normal and inferior goods
Diminishing marginal productivity	Opportunity cost
Excess demand	Relative cost
Excess supply	Specialization
Exchange rates	Substitution effect and income effect
Expectations	Transport costs

KEY POINTS

- International markets clear at prices where excess demand in the importing nation equals excess supply from the exporting nation.
- Excess demand is the difference between the quantity demanded and quantity supplied across the range of prices. Excess supply is the difference between quantities supplied and demanded at every price.
- Changes in the demand or supply for a traded good affect its international excess demand and excess supply, international price, and the level of trade.
- The balance of trade equals export revenue minus import expenditure. A trade deficit (surplus) occurs if import expenditure is greater (less) than export revenue.
- A nation has a comparative advantage in producing a good if its relative price or opportunity cost of the good is lower than in other nations.

REVIEW PROBLEMS

1. Diagram what will happen to the price and quantity of traded oil when OPEC restricts supply, using a diagram based on Figure 1.4.
2. By tradition, Japanese businesses deal only with Japanese banks. Japan is a net importer of banking services. If Japanese businesses begin dealing more with U.S. banks, show what will happen in the market for banking services between the two trading partners.
3. Diagram what will happen in the current international market for cars if the United States announces a stricter quota on imports that will take effect with next year's models. (Hint: This can affect both the excess demand in the United States and the excess supply from Japan.)

4. Diagram what will happen in the market for wheat between the United States and Russia when a forecast says Russia will have a long, cold winter and a spring drought. Russia is the importer of wheat.

5. Illustrate what will happen in the international market if the Buy American campaign aimed at U.S. consumers changes domestic tastes for clothing, which is initially a U.S. import.

6. The United States is an exporter of business services and is trying to get other nations to lower their protection of these services. Show what will happen in the international market for business services if foreign nations increase their demand for U.S. business services. Will domestic consumers of services enjoy the changes?

7. Illustrate what will happen in the international market for autos as incomes rise in China. Treat China as the home nation, and Japan and the United States as the foreign producer.

8. Show what will happen in the international market for autos if technology for auto production improves in the United States (a net importer of autos).

9. Illustrate what will happen in the international market for gold if news of war causes buyers *and* sellers to expect higher prices in the future.

10. Suppose U.S. and Venezuelan demands for steel are approximately the same. The domestic and foreign autarky prices are $500 and 22,500 bolivar respectively, and the exchange rate is bolivar/$ = 50. Determine the likely exporter. Illustrate international excess supply and demand when the international traded price is $475, the volume of trade 100, U.S. production 100, and Venezuelan production 300. Find the level of consumption in each nation.

11. In Problem 10, find the U.S. import expenditure on steel. How many bushels of wheat would we have to export at $2.50/bu to balance trade? At $2/bu?

12. Explain whether you think a BOT surplus or deficit should be preferred for the United States at this time. Would any governmental policy help to reach this goal?

13. What can be said about the following pattern of labor inputs between the United States (U.S.) and Europe (EUR)? Who has the absolute and comparative advantage in each good? Predict the pattern of trade.

	U.S.	EUR
S	2	3
M	3	4.5

14. Justify your opinion about the goods in which the United States has a comparative advantage: oil, insurance, new cars, thread, accounting, textiles, engineering, clothing, olive oil, economic forecasting, chemicals, wheat, telecommunications, warm winter vacations, cool summer vacations, citrus fruits, fast food, architectural design, and education.

READINGS

Paul Gregory and Roy Ruffin, *Basic Economics,* Scott, Foresman, Glenview, IL, 1989. An excellent principles text. Sections on the global economy are especially relevant. Students wanting to review economics principles would benefit from this text.

Roy Ruffin, *Modern Price Theory,* Harper Collins, New York, 1992. A clearly written intermediate text that develops the tools of modern microeconomics.

John Adams, *International Economics: A Self-Teaching Introduction to the Basic Concepts.* Riverdale, Wellesley Hills, MA, 1979. A handy paperback that drills the student on the essential quantitative relationships in international economics.

John H. Jackson, *Competition in Services: A Constitutional Framework,* AEI Press, Washington, DC. 1988. Explores increasing international trade in services and proposes trade liberalization through the General Agreement on Tariffs and Trade (GATT).

Joseph McKinney and Keith Rowley, *Readings in International Economic Relations,* Stipes, Champaign, IL, 1989. A handy collection of readings on trade policy, international finance, and multinational firm activity.

CHAPTER 2

Constant Cost Production and Trade

CHAPTER PREVIEW

The important principle of comparative advantage was formulated in the late 1700s by David Ricardo, an English economist who wanted to understand the basic cause of international trade in as simple a way as possible. Ricardo developed a constant cost model of production, with fixed inputs per unit of output. Applications and extensions of the constant cost model remain at the forefront of economic research. This chapter covers:

    (a) The *constant cost* model of production and trade
    (b) The *gains from trade* in a constant cost economy
    (c) Comparisons of *labor productivity* and *international wages*
    (d) *Applications and tests* of the constant cost model

INTRODUCTION

Ricardo's efforts in the late eighteenth century were among the first to investigate systematically the fundamental causes and effects of international trade. Mercantilism, the most popular economic doctrine in Ricardo's day, holds that a nation's wealth is equivalent to the stockpile of gold and other assets it amasses. According to mercantilism, exports create revenue while imports squander wealth to other nations. Economic policy should promote exports and restrict imports. Mercantilists in Ricardo's day were typically industrialists who enjoyed foreign consumers while wanting protection from foreign competition. The mercantilist vision is generally shared by modern industrialists.

    Adam Smith had argued against the mercantilists (*The Wealth of Nations*, 1776) pointing out that national wealth is more correctly viewed as the nation's capacity to produce goods and services. To increase its wealth, Smith argued, a nation should increase its productivity. Smith believed this required producing goods in which the country has an absolute cost advantage and trading these goods for cheap goods on international markets. Smith believed the *invisible hand* of international competition would lead a nation in this direction, if government economic policy could be kept out of the way. He presented forcible arguments against interference with the market mechanism.

Ricardo took Smith's ideas a step further. Ricardo realized that gains could be made from trade even by a country that was inefficient in an absolute sense compared with all other countries in producing every good. To enjoy returns from specialization and trade, only *comparative advantage* would be required. Every nation must have a relative edge in efficiency in some activities. Comparative advantage and the gains from specialization and trade have proved to be the most profound and lasting principles in all of the social sciences.

Ricardo constructed one of the first and most successful scientific models. His model of specialization in production and trade has offered each generation of economists a solid foundation on which to build the study of international economics.

A theory of production must lie at the heart of any understanding of trade. In Ricardo's theoretical economy, one input (labor) is used in fixed amounts per unit of output. In the simplest model, two goods can be produced by two nations, home and foreign. Both nations are found to gain through specialization according to their comparative advantage.

Fundamental relationships among international wages, international productivity of labor, and exchange rates are developed in the constant cost model. The model has been extended to include many goods. Current efforts to apply and test the constant cost theory of production and trade support Ricardo's insights.

A. CONSTANT OPPORTUNITY COSTS OF PRODUCTION

Ricardo visualized an economy as composed of all the productive processes taking place. Inputs are hired by firms in each industry to produce outputs for consumption. Ricardo postulated a production process with a single input to see clearly the basics involved in production and international trade. A preliminary step in the scientific method is to construct a testable theory. Ricardo's effort was one of the first to approach the understanding of something very complicated through building a simple abstract model.

1. Labor in the Constant Cost Model

The most critical assumption is that there is only one productive input, labor. While any productive process has numerous inputs, this assumption creates the simplest possible theoretical situation. Other inputs such as capital machinery and equipment, natural resources, and entrepreneurship are implicitly being held constant.

Ricardo wrote about the importance of various inputs. In an abstract sense the other inputs embody the labor used in their own production. In the labor theory of value the source of all value ultimately arises from labor. The assumption of a single input, labor, vastly simplifies the real world, as does any theoretical assumption. With *fixed input proportions* the amount of labor required to produce each unit of output does not vary as the level of output or the wage varies.

> Constant cost theory assumes that a single input (labor) is used in fixed proportions in the economy's production processes.

Suppose the amount of labor it takes to produce a unit of services is 2 and the amount of labor it takes to produce a unit of manufactures is 3. The units of labor could be person-years. It takes 3 people 1 year or 1 person 3 years to make a unit of manufactured goods. This unit of manufactures can be thought of as a standard composite basket of manufactures produced in the economy.

Ricardian labor inputs are expressed by this notation:

$$L/S = 2 \quad \text{and} \quad L/M = 3$$

The way to read this notation is "labor per unit of services is equal to 2" and "labor per unit of manufactures is equal to 3." Labor inputs are simply taken to be fixed constants. Since labor is the only input, substitution with other inputs is impossible. These labor inputs describe the economy's *constant cost technology.*

The total amount of labor employed in the service sector is written $2S$. It takes 2 workers to produce a unit of services, and S units are produced. For instance, if output in the service sector is equal to 30, the service sector must employ $2 \times 30 = 60$ workers. It takes 2 workers to produce a unit of services, and 30 units are produced, which means 60 workers must be employed in service production.

The entire labor force is fully employed in both sectors. Quantities of outputs are represented by S in services and M in manufactures. If the total amount (endowment) of labor, L, in the entire economy equals 120,

$$L = 120 = 2S + 3M$$

Since it takes 3 workers to produce a unit of output in manufactures, $3M$ workers are employed in manufacturing. Employment in services ($2S$) plus employment in manufactures ($3M$) must sum to the entire labor force ($L = 120$). The economy is limited in the outputs it can produce. With only a certain quantity of labor and given labor input requirements, more output in one sector means less output in the other sector.

2. The Constant Cost Production Possibilities Frontier

Given this simple production structure, the economy's exact production possibility frontier (PPF) is easily derived. The PPF shows the various combinations of output (M and S) that the economy can produce given its resources and technology.

In Figure 2.1, manufactured output is measured on the vertical axis, and service output is measured on the horizontal axis. If the entire labor force worked in manufacturing, service output S would be zero and 120/3 = 40 units of M could be produced. One end of the PPF is at 40 on the vertical M axis. At the other extreme, if no M were produced, 120/2 = 60 units of S could be produced. This reasoning gives the two endpoints of the PPF: $(M, S) = (40, 0)$ on the vertical axis and $(M, S) = (0, 60)$ on the horizontal axis.

Since the labor inputs per unit of output do not vary, the PPF is the straight line joining these two endpoints. Each additional unit of S produced costs the same amount of sacrificed M down along the PPF. This is the sense in which costs are constant. The opportunity cost of additional output is constant throughout the range of production.

The domestic relative price of services in autarky is the absolute value of the slope of the frontier, $|-40/60| = 2/3$. This price is the same all along the frontier, since the labor input per unit of output and the opportunity cost of production are constant. The same amount of M must be given up to acquire an additional unit of S everywhere along the frontier. To produce an extra unit of S requires 2 units of labor. Since the economy has full employment, these 2 workers must come from the manufacturing sector. Output of manufactures will drop by less than 1 unit because 3 workers are

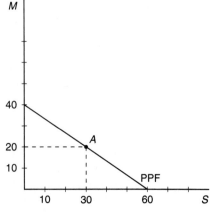

Figure 2.1. A Constant Cost Production Possibility Frontier With constant input requirements, the opportunity cost of production remains constant as output moves along this straight production possibility frontier (PPF). In this example the labor force is 120 and labor inputs are L/S = 2 and L/M = 3. The economy can produce at the endpoints $(M,S) = (40, 0)$ or $(0, 60)$ or at any point in between. At point A, production and consumption is $(M,S) = (20, 30)$.

required to produce 1 unit of M. When the 2 workers leave manufacturing, output drops by 2/3 of a unit. Opportunity costs are constant along the PPF, since the unit labor input requirements remain constant. The equation of the PPF is

$$L = 2S + 3M$$

Constant costs of production are illustrated by a straight PPF. The opportunity cost of additional output is a given amount of the other output throughout the range of production.

Home consumers in autarky must choose a point along the constant cost PPF in Figure 2.1. Consumers choose among available goods and services according to the satisfaction or utility they provide, given prices of the goods and a limited income.

For simplicity, suppose consumers in the economy of Figure 2.1 always spend an equal share of their income on the two goods. Each unit of S is valued at 2/3 of an M. In terms of M, the total amount of S consumed is worth 2/3 S. An equal share of income is spent on each good when 2/3 $S =$ M. Combining this with the equation for the PPF,

$$L = 120 = 2S + 3 \ (2/3S) = 4S$$

which implies $S = 30$. Consumption of M must then be 20, which is illustrated by point A in Figure 2.1. Since consumers will spend half their income on each good, half the labor force must work in each sector. Output and consumption of both goods are easy to find under these simplifying assumptions.

3.   Improved Technology and Economic Growth

Improved technology in this Ricardian production structure is illustrated by a decreasing unit labor input. Improved technology in services would lower the unit input from its current value of 2 and expand the production frontier along the S axis. When the unit labor input in services drops to 1.5 from 2, the production frontier expands from PPF to PPF' in Figure 2.2. The equation for the PPF becomes

$$L = 120 = 1.5S + 3M$$

Total potential output in services has become $120/1.5 = 80$. As apparent in Figure 2.2, more of both goods can potentially be produced with the improved technology in one sector. The domestic relative price of services falls to $|-40/80| = 1/2$. Increased supply of S relative to M has led to a

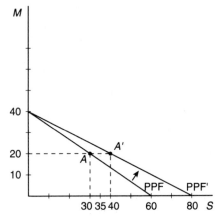

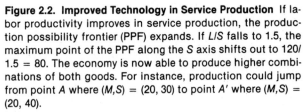

Figure 2.2. Improved Technology in Service Production If labor productivity improves in service production, the production possibility frontier (PPF) expands. If L/S falls to 1.5, the maximum point of the PPF along the S axis shifts out to $120/1.5 = 80$. The economy is now able to produce higher combinations of both goods. For instance, production could jump from point A where $(M,S) = (20, 30)$ to point A' where $(M,S) = (20, 40)$.

lower price of S in terms of M, similar to an increase in the supply of services.

> Improved technology in one sector expands the PPF in that direction, lowers the relative price of that good, and raises the economy's potential to produce all outputs.

Economic growth in this model with one input simply means a larger labor force. Growth is pictured by a parallel outward shift of the PPF. In Figure 2.3, the labor force has expanded from 120 to 144. Input requirements are back at $L/S = 2$ and $L/M = 3$. The equation for the PPF is now

$$L = 150 = 2S + 3M$$

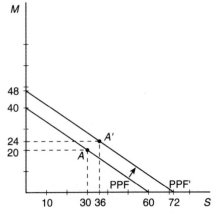

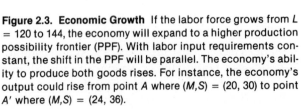

Figure 2.3. Economic Growth If the labor force grows from $L = 120$ to 144, the economy will expand to a higher production possibility frontier (PPF). With labor input requirements constant, the shift in the PPF will be parallel. The economy's ability to produce both goods rises. For instance, the economy's output could rise from point A where $(M,S) = (20, 30)$ to point A' where $(M,S) = (24, 36)$.

At the extremes a total of 144/2 = 72 units of S or 144/3 = 48 units of M could be produced with the higher labor force. These are the new endpoints on the M and S axes. The relative price of S in terms of M remains at 2/3. With either improved technology or growth, the economy can produce more of both goods. If consumers spend half their income on each good, consumption shifts to (M,S) = (24,36).

Economic growth is pictured by an outward shift of the PPF.

4. International Differences in Opportunity Costs

Consider a foreign nation that has its own particular unit labor inputs and relative price. The foreign unit labor input in service is assumed to be $L*/S = 6$, and the foreign unit labor input in manufactures $L*/M = 4$. The foreign labor force is assumed to be $L* = 240$. Note that the asterisks signal variables of the foreign country. The foreign production frontier PPF is drawn in Figure 2.4 with endpoints 240/4 = 60 $M*$ and 240/6 = 40 $S*$. The equation of the foreign PPF* is

$$L* = 240 = 6S* + 4M*$$

The relative price of services in the foreign nation is $M/S = |-60/40| = 3/2$.

Note that in this example the unit labor input requirements are higher for both goods in the foreign country: $L*/S > L/S$ and $L*/M > L/M$. This means the home country has an absolute advantage in producing both manufactured goods and services. It might seem that it would not be in the interest of the more efficient home country to trade at all with the inefficient foreign country. If we can produce goods more efficiently than the foreign country, why bother with importing anything from them? It will, nevertheless, pay the home country to specialize just as it will pay the for-

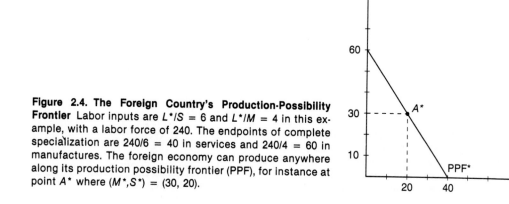

Figure 2.4. The Foreign Country's Production-Possibility Frontier Labor inputs are $L*/S = 6$ and $L*/M = 4$ in this example, with a labor force of 240. The endpoints of complete specialization are 240/6 = 40 in services and 240/4 = 60 in manufactures. The foreign economy can produce anywhere along its production possibility frontier (PPF), for instance at point $A*$ where $(M*,S*) = (30, 20)$.

eign country. Comparative advantage, not absolute advantage, determines the potential gains from trade.

The relative autarky price of services is higher in the foreign country than in the home country because the labor input requirement in service production is higher in the foreign country. The opportunity cost of service production is higher in the foreign country in that more manufactures must be given up to produce an extra unit of services. By the same token, the opportunity cost of service production is lower in the home country. Relative price differences provide the foundation for international specialization and trade.

If foreign consumers also spend half their income on each good, the foreign labor force will be split equally between sectors. With 120 workers in each sector, foreign consumption of services will be $120/6 = 20 = S^*$ in autarky, while consumption of manufactures will be $120/4 = 30 = M^*$.

It is important to realize that consumers in each nation are constrained to consume along their country's PPF when there is no international trade. Consumers must choose the point that they enjoy the most along their own PPF when there is no trade. Each economy, on its own, will value a good according to its opportunity cost of production. When production of one good increases, production of other goods must decline. The lost output represents the true value of increased production. If consumers were identical in the two countries, they would consume different ratios of the two goods given the different technologies and opportunity costs of production in the two countries without international trade. Consumers would push each economy along its PPF until the optimal combination of goods was produced.

Figure 2.5 summarizes autarky production and consumption for both the home and foreign nations. The home country produces 20 units of M and 30 units of S, consuming at point A. The foreign country produces 30 units of M^* and 20 units of S^*, consuming at point A^*. Consumers in both

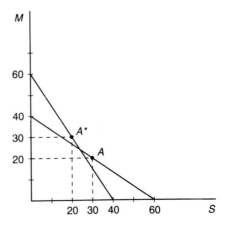

Figure 2.5. Production and Consumption without Trade Production and consumption in autarky occur at point A in the home country and point A^* in the foreign country. Services are relatively cheap before trade in the home country, while manufactures are relatively cheap in the foreign country.

countries spend half of their income on each good. The autarky relative prices of services are 2/3 at home and 3/2 abroad. Services are relatively cheap in the home country, and manufactures are relatively cheap in the foreign country. Note that neither country can consume the bundle of goods consumed by the other country, since it is beyond its own PPF.

> In a constant cost economy, potential output is determined by the total input supply and the input requirements in each productive activity. In autarky, consumers choose the optimal output combination along their PPF.

EXAMPLE 2.1   Productivity Growth in U.S. Industries

These figures show the growth rate of unit labor inputs in various U.S. industries as reported by Matthew Shapiro (1987). Decreases in L/Q indicate industries where investment and innovation are high. Unit labor inputs have recently fallen the fastest in communications, agriculture, manufacturing, and utilities. Increases in L/Q typically indicate sagging industries where investment and growth are small. The largest increases have occurred in mining and construction. When unit labor inputs fall, the PPF expands. When unit labor inputs rise, the PPF contracts. The PPF of the United States has expanded in its capacity to produce goods at the first of the list, while it has contracted in its capacity to produce goods at the end of the list.

	1974–1985
Communications	−2.3%
Agriculture	−1.4%
Manufacturing	−1.4%
Utilities	−1.2%
Transportation	−0.1%
Retail trade	0.4%
Wholesale trade	0.5%
Finance, insurance	0.6%
Construction	1.1%
Mining	4.3%

Problems for Section A

A1. Draw the production frontier for a nation whose unit labor inputs are $L/S = 4$ and $L/M = 5$ with a labor force $L = 220$. Find the relative price of S in terms of M. Find the relative price of M in terms of S.

A2. Find consumption for the economy in the previous problem when consumers spend half of their income on each good.

A3. In the previous problem, suppose technology improves in manufacturing until $L/M = 4.4$. Draw the revised production possibility frontier. Suppose the economy then grows until the labor force $L = 264$. Draw the new frontier.

B. SPECIALIZATION AND GAINS FROM TRADE WITH CONSTANT COSTS

Two economies with constant costs can typically both enjoy increased consumption if they specialize and trade with each other. Differing relative prices are the stimulus to specialize, leading to an efficient global pattern of production. The gains from trade are illustrated by an expanded income line for each trading economy. Consumers in trading economies have the potential to consume more of all goods.

1. Relative Prices and Specialization

The home relative price of services in terms of manufactured goods in the example from the previous section is less than the foreign relative price. Services are relatively cheap in the home country in the fundamental sense that less of other goods must be given up to produce more service output. Manufactured goods are relatively cheap in the foreign nation because their opportunity cost (what is given up to produce them) is lower there.

This comparison of opportunity costs suggests that the home nation is relatively more efficient in producing services, while the foreign nation has an efficiency advantage in manufactures. Ricardo suggested that nations should specialize in producing the goods in which they have this comparative or relative efficiency advantage. These three ideas are equivalent:

(a) Lower opportunity costs
(b) Relative efficiency
(c) Comparative advantage

Comparative advantage arises when relatively less of other goods must be sacrificed to produce a unit of the specialized good. The global potential to produce goods increases with specialization.

Relative prices or opportunity costs indicate the efficient pattern of specialization. Countries tend to specialize in producing those goods whose relative prices are lower than in other countries.

In this example the home country begins sacrificing manufactures to produce more services. Resources are rearranged as the service industry grows with new and expanding firms. Labor (along with the background resources in the economy) begins moving into the service sector, where its output is more highly valued. The manufacturing industry declines and ultimately shuts down because costs do not change as the nation expands production of its comparative advantage good.

Figure 2.6 shows the home nation in a position of *complete specialization* in services at point *P*. The economy has moved down along its PPF to produce only services. It will enjoy gains from specialization and trade because services can be traded internationally at a price above the domestic price of 2/3. The high relative price of services on the international market is the stimulus for specialization. The rest of the world values services more than the home economy. Suppose the world relative price of services is given by the terms of trade line *tt* = 1 in Figure 2.6. From point *P*, the economy can trade up along *tt* = 1 and consume beyond its PPF. More of both goods can be consumed on the terms of trade line.

When two specialized countries trade with each other, the terms of trade are determined by the interaction of demand. Relative demands for the two goods in the two nations will set the terms of trade. It is certain that the home nation will want more than 2/3 of a unit of *M* per unit of exported *S* to make specialization and trade worthwhile. From the viewpoint of the home country, *tt* = *M/S* must be above 2/3. It is also certain that the foreign nation of Figure 2.4 will only offer less than 3/2 of a unit of *M* for each unit of *S* it receives. From the viewpoint of the foreign country, *tt* must be less than *M/S* = 3/2.

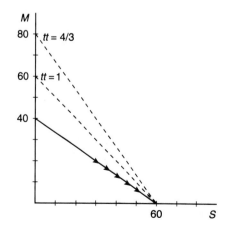

Figure 2.6. Complete Specialization for the Home Country
The high international price of services pushes the home country into complete specialization at point *P*. All inputs are used in service production, and the domestic manufacturing industry completely collapses. From point *P*, the economy can trade up along its terms of trade (*tt*) line. Every unit of exported services brings in 1 unit of manufactures along *tt* = 1. Exporting all 60 units of produced services would bring in 60 units of imported manufactures. If *tt* = 4/3, exporting all 60 units of services would bring in 80 units of imported manufactures.

The *limits to the terms of trade* are these minimally acceptable prices of exports for the two trading partners:

$$3/2 > tt > 2/3$$

The terms of trade must fall between these limits for trade to be mutually beneficial. In Figure 2.6, the *tt* line must fall between the home PPF with slope 2/3 and the dotted line with slope 3/2, which represents the foreign relative autarky price.

In the late 1700s, John Stuart Mill contributed to Ricardo's model by showing how the terms of trade could be decided. Mill assumed that consumers in both nations spend an equal share of their income on each good. Since the relative price will be the same in both countries with trade, each nation will export half of its product. The terms of trade in this example will be 30 *M* from the foreign country exchanged for 30 *S* from the home country, or 30/30 = 1. This terms of trade falls within the limits to the terms of trade. Mill's insight led to the idea of consumer utility, the basis of the theory of consumption.

The terms of trade line representing 1 unit of *M* for each unit of *S* is pictured in Figure 2.7. Think of the two nations as coming to terms at this relative price. Each unit of exported *S* brings in a unit of *M* when *tt* = 1. Consumption takes place up along the terms of trade line *tt* = 1 beyond the home economy's PPF. With the home economy exporting 30 units of *S*, 30 units of *M* are imported.

The *trade triangle* in Figure 2.7 has 30 units of exported *S* along its base (measuring left from the production point *P*) and 30 units of imported *M* trading up the *tt* line. Consumption takes place at point *C* in Figure 2.7. The trade triangle shows imports and exports. The home economy is left consuming 60 − 30 = 30 units of *S*. Imports of *M* are 30 units. If all 60 units of *S* were exported, the home country could import 60 units of *M*. It

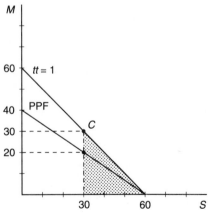

Figure 2.7. Consumption with Specialization and the Trade Triangle Consumers choose the point along the terms of trade (*tt*) line that they most prefer. In this example, they choose (*M,S*) = (30, 30) at point *C*. The 30 units of exported services exchanges for 30 units of manufactures on the international market. The trade triangle illustrates both the volume of trade and the terms of trade.

is apparent that consumers in the economy will be better off with trade, since they can choose among combinations of goods along the $tt = 1$ line that lies beyond their PPF.

2.   The Real Gains from Trade

The real gains from consumption at point C in Figure 2.7 are measured using the domestic autarky price of $M/S = 2/3$. This price line is labeled d in Figure 2.8. It is drawn through point C parallel to the economy's PPF.

The value of consumption with trade in terms of M is

$$30\,M + (2/3 \times 30S) = 30M + 20M = 50M$$

The 30 units of S consumed are worth 20 units of M at the domestic autarky price. Added to the 30 units of M consumed with trade, the value of consumption is 50 units of M. The value of autarky consumption in terms of M is only 40, the endpoint on the PPF. The gains from trade are measured as the difference $50 - 40 = 10\ M$, which amounts to a $10/40 = 25\%$ real gain from trade.

The real gains from trade can also be calculated in terms of services. The value of consumption in terms of services after trade is

$$(3/2 \times 30M) + 30S = 45S + 30S = 75S$$

The 30 units of S are produced and retained for consumption after exports. Imports of $30M$ are valued at 45 units of S by the high autarky price of M. Total consumption is valued at 75 units of S. This is a gain of $75 - 60 = 15\ S$, which in percentage terms is $15/60 = 25\%$.

The real gains from trade can be measured in terms of any good. Note that the endpoints of the autarky price line in Figure 2.8 are $75S$ on one

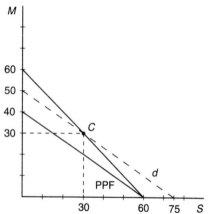

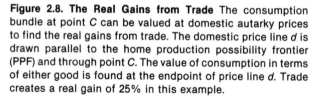

Figure 2.8. The Real Gains from Trade The consumption bundle at point C can be valued at domestic autarky prices to find the real gains from trade. The domestic price line d is drawn parallel to the home production possibility frontier (PPF) and through point C. The value of consumption in terms of either good is found at the endpoint of price line d. Trade creates a real gain of 25% in this example.

end and 50 M on the other. The gains from trade are found graphically by projecting the consumption point to either axis using the domestic relative price. The real gains from trade for the home country in this example are 25%.

In the foreign nation as well, real gains result from trade. Specialization pushes the foreign nation into the production of manufactures. With only two nations in the world, home imports exactly equal foreign exports and home exports exactly equal foreign imports. Foreign exports in this example must be 30 units of M. The value of each unit of exported M on the world market is 1. The 30 units of exported M trade for 30 units of S, which the home nation exports.

It is good practice at this point to sketch the foreign nation's PPF from Figure 2.4, its specialization point P^*, terms of trade line tt, and consumption point C^*. These can all be derived from the observed levels of trade and consumption. With the international trade in this example, foreign consumption takes place at $C^* = (M^*, S^*) = (30,30)$, which is beyond its production frontier. the gains from trade in the foreign country can be measured in terms of either M or S. In this example the foreign country also enjoys real gains from trade of 25%.

> The real gains from trade can be measured in terms of either imported or exported goods. Every country involved in trade enjoys real gains from trade.

The foreign nation in this example has the same real gains from trade as does the home nation. This might be anticipated because the terms of trade $M/S = 1$ are about halfway between the home autarky price of 2/3 and the foreign price of 3/2. If the terms of trade had been closer to 2/3, the home country would have gained more. If the terms of trade had been closer to 3/2, the foreign country would have gained more.

A general lesson is that the more highly valued a nation's exports are on the world market, the greater will be the gains from trade. Graphically, the farther the tt line swings away from a country's PPF, the larger will be the country's gains from trade. Gains from trade are thus partly due to the influence of international demand. In this example, home and foreign consumers both value the two goods similarly. Suppose home consumers value foreign manufactures more than foreign consumers value home services. The terms of trade would then move more in favor of the foreign country. The foreign nation would be in a better bargaining position than the home nation because of the international pattern of tastes. Trade would drive up the value of foreign manufactures more than the value of home services.

If a big nation enters into trade with a smaller one, which can expect to gain more? A common opinion is that international trade benefits large nations more than small ones. Large nations are sometimes pictured as dominating both the level and terms of trade, exploiting available resources and cheap labor in small countries. The terms of trade, however, will not vary much from a big nation's autarky price when it trades with a small country. The small nation adds little to the demand for the big nation's exports, but the demand for the small nation's export jumps substantially. The small country gains more because the terms are farther from its PPF. The large nation would gain less from trade because the terms of trade would be close to its autarky price.

EXAMPLE 2.2   Unit Labor Inputs and Specialization in Iron and Steel

It is generally possible to understand or predict the pattern of international trade through an examination of labor inputs. Figures from Mordechai Kreinin (1984) compare unit labor inputs across nations in iron and steel. In each nation the Ricardian labor input in iron and steel (L/I) is set equal to 10 in 1964. The reported figures for 1980 show substantial improvements in labor productivity in Japan, Germany, and France. Constant cost theory would predict that the United States and the United Kingdom would not be specializing and exporting as much iron and steel as they were in 1964, given their relative decline in productivity. In fact, the United States and the United Kingdom have become net importers of iron and steel. Japan has seen the most dramatic increase in steel production and exports. Japan switched from being a large steel importer to a net exporter between 1964 and 1980.

	U.S.	U.K.	France	Germany	Japan
L/I	8.4	8.4	4.5	4.4	2.8

Problems for Section B

B1.   Completely diagram the foreign nation in the example from the text. Show production point P^*, the terms of trade line tt, consumption with trade C^*, and the foreign trade triangle. Find the gains from trade in terms of each good and in percentage terms.

B2.   Suppose the home economy is characterized by $L/M = 4$ and $L/S = 5$, and the foreign economy by $L^*/M = 5$ and $L^*/S = 6$. Which country has the comparative advantage in S? Find the relative prices of S in both countries. Find the limits to the terms of trade.

C.   EXTENSIONS OF CONSTANT COST TRADE THEORY

This section applies the constant cost model of trade to issues of international relative wages and exchange rates. Two avenues are available to improve home wages relative to foreign wages: improved terms of trade and increased labor productivity. For trade to occur, the exchange rate is constrained within limits set by the wages and productivity of trading partners. Finally, constant cost trade theory is extended to include many different types of goods.

1. International Differences in Labor Productivity and Wages

The picture of production and trade with constant costs teaches lessons that lie at the foundation of understanding of the causes and effects of international trade. One primary lesson of the Ricardian model involves the link between labor payments across trading partners. Trade influences the relative price of outputs and payments to productive resources. Relative wages across trading partners are linked by productivity differences and the terms of trade.

In the long run, zero economic profit is expected when there is free entry and free exit of firms in a competitive industry. Accounting profits may be positive, but no excess profits will develop. The price of a good in competition moves to the cost of producing it. In other words, price equals average cost: $P = AC$.

With complete specialization the international value of each good is determined in the nation where it is produced. The price of services in the example of the home country specializing in services is the average cost of producing services in the home nation,

$$\$/S = (L/S)(\$/L) = (L/S)w = 2w$$

To produce a unit of services, 2 units of labor are required and each unit of labor is paid the home wage w. The price and the average cost of producing a unit of services equals $2w$.

Manufactured goods produced in the foreign nation have a dollar price that depends on the foreign wage rate, the foreign unit labor input, and the exchange rate. Suppose Canada is the foreign country, and the Canadian dollar C$ is the foreign currency. The price of manufactures in Canadian dollars is the Canadian unit labor input in manufactures ($L*/M = 3$) times the Canadian wage $w*$,

$$C\$/M = 3w*$$

The Canadian wage rate $w*$ is the price of Canadian labor in Canadian dollars: $C\$/L*$. The dollar price of Canadian manufactured goods is found through the exchange rate $e = \$/C\$$, the value of Canadian dollars in terms of dollars:

$$\$/M = (\$/C\$)(C\$/M) = e3w*$$

The expression $e3w^*$ represents the U.S. dollar price of manufactured goods from Canada.

The *Ricardian terms of trade (tt)* or the relative price of services in terms of manufactured goods equals the ratio of these two dollar prices from the countries of origin:

$$tt = (\$/S)/(\$/M) = M/S = 2w/e3w^*$$

A clear relationship among wages in the two countries, the exchange rate, and the terms of trade emerges.

The relative wage in U.S. dollars is written w/ew^*. Solving for the relative U.S. wage using the expression for the terms of trade,

$$w/ew^* = (3/2)\ (M/S) = 1.5\ tt$$

The term w/ew^* is the U.S. wage rate relative to the Canadian wage rate, both expressed in U.S. dollars. If it is less than 1, Canadian wages are higher than U.S. wages. One limit to the terms of trade in this hypothetical example is that $tt > 2/3$. It follows that $w/ew^* > 1$, which implies that the U.S. wage must be higher than the Canadian wage if the two countries are to trade in this example.

The implications of this little bit of algebra and economic reasoning are fundamentally important. The wage of home workers relative to foreign workers can be increased through only two routes: labor productivity and the terms of trade. Remember that the labor productivities in the two countries lead to the term $1.5 = 3/2 = (L^*/M)/(L/S)$.

Changing productivity affects relative wages across trading partners. Suppose home labor becomes more productive, with L/S falling from 2 to 1.5 in this example. Less home labor is required per unit of service output. Then $tt = 1.5w/3ew^*$, and w/ew^* rises to $2tt$. The identical outcome occurs if foreign labor becomes less productive, with L^*/M rising from 3 to 4. In both circumstances, home labor becomes more productive relative to foreign labor, resulting in a relatively higher home wage. The home wage will decline relative to the foreign wage if home labor becomes less productive or foreign labor becomes more productive. This link between labor productivity and the international relative wage is fundamentally important.

Terms of trade improve for the home nation if tt rises. Remember tt equals M/S, in the international relative price of home exports. If tt rises, services have become more valuable and home labor will receive higher wages relative to foreign labor. At the same time, foreign workers will become worse off relative to home workers. A terms of trade improvement for the foreign nation, tt falling, would make foreign workers better off relative to home workers.

The terms of trade depend partly on demand between the two nations. A nation that increases its demand for foreign products will see its relative wage falling. There is a lesson here for the United States in its trade with Japan. When demand for Japanese manufacturing goods in the United States rose because of their reputation for quality, the terms of trade worsened for the United States and wages in Japan rose relative to those in the United States.

> Higher productivity and better terms of trade increase home wages relative to foreign wages. Falling productivity and worse terms of trade decrease home wages relative to foreign wages.

The burden in practice does not fall entirely on labor to increase its own productivity through effort. The quality and quantity of other inputs directly affect labor productivity. With better machines and training, labor will be more productive in manufacturing and services. With better equipment and farmland, labor will be more productive in agriculture. Investment spending by firms on physical capital and by workers on human capital (education) is required to increase labor productivity. Trying harder may not increase productivity if the right tools and training are not available.

These lessons are fundamental:

(a) Payments to productive resources are linked between trading partners.
(b) A factor's payment is ultimately tied to its productivity.
(c) A change in the domestic demand for foreign products alters the terms of trade and the domestic wage relative to the foreign wage.

EXAMPLE 2.3   The Relative U.S. Wage

The term w/ew^* can be calculated from data on production workers. The Bureau of Labor Statistics reports international relative wages. The U.S. wage has recently risen and then fallen relative to the German wage. In 1981 the West German wage was equal to the U.S. wage. By 1983 the U.S. wage had risen 30% relative to the German wage, mainly because of dollar appreciation. By 1988 the U.S. wage had fallen to 80% of the German wage because of dollar depreciation. The same pattern has been true for U.S. and Japanese wages, which were equal in 1988. For Taiwan and South Korea, the U.S. wage remains much higher but has undergone a marked decline. Wages in Taiwan and South Korea were only 1/13 of the U.S. wage in 1983 but had risen by 50% by 1988.

	1981	1983	1988
West Germany (former)	1.0	1.3	0.8
Japan	1.8	2.2	1.0
Taiwan, South Korea	11.0	13.0	6.5

EXAMPLE 2.4   Comparison of U.S./Pacific Rim Competitiveness in Manufacturing

Wages and unit labor inputs can be used to make international comparisons of the cost of producing manufactured goods, which typically require a good deal of labor input in assembly line operations. Susan Hickock and James Orr (1989) report on a comparison of U.S. manufacturing with four newly industrialized countries in the Pacific Rim. Wages in the United States are substantially higher than in these countries. The unit labor input requirements L/M depend on the actual goods produced and the level of capital input. While L/M is lowest in the United States, the other countries have a comparative advantage in manufactures production. The high wage in the United States causes higher labor cost per unit of output.

	1988 Wages (in U.S. dollars)	L/M	Unit Cost
Taiwan	$2.71	3.8	$10.30
South Korea	$2.52	4.3	$10.84
Malaysia	$.81	4.8	$3.89
Thailand	$.86	8.3	$7.14
United States	$13.90	1.0	$13.90

Manufacturing growth rates are high (8% to 12%) in these four countries because of the high levels of growth in investment goods or capital machinery used with the labor input. While the low L/M in the United States is due to the high level of capital in the United States, these four countries are investing heavily and will continue to increase their manufacturing output rapidly. Each of these countries has recently had a balance of trade surplus with the United States.

2. Exchange Rates and International Wages

Another link is found in the Ricardian trade model between exchange rates and wages across trading economies. For the home economy to export services, the price of services must be lower at home than abroad. The price of services produced by the competitive home industry is $\$/S = w(L/S)$. This home price must be less than the price of services that could be produced in the foreign country. Remember, e is the exchange rate ($\$/C\$$), and w^* is the foreign currency price of labor ($C\$/L^*$). The dollar price of foreign labor is $ew^* = \$/L^*$. The dollar price of services produced in the foreign country is the exchange rate times the foreign price of services: $ew^*(L^*/S)$.

If the home country exports services, the dollar price of services produced at home must be less than the dollar price of services produced in the foreign country: $w(L/S) < ew^*(L^*/S)$. Solving for e, we have

$$e > \frac{w(L/S)}{w^*(L^*/S)}$$

The value of the Canadian dollar has this lower limit if the home country is to export services. Otherwise, services will be cheaper in Canada.

For the foreign nation to export manufactures, the domestic currency price of manufactured goods produced in the foreign country $ew^*(L^*/M)$ must be less than the domestic price $w(L/M)$. Manufactured goods will be cheaper from the foreign country if

$$\frac{w(L/M)}{w^*(L^*/M)} > e$$

Summarizing these two conditions, if the home country is to export services and the foreign country is to export manufactures, the exchange rate has these bounds:

$$\frac{w(L/M)}{w^*(L^*/M)} > e > \frac{w(L/S)}{w^*(L^*/S)}$$

Nothing has been said here about the foreign exchange market and how e is determined in practice. An international gold standard, fixed exchange rates, or floating exchange rates could be used. However e is determined, it must fall within these limits if the two countries are to trade according to their comparative advantage. Figure 2.9 illustrates these limits to the exchange rate.

Suppose $w = 14$ and $w^* = $ C\$10 with the unit labor inputs from the example in the text: $L/S = 2$, $L/M = 3$, $L^*/S = 4$, and $L^*/M = 3$. The exchange rate e would then have to be between $14/10 = 1.4$ and $(14/10)(2/4) = 0.7$ for the two economies to trade. If $e = 2$, both services and manufac-

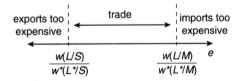

Figure 2.9. Ricardian Limits to the Exchange Rate If the exchange rate e is too low (the dollar is valued too high), exports will cost too much abroad. If e is too high (the dollar is valued too low), imports will cost too much. Only a limited range of e is consistent with trade. Looked at another way, home wages must fall within a range defined by the exchange rate, foreign wages, and international labor inputs.

tured goods would be cheaper in the United States. The price of services from the home country would then be $\$/S = 2w = \$28$, while in the foreign country $\$/S = 4ew^* = \$80$. The price of manufactures would be $\$/M = 3w = \$42$ in the home country and $\$/M = 3ew^* = \$60$ in the foreign country. At the other extreme, if $e = 0.5$, both manufactures and services would be cheaper in the foreign country. Convince yourself that if $e = 0.5$, $\$/S$ would be $\$28$ in the home country and $\$20$ in the foreign country, while $\$/M$ would be $\$42$ in the home country and $\$15$ in the foreign country.

> Limits to the exchange rate must be maintained if two economies are to trade with each other. If the exchange rate goes out of line, international trade becomes unprofitable and ceases.

Given the substantial gains from trade, the exchange rate is bound to fall within this range. If a currency appreciates too far, the price of the nation's exports is no longer below the international traded price. If a currency depreciates too far, other nation's exports become too expensive at home. These limits to the exchange rate can be made more realistic by including indirect labor inputs and the labor content of intermediate and capital inputs and by allowing partial specialization. These modifications do not alter the basic lesson that exchange rates must have limits for trade to take place.

The limits on the exchange rate can be interpreted another way. For a given exchange rate, a nation's wage can be only so high if it is to continue trading with its partners. If wages rise too far, the economy loses any cost advantage it has compared with its trading partners. In this example, suppose the foreign wage $w^* = 10$ and the exchange rate $e = 1$. Then w must be between $\$10$ and $\$20$ if trade is to take place. Wages outside this range will cause trade to cease.

Home wages are limited by labor productivity in the home country relative to the foreign country. If home labor becomes more productive, the home unit labor inputs L/S and L/M fall. This improvement in home labor productivity will lower the range of e, meaning a possible long-run dollar appreciation.

In an open economy, home wages are constrained by foreign wages, the exchange rate, and labor productivity. The constant cost model provides a simple, useful tool for gaining insight into the nature of international competition. Governments are constrained in their exchange rate policy because trade will cease if e moves outside its limits. If the dollar depreciates too far, imports become too expensive and trade is curtailed. If the dollar appreciates too far, exports become too expensive abroad and trade is curtailed. With free trade, central banks have limited discretion for exchange rate manipulation without affecting the pattern of international trade. Exchange rate policy can be used as a form of protection if it is pursued beyond these limits.

3. Trade with Many Goods

Assuming there are only two types of goods simplifies matters but raises the question of whether results hold when there are many goods. Given the structure of Ricardian trade, most results do follow when there are many goods. The basic lessons with many goods can be learned from an example with three goods. The three major industrial categories in modern economies are services S, manufactures M, and agriculture A.

Comparing two nations, home and foreign, suppose the unit labor inputs are those in Table 2.1. Looking at the opportunity costs of one good in terms of another good creates some confusion because each country has two sets of independent opportunity costs. For instance, the opportunity cost of one unit of M in the home country is 3/2 S or 3/4 A. In the foreign country the opportunity cost of one unit of M is 4/3 S or 2 A. In terms of agricultural goods, M is cheaper at home. In terms of services, M is cheaper abroad.

This ambiguity can be eliminated by making a comparison between nations for each commodity to see how much labor is required in one nation relative to the other. For instance, using the figures on services in Table 2.1, the home input relative to the foreign input is $(L/S)/(L*/S) = 2/3$. It takes 2/3 of a worker at home to produce as much service output as 1 worker produces abroad. In manufacturing, it takes 3/4 of a home worker to match 1 foreign worker. In agriculture, 2 workers at home are required to match the productivity of 1 worker abroad.

In this example the home economy has a clear comparative advantage in services, since home labor is relatively most efficient in that activity. In services it takes 3/2 foreign workers to match a home worker. The foreign nation has a clear comparative advantage in agriculture, since it takes only 1/2 of a foreign worker to match the output of a home agricultural worker.

In manufacturing, 4/3 foreign workers match 1 worker at home. Manufactures represent a middle ground between services and agriculture and could be exported by either country or not traded at all. The pattern of production and trade in manufactures depends on the size and the levels of demand of the two economies. Manufactures would not be traded at all if the prices of manufactures in the two countries happened to match.

Figure 2.10 illustrates the home country's constant cost PPF when there are three goods. The home endowment of labor in this example is 120. The

TABLE 2.1. Unit Labor Inputs with Three Industrial Sectors

	L/S	L/M	L/A
Home	2	3	4
Foreign	3	4	2

L = labor; S = services; M = manufactures; A = agriculture.

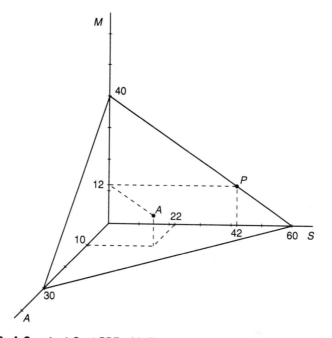

Figure 2.10. A Constant Cost PPF with Three Goods Labor inputs in this example are those listed in Table 2.1. The labor force in this economy is 120 workers. With three goods, the production possibility frontier (PPF) is a flat surface or triangle. Autarky production and consumption occur at point A where (M,S,A) = (12,22,10). With complete specialization the economy moves to point P where (M,S,A) = (12,42,0). Agriculture shuts down, manufacturing stays the same, and services expand. Trading services for agricultural good would subsequently move consumption out beyond the PPF.

line between the M axis and the S axis is the same in Figure 2.1. If all home labor were in agriculture, 120/4 = 30 units of A could be produced. The PPF is the triangle connecting the endpoints of complete specialization in each industry.

In autarky, domestic consumers would determine the point of production and consumption at a point such as A on the surface of the PPF. Note that 22 units of S and 10 units of A are produced, requiring 2 × 22 = 44 workers in sector S and 4 × 10 = 40 workers in sector A. This leaves 120 − 84 = 36 workers for the manufacturing sector, which means 36/3 = 12 units of M are produced. Point A rests on the PPF and is the point (M,S,A) = (12,22,10).

With specialization the home economy drops agricultural production and moves to a point such as P. Suppose manufactures are not traded and output remains at 12. Service output rises to 84/2 = 42 with the 40 workers coming from agriculture. If the terms of trade are 1 unit of A for each exported S, the economy could trade 15 units of S and consume at the point

$(M,S,A) = (12,27,15)$ beyond its PPF. The principles of trade remain the same when there are many goods.

When there are many goods, they can be arranged in a labor input rating. Each nation will export those goods near the end of the ranking where the nation's industries are relatively more efficient. Consider a hypothetical comparison of the United States and Mexico across 10 types of manufactured goods. Suppose $L/M < L^*/M$ for every one of the 10 goods. In other words, the United States is more efficient than Mexico in producing every good. Still, the 10 goods could be ranked according to $(L/M)/(L^*/M)$, which would all be less than 1. Mexico would specialize in the goods at the high end of the ranking, while the United States would specialize in the goods toward the low end. This application of the Ricardian model has found wide-ranging support.

4. Trade among Many Countries

The Ricardian model of trade can also be applied to situations with many countries. When there are two goods, M and S, the opportunity cost of a unit of S can be found from each country's labor inputs. Countries with a low opportunity cost of S will export S, and those with a high opportunity cost of S will import S.

To illustrate, suppose there are three countries, labeled 1, 2, and 3. Table 2.2 shows the unit labor inputs for M and S in each of the three countries. The relative price of S across countries can be ranked

$$4/3 \text{ in country } 3 > 3/4 \text{ in country } 2 > 2/3 \text{ in country } 1$$

The relative price of services is $2/3$ M in country 1, $3/4$ M in country 2, and $4/3$ M in country 3.

Country 1 has the lowest opportunity cost of services and will export S in free trade. Country 3 has the lowest opportunity cost of manufactures and will export M in free trade. Country 2 maintains an intermediate position. The international terms of trade will determine the exports and imports of country 2. Demand across the three countries will contribute to the terms of trade and determining the production of intermediate country 2. If the terms of trade are above $M/S = 3/4$, country 2 will export services.

TABLE 2.2. Unit Labor Inputs with Three Countries

	L/S	L/M
Country 1	2	3
Country 2	3	4
Country 3	4	3

L = labor; S = services; M = manufactures.

If *tt* is less than 3/4, country 2 will export manufactures. The limits to the terms of trade come from the extreme countries:

$$4/3 > tt > 2/3$$

When there are many goods and many countries, unit labor input rankings potentially indicate which goods could be exported. In Table 2.3 a situation with three goods and three countries is pictured. The labor input ranking L_1/L_2 between countries 1 and 2 in each of the goods is

$$(4/2)_A > (3/4)_M > (2/3)_S$$

This is exactly like the example in Table 2.1. Country 1 will export good S to country 2 in exchange for good A. Between countries 2 and 3,

$$(4/2)_M > (3/4)_S > (2/3)_A$$

Country 2 will export good A to country 3 in exchange for good M. Finally, comparing Ricardian labor inputs between countries 1 and 3, we have

$$(3/2)_M > (4/3)_A > (2/4)_S$$

Country 1 will export good S to country 3 in exchange for good M.

The pattern of trade that emerges in this example is clear. Country 1 specializes in S, country 2 specializes in A, and country 3 specializes in M. This pattern of trade is illustrated in Figure 2.11.

Predicting the pattern of trade may not work out as neatly as in this example when many countries and many goods are involved. Additionally, international differences in demand can play a role in determining patterns of specialization and trade when there are many factors and goods. Still, there will be goods in which each country holds a definite comparative advantage relative to all other countries. Gains will come if the country specializes according to this comparative advantage. As the saying goes, there is a place in the sun for everyone.

TABLE 2.3. Unit Labor Inputs with Three Countries and Three Goods

	L/S	L/M	L/A
Country 1	2	3	4
Country 2	3	4	2
Country 3	4	2	3

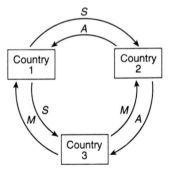

Figure 2.11. Trade with Three Countries and Three Goods With the unit labor inputs in Table 7.3, this pattern of international trade emerges. Country 1 has a consistent comparative advantage in good *S* relative to the other countries. Country 2 has the comparative advantage in good *A*. Country 3 has the comparative advantage in good *M*. Global efficiency and income increase with this pattern of international specialization and trade.

EXAMPLE 2.5   Improving Labor Productivity through Research and Development

One way to improve productivity or lower unit labor inputs is through research and development (R&D). Especially relevant for international economics is *technology transfer* that occurs from the developed to the developing nations. These figures from the *Trade and Development Report—1987* of the United Nations Conference on Trade and Development (UNCTAD) reveal the changing pattern of R&D expenditures. Total world expenditure on R&D in 1983 was $265 billion, about 8% of U.S. gross national product (GNP). The percentages listed below are each country's share of total R&D spending. Nearly all R&D is carried out in the developed nations. The implication is that developing nations must acquire new technology from the industrial nations. Furthermore, since 1970 Japan has stood out with increased spending on R&D and the United States with decreased spending. These trends take on importance when it is remembered that relative wages rise as labor productivity improves.

	1970	1975	1980	1983
European Economic Community	20%	22%	22%	21%
Japan	7%	10%	12%	13%
U.S.	40%	33%	34%	33%
USSR (former)	19%	21%	18%	18%
Developing nations	2%	3%	3%	3%

EXAMPLE 2.6   Capital and Productivity

Productive capital can account for changes in labor productivity. According to figures from the Federal Reserve Bank of St. Louis (*National Eco-*

nomic Trends, December 1989) growth in the stock of productive capital (machinery and equipment) relative to the labor force slowed during the 1970s and 1980s from what it had been during the 1950s and 1960s. While labor productivity continued to increase, its rate of increase slowed. In this table, both the capital-to-labor ratio and the labor-to-output are rescaled to 1 in 1950. While the ratio of capital to labor in the economy (*K/L*) has continued to rise, its growth has slowed since the 1950s and 1960s. Labor input per unit of output (*L/Q*) in the economy fell more in the 1950s and 1960s than it did during the 1970s and 1980s.

	K/L	*L/Q*
1950	1.00	1.00
1960	1.03	.97
1970	1.05	.94
1980	1.06	.93
1988	1.07	.92

Problems for Section C

C1. Suppose foreign labor inputs are $L^*/M = 5$ and $L^*/A = 3$, while home labor inputs are $L/M = 2$ and $L/A = 3$. Find the international pattern of specialization. Find the relative wages w/ew^* if the terms of trade are 1.

C2. Find the limits to the exchange rate with the unit labor inputs in the previous problem when $w = \$10$ and $w^* = 1000$ pesos.

C3. If $w = \$15/L$, $e = \$/A\$ = 0.75$ (the value of the Australian dollar), and $w^* = A\$15$, find the dollar prices of the three types of goods S, M, and A using the unit labor inputs in Table 2.1. Predict the pattern of trade.

C4. Diagram the foreign country's PPF when $L^* = 228$ and the unit labor inputs are those in Table 2.1.

D. EMPIRICAL APPLICATIONS OF CONSTANT COST TRADE THEORY

Consumers and firms in the United States are becoming increasingly aware of the vital nature of international trade. Still, by most nations' standards, the U.S. economy is relatively closed. In 1985 the ratio of imports to GNP in the United States was 8%, while it was 11% in Japan and 21% in Germany. For most nations this percentage ranges from 20% to 50%. The United states is the world's largest exporter, with exports valued at $213 billion in 1985, ahead of Germany's $183 billion. These exports were only

TABLE 2.4. U.S. Exports by Percentage

Machinery	31%
Agriculture	11%
Aircraft	9%
Computers	8%
Chemical	7%
Metal products	6%
Other	28%

SOURCE: From *Survey of Current Business*, p. 53; U.S. Department of Commerce, March 1991, Washington, DC: U.S. Government Printing Office.

5% of U.S. GNP, compared with 29% for Germany. As an extreme example, the Netherlands exports 69% of its GNP. The United States is also the world's largest economy, with imports of $321 billion in 1985 accounting for 14% of total world imports. Germany's imports the same year were 10% and Japan's imports were 7% of the world total. The U.S. economy has been described as a closed giant. This section examines tests and applications of the Ricardian model to the U.S. economy.

1. Exports and Imports of the United States

The value of exports of agricultural and some important manufactured goods from the United States is presented in Table 2.4. These figures are percentages of the total value of exports. The other exports in manufactures and agriculture are highly diversified.

The largest buyers of U.S. exports are shown in Table 2.5. Canada is the largest buyer. More than a third of U.S. exports are shipped to Canada and Mexico.

A breakdown of the largest categories of imports of goods to the

TABLE 2.5. Buyers of U.S. Exports by Percentage

Canada	22%
Japan	12%
Mexico	6%
United Kingdom	6%
West Germany	5%
Netherlands	3%
Other	46%

SOURCE: From *Survey of Current Business*, p. 51, U.S. Department of Commerce, March 1991, Washington, DC: U.S. Government Printing Office.

TABLE 2.6. U.S. Imports by Percentage

Capital goods	24%
Consumer goods	21%
Autos	17%
Oil	12%
Iron & steel	6%
Food & beverages	4%
Other	16%

SOURCE: From *Survey of Current Business*, p. 54, U.S. Department of Commerce, March 1991, Washington, DC: U.S. Government Printing Office.

United States is shown in Table 2.6; the other 16% of imports is highly diversified across many types of goods. Consumer goods are typically manufactured on assembly lines, as are autos. Imports of oil, coffee, and cocoa are best understood as arising from the availability of natural resources.

The United States imports the most from the countries in Table 2.7. A quarter of U.S. imports comes from North America. Imports from Japan are largely autos and electronics. Mexico and South Korea have grown in recent years as suppliers of U.S. imports.

Given the high level of diversification indicated in these tables, economists studying international trade have developed models with many types of goods and many nations. The examples with three goods and three countries in the last section should convince you that constant cost models of trade with many types of goods can be used to predict the direction of trade, exchange rates, relative international wages, and so on. Bilateral trade comparisons are simple enough, but multilateral trade among many nations creates theoretical difficulties. Still, the fundamental principles are valid enough to be accepted even when international trade involves many goods and many countries.

TABLE 2.7. Suppliers of U.S. Imports by Percentage

Canada	19%
Japan	18%
West Germany	6%
Mexico	6%
Taiwan	5%
South Korea	4%
Other	42%

SOURCE: From *Survey of Current Business*, p. 52, U.S. Department of Commerce, March 1991, Washington, DC: U.S. Government Printing Office.

The text has concentrated on the example of exported services. There is good reason to do this for the United States. Services include banking, transportation, shipping, motion pictures, tourism, lodging, insurance, advertising, engineering, architecture, construction, computer services, communications, accounting, wholesaling, and retailing. These services represent more than 70% of the U.S. economy's jobs and 30% of U.S. exports. Indeed, these are activities in which U.S. firms are especially efficient and internationally competitive.

Before 1900, most workers in the United States were in agriculture. Since then, manufacturing has accounted for about 30% of all jobs, with the service sector growing from 31% to 70% and agriculture shrinking from 38% to 4%. Trade in services goes beyond the trade in goods covered in Tables 2.4 through 2.7.

International trade in services accounts for about one-quarter of total world trade. The United States is the world's leader in service exports. In 1980 the United States exported $38 billion worth of services, amounting to 16% of merchandise exports. Of the total service exports, 37% was in passenger fares, 27% in travel and tourism, and 12% in shipment. The share of services in exports has been growing in the United States. Japan and West Germany are net importers of services. Studies in the developing pattern of international trade that disregard services miss the overall picture for the United States. It is apparent that the United States is moving into international specialization in service production.

2. Attempts at Testing Constant Cost Theory

Is simple constant cost theory able to predict actual trade statistics? A pioneering article by G.D.A. MacDougall (1951) compared exports from the United states and the United Kingdom in 1937. When labor productivity was higher in a particular industry in one of the two nations, that nation's share of that export market was consistently higher. This is the essential prediction of constant cost trade theory. Labor productivity determines comparative advantage, which in turn underlies the pattern of trade. Other, more recent studies have confirmed MacDougall's tests for other countries and for many types of goods.

Herbert Glesjer et al. (1982) have recently complete studies that compare nations in Europe before and after they joined the European Community (EC). When nations join the EC, trade restrictions among them are largely eliminated. Nations with lower opportunity costs of goods before joining the EC were found to export just those goods to other member countries after joining. Again, this is the prediction of the theory.

High-tech goods are defined as those involving relatively high degrees of R&D. Included in the category of high-tech goods are electronics, chemicals, aircraft, computers, and specialized machinery. The figures in Table 2.8 may help explain Japan's evolution into an international supplier of

TABLE 2.8. An International Comparison of Unit Labor Inputs in High-Tech Products

	1963	1970	1978	1984
European Community	1.25	1.34	1.44	1.46
United States	1.00	1.08	1.00	1.06
Japan	1.76	1.18	1.00	0.92

SOURCE: *Annual Economic Report 1984-5*, p. 47, European Economic Community, 1985, Brussels: EEC.

high-tech products. These figures are the unit labor inputs L/H, where H represents a unit of high-tech output. The unit inputs are rescaled so that $L/H = 1$ in the United States in 1963. Note that the EC has declined in its productivity of high-tech goods. The United States has essentially held its position, while Japan has improved productivity.

The EC's concern is with the decline of Europe in its position as a supplier of high-tech products. Japan's improvement has been due to its investment in human capital (education) and a high level of investment in capital equipment. In 1963, Japan was the most relatively inefficient producer of high-tech products, having the highest labor input requirement. The United States was then the most efficient producer. While technology in the United States remained fairly constant, Japanese technology improved dramatically. The Japanese PPF has been expanding along its high-tech axis.

The 1970s was a decade of serious decline for the U.S. auto industry. An examination of unit labor inputs largely explains why. Imports of Japanese cars rose from less than half a million in 1970 to almost two-and-a-half million in 1980. Japanese autos went from less than 5% to more than 20% of the U.S. retail market. Labor productivity in Japan has increased tremendously, as reflected by data from the Japanese Ministry of International Trade and Industry (MITI) and the U.S. Bureau of Labor Statistics (BLS). Rescaling units so $L/\text{auto} = 1$ in the United States in 1970, the Japanese unit input was $L^*/\text{auto} = 1.5$ the same year. Over the decade, L/auto in the United States rose to 1.15 while the Japanese L^*/auto fell to 0.75. The improvement in Japanese automobile productivity is attributed to their high investment over the period, with the stock of capital in the auto industry rising 225% in the 1970s.

The 1980s witnessed radical changes in the U.S. automobile market. About 30% of all new cars in the United States are foreign. In fact, the distinction between domestic and foreign cars is blurred, with 30% of the value of a typical domestic car accounted for by its foreign parts. On the Ford Escort, only the glass, valves, wheel nuts, and tappets are made in the United States. The future promises wider dispersion in the world auto market, with newly industrializing countries producing their own cars and entering into international competition. The theory of comparative cost would predict that since the United States is losing its comparative advantage in autos, imports of autos will continue to increase.

EXAMPLE 2.7   U.S. Trade in High-Tech Goods

Mordechai Kreinin (1985) has estimated the opportunity cost of high-tech goods in terms of all manufactured goods in 1980 for the United States, Japan, and West Germany. The numbers below represent the labor inputs per unit of high-tech goods L/H divided by the labor input for all manufactured goods L/M. This gives the opportunity cost M/H of high-tech goods in terms of all manufactures in each of the three countries. The United States has a slight comparative advantage in high-tech manufactures, but Japan's increased spending on R&D has put it close:

$$0.90_{\text{US}} < 0.95_{\text{Japan}} < 1.08_{\text{West Germany}}$$

EXAMPLE 2.8   U.S. Service Firms

One statistic that reflects the underlying comparative advantage the United States has in services is the U.S. share of the world's largest firms in various service sectors. In some instances, such as construction, this indicates a high degree of existing international specialization. In others, such as retailers, the U.S. firms operate inside the United States, and little export of the services occurs. Even in these instances, however, the United States has developed successful techniques and has experienced and specialized labor that can be applied in foreign markets. These statistics are reported in *Foreign Direct Investment and Transnational Corporations in Services* (United Nations, 1989). The list below shows the number of firms in the 10 largest worldwide firms in each category. U.S. regulations inhibit the size of U.S. banks, which are important to the world banking system even though they do not show up in the world's top 10. All of the world's largest trading companies, which specialize in international arbitrage, are Japanese. During the 1980s services became increasingly important in the United States. Looking ahead to the 1990s and beyond, the U.S. economy will become more oriented toward service export.

Sector	*U.S. Firms in Top 10*
Restaurant chains	10
Retailers	9
Securities	9

Accounting	8
Hotels	8
Market research	8
Advertising	7
Airlines	6
Law firms	6
Transport	6
Insurance	5
Publishing	5
Construction	4
Reinsurers	4

Problems for Section D

D1. Which four countries are the largest trading partners of the United States, considering both imports and exports?

D2. High-tech manufactured goods require a large input of skilled labor. Why might the United States be able to produce relatively cheap high-tech goods?

D3. Investment spending in the U.S. automobile industry lagged far behind its competitors in the 1960s and 1970s. How would this account for the relatively high cost of producing autos in the United States during the 1980s?

CONCLUSION

In the modern theory of production, firms combine various inputs to minimize cost and to produce maximum profit from output. Firms vary their input mix according to the prices they must pay for inputs. If labor becomes more expensive, firms naturally want to substitute toward other inputs. If the price of capital rises, firms would switch toward more labor-intensive techniques. As a radical example of switching between inputs according to their prices, compare farms in the United States and India. Farms in the United States use much machinery and little labor because labor is relatively expensive and machinery relatively cheap. In India, where labor is relatively cheap and machinery relatively expensive, much labor is combined with little machinery. The constant cost model does not allow this substitution process.

The constant cost explanation of international trade strips matters to the simplest level. While the theory is workable, it has obvious shortcomings. Why does one nation have lower labor inputs than another? What would cause these inputs to change over time? Does including other inputs alter the fundamental predictions of the model? Is complete specialization often observed? Modern theories, which include increasing costs of production, various inputs, and different types of industrial structure, answer some of these questions. In the end, constant cost trade theory stands as a fundamental and useful way of understanding international trade.

KEY TERMS

Absolute advantage
Comparative advantage
Complete specialization
Constant costs
Invisible hand
Labor input ranking

Limits to the exchange rate
Limits to the terms of trade
Mercantilism
Opportunity cost
Relative price

KEY POINTS

- Constant cost production possibility frontiers can be drawn when factor mix terms do not change. The slope of a constant cost PPF represents the relative price of goods in the economy.
- Trade with constant costs involves complete specialization according to comparative advantage. The gains from trade can be illustrated by the increased value of goods consumed. Specialization and trade create the opportunity to consume more of every good.
- Constant cost trade theory illustrates fundamental international links among wages, productivity, and exchange rates.
- Unit labor inputs are an indicator of comparative advantage and contribute to an understanding of observed patterns of trade.

REVIEW PROBLEMS

1. Comparing Figures 2.1 and 2.4, which nation has a lower opportunity cost of manufactures? Which nation would you expect to export manufactured goods?
2. Suppose the economy Delta is characterized by unit labor inputs of $L/M = 4$ and $L/S = 5$. Compare Delta with the home country in Figure 2.1 and predict the pattern of specialization. Make a similar comparison between Delta and the foreign economy in Figure 2.4.
3. The workforce of the United States totals about 150 million, while the workforce

of Japan is about 60 million. Find the amounts of high-tech goods these economies could produce over the years in Table 2.8 if a quarter of each labor force was in high-tech manufactures.

4. Suppose the home economy is characterized by $L/M = 4$, $L/S = 5$, and $L = 260$. The foreign economy's production structure is given by $L^*/M = 6$, $L^*/S = 5$, and $L^* = 300$. Find the pattern of comparative advantage and specialization. Suppose each nation exports half of its production to the other with free trade. Find the terms of trade and both nations' trade triangles.

5. Evaluate the gains from trade for both economies in the previous problem in terms of S. Evaluate the gains from trade for both nations in percentage terms. Explain which country enjoys the largest gains from trade.

6. Find the percentage gains from trade in this same example if the terms of trade turn out to be $M/S = 1$ and the same 30 units of S are exported by the foreign country. Explain the difference in the gains compared with the previous problem.

7. If the terms of trade $tt = M/S = 1.4$ between the home economy in Figure 2.1 and the foreign economy in Figure 2.4, find the relative wages w/ew^* implied by free trade. Find the relative wage if $tt = 0.7$. Explain the effect of this change in the terms of trade on the relative wage.

8. Using the information in the previous problem with each terms of trade, find w if $w^* = 1,100$ yen and $e = \$/yen = 0.008$. Compare the limits to the exchange rate under each of the two terms of trade.

9. In the home economy, unit labor inputs are $L/M = 2$ and $L/A = 3$ for manufactures (M) and agriculture (A). In the foreign economy, unit labor inputs are $L^*/M = 4$ and $L^*/A = 5$. The terms of trade are $tt = A/M = 3/4$. Find the relative wages implied by trade.

10. Find the limits to the exchange rate for the two trading economies in the previous problem.

11. Find the home wage w if the foreign wage $w^* = 10,000$ pesos and $e = 0.001$ in the previous problem. Show what happens to w if
    (a) The tt worsens for the home country, falling to 7/10
    (b) The home labor input L/M subsequently improves to 1.5

12. Suppose the unit labor inputs for three goods are

	Good 1	Good 2	Good 3
Home	3	5	3
Foreign	2	1	3

Predict the pattern of trade.

13. If the foreign wage is 2,250 yen and exchange rate $e = 0.008$ in the previous problem, find the home wage w that makes the price of the middle good the same in both economies. Given this home wage, find the prices of the two traded goods produced in each country. Verify the direction of trade.

14. Find the limits to the exchange rate in the previous problem.

15. Consumer goods such as appliances and clothing require relatively low levels of investment and high levels of unskilled labor. Why would the United States have little cost advantage in such goods?

READINGS

William Allen, *International Trade Theory: Hume to Ohlin,* Random House, New York, 1965. A short paperback with readings from David Hume, Adam Smith, David Ricardo, John Stuart Mill, and others.

David Ricardo, *The Principles of Political Economy and Taxation,* Everyman's Library, New York, 1969 [1817]. Chapter 3, "On Foreign Trade," contains Ricardo's own masterly presentation.

PART TWO

Neoclassical Trade Theory

CHAPTER 3

The Gains from Trade

CHAPTER PREVIEW

This chapter develops the tools to study the gains from trade. Economists believe international trade generates overall gains. The arguments for free trade are presented in this chapter. Topics covered are:

(a) The *production possibility frontier* with increasing costs
(b) Measuring the gains from trade with *social welfare* and *real income*
(c) The importance of international trade in *developing economies*
(d) The potential role of *industrial trade policy* in the form of subsidies and other devices aimed at promoting export industries

INTRODUCTION

A nation's firms and industries are ultimately limited in the quantity they can produce because labor, capital, and natural resources are limited. The available resources or factors of production play a critical role in determining a country's comparative advantage and the pattern of trade.

There are many different kinds of labor. Capital goods such as machinery and equipment come in many varieties and must themselves be produced. Natural resources are as different as Kansas farmland, Kuwaiti crude oil, Colombian rain forests, and sunny Italian hillsides. The technology used to combine labor, capital, and natural resources into goods and services is constantly evolving. All of these elements come together in determining a nation's production possibilities and comparative advantage.

When relative prices of goods and services change, resources shift from one industry to another. If the price of copper increases, for instance, mining firms raise wages, hire more workers, and invest in more equipment to increase their output. The opposite occurs when copper prices fall: workers are laid off, wages fall, capital equipment is sold or left idle, and output falls. The overall limits to what can be produced are described by the economy's production possibilities frontier (PPF).

When output in an industry rises, resources shift into it and output in other industries must fall. If this shift continues, the decrease in other outputs may accelerate. If so, the opportunity cost of the good increases as its output increases. The PPF in this situation is a curved line, bowed away from the origin. Costs of production increase.

Consumers in an economy choose between available goods according to relative prices, making choices subject to their budget constraints. When the relative price of a good increases, consumers switch to substitutes and suffer reduced real income. The demand for a good falls as the price rises. As a whole, consumers influence prices through demand. Firms likewise respond to price changes, continually switching their efforts to more profitable activities. When the price of a particular good rises, profit opportunity increases, causing individual firms to increase output and perhaps inducing new firms to enter the industry. Falling prices create losses, causing firms to cut back production and potentially exit the industry. In the general equilibrium, prices determine output through the interaction of supply and demand.

When a small economy trades with the rest of the world, it accepts international prices for the traded goods and services. A small economy cannot influence worldwide or global supply or demand. International markets determine prices of traded goods. When a small economy begins to buy a good or service traded on a large international market, it has no effect on international excess demand or price and accepts the international price. Industries inside the small economy must rearrange their activities toward outputs more highly valued on the international market. A trading economy moves toward specialization in producing goods in which it has a comparative advantage relative to the rest of the world. The underlying structures of production are the basis for this comparative advantage.

Goods and services that a nation can produce relatively cheaply are exported while those that are cheap in the rest of the world are imported. Another inducement to import is the quality of foreign goods. Consumers in an open economy end up with a mix of domestic and foreign goods. The question arises whether they are better off than they were without trade. If they end up with more of every sort of good, they are better off indeed. One measure of whether there are gains from trade is whether consumers can consume more of every good after trade. Another measure uses the notion of community welfare or utility. Techniques of measuring community welfare are introduced in this chapter.

A move to free trade may bring overall gains, but adjustments in the economy must be made. The production processes have to be reorganized according to international prices. Firms expand output in one industry and reduce output in another. New firms may enter an expanding industry, while old firms shut down in a shrinking one. Business is a risky business. Workers are forced to retrain or relocate. The overall long-term gains for the nation are offset in part by these short-term adjustment losses. Workers who have held jobs in the same industry for 20 years will not want to see their industry declining because of international competition. An appeal to overall economic efficiency will not warm their hearts.

The tools developed in this chapter prove fruitful in the study of economic development. Trade has played a vital role in the development of most economies. Most economists who study development view trade as an engine of growth. The United States provides a prime example of a developing nation that relied on trade to build a foundation for growth. Cheap agricultural products based on abundant and fertile land were exported during the country's early development. High tariffs were placed on manufactured goods both to raise revenue and to give the nation's infant industry a chance to become established. The infant industry tariff is an example of industrial trade policy aimed at reorganizing the economy toward activities that ultimately will become more profitable. The tools of this chapter are used to study export subsidies and other industrial trade policies.

A. THE PRODUCTION POSSIBILITIES FRONTIER AND REAL INCOME

The PPF summarizes an economy's potential to produce goods. It illustrates the influence of relative prices on the pattern of production and lays the foundation for finding the gains from trade. This section develops the ideas of

(a) increasing opportunity costs
(b) an economy's real income and welfare

1. Activities in an Economy

Other things being equal, productive resources move to the firm or industry where they are paid the highest. A firm hires an extra worker or other input according to the value of the resulting additional output. The price of the firm's output and the productivity of the input itself determine the value of the additional output an input produces. The productivity of any input, labor for instance, depends on the quantity and quality of the firm's other inputs (capital, management, intermediate inputs, resources) and the technique used to combine the inputs into output.

Consider an economy producing two sorts of goods—manufactures and services. Prices and outputs of both goods are determined in two distinct markets. Also payments to factors of production (labor, capital, and natural resources) and employment are determined in markets for each of the economy's inputs. Owners of the productive resources sell their factors of production to firms. Firms combine the factors into outputs, which are ultimately sold to consumers who have earned income by supplying their factors of production. The factor markets and output markets are linked in various ways and make up the economy.

This activity is summarized by the flow of economic activity pictured in Figure 3.1. The arrows show the flow of goods and services. Payments flow in the opposite direction. Factor markets are represented by dotted arrows. Some firms sell intermediate goods, which are used to produce other goods, to other firms. The government acts much like a firm, hiring productive factors and providing services (mainly public goods such as national defense, parks, and public health). Figure 3.1 is a flow diagram for an open economy. International economics is concerned with the transactions that cross the national boundary. Foreign firms enter the picture by selling their goods to domestic firms, consumers, and the government. Foreign firms also buy intermediate inputs from domestic firms. Factor owners can supply their labor, rent their capital, or sell their natural resources to foreign firms and the foreign government.

2. Production Possibilities Frontiers with Increasing Opportunity Costs

It would be tedious to analyze each market individually, even in a simple economy producing only two types of goods. The PPF summarizes the entire economy.

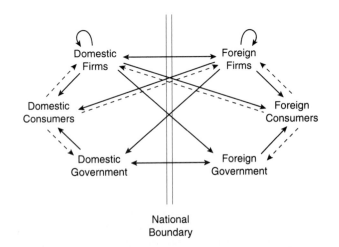

Figure 3.1. The Circular Flow of Economic Activity In a general sense, national boundaries are incidental to economic activity. The arrows show flows of goods and services from firms and governments to consumers. The arrows between firms illustrate trade in intermediate goods. The dotted arrows indicate factor markets, with individuals selling their labor, capital, and natural resources to firms and governments. International economics is the study of transactions that cross the national boundary.

In Figure 3.2, an economy at point *C* produces 300 units of manufactured goods *M* and no services *S*. All of the economy's resources are put into manufacturing in this situation of complete specialization. Suppose this economy is producing at point *C*. Consider what must happen as the economy moves down along the PPF from point *C* toward point *B*. A rising price of *S* relative to *M* would induce such a movement. Resources are bid away from their employment in the manufacturing sector by higher payments in the service sector. Firms in the service sector will want to hire inputs that are most productive in services.

The economy reaches point *B* when enough resources have been shifted to services so that output in that sector climbs to 50 units. Note that output of *M* has dropped from 300 to 275. The *opportunity cost* of the first 50 units of *S* is the lost 25 units of *M*. In the transition from point *C* to *B*, 1/2 of an *M* is given up on average for every unit of *S* produced.

At any point of the PPF, the slope of the PPF is an estimate of the opportunity cost of *S* in terms of *M*. The tangent at point *B* estimates how much *M* production an extra unit of *S* would cost. The slope of the PPF is called the *marginal rate of transformation* (MRT). The MRT is an estimate of how many units of *M* must be given up to produce another unit of *S*.

> The PPF shows the potential of the economy to produce goods when there is full employment and efficient production. The slope of the PPF is the marginal rate of transformation (MRT).

If the relative price of *S* continues to rise, more resources will shift into services. Resources most productive in services go to that sector first. Firms in the service industry must bid resources away from their employment in manufacturing. This means offering a factor payment above what is received in manufacturing. Firms in the service sector will seek out factors

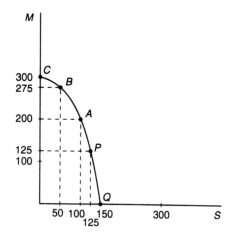

Figure 3.2. A Production Possibilities Frontier with Increasing Costs Increasing opportunity costs of production result in a production possibility frontier that is bowed away from or concave to the origin. The opportunity cost of additional production of (S) rises from 25/50 = 0.5 between points *C* and *B* to 125/25 = 5 between points *P* and *Q*. The opportunity cost of the production of *S* rises with the level of the production of *S* when costs are increasing. The same can be said for the production of *M*.

most suited to the production of services. The economy moves down along the PPF toward point A. At point A, another 50 units of S are produced while output of M has dropped to 200. The opportunity cost of these additional 50 units of S is $275 - 200 = 75 M$, or $75/50 = 1.5$ units of M for every S. Note that the opportunity cost has increased from what it had been between point C and B. The MRT of good M for good S increases moving down along this PPF. This increasing cost is reflected by the bowed-out PPF.

With *increasing opportunity costs,* the PPF is concave to (bowed away from) the origin. If the relative price of services continues to rise, production responds by shifting down toward point P. The opportunity cost of producing the 25 additional units of S to point P is $200 - 125 = 75 M$, or $75/25 = 3 M$ per unit of S. Moving finally to point Q, the opportunity cost of the last possible 25 units of S is $125 M$, or $5 M$ per unit of S.

Note that the PPF is concave all the way from point C to point Q. Sound theoretical reasons and empirical evidence suggest that increasing costs prevail and that the PPF should be concave to the origin. It is important to realize that the opportunity cost of S increases moving down the concave production frontier. Technically, this is due to *diminishing marginal productivity* of the inputs. With other inputs constant, the *marginal product* or addition to output of an extra worker diminishes as more workers are hired. The same is true for all inputs. As inputs shift between sectors along the frontier, diminishing marginal productivity creates a concave PPF. For incremental 1-unit increases in the output of services, the MRT approximates opportunity cost.

> Increasing costs of production (a concave PPF) are due to diminishing marginal productivity of the inputs.

In autarky, consumers choose the point along the PPF they want, according to their demand for the goods. Imagine supply and demand at work for each good, determining prices and outputs of the two goods. Producer choice is represented by the production frontier. Consumer choice is the process of choosing the most desired bundle of goods along the production frontier. The interaction of consumer and producer choice determines the relative price of services or the amount of M that trades for a unit of S. Factor markets are at work in the background, determining payments to the owners of labor, capital, and natural resources. Incomes of the factor owners influence their demand for final products.

3.   Indifference Curves and Consumer Equilibrium

The process of choice carried out by consumers can be understood with *indifference curves.* Imagine consumers are indifferent between the combinations of M and S along the indifference curve labeled *I* in Figure 3.3. Similarly, consumers equally prefer any point along indifference curve *II*. Since

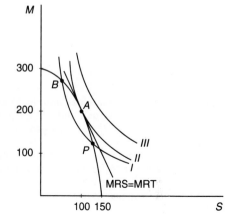

Figure 3.3. Maximizing Welfare and Consumer Choice Indifference curve *I* represents a low level of utility, *II* an intermediate level, and *III* the highest. Consumers maximize utility subject to the constraint of having to remain on their economy's production possibilities frontier (PPF). Point *A* represents the optimal consumer equilibrium where the slope of the indifference curve (the marginal rate of substitution, or MRS) equals the slope of the PPF (the marginal rate of transformation, or MRT).

curve *II* lies beyond curve *I*, consumers would prefer consuming at any point on *II* to consuming at any point on *I*. Of the three indifference curves, *III* represents the highest level of welfare or consumer satisfaction.

Consumers are constrained to choose a point along the PPF in autarky. Bundles *B* or *P* on the PPF and on indifference curve *I* could be chosen, but that would be inferior to the choice of point *A* on indifference curve *II*. Consumers would like to be on indifference curve *III*, but it lies beyond their economy's PPF. The optimal choice in Figure 3.3 is clearly point *A*, where welfare or utility is maximized subject to the constraint of remaining on the PPF. Indifference curve *II* and the PPF are tangent at point *A*. Their slopes at point *A* are equal.

The slope of an indifference curve is called the marginal rate of substitution (MRS). The MRS shows how many units of *M* consumers are willing to sacrifice for an extra unit of *S*. At the consumer optimum (point *A*) the MRS equals the MRT along the PPF. Consumers value an extra unit of *S* exactly the same as its opportunity cost in production.

At point *B* the MRS is greater (in absolute value) than the MRT. Consumers value an extra unit of *S* more than its opportunity cost in production, and the relative price of *S* would be bid up. At point *P* the MRS is less than the MRT. Consumers value an extra unit of *M* more than its opportunity cost in production, and the relative price of *S* would be bid down.

At the consumer equilibrium the MRS along an indifference curve equals the MRT along the PPF.

4. Finding Real Income

In Figure 3.4 the slope of the tangency at the optimal point *A* on the PPF is found from the endpoints of the tangent at point *X*. Slope equals the rise over the run, or $-400/200 = -2$. The negative sign indicates that about 2

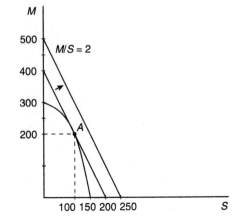

Figure 3.4. Relative Price Lines and the Value of National Income Suppose production and consumption take place in autarky at point A. The line tangent to the production possibilities frontier at point A is the relative price line. Its endpoints show the value of national income in terms of that particular good. National income is valued at 400 M or 200 S. The parallel outward shift in the price line represents an increase in national income at the same relative price M/S = 2.

units of M must be given up for the extra unit of S at point A. The endpoints of this *domestic price line* indicate the value of national product or income expressed in units of either good.

The value of national income at point A equals 400 units of M. Consumption at point A is 200 units of M and 100 units of S. Each unit of S is valued at 2 M, so the 100 units of S produced and consumed are worth 2 × 100 = 200 units of M. Total output and consumption are thus valued at 200 M + (2 × 100 S) = 400 M. Likewise, production, consumption, and national income are valued at 200 S.

Valuing national income in terms of one good or the other may seem unusual. Indeed, national income is typically expressed in the national currency. When income is expressed in terms of goods, it is referred to as *real income*. Nominal income is expressed in terms of the domestic currency. Suppose the nominal price of manufactures in the economy of Figure 3.4 is $2. Remember that the relative price of a unit of S at point A is M/S = 2. The nominal price of a unit of S must then be $2/M × 2 = $4. National income valued at 400 M could be nominally valued at $2/M × 400 = $800. Alternatively, national income of 200 S can be stated nominally as $4/S × 200 = $800.

Comparison of nominal valuations across time must take into account the changing value of currency. Inflation leads to rising prices and higher nominal income, even with constant real income. Valuing national income in real terms drives home the point that changes in real income matter.

> Real national income, evaluated in terms of one good or the other, is found at the intersection of the relative price line (tangent line) of the PPF with either axis.

At the same relative price, higher income is reflected by a price line farther from the origin. Such an increase in income is illustrated by the price line running from 500 *M* to 250 *S* in Figure 3.4. Note that the relative price is unchanged, since $M/S = 500/250 = 2$. National income would have risen to 500 *M,* 250 *S,* or $1,000 at the same nominal prices. This level of income is unattainable in autarky given the economy's PPF.

A straightforward way to measure the gains from trade will be to see whether trade increases national income valued at domestic prices. In other words, if through international trade consumers end up with a bundle of goods valued higher at their original domestic prices, trade has shown overall gains. Consumers clearly gain if they have the potential to consume more of every good after trade. If so, there are obviously gains from trade. Alternatively, welfare or utility increase if consumers can move to a higher indifference curve with trade.

EXAMPLE 3.1   The U.S. Production Frontier

Output of services relative to manufactures in the United States has been growing steadily since 1950. The ratio of service to manufacturing output has grown from 2.8 to 3.5, as estimated by Patricia Beeson and Michael Bryan (1986). Valued in constant 1982 dollars, real output of services has grown from $625 billion to $2,200 billion (a 252% increase) since 1950. Manufacturing output has grown from $225 billion to $625 billion (a 178% increase) over the same time. The higher ratio of service output reflects a switch toward consumption of services with higher personal income as well as a tendency to specialize internationally in services. It also partly reflects a tendency of firms to hire business services such as accounting and consulting, rather than performing those activities inside the firm. Over the years 1969 to 1985, the average price of manufactured goods relative to other goods (services and agriculture) fell by 26%, according to Lynn Brown (1986).

The PPF of the United States has greatly expanded over the years because of economic growth or development and has shifted away from manufactures because of their falling relative price. This analysis downplays the positive influence of new goods and services. Many goods available now were not around 40 years ago. Dividing economic activity into two simple categories oversimplifies and distorts reality somewhat, but insight is gained by looking at these broad trends. With competition from the manufacturing industries in developing nations where wages are low, the relative price of manufactures cannot be expected to rise in the future.

EXAMPLE 3.2   Investment by Sector in the United States

Underlying the shifting U.S. PPF is the investment in capital (machinery, equipment, and structures) in the different sectors. Expanding output requires more capital input. Figures from *Fixed Reproducible Wealth in the US 1925–85* published by the U.S. Department of Commerce (1987) show the percentage of investment spending by sector in the United States over 10-year periods starting in 1956:

	Agriculture	*Manufacturing*	*Services*
1956–1965	4%	32%	64%
1966–1975	13%	16%	71%
1976–1985	−7%	10%	97%

A large and increasing percentage of investment is aimed at the service industry. Investment in manufacturing, on the other hand, has been steadily declining. Agriculture has had an uneven trend in investment and had disinvestment in the period 1976–1985. Stocks of existing capital in 1985 were reported as:

	Agriculture	*Manufacturing*	*Services*
Stock	$11 billion	$81 billion	$351 billion
Percentage of total	3%	18%	79%

This distribution of the labor force in the U.S. economy is mirrored by the distribution of capital. According to the 1989 *Economic Report of the President,* 69% of all workers are in services (personal and business services, transport, utilities, finance, trade, government, military, etc.), 28% are in manufacturing, and 3% are in agriculture. In 1960, 52% of all workers were in services, 41% were in manufacturing, and 7% were in agriculture.

EXAMPLE 3.3   Patterns of Specialization

This table from the *World Development Report 1988* of the World Bank reports the changing structure of production for developing and industrial nations. The numbers reported are percentages of gross national product (GNP) in services S and manufactures M. Note the growth in manufacturing for the developing nations and the corresponding decline in the industrial nations. The industrial nations are specializing more in services. The residual GNP is agriculture, which has fallen from 30% to 19% in the developing nations and from 5% to 3% in the industrial nations.

	1965			1980			1987		
	S	*M*	*A*	*S*	*M*	*A*	*S*	*M*	*A*
Developing nations	41%	29%	30%	44%	37%	19%	46%	35%	19%
Industrial nations	55%	40%	5%	61%	36%	3%	62%	35%	3%

Problems for Section A

A1.   Diagram a production possibility frontier with these points on it: $(M,S) = (100,0), (90,25), (70,50), (40,75),$ and $(0,100)$. Show that it has increasing opportunity costs of production.

A2.   From your diagram in problem A1, *estimate* the MRT when consumption is $(M,S) = (90,25)$. (Hint: Draw the relative price line.) What is the value of consumption in terms of S? What is the value of national income in terms of M? If the price of M is $\$/M = 3$ billion, find nominal national income.

A3.   Estimate the relative price needed to shift consumption from $(90,25)$ to $(40,75)$ along the PPF in problem A1.

B. SPECIALIZATION AND THE GAINS FROM TRADE

When an economy begins to trade internationally, it opens itself to international prices. These new prices rearrange production, pushing the economy into specializing in producing the goods the rest of the world values more highly. Imports enter the economy, causing cutbacks in the domestic industries that compete with imports. This section stresses that specialization and trade lead to overall gains, manifested as the potential to consume more of every type of good. Real income increases with trade, and consumers move to a higher level of satisfaction and a higher indifference curve.

1. Domestic Autarky Prices and International Prices

The supply side of an economy is pictured by the PPF. The upper limits of production with efficiency and full employment of all resources are laid out along the economy's PPF. The demand side of an economy is made up of consumers and their desires for all of the various goods and services, represented by indifference curves. The interaction of supply and demand determines relative prices, the optimal choice along the production frontier, and the value of national income.

Given that the economy is operating on its PPF, there are two ways for the economy to provide more goods for its consumers and to enjoy higher national income and welfare. One way is economic development through expanding the resource base or improving technology. Economic development pushes the production frontier out from the origin. The only other way to attain higher national income and welfare is through international trade.

Suppose the economy's autarky relative price of services M/S is 2 at point A (for autarky) in Figure 3.5. The economy produces and consumes 200 units of M and 100 units of S at point A in autarky. Suppose additionally there is an international market for services where each unit of service output is worth 4 M. As the economy opens to free trade, firms producing S have the option of selling at a relative price of either 2 or 4. If the nominal or home currency price of a unit of M is \$2, the nominal price of S is \$4 on the home market and \$8 on the international market. It is easy to see in which market the domestic firms producing services will want to sell. This is the predominant incentive to export.

In Figure 3.5 the *international price* of $M/S = 4$ is sketched along with the economy's PPF. This international price is assumed to remain the same whether or not the economy trades internationally. The economy, in other words, is assumed to be small relative to the international market.

Industry inside the economy will respond to the higher international price of services through increased output or *specialization* in that sector. Resources shift into services, with output rising from 100 units of S at autarky point A to 125 units of S at specialized point P. Resources leave manufacturing, causing its output to drop from 200 to 125. The economy moves from autarky production point A to production point P with trade, specializing in the good that is relatively more expensive on the international market.

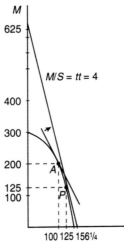

Figure 3.5. International Prices and Specialization The price line $M/S = 4$ represents the international price of services. It is higher than the domestic relative price of 2. An open economy will specialize in the production of S, moving from point A to point P. The domestic service industry expands and the domestic manufacturing industry contracts as the economy specializes into free trade.

2.   Finding the Real Gains from Trade

Trade takes place at international or world prices with free trade. For every unit of S exported, 4 units of M are imported in this example. This sounds like barter, with one good being directly traded for another. Money facilitates exchange. In international trade the two monies involved are traded in the foreign exchange market. Domestic service firms sell their product on the international market. Foreign importers of services must buy domestic currency on the foreign exchange market, selling their own currency. Domestic importers of manufactures go to the foreign exchange market to buy foreign currency, ultimately selling the imported goods to domestic consumers.

The internationally specialized economy produces 125 units of M and 125 units of S, trading services for manufactures at the international price. In Figure 3.6 the international price line is labeled tt for *terms of trade*. Its slope is −4, representing the 4 units of M that are received for every unit of exported S. In this example the economy takes the terms of trade, adjusts production to point P, and trades to the most desired point T along the terms of trade line tt.

Consumer choice determines point T. Point T represents the highest indifference curve consumers can attain along the terms of trade line tt. Point T is a tangency between the tt line and the highest indifference curve that touches the tt line. At point T the marginal rate of substitution along indifference curve III equals the terms of trade. In autarky, consumers maximize their welfare or utility subject to the constraint of being on their economy's PPF. Consumption at point A results in the welfare level represented by indifference curve II as in Figure 3.3. Consumption at point T results in higher welfare.

In free trade, production takes place where the marginal rate of transformation (MRT) along the PPF equals the terms of trade (tt). Con-

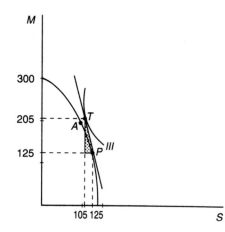

Figure 3.6. Production and Consumption with Free Trade With international specialization at point P, consumers in the economy can consume anywhere along the tt line. In this example, 20 units of S are exported in exchange for 80 units of M. At point T, consumption of both goods has increased relative to the autarky position at point A. Consumers move to a higher level of welfare and a higher indifference curve at point T.

sumption takes place where the marginal rate of substitution (MRS) along a tangent indifference curve equals *tt*.

In this example, 205 units of *M* and 105 units of *S* are consumed with free trade at point *T*. Production takes place at point *P* where $(M,S) = (125,125)$. Note that consumers would be forced to a lower level of utility (indifference curve *I* in Figure 3.3) if they had to consume what the economy produces at point *P*. Exports of services amount to $125 - 105 = 20$ units of *S*. Imports of manufactures are $205 - 125 = 80$ *M*. This trade reflects the international terms of trade *tt*, since $80/20 = 4$ *M/S*.

The shaded triangle in Figure 3.6 with exports as the base and imports as the height is the *trade triangle*. Note that consumers enjoy more of both goods in free trade relative to autarky in this example. Point *T* is northeast of point *A*. The same would be true for other economies specializing and trading. The world economy must be operating more efficiently than it does without trade. Consumers around the world can potentially consume more of every good with free trade.

> International prices determine the pattern of output and the possibilities in consumption for an open economy.

The *real gains from trade* are found by valuing the goods consumed with trade at the original domestic autarky prices. The autarky relative price of *M* for this example economy is 2 from Figure 3.4. Each unit of *M* consumed can be valued at the domestic autarky price of 1/2 *S*. With the trade in Figure 3.6, the value of consumption in terms of services is $105\ S + (205\ M \times 1/2) = 207.5\ S$. The 205 units of *M* consumed are valued at 102.5 units of *S*. Along with the 105 units of *S* consumed, the value of consumption with trade totals 207.5 units of *S*. This is beyond the level of 200 units of *S* obtained with autarky in Figure 3.4. The gains from trade in this example amount to 7.5 units of *S*.

The gains can similarly be calculated in terms of *M*. Even if less of some particular good is consumed, there can be overall gains from trade. Remember that consumers choose the point along *tt* that they prefer. Consumers have the potential to consume more of both goods with trade.

> The real gains from trade, valued in a standard (numeraire) commodity, show the increased level of consumption through specialization and trade.

Trade clearly generates gains if more of every good can be potentially consumed. Trade generally provides the potential to consume more than can be produced in any economy on its own. Trade has the same effect on consumption as economic development, which expands the PPF. Trade allows consumers to enjoy combinations of goods beyond the economy's PPF.

Thousands of goods and services are traded internationally. This simple example with two types of goods illustrates the main point that international trade results in a more efficient worldwide pattern of production and higher levels of consumption. International trade helps an economy perform its basic function, providing goods and services. From the viewpoint of global economic efficiency, international boundaries introduce frictions and distortions that decrease the capacity to produce goods and services.

3. Production Adjustment with Free Trade

Domestic manufacturing firms are forced to face foreign competition when the economy opens to free trade. Foreign industry must have a cost advantage in producing the goods a country imports. A positive role for economic policy is to assist workers in switching from one sector to another as the economy adjusts to foreign competition.

Many domestic manufacturing firms will go out of business with the adjustment to free trade from point A to point P in Figure 3.5. Many manufacturing workers will have to retrain or relocate. Stockholders and investors in the domestic manufacturing industry will lose. Only the more efficient domestic manufacturing firms survive. These costs of adjustment can be sizeable, but in the long run they are outweighed by the efficiency gains resulting from free trade.

> When an economy opens to trade, it will move along its PPF toward producing goods with relatively higher international prices.

In the example of Figure 3.5, domestic output of manufactures falls and output of services rises. Services are more expensive on the international market, and manufactures are cheaper. Consumers will want the right mix of the two goods. Viewed as a whole, the economy exports its internationally dear services in exchange for internationally cheap manufactures. Each unit of manufactures is valued at 1/2 S at home but only 1/4 S internationally. Importing firms buy the cheap manufactures from abroad to sell in the domestic market, forcing the domestic manufacturing industry to lower its output. In practice, the same domestic firms often switch some of their activity from production to importing.

The PPF illustrates the long-run possibilities in the economy. The friction of adjustment pushes the economy temporarily below its PPF as pictured in Figure 3.7. The economy will move along the path with arrows in the adjustment process. Resources in the manufacturing sector may not readily transform into inputs for the service sector. These resources may be labor with specialized skills or manufacturing capital machinery and equipment not suited to service production. These resources may be located away from the growing commercial centers where service production takes place. The costs of retraining, retooling, and relocating must be paid through the use of scarce economic resources. The economy temporarily produces less than it would if there were no adjustment friction. As adjustments are made, the economy moves to production point P.

The ultimate gains from free trade make the transition costs worth paying. When firms in an economy are open to competition, they learn to adjust to changing conditions in their market, the economy, and the world.

EXAMPLE 3.4   From Autarky to Free Trade: Japan after 1858

A classic example of the benefits of trade is provided by Japan's entry into world markets in the 1800s, examined by Richard Huber (1971). Before 1858 and the arrival of a fleet of U.S. warships, Japan had been isolated during a half century of trade restrictions. When trade opened, the volume of trade increased 70 times by 1890, to about 70% of national income. Most of Japan's exports of that era were silk and tea. Copper, dried fish, and coal were other Japanese exports. Prices of these exports rose 33% with the move to free trade. Imports of sugar, cotton, and metals (virtually all from Great Britain) fell in price to 39% of their autarky levels. This means that the world relative price of Japanese exports in terms of Japanese imports was about 3.5 times the autarky price inside Japan. World prices were apparently not affected by Japan's entry into world trade. Japan, in other words, was a small economy. Huber esti-

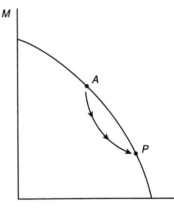

Figure 3.7. Adjustment Frictions Production may be forced to take the path indicated by arrows below the production possibilities frontier in its adjustment to international prices and production point P. These short-run adjustment costs must be paid, pushing the economy temporarily below its long-run potential. National income falls during the adjustment period.

mates that real national income rose in Japan by 65% with the move to free trade.

EXAMPLE 3.5   Estimating Gains from Trade: Compact Trucks

Robert Feenstra (1988) presents a method for calculating the gains from trade. Compact pickup trucks, first built in Japan, were imported from Japan into the United States during the late 1960s and 1970s. The tariff on these trucks increased from 4% to 25% in 1980. It is little surprise that U.S. automakers were soon domestically producing compact pickups. From 1979 to 1984 the number of standard size U.S. pickups produced fell from 1.9 million to 1.3 million. Even with the tariff, yearly imports of Japanese compact pickups rose from 464,000 to 649,000 over these same years. Feenstra estimates the consumer gain from the Japanese trucks to be $628 per truck in 1979 and $582 in 1980 before the tariff was put in place. This gain is estimated by figuring what U.S. consumers would have had to pay for similar trucks had they been produced domestically. This gain represents about 20% of the average price of the imported trucks. With the tariff the gain per truck fell to about $200 because the price of the trucks increased. Based on quality differences, the gains from consuming compact U.S. trucks were only about 15% of the gains from consuming Japanese trucks. Consumers paid for the protection of the domestic truck industry through higher prices and decreased quality.

Problems for Section B

B1.   Evaluate the gains from trade in terms of manufactured goods comparing Figures 3.4 and 3.6.

B2.   Starting with Figure 3.4, suppose the terms of trade tt are 0.9 M for every unit of S. In which good will the economy specialize? Illustrate with a diagram. Show the short-run adjustment path.

B3.   At $tt = M/S = 0.9$, suppose production moves to point B from point A in Figure 3.2. If 72 units of M are exported, diagram the trade triangle. Find the consumption of both goods after trade. Find the real gains from trade in terms of S.

C.   ECONOMIC DEVELOPMENT AND INTERNATIONAL TRADE

With most of the world's population living in poverty, economic development may be the most important branch of economics as the next century approaches. International trade and finance have proved indispensable for economic development. Economies that try to develop closed to outside influences are like gardens trying to grow without sunshine. This section examines the role of international trade in economic development.

1.   Export Promotion versus Import Substitution

Economies develop by increasing or improving their productive resources, such as capital and skilled labor, or by improving their technology of production. Technology refers to the techniques used in combining various inputs into an output. *Human capital* or labor skills can be acquired through education and training. Capital equipment and machinery are accumulated through investment spending by firms. In open economies, investment often comes from abroad. Since there is relatively little capital in the typical developing economy, the return on investment can be quite high. Development is a gradual process. There are no shortcuts to acquiring the human and physical capital required to develop and increase productivity.

Economic development is pictured by an expanding PPF. The economy is potentially able to produce more of every good as it develops. Indeed, a developing economy may establish new industries.

International trade plays a vital role in the development of most successful nations. As an economy specializes and exports, it may be better able to attract foreign investment. Foreign firms are often the stimulus to move into outward-looking or exporting industries. As the economy opens, workers must intensify their training to compete effectively in international markets. The PPF evidently expands faster when the economy concentrates on its export industry. Export-led growth occurs when growth in the economy is biased toward its export sector. Policy aimed at pushing the economy more into international specialization is called *export promotion.*

Some economies have tried to develop through *import substitution,* replacing imports with domestically produced goods. The basic motivation behind this approach to economic development is the belief that the economy should be able to provide for itself. "The rich developed nations have automobile industries, so we must have one if we are to be successful" seems to be the reasoning.

In practice, import substitution often amounts to little more than slightly disguised protectionism. High tariffs are imposed to protect the domestic industry, which is supposed to provide a full range of goods and services. Even regions as large and diverse as the United States or Europe do not produce, and must import, many types of goods. A domestic import competing industry can never catch up entirely with the rest of the world unless it has some underlying comparative advantage. Protected industries in a developing nation operate relatively inefficiently but make profits because of the artificially high price. The economy may fail to develop as fast as it would if attention were focused on the export industry. Large gains from trade are bypassed, and consumers continue to lose.

The Eastern Bloc nations basically tried to develop through import substitution, which accounts in large part for their poor economic performance. As these economies begin to liberalize, international trade and investment will play increasingly important roles. Mexico has attempted to develop an auto industry, allowing German and Japanese firms to set up plants for the Mexican market as well as for export. India has followed the same strategy, with little success. England has a history of import substitution policy in steel and shipping. Policies of import substitution are difficult to separate from policies of protection.

Figure 3.8 illustrates the losses that arise with import substitution. Suppose the economy is operating in free trade at production point P, specializing and exporting S. Import substitution policy will induce the economy to move up its PPF toward autarky point A, to produce at point IS (import substitution). The economy then trades at the international terms of trade, along line tt', which is parallel to tt.

Note that tt' lies below the terms of trade line tt, which starts at point P. Consumers are constrained to pick a bundle of goods below their consumption possibilities with free trade. For illustration, consumption with free trade is labeled T and consumption with import substitution policy is labeled T'. Consumers are forced to a lower indifference curve (not drawn), and real income falls in the move from point T to T'.

As inefficient as import substitution policies have proved, there is nevertheless sentiment that less developed countries (LDCs) should not depend on the developed countries (DCs). Such dependence is often labeled exploitation. If a large foreign multinational firm builds a plant and produces goods that are exported, cries of exploitation of cheap labor are heard. This sentiment is promoted by the firms inside the LDCs that would benefit through avoiding the international competition. These domestic firms themselves would like to carry out the production and export.

National pride seems to be hurt if, for instance, a domestic automobile

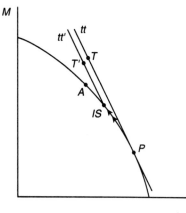

Figure 3.8. Import Substitution Import substitution encourages the economy to shift resources away from production point P in free trade. Output shifts toward the imported good to point IS. Trade then occurs up along the terms of trade line tt', which lies below tt. Consumption point T' will lie below T, real income falls, and consumers are forced to a lower indifference curve.

or steel industry cannot establish or maintain itself. Never mind that a huge competitive international market already exists. LDCs desire to emulate the larger industrialized nations that are diversified.

Each developing nation has its own particular situation, so a general prescription for growth is difficult to formulate. The simple advice of opening to international trade and investment, however, will universally increase income.

> The development strategy of import substitution has proved wasteful and unsuccessful, creating more problems than it solves. Developing economies should be encouraged to adjust to international competition.

An economy's direction of development is determined by fundamentals such as the availability of capital and natural resources, the training and background of labor, and changes in technology. Nations like Australia, with mineral and gem deposits, naturally have the potential to develop mining as well as industries that use the minerals and gems directly as inputs. Nations with fertile land and agreeable climate are best suited to develop agricultural industry.

The United States will never produce bananas or coffee for export. Costa Rica will never export wheat. The point is not that these goods cannot possibly be produced in the countries. They could be, but only at a great expense. Hothouses can be built for bananas or coffee in the United States. Rain forests can be cleared and hills flattened to grow wheat in Central America. Such projects have been carried out, but the goods are too expensive to compete with imports from regions where natural conditions are suited. Manufactured goods and traded services can be produced virtually anywhere. All that is needed is the investment or capital goods, management, labor, and entrepreneurship to begin production.

2. Export-led Growth

In Figure 3.9, economic development is biased toward manufactures. The production frontier expands outward, with the expansion biased toward the manufacturing sector. The terms of trade tt determine production for an open economy as development occurs.

In Figure 3.9 the terms of trade tt stay the same as development occurs. The economy starts at point P, producing according to the international price tt and trading to point T. As the economy develops, its potential to produce manufactures grows more rapidly than its potential to produce services S or agricultural goods A. This bias in growth can be due to international investment or the use of improved technology in manufacturing.

After development the economy will produce at point P' and trade at the same terms of trade tt. Note that the two terms of trade lines are parallel.

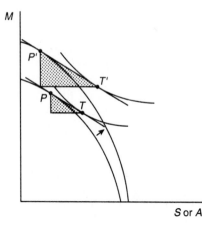

Figure 3.9. Export-led Growth Concentrating on the production of manufactures may lead to enhanced potential to produce manufactures in the long run. This expansion is illustrated by a production possibilities frontier that expands more toward the specialized export good.

The economy trades off from point P' to point T'. With development, consumers enjoy a higher level of welfare or utility on a higher indifference curve.

Growth leads to gains because more of both goods can be consumed. The potential for growth may be greater, however, given the potential to specialize. With export-led growth, production frontiers evidently can expand faster. When the economy trades freely, incentive and opportunity for the export sector to expand are increased.

If the domestic manufacturing industry were protected, the PPF would expand more slowly and there would be less bias toward developing technology and resources for manufactures. Ultimately, less of both goods is consumed under protection.

The *developmental gains* from trade refer to the enhanced growth in the production frontier that results from improving technology and expanding resources with specialization. Developmental gains from trade are difficult to analyze because the results of specialization are difficult to compare with what could have happened without it. In the case of a protected economy using import substitution as its strategy, the outcome of free international trade and investment is difficult to project.

Gains from specialization and trade occur as the economy adjusts production along its PPF. Developmental gains from trade go beyond movement along the economy's current PPF and refer to the expansion of the PPF induced by free international trade and investment.

Growth biased toward the export industry has the potential of lowering the price of the exported good when the economy is a major supplier on international markets. Examples of such nations and goods could be Chile and copper, Saudi Arabia and oil, South Africa and diamonds, or Colombia and coffee. As such an economy expands, the international supply of its export rises. This lowers the price of the export, which means falling terms of trade. If the terms of trade fall considerably, the nation may end up worse off after growth and trade. This outcome is an example of what is called *immiserizing growth.*

Figure 3.10 pictures an immiserizing expansion of the manufacturing export sector. Before growth the terms of trade *tt* led the economy to produce at point *P* and consume at point *C*. With growth and increasing exports the terms of trade fall to *tt'* as the economy's supply of its export increases on the international market. This decline in the terms of trade is more apt to happen when international demand for the country's export is inelastic. The terms of trade fall to *tt'*, with production ending up at *P'* and consumption at *C'*.

Most nations do not grossly affect their terms of trade through expanding their exports. While there is potential for immiserizing growth, it has not been realized in practice.

3.   Foreign Investment and Economic Development

The potential to specialize and export is an incentive for investment in the expanding export sector. Most often LDCs depend on rich, developed countries for the initial investment to begin the economy's expansion. For instance, rapid development in the United States began with the influx of foreign investment into railroads in the 1800s. Multinational firms provide both physical and human capital in the forms of equipment, skilled labor, and management. The most successful multinational firms adapt well to the foreign customs and laws in the host country. Setting up a branch operation can be risky, but the returns to the firm can be high.

Despite some reluctance to "sell out" to foreign interests, the gains from growth and trade are too great to be pushed aside entirely. Mexico, Greece, and many other nations have historically limited the percentage of foreign ownership in firms and thus curtailed multinational investment. Viewed from the perspective of long-term income or welfare potential, this

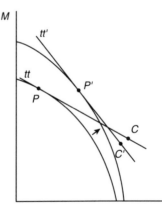

Figure 3.10. Immiserizing Growth Export-led growth can lead to a fall in the terms of trade if the economy is a major supplier of the exported good on the world market and world demand is inelastic. The fall in the terms of trade from *tt* to *tt'* forces the economy into consuming an inferior bundle of goods at a *C'*. Evidently, however, immiserizing growth rarely occurs.

policy is seriously flawed. The potential for growth and increased income or welfare leads to expansion in the export industries, potentially greater production possibilities, and ultimately higher income.

4. Newly Industrializing Countries, Less Developed Countries, and Developed Countries

Newly industrializing countries (NICs) like Brazil, Korea, Mexico, Taiwan, Hong Kong, and Singapore rely heavily on manufactured exports. From a global efficiency standpoint, these are the nations where a large part of assembly line production should be taking place. Most manufacturing jobs require little training. Manufacturing typically uses a high degree of unskilled labor. The machinery and techniques of production are developed and readily available.

Developed countries (DCs) like the United States, Japan, and the nations of Western Europe have relatively high wages for handlers and assemblers and cannot compete with the low manufacturing wages in the NICs.

One predominant difference between the LDCs and the NICs is that NICs have turned to policies of export promotion, while LDCs are often stuck on policies of import substitution.

It is unfortunate that the DCs (the United States, Japan, and the European nations) protect their manufacturing sectors, since the LDCs and NICs view this as a direct hindrance to development. Protection is also unfortunate for the general interest of the DCs and for global economic efficiency. As reported by the General Agreement on Trade and Tariffs (GATT), tariffs on imports of manufactures from developing nations average 9% in the United States and 7% in both Japan and Europe. This may not seem like a high rate of protection, but it can keep a developing nation from selling in these large markets. Tariff rates on some goods are much higher.

Protection of the basic industries like textiles, apparel, and footwear is higher in the DCs than the average levels of protection. Protection is high in precisely the industries that would potentially be exported by LDCs and NICs. Nontariff barriers (quotas and other restrictions) of the DCs also seriously inhibit trade. A study by the World Bank shows that 14% of manufactured imports from DCs into the United States are subject to nontariff protection. In Europe 21% of manufactured imports from DCs are subject to nontariff barriers. A full 65% of textile and clothing imports from DCs are subject to nontariff protection in the United States and Europe. Developing nations may not take the industrial nations too seriously when they preach the virtues of free trade!

Imagine yourself an entrepreneur or manager in a manufacturing firm in a poor developing country. Wages and costs are low, but you are unable to sell your goods in the United States because of the tariff that must be paid. When U.S. officials or economists talk about the benefits of free trade, it will sound hypocritical.

EXAMPLE 3.6   Manufactured Exports of Newly Industrializing Countries

These figures from the *Yearbook of International Trade Statistics* (1981) of the United Nations shows the percentage of each nation's exports made up of manufactured goods. NICs show a clear tendency to expand into the production and export of manufactured goods.

	Percentage of Manufactured Goods in Exports	
	1965	*1980*
Brazil	8%	39%
Hong Kong	94%	97%
Korea	59%	90%
Mexico	16%	40%
Singapore	35%	54%

EXAMPLE 3.7   Capital Goods and Growth

Machinery is an important input, generally thought to be essential for economic development. Bradford DeLong and Larry Summers (1990) studied 61 countries and showed that countries with abundant and cheap machinery develop faster. From 1965 to 1980, Japan invested 12% of its annual income in new machinery, which explains almost all of its very high 5.4% annual growth in output. At the other end of the spectrum, Argentina invested 2% of its annual income in new machinery and grew at only 0.9% per year. Protection of the domestic industries producing machinery is found to slow growth by making machinery more expensive.

EXAMPLE 3.8   Shifting Patterns of Specialization and Exports

This table from the *World Development Report 1986* of the World Bank provides one look at the changing international pattern of specialization and export. LDCs remain primarily agricultural but are specializing into manufacturing. NICs are specializing more in manufacturing and are moving away from agriculture, which accounts for roughly half as much export as in the LDCs. All but 7% of the manufacturing exports in the

oil exporters was oil extraction in 1984. The oil exporters should be analyzed separately because they rely on agricultural imports and are expanding their service exports. The United States and Canada specialize
in services to a higher degree than the other DCs listed. Every DC specialized away from manufacturing over the period.

| | Percentage of Exports by Sector | | | | | |
| | Agriculture | | Manufacturing | | Services | |
	1965	1984	1965	1984	1965	1984
LDCs	43%	37%	29%	34%	28%	29%
NICs	21%	15%	31%	36%	47%	49%
Oil exporters	5%	2%	65%	61%	30%	37%
U.S.	3%	2%	38%	32%	59%	66%
Canada	5%	3%	34%	24%	61%	72%
Japan	9%	3%	43%	41%	48%	56%
U.K.	3%	2%	38%	32%	59%	66%

Problems for Section C

C1. Illustrate export-led growth in services with an expanding PPF
and trade.

C2. With growth biased toward manufactures as in Figure 3.9, what
happens to the opportunity cost of a unit of manufactures when the ratio
of outputs is constant? (Hint: The ratio of outputs is constant along a line
from the origin.) How does this reflect biased growth?

C3. Growth is unbiased across sectors when it is not biased toward
any sector. Illustrate unbiased growth with an expanding PPF. What happens to the level of trade in a small nation exporting manufactures?

D. INDUSTRIAL TRADE POLICY

Given the potential gains from trade, industrial trade policy has the goal of
managing the composition and direction of trade to the country's advantage. Governments around the world try to help domestic industry by establishing laws and policies that favor domestic production. Production of exports is encouraged through subsidies and other sorts of arrangements.
Monopolies and cartels are encouraged in European and most other nations, unlike the situation in the United States. This section examines var-

ious sorts of industrial trade policy, including subsidies, tax and tariff policies, free trade zones, free enterprise zones, price supports, and subsidized loans.

1. Export Promotion

Most governments try to devise ways to promote exports of particular goods, aiming to make industry in the country expand in international markets. At the same time, industries that compete with imports are sheltered with protection. This overall *industrial trade policy* is typically carried out under pressure from the export industry and the industry that competes with imports. Political and financial support, after all, keeps politicians in office.

Often underlying the policy is a desire to increase export revenue and decrease a trade deficit. Promoting the export industry may seem more desirable than a devaluation, which increases the price of imported intermediate inputs and consumer goods and might discourage incoming foreign investment.

A *subsidy* is any device that lowers the cost or increases the revenue of a firm exporting to the international market. The simplest type of subsidy is a direct payment per unit of good produced or exported in the targeted industry. Other subsidies come in the form of reduced corporate taxes on profits of exporting firms or waivers on tariffs of imported intermediate products. Labor can also be subsidized in export industries through direct payments per worker to exporting firms. Another common device is government-sponsored research and development (R&D), which lowers cost in the export industry. The U.S. Department of Agriculture and the land grant universities in the United States historically have subsidized U.S. agriculture in this manner.

These cost-reducing subsidies enable exporting firms to sell at a lower price on the international market. Foreign competing industries view subsidies as unfair.

> Export subsidies are aimed at making a nation's exported goods cheaper on international markets and increasing revenue or profit in the export sector.

Through subsidies a government spends tax revenue working directly with industry to make goods cheaper for foreign consumers. Stated this way, the industrial trade policy of export promotion sounds almost ridiculous. Such policies tax domestic consumers, with the transfer going to foreign consumers.

Nevertheless, some sentiment has arisen to develop a comprehensive industrial trade policy for the United States. This may be due to the trade deficits of the 1980s and to the perception that foreign governments "unfairly" subsidize their export industries. If foreign taxpayers are willing to subsidize our consumption through government subsidies funded by taxes in their countries, it may not be so smart to retaliate by subsidizing their consumption. U.S. industries seeking protection often claim that the Japanese government (and taxpayers) unfairly subsidize targeted Japanese export industries. Japanese taxpayers' willingness to subsidize our consumption in the United States, is not clearly cause for alarm.

Governments of the rich DCs subsidize export industries in various ways. *Foreign aid,* simply giving money to governments of poor countries, often results in the export of domestically produced goods. The countries receiving the aid may, in other words, turn around and buy domestic goods. The United States offers *military aid* that is often tied to the purchase of U.S. weapons. Since revenue for this foreign and military aid comes from taxpayers, it is, in effect, a subsidy to firms producing the exports.

The little-publicized Export-Import (Ex-Im) Bank is backed by the U.S. Department of Commerce and makes loans at low interest rates to exporting firms, particularly in the aerospace industry. Agricultural price supports subsidize the export of agricultural goods. Government sponsored R&D, performed in government labs or in state-supported universities, leads to product development, often in export industries.

The main point is that the United States and other industrial countries already have an extensive industrial policy. Whether it should be expanded through a particular program depends on the costs and benefits of the program itself. Proponents of industrial trade policy are often firms that are finding it difficult to meet foreign competition head on.

The evidence of subsidies across nations is increasing. The political pressures leading to industrial trade policies are having some effect.

2. Costs of Export Subsidies

An export subsidy lowers the cost of production for domestic exporting firms. In Figure 3.11 the domestic supply of services increases from S to S' with a production subsidy. Suppose the international price of this exported good is $10. The export industry will increase its output from 100 to 120 units because of the subsidy. With the domestic quantity demanded unchanged at 50, excess supply or export rises from 50 to 70. Export revenue increases from $10 × 50 = $500 to $10 × 70 = $700 as a result of the subsidy.

Firms along the supply curve benefit from the subsidy. Some firms that would not have produced at all enter the industry. The subsidy encourages relatively inefficient productive activity. Moreover, the government subsidy does not come from thin air. Taxes must be levied to support it. A subsidy of $2 per unit, the vertical distance between S and S', costs taxpayers $2 for every unit produced. The tax burden of this subsidy is $2 × 120 = $240, the shaded rectangle.

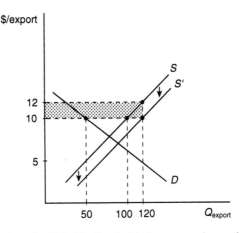
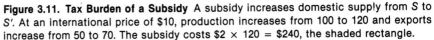

Figure 3.11. Tax Burden of a Subsidy A subsidy increases domestic supply from S to S'. At an international price of $10, production increases from 100 to 120 and exports increase from 50 to 70. The subsidy costs $2 × 120 = $240, the shaded rectangle.

Both the costs and benefits of a potential subsidy should be considered. Taxpayers need to be aware of the tax burden imposed by any sort of export subsidy.

A subsidy can lead to long-run gains if it successfully biases growth of the PPF toward the export industry. In Figure 3.12 the PPF expands along

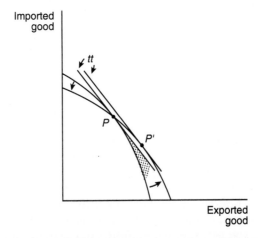

Figure 3.12. A Shift of the Production Possibilities Frontier (PPF) with an Export Subsidy The long-run effect of a subsidy can be a bias of the PPF toward the exported good. The value of production increases as production shifts from point P to point P' in this example. If production instead moves into the shaded region, the value of production falls.

the export axis but contracts along the import axis. This biased development can occur through improved technology because of research or subsidized training of the labor force in the export industry. The terms of trade are taken to be constant for the small economy in Figure 3.12. If production moves out beyond the original *tt* line to point *P'*, long-run dynamic gains will be made in real income or welfare because of improved technology in the export industry. If, however, production moves to a point in the shaded region below the original *tt* line, real income and welfare will ultimately fall with the subsidy.

Subsidies generally cannot be used successfully to target growth industries. Economic growth is a complicated process, and governments cannot direct this process better than markets.

Even if national income increases with the subsidy and improved technology, income will be redistributed by the tax and subsidy. This raises the important issue of income redistribution. Clearly firms, stockholders, and workers in the export industry will enjoy the subsidy at the expense of others in the economy. In shaping industrial trade policy, income redistribution is typically as important as real income or overall welfare. The basic tools used to examine the income redistribution caused by trade, protection, and industrial trade policy are developed in the coming chapters.

3. Free Trade Zones and Free Enterprise Zones

Another tool of industrial policy is the *free trade zone* (FTZ), a location inside the country made exempt from tariffs on imported intermediate inputs and capital goods. Taxes on foreign investment can also be lowered or eliminated inside an FTZ. Developing nations, particularly around the Pacific Rim, use FTZs to encourage the entrance of foreign multinational firms and the production of exports. FTZs encourage international trade and investment by skirting protectionistic laws that apply to the rest of the country.

FTZs can be found close to every port and international airport. Goods are brought there for storage, inspection, reshipping, and manufacturing. All the costly and cumbersome customs procedures are avoided. In the United States the FTZ Board, part of the executive branch of the government, approves and oversees FTZs. This gives the president a subtle degree of power to skirt the protectionistic bent of Congress.

Consumers can enter and shop inside *free enterprise zones* (FEZs), which are designated areas where all protectionism is relaxed so goods and services can be traded freely without tariffs, quotas, or administrative hassle. Most major cities around the Pacific Rim have FEZs. The idea is gaining in popularity elsewhere. The bustling cities of Hong Kong and Singapore are classic examples of what can happen when hindrance to international trade and finance is limited.

For the sake of efficiency, economists favor FTZs and FEZs. If an entire country were an FEZ, there would be free trade.

4.   The New International Economics

Currently under debate is whether a nation should have a comprehensive industrial trade policy, which would include export subsidies, protection, and other measures to manage the content and direction of trade. Proponents have labeled this a "new" approach to international economics. Japan, European countries, the United States, and other nations are involved in the debate.

The fundamental issues of the debate are as old as economics itself. The debate over protectionism has raged for centuries. When it comes to export promotion, taxpayers would be unlikely to lend their support if they realized they were subsidizing the real income of foreign consumers. Industries receiving support, of course, would be receptive and continue to lobby for protection.

Examined on a case-by-case basis, any particular policy should have to pass the economic test of weighing its costs versus its benefits. Economic theory and evidence from the development of nations favor a preliminary bias against hindering free trade and the use of subsidies. In complex market economies like the United States, governments have not demonstrated the ability to design and implement successful industrial trade policy.

EXAMPLE 3.9   Free Trade Zones in the United States

Jafar Alavi and Henry Thompson (1988) reported on the hundreds of FTZs in the United States. Based on a law dating to the 1930s and the time of the radical Smoot-Hawley tariff, manufacturers began using FTZs heavily in the late 1970s. Today almost 2% of GNP is produced inside these FTZs. Many industries in the United States have been able to institute an inverted tariff structure that insulates them from foreign competition. With inverted tariffs, tariff rates are higher for intermediate goods than for finished goods. Automobiles, office equipment, electronics, and printing are examples of industries that have inverted tariff structures. Much of the current activity in the FTZs of the United States is aimed at avoiding this inverted tariff structure. Intermediate goods are imported without duty into the FTZ, where they are assembled and "exported" into the country. Roughly 80% of the goods shipped from FTZs land in the United States. This is unlike the typical use of FTZs in the LDCs and NICs, where goods must be exported by law. Curiously, the first automaker in the United States to receive FTZ status was Honda. Today all of the auto plants are FTZs. No general theory can explain all of the effects of FTZs. Basically FTZs open part of the nation to free trade, so their net effect must be a movement toward increased international specialization and trade.

EXAMPLE 3.10   Increasing Subsidies of Industrialized Nations

This table shows estimated total subsidies as a percentage of gross domestic product (GDP), as reported by the OECD in *National Accounts,* 1982. Note that the United States has lower subsidy levels than the other industrial nations. All nations except France have increased their subsidy levels since the 1950s, but France has historically had high levels of subsidies. The tax burden of subsidies in some of these nations is sizeable. There is some truth in the claim of U.S. firms that the field of international competition is not level because foreign governments subsidize their industries heavily. The issue is whether U.S. taxpayers should retaliate by subsidizing foreign consumption in return. If foreign taxpayers are willing to subsidize our consumption, should we elect to subsidize their consumption of our exports?

	Total Subsidies as Percent of GDP			
	1956	*1964*	*1972*	*1980*
Canada	0.4%	0.9%	0.8%	2.3%
France	2.7%	2.0%	2.0%	2.5%
Germany	0.2%	1.0%	1.5%	1.6%
Italy	1.3%	1.2%	2.3%	3.0%
Japan	0.3%	0.7%	1.1%	1.3%
U.K.	1.8%	1.6%	1.8%	2.3%
U.S.	0.2%	0.4%	0.6%	0.4%

EXAMPLE 3.11   Wartime Economic Policy and International Trade

During World War II, wages and prices were set in an effort to control inflation and funnel resources into the war effort. The following story was reported in *Business Week* (October 23, 1943). Price ceilings on corn resulted in corn feed shortages on hog and dairy farms. Imports of Canadian wheat increased to substitute for the lost corn. These imports, however, displaced iron ore on Great Lakes freighters, which led to iron ore shortages. Wheat that had been used to produce industrial alcohol and synthetic rubber was directed to feed. Alcohol producers substituted molasses for wheat as a raw material. This molasses was imported from the Caribbean on freighters that had been carrying petroleum products from the Gulf Coast. Meanwhile, hog farmers substituted skim milk for corn feed to an extent. Casein, used to make adhesives, is made from skim milk and suddenly had to be imported from Argentina. Arbitrary industrial trade policy (a price ceiling on corn in this case) can have unforeseen and far-reaching effects!

Problems for Section D

D1. In what ways is a currency devaluation like an export subsidy? How are they different?

D2. As a consumer, would you prefer to live inside an FTZ or an FEZ?

D3. Predict the effects of a subsidy to an industry competing with imported goods.

CONCLUSION

Overall gains can be enjoyed from free international trade. Why is it, then, that every nation restricts trade with tariffs, quotas, exchange controls, and a host of other methods? Protectionism is perhaps the oldest topic in economics and is taken up in the next chapter. The gains from trade have been illustrated with an economy facing given international prices or terms of trade. Some nations, however, are large in the international markets for their exported and imported goods. Large nations have power to influence international prices or the terms of trade. Chapter 5 examines how countries facing each other bargain to determine their terms of trade. Following chapters develop the basic sorts of production structures that underlie the shape of the production possibilities frontier. The ultimate goal of the coming chapters is to develop tools for analyzing income redistribution caused by international trade, protectionism, and industrial trade policy.

KEY TERMS

Developmental gains from trade
Diminishing marginal returns
Diversification
Domestic relative prices
Export promotion
FTZs and FEZs
Gains from trade
Human capital
Immiserizing growth
Import substitution

Increasing opportunity cost
Industrial trade policy
LDCs, DCs, and NICs
Marginal productivity
Marginal rate of substitution
Marginal rate of transformation
Nominal prices
Subsidy
Terms of trade
Trade triangle

KEY POINTS

- The production possibilities frontier (PPF) illustrates the limited resources of an economy and the increasing opportunity costs of production. Relative prices in the economy determine the composition of output.
- Specialization and trade allow a nation to consume a more highly valued bundle of goods. This is the fundamental source of the gains from trade.
- Economic development is illustrated by an expanding PPF. There is solid evidence that export-led growth creates more productive economies with higher income.
- Inefficient export subsidies are used in many nations. Industrial trade policy refers to the comprehensive plan of export promotion and import protection in a nation. A comprehensive trade industrial policy in the United States, promoted by some industrialists and politicians, would decrease economic efficiency.

REVIEW PROBLEMS

1. If income rose to a value of 220 S in Figure 3.4 with the same relative price of S, find the value of income in terms of M.
2. From example 3.1 of the changing U.S. production frontier and the shift from manufactures to services in the United States, sketch the PPFs and the outputs in 1950 and 1986. Show the underlying rise in the relative price of services, the decline in the ratio M/S of outputs, and the growth in the economy.
3. Sketch a PPF with constant costs of production. Use a maximum manufacturing output of 200 as the basis. What is the relative price of M along your PPF? Does the law of diminishing marginal returns hold in this economy?
4. Sketch a PPF with increasing costs of production, using outputs of M of 200, 150, 100, 50, and 0. Find the opportunity costs of increased production of M at each step of 50 units. What determines where production takes place in this economy?
5. Suppose the domestic autarky relative price $M/S = 1$ and autarky consumption takes place at $(M,S) = (100,100)$. If production with free trade takes place at $(M,S) = (50,160)$ with 50 units exported and 60 units imported, find the consumption bundle (M,S). Sketch the trade triangle. What are the terms of trade? Find the gains from trade in terms of good M.
6. Find the terms of trade and the percentage gains from trade in the previous problem.
7. Illustrate consumer choice and the welfare gains in the previous problem with indifference curves.
8. Comparing unbiased growth with biased growth, which leads to higher gains from trade? Which leads to higher national income?
9. Distinguish between the gains from trade along the current PPF and developmental gains from trade.
10. Free trade zones allow foreign intermediate inputs to enter the nation freely. There is a large FTZ in McAllen, Texas, on the Mexican border. Along the border, workers pass freely in both directions. If you were a firm, what would you con-

sider in deciding whether to operate the FTZ inside the United States or across the border in Mexico?

11. Suppose the entire state of California wanted to declare itself an FEZ. What would be the effects in California? What would be the effects on the entire United States?

12. The most heavily subsidized industry in the United States is agriculture. There are price supports, government research, direct subsidies, and so on. What would happen to the pattern of trade and income distribution in the United States if this subsidization were reduced?

READINGS

Robert Lawrence, *Can America Compete?*, Brookings Institution, Washington, DC, 1983. Examines forces behind the changing structure of U.S. industry, showing the trend to specialize in products using large amounts of R&D.

Trade Policies for a Better Future, GATT Study Group, General Agreement of Tariffs and Trade, Geneva, 1985. A general argument for the gains from trade is put forth in "Why Open Trade Is Better Trade."

Anne Krueger, *Trade and Employment in Developing Nations: Synthesis and Conclusions*. Chicago, University of Chicago Press, 1984. An excellent summary of the forces of international trade and development.

Gerald Meier, *Leading Issues in Economic Development*, Oxford, Oxford University Press, 1989. A fine collection of readings on various topics in the economics of development.

CHAPTER 4

Protectionism

CHAPTER PREVIEW

The goal of this chapter is a general understanding of the causes and effects of protectionism in international trade. Specifically, this chapter covers:

(a) The effects of *tariffs* on an import market
(b) *Quotas* and other *nontariff barriers* to trade
(c) The *distortion* of protection on the pattern of production
(d) The *political economy of protection,* or causes of protection

INTRODUCTION

The topic that began debate and writing about the effects of economic policy was government protection of domestic industry from foreign competition. Economists have long favored free trade and developed the arguments favoring free trade in the previous chapter. Industrialists, however, have been resourceful when it comes to finding arguments for protecting their own particular industry, pointing to the costs that arise when a firm or factory closes because of foreign competition: households are left without income and workers must retrain or relocate. Nevertheless, international economists have consistently advocated facing international competition through free trade.

This chapter studies protectionism, which alters the pattern of production and redistributes income. Protection of an industry creates gains for some and losses for others. Those who would enjoy the gains can be expected to favor protection.

Both theory and evidence suggest that national income rises and is more evenly distributed when the nation pursues free trade. Comparative advantage is the foundation of international trade and perhaps the most universal principle in the social sciences. Nations, firms, or individuals who ignore their comparative advantage will be less than efficient and ultimately poorer than if they were to specialize and trade. Protectionism restricts the ultimate beneficial effects of exploiting comparative advantage through free international trade. Protectionism restricts free international trade, lowering national income and distributing income more unevenly.

After years of preaching, economists have yet to persuade governments to give up protectionism. Tariffs, quotas, and other nontariff barriers on imports are common policy. The ultimate reason for protectionism is simple. Those who benefit from the policy, the factory owners and workers in the protected industries, are organized and willing to spend resources to lobby and influence political decisions in their favor. Disorganized consumers and taxpayers do not generally realize the extent of their loss. The amount of the loss for each individual consumer is not large enough to spend an undue amount of resources lobbying against the harmful policy. The benefits of protectionism are concentrated while its costs are spread, allowing the overall inefficiency to prevail.

The partial equilibrium picture of protectionism is developed in this chapter using the tools of market supply and demand. If the nation levying a tariff is small in relation to the world market, the price of the taxed imported good remains at the world level. The partial equilibrium approach concentrates on the protected market isolated from the economy, and remains a widely used tool in applications.

The production possibilities frontier (PPF) is used to develop the picture of adjustment across the economy to protectionistic policy. The following chapters examine adjustment in international prices and production across economies, and the patterns of income redistribution resulting from protectionism with various structures of production.

The study of international trade is in large part the study of the effects of trade restrictions. National income in the United States is lower than it would be without the current level of protectionism. Resources are wasted on relatively inefficient activities. Jobs in some industries depend on the continued political favor of protection. Taxpayers subsidize the consumption of foreigners. Developing nations see protection in the United States as a direct hindrance to their progress, since many of the goods they can produce relatively efficiently are screened out of the United States.

Because trade policy affects all of us in measurable ways, we should learn as much as possible about its causes and effects. Most U.S. firms, even those selling strictly in the domestic market, face competition from firms in Europe, Japan, and the rest of the world. An acquaintance with the fundamentals of protectionism is fundamentally important.

A. TARIFFS: TAXES ON IMPORTS

A *tariff* is first and foremost a tax levied on a good imported across the national border. As with any kind of tax, the consumer ends up paying a higher price. The average tariff rate in the United States is about 4%, falling from about 10% in the 1960s and 15% in the 1950s. This reduction in the average tariff is due mainly to the agreements reached through the international negotiations organized under the General Agreement on Tariffs and Trade (GATT). Seventy-eight nations are committed in principle to lowering their levels of protection through GATT. The president of the United States is given authority to influence international trade through the Reciprocal Trade Agreements Act, which is U.S. law. As part of this authority, the United States has taken part in the Multilateral Trade Negotiations of GATT since the end of World War II.

The Escape Clause, Section 201 of the Trade Act of 1974, allows Congress to enact temporary protection in the "national interest" for an industry that can prove to the International Trade Commission (ITC) that it is being damaged by imports. Some industries also obtain *special protection* despite the general agreement to lower protection under GATT. While the current average tariff rate of 4% may sound low, tariffs on some goods are much higher, and the costs associated with the distortion from protection are quite high.

Tariffs have the double attraction to governments of being inconspicuous and easy to collect. It should be no surprise that tariffs have historically been a popular way for governments to raise revenue. Many governments have raised most of their revenue through tariffs. The U.S. government earned more than half of its revenue through tariffs up until 1870, and more than 25% until the 1920s. Business and personal income taxes now account for most of the U.S. government's revenue, with tariffs producing less than 2%. Many developing countries and newly industrializing countries rely on tariffs as the major source of government revenue.

1. The Cost of a Tariff

Some idea of the everyday effect of tariffs on the prices of goods we all consume can be gained from the examples in Table 4.1 from Murray Weidenbaum and Michael Munger (1983). The higher price is a windfall to the domestic industry that competes with imports. Domestic production that is inefficient relative to foreign production and relative to the lost production opportunities at home is encouraged. The government receives some revenue through the taxation of consumers, who suffer by having to pay a higher price for the imported goods.

Tariffs can be levied on finished goods like cars and stereos, or they can be hidden as a tax on imported intermediate goods like fabric or elec-

TABLE 4.1. Estimated Price Effects of Tariffs

	Free Trade	With Tariffs
Autos	$7,500.00	$10,000
Box of candy	$2.00	$5
Bluejeans	$14.50	$18

SOURCE: "Protection at Any Price?" *Regulation*, 1983.

tric motors. These components or intermediate products are imported and included in goods that can be labeled "Made in the USA." The rates of *effective protection* include protection on intermediate goods as well as price increases associated with quotas and other nontariff barriers. Quotas are quantitative restrictions on the import of goods. Nontariff barriers are other devices, such as voluntary export restraints or artificially tough health and safety regulations, used to limit imports.

Effective protection is the net percentage of a good's domestic *value added* that is shielded by tariffs. Domestic value added refers to the share of the price of a final good added by domestic inputs. Let V be domestic value added. Protection will be valued relative to V. If P^* is the international price of the finished good and T the tariff rate on the finished good, the tariff raises price inside the country by TP^*. Relative to V, the tariff affords protection of TP^*/V.

Domestic producers may use foreign intermediate inputs in their production process. Let p^* be the international price of the intermediate input and t the tariff rate on the intermediate input. The tariff raises the cost of the intermediate input by tp^*. The effective rate of protection (ERP) would be

$$ERP = (TP^* - tp^*)/V$$

Note that a high enough tariff on intermediate goods can result in a negative rate of effective protection for a domestic producer.

As an example of the rate of effective protection, suppose the international price of a shirt is $20 and the tariff on shirts is 10% ($2 per shirt). A domestic shirtmaker imports materials worth $12 to make a $20 shirt, adding domestic value of $8. The $2 shirt tariff effectively protects domestic value added by $2/$8 = 1/4 = 25%. A 5% tariff on imported materials would tax the shirtmaker by $12 × 0.05 = $.60, reducing the effective rate of protection to ($2.00 − $.60) / $8 = 17.5%. A higher tariff on imported materials would reduce the effective rate of protection.

The effective rate of protection can be negative if the tariff on imported materials is high enough. A tariff rate of 20% on the imported materials would raise their cost by $2.60 = 0.2 × $12. The ERP becomes negative: ($2.00 − $2.60) / $8 = −7.5%. The domestic producer would operate at a net disadvantage because of the pattern of tariffs.

Estimates of effective protection in Table 4.2 from Alan Deardorff and Robert Stern (1984) compare the United States, Japan, and Europe. Effective rates of protection are generally higher than nominal or stated tariff rates. As the examples show, rates of effective protection are very high on dairy products, wool fabrics, leather, and cotton fabrics. As the manufacturing process proceeds, the protection of intermediate inputs in each stage is included in the final level of protection. This is why the rates in Table 4.2 are much higher than the average U.S. tariff rate of only 4%.

On a more detailed level, a study by A.J. Yeats (1974) finds significant variation in effective rates of protection. In the United States, mill feed products (111%), cottonseed oil (466%), soybean oil (253%), cigarettes (113%), and soft drinks (−10%) are outstanding examples. In the European Community (EC), sea foods (53%), milk (60%), vegetable oils (138%), cigarettes (147%), and soft drinks (−20%) stand out. In Japan, milk (249%), processed food (59%), cocoa (81%), woven fabrics (65%), cottonseed oil (200%), soy bean oil (286%), cigarettes (406%), and animal fats (−2%) are radical examples of ERP.

> Protectionism costs consumers. Prices are made higher than they would be without protection. All forms of trade protection act like a tax on consumers.

2. Market Analysis of a Tariff

The theoretical effects of a tariff on the domestic market are pictured in Figure 4.1. The price of $p^* = \$5$ is the international price of the manufactured good M. The nation can import as much as it likes at a price of $5. Under this condition the economy is said to be a price taker in this international market. At the international price the difference between the quantity demanded (300) and the quantity supplied (100) is imported. If the

TABLE 4.2. Effective Rates of Protection

	U.S.	Japan	Europe
Clothing	43%	42%	19%
Textiles	18%	2%	9%
Footwear	15%	50%	20%
Food and tobacco	11%	50%	18%
Furniture	6%	10%	11%
Agriculture	2%	21%	4%

SOURCE: *The Structure and Evolution of Recent U.S. Trade Policy*, University of Chicago Press, 1984.

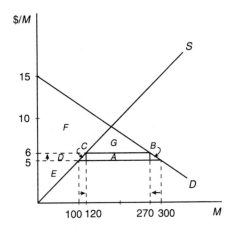

Figure 4.1. The Market Effects of a Tariff A 20% tariff raises the domestic price to $6 from the world price of $5. The level of imports drops to 150, and tariff revenue of $150 in area *A* is created for the government. Domestic firms enjoy the increased producer surplus represented by area *D* ($110). Consumer surplus falls with the tariff by area *A* + *B* + *C* + *D* = $285. The deadweight loss of the tariff is the area of the triangles *B* + *C* = $15 + $10 = $25.

economy is open to free trade in this good, 200 units are imported and the domestic price equals the international price of $5.

When a tariff is placed on good *M*, its domestic price increases. Suppose a 20% tariff is levied on good *M*. With $t = 0.2$, the domestic price of *M* rises to $5 \times 1.2 = $6. Consumers respond to this higher price by switching to substitutes and reducing the quantity of *M* demanded from 300 to 270, up the demand curve. Producers respond to the higher price of *M* with an increase in the quantity supplied domestically from 100 to 120, up the supply curve. Imports drop to the difference between the quantities demanded and supplied domestically: $270 - 120 = 150$. This tariff reduces the level of imported *M* by 25%, from 200 to 150.

Tariff revenue for the government in this example will be $150, which is found by multiplying the tariff per unit ($1 = 0.2p* = 0.2 \times 5) times the level of imports 150. This is represented in Figure 4.1 by the rectangle labeled *A*.

Consumers must pay a higher price and end up consuming fewer goods with the tariff. To gauge the loss of consumers, the concept of *consumer surplus* is used. When the price of *M* is $5, 300 units are demanded. Note that consumers located back up along the demand curve would pay more than the $5 price. One unit of *M*, for instance, could be sold at just under $15. As the price falls from $15, more and more consumers buy the good. At the world price of $5, all of the consumers up along the demand curve are able to acquire the good for less than they would be willing to pay. The area *A* + *B* + *C* + *D* + *F* + *G* in Figure 4.1 is a measure of the gains to consumers from buying at the market price of $5. This area is called the consumer surplus. In this example, the consumer surplus equals $1/2[($15 - $5) \times 300] = $1,500$.

Consumers lose the entire area *A* + *B* + *C* + *D* in Figure 4.1 with the tariff. This area is a measure of the loss forced on consumers by the tariff. It is a measure of the loss in consumer surplus. Some consumers are squeezed out of the market, while those remaining must pay a higher price. When the price rises from $5 to $6 with the tariff, the consumer surplus is reduced by the area between $5 and $6 over to the demand curve. With the tariff the consumer surplus falls to area $F + G$, which equals $1/2[(\$15 - \$6) \times 270] = \$1,215$. The loss in consumer surplus with the tariff thus equals $1,500 - $1,215 = 285.

Producers gain area D in Figure 4.1, since they end up selling more goods at a higher price. This is a gain in *producer surplus*. Firms already in the market enjoy the higher price with the tariff. Other firms may enter the industry, attracted by the higher price. Firms are able to sell at a price above what they would be willing to accept. The area above the supply curve and below the price measures these gains to firms, the producer surplus. When the price is $5, producer surplus is area E, equal to $1/2(\$5 \times 100) = \$250$. When the price rises to $6 with the tariff, producer surplus increases to area $E + D$, which equals $1/2(\$6 \times 120) = \$360$. Area D, the gain in producer surplus, thus equals $360 - $250 = 110.

This leaves triangles B and C as the *deadweight loss* resulting from the tariff. These are consumer losses that are not offset by government tariff revenue or gain in producer surplus. Rectangle A ($150) of the total consumers' loss ($285) goes to the government as tariff revenue, and area D ($110) goes to the domestic industry. Since the government spends its revenue and any excess profit is ultimately spent, the income represented by areas A plus D ($260) is redistributed among individuals in the economy. Triangles B and C, however, represent losses that are not offset. These losses amount to $B = $15 plus $C = $10, or a total deadweight of $25. The redistributions of income as a result of tariff in Figure 4.1 are summarized in Table 4.3.

Tariffs are taxes that redistribute income and cause net losses because of inefficiency.

Domestic consumers of the manufactured good in Figure 4.1 are definitely hurt by the tariff. Domestic firms that compete with imports are definitely helped. As a group, workers for these manufacturing firms may stand to gain, as do owners of the capital employed in the industry. Gene Grossman and Jim Levinshon (1989) find empirical evidence that tariffs increase the value of the stocks of firms in the protected industries. Shareholders

TABLE 4.3. Income Redistribution Resulting from the Tariff in Figure 4.1

Consumer Loss	Producer Gain	Government Revenue	Deadweight Loss
$A+B+C+D$	D	A	$B+C$
$285	$110	$150	$15 + $10 = $25

have an interest in keeping their industry protected. There is also empirical evidence that protection elevates the wages of labor in protected industries.

It is easy to spot the few winners from a tariff. Since the gains can be sizeable, the winners find it worthwhile to spend resources lobbying for protection in Congress. Political support and contributions explain the typical Congressional representative's bias toward protectionism.

3.   Protection versus Free Trade

Economists have estimated the deadweight losses from tariffs in the United States. Studies use these partial equilibrium market techniques to estimate the areas of the deadweight triangles in Figure 4.1. Yearly losses resulting from higher prices paid by consumers are conservatively set at $255 per person by Murray Weidenbaum and Tracy Munger (1983). Other studies come up with similar figures. Tariffs are an implicit although not generally recognized tax on consumers.

The inefficient organization of production resulting from a tariff creates serious losses. Firms that cannot compete effectively with firms in the rest of the world are encouraged to continue operation. Valuable productive inputs like labor, capital, and natural resources are spent producing goods and services that could be obtained more cheaply on international markets. The economy produces less of the goods that the rest of the world values more highly, thus losing valuable income. Instead of concentrating on profitable export production, the economy produces substitutes for the goods it could be importing. The gains from moving to free trade include the improved pattern of production.

Losses are also incurred through the lobbying activity of industry and the interested groups of labor. Protected industries employ hundreds of lobbyists, spending millions of dollars to bend the ears of politicians in Congress. Lobby groups also advertise to win popular support for their desired protection. A rational change of political structure would allow the executive branch, which has the interest of the entire nation rather than some Congressional district at heart, to set international trade policy. The final section in this chapter looks deeper into the political economy of protectionism.

Economic efficiency calls for an end to protectionism and an opening to international competition. Economists have been making this argument as long as economics has existed. The political process of lowering protection has proved lengthy and difficult. The danger of being sucked back into protectionist arguments is constant, especially in times of trade deficits and sagging local industries. In the final analysis, there is no way to avoid facing international competition. Protectionism is a quick fix that undermines economic efficiency in the long run.

Tariffs are inefficient but remain part of the political landscape because of the influence of those who gain from protection.

The United States has witnessed declines in what have been called the "basic" manufacturing industries. Between 1974 and 1982 the following average yearly percentage declines in the outputs of these U.S. industries are reported in the *Yearbook of Industrial Statistics* published by the United Nations:

Iron and steel	−6.0%
Footwear	− 4.3%
Nonferrous metal	−2.0%
Textiles	−1.5%
Apparel	−1.1%

These industries have been forced to face increasing competition, largely from less developed countries and newly industrialized countries where wages are low.

Alarmists claim the United States is "deindustrializing." Certainly some reorganization of U.S. industrial structure took place in the 1970s and 1980s. Proponents of these sagging industries, their managers, stockholders, and workers, are clamoring for protection. Since the 1950s manufacturing employment has dropped from approximately 35% of the U.S. workforce to 25%, while employment in services has risen from 50% to 70%. This trend partly reflects the underlying comparative advantage and increased international specialization of the U.S. economy. Manufacturing employs high levels of unskilled labor, an abundant and cheap input in developing and newly industrializing countries. Rather than using a patchwork of protection for our relatively inefficient industries, trade policy should retrain and relocate workers into activities that are internationally more efficient.

The European nations are moving toward a free trade area with few internal restrictions by the end of 1992. The United States and Canada have formed a free trade area. Both the United States and Canada are negotiating with Mexico on creating the North American Free Trade Area. There is some discussion of such a free trade area between the United States and Japan. The United States and Israel have had a free trade agreement for some time. South America, Africa, and Southeast Asia all have regional free trade areas.

While national governments may be convinced that free trade promotes economic efficiency and believe it redistributes income more fairly, local politicians are subject to the constant pressures of protectionism. President Reagan was a firm believer in free trade, but the record shows his administration turned the United States slightly back toward protectionism. Everywhere there are local protectionists disguised as global free traders. The oldest issue in economics promises to remain one of the most current and pressing.

EXAMPLE 4.1   Personal Income Distribution with Protection

Economists have long argued that tariffs are a *regressive* form of taxation. Individuals with low income spend a larger share of their income on basic items like food, clothing, autos, and shoes. These goods are among the most highly protected. A recent study by Susan Hickok (1985) studies the regressive form of protection. Imagine the implicit tax imposed by a tariff were converted to an income tax surcharge, tacked on after regular income taxes had been paid. The list below shows the percentage income tax surcharges that would be equivalent to current levels of protection. People with the lowest incomes ($7,000 to $11,700) would have to pay an additional 57% of their income tax bill to match the taxes they pay on tariffs and other protection. People with income of $58,500 and above would have to pay only 5% additional income taxes to match the current levels of protection. If such a regressive income tax surcharge were suggested, it would be labeled politically unfair.

Income	Equivalent Income Tax Surcharge
$ 7,000 to $11,700	57%
$11,700 to $16,400	36%
$16,400 to $23,400	26%
$23,400 to $35,100	19%
$35,100 to $58,500	12%
$58,500 and up	5%

EXAMPLE 4.2   Average U.S. Tariffs

Tariff protection in the United States is at an all-time low, mainly because of the international cooperation afforded by GATT. This table from the *Statistical Abstract of the United States* presents a brief history of average tariffs in the United States since 1830. In the early years, high levels of protection of manufactured goods significantly reduced real income in the agricultural South, accounting in no small part for the Civil War. Until income taxes were legalized in the 1920s, tariffs accounted for more than a quarter of government revenue. Note the high level of protection imposed by the Smoot-Hawley Tariff Act of 1930. International trade subsequently came to a virtual halt, largely explaining the Great Depression. Since the cooperative agreement of GATT began in 1946, tariffs have generally declined. Quotas and other nontariff trade barriers, however, have been increasing in recent years.

Year	Average Tariff
1830	62%
1850	27%
1865	48%
1900	49%
1910	40%
1920	16%
1932	59%
1940	36%
1950	13%
1960	12%
1970	10%
1985	4%

EXAMPLE 4.3 Learning How to Import and Export

Customs laws and practices present a formidable hindrance to international trade. Anyone who wants to export or import must become familiar with the "ins and outs" of customs practice. The American Association of Exporters and Importers (AAEI) was founded in 1921 to lobby for international traders and to offer technical assistance to traders. It has 1,200-member firms and publishes the *U.S. Customs House Guide,* a formidable 1,500-page tour through the intricacies of U.S. trade policy. A complete guide to tariffs on every good imaginable is included. On its papers, we learn the following about tariff rates:

Wheeled toys designed to be ridden by children and parts and accessories thereof:

Chain-driven wheeled toys	free
Other	3.6%
Dolls' carriages, dolls' strollers, and parts and accessories thereof	7.8%

Dolls representing only human beings and parts and accessories thereof:

Dolls, whether or not dressed:

Stuffed	12%
Other	12%
Parts and accessories thereof	8%

It is not mentioned which parts the dolls may represent. Have you ever wondered why tennis rackets are displayed without strings?

Lawn-tennis rackets, whether or not strung, and parts and accessories thereof:

Rackets, strung	5.3%
Rackets, not strung	3.9%
Parts and accessories	3.1%

The AAEI lobbied against footwear protection in 1985. It consistently lobbies with Congress and the Department of Treasury for reasonable guidelines and policies. It runs a quota alert system that informs members about the imposition and lifting of quotas. The *Guide* contains a full statement of all U.S. trade laws including tariffs, quotas, and other regulations, all necessary certificates and forms for importing and exporting, and articles on the changing face of international trade.

Problems for Section A

A1.   Suppose a 40% tariff is levied on the market for the imported manufactured good in Figure 4.1. Find the level of imports, tariff revenue, change in producer and consumer surplus, and deadweight loss.

A2.   Why are automobiles highly protected in the United States while toys and games are not?

B.   QUOTAS AND OTHER NONTARIFF BARRIERS

A *quota* is a quantitative restriction on the level of imports. The level of imports cannot exceed a quota when one is imposed, even if the goods are given away free. Quotas force all subsequent adjustment onto domestic price, generally providing more protection than tariffs for the domestic import competing industry. If domestic supply or demand for the imported good changes, quotas keep the level of imports constant and force all adjustment onto price. In markets with growing demand, prices paid by consumers will be higher with a quota than they would be with a tariff. Other *nontariff barriers* act much like quotas.

1. Market Analysis of a Quota

In Figure 4.2 a quota of 150 units of good M is in effect. The international price of M is $5. In the absence of the quota, 200 units of M would be imported. The quota of 150 pushes the domestic price above the international price, bringing about inefficient production at home and costing consumers.

Check the similarity between Figures 4.2 and 4.1. The quota in Figure 4.2 and the tariff in Figure 4.1 make the general point that quotas and tariffs can have equivalent effects on the market. Quotas, however, are typically set at levels that would be equivalent to high tariff rates. Quotas are harsh measures.

A quota generates no government revenue. Suppose the import market is switched from free trade to a quota. Consumer surplus falls by area $A + B + C + D$ in Figure 4.2, with area D transferred to producer surplus. Area $A + B + C$ is the deadweight loss from the quota. If this import market is subsequently switched from a quota to its equivalent tariff, consumers and firms would be indifferent while the government gains the revenue in area A.

Foreign exporters are able to sell at the higher price of $6 with the quota in Figure 4.2. Before the quota, foreign export revenue on the sale of M was $5 × 200 = $1,000. With the quota, foreign export revenue falls to $6 × 150 = $900. If home imports were inelastic, foreign export revenue would rise with the quota. Area A amounts to a *transfer* from domestic consumers to foreign exporting firms.

Area A equals $150, and triangles B and C each have a combined area

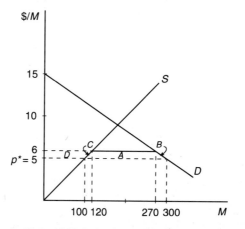

Figure 4.2. Quota on Imports of M A quota of 150 pushes the domestic price up 20% from the world level of $5. This quota is similar to a 20% tariff except that no tariff revenue is generated for the government. The deadweight loss of this quota is the area $A + B + C = 175, compared to only area $B + C = 25 for a tariff.

of $25. The deadweight loss in the home country resulting from the quota in Figure 4.2 is the sum, $175. With a tariff, revenue of $150 in area *A* would go to the government while the $25 in areas *B* and *C* would be the deadweight loss. Quotas are more costly than tariffs, since the deadweight and transfer loss is greater. This quota costs the economy $150 compared with the tariff. The tariff costs the economy $25 compared with free trade.

Governments can, however, raise revenue through *licensing* quotas to firms offering the highest bid. Being able to buy at a low international price and sell at an artificially high domestic price may give the foreign exporter (or domestic importing firm) higher potential profit. Suppose domestic importing firms buy *M* at the international price of $5, then turn around and sell at the artificially high price of $6. Another set of domestic firms produce 120 units of *M*. Domestic producers of *M* gain area *D* in producer surplus. Importing firms make a profit of $150 in area *A*. If importers were forced to bid for the right to import, the government could appropriate area *A*. Firms would be forced to pay this price in a competitive bid for the privilege to import, and their profit from importing would be normal.

2. Market Adjustment with a Quota

Another fundamental difference between tariffs and quotas is that adjustment to any change in the market is forced entirely on price when a quota is imposed on the import market. Suppose the domestic demand for manufactured good increases as in Figure 4.3, perhaps because of rising income.

When a tariff is imposed, the domestic price will remain at $6, the world price of $5 plus the $1 per unit tariff. Since price is unchanged, domestic suppliers continue to produce 120. Quantity demanded rises to 320. The level of imports would jump to 200 = 320 − 120 with a tariff.

When the quota is 150, the increase in demand forces price to rise to $7. Imports are forced to remain at 150 as domestic production is spurred

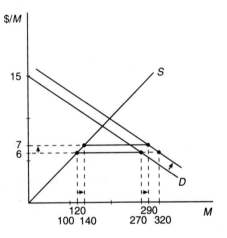

Figure 4.3. Market Adjustment with a Quota With a quota of 150 in place, an increase in the demand for imports forces all adjustment onto price. Domestic production increases from 120 to 140, but only 150 units of *M* can be imported. The domestic price is pushed up from $6 to $7.

to 140. Consumers are worse off with the quota than with a tariff, consuming 30 fewer units at the higher price of $7. Consumption with the tariff is 320. With the quota, consumption is only 290.

Protected industries would generally prefer a quota over a tariff when the international price of a good is falling, when domestic demand is rising, or when domestic supply is falling. In these circumstances the industry can maintain its output level with a quota. Industries would lobby for tariffs rather than quotas when the international price is expected to rise, when domestic demand is expected to fall, or when domestic supply is expected to rise. In these circumstances a quota might become ineffective but a tariff continues to offer its margin of protection.

> For any quota there is an equivalent percentage tariff rate that creates the same production, consumption, imports, and domestic price. Quotas have the disadvantages of not producing tariff revenue for the government and forcing all international adjustment onto domestic price.

EXAMPLE 4.4   Costs of Quotas

David Tarr and Morris Morkre (1987) of the Federal Trade Commission have estimated the deadweight losses resulting from U.S. quotas. The quota on Japanese autos is estimated to have an annual loss to consumers of $1.037 billion (area $A + B + C + D$ in Figure 4.2) and a cost-to-benefit ratio of 24 to 1 (the ratio of areas $A + B + C$ to area D in Figure 4.2). Japanese automakers enjoy higher prices in the United States, receiving an estimated $860 million in annual profit. Import demand for autos in the United States is inelastic. Sugar quotas cost consumers $767 million annually (about $8.50 per household). Quotas on textile imports from Hong Kong alone cost consumers $401 million annually with a cost-to-benefit ratio of 19 to 1. Steel quotas cost $1.145 billion annually (about $12.70 per household) with a cost-to-benefit ratio of 115 to 1. On average, current quotas are estimated to amount of an 18.5% tariff with potential government tariff revenue transferred to foreign producers and an overall cost-to-benefit ratio of 35 to 1. Quotas promote a sizeable amount of economic inefficiency.

3.   Nontariff Barriers

There are other sorts of *nontariff barriers* (NTBs) besides quotas. Since the United States and other industrialized nations are committed to lowering levels of protection under GATT, more subtle forms of protection afforded by these NTBs have become popular. Governments are constantly under pressure from industries for protection and are quick to devise ways to skirt the GATT agreement.

A popular form of NTB in the United States is the voluntary export restraint (VER). Japanese automobile exporters "voluntarily" limited their quantity of exports in the 1980s, often under threat of tougher protectionist measures against Japanese imports into the United States. The U.S. auto industry put pressure on the U.S. government, the U.S. government put pressure on the Japanese government, which in turn put pressure on Japanese automakers for "voluntary" agreements.

A VER has the same basic effects as a quota inside the nation, but it discriminates between trading partners. European auto exporters to the United States benefit greatly with the Japanese VER because they are not subject to quantity restrictions and enjoy the higher auto prices created in the United States. Furthermore, VERs have the effect of creating a cartel for the exporting country. The Japanese government is forced to work with Japanese automakers to restrict competition among themselves inside the U.S. market. The VER gives monopoly power to the Japanese auto industry. Monopolies maximize their profit by restricting output and raising price. A VER inadvertently gives monopoly power to the foreign industry. With restraint on competition, profit for the Japanese auto industry may rise.

Empirical evidence and theoretical arguments lead to the expectation of *quality upgrading* with a VER or quota. If Japanese automakers agree to export a limited number of cars per year, it may make sense to aim at the high quality end of the auto market, where the profit per car may be higher. Cars imported from Japan now have all the luxury extras, unlike the simple utilitarian models of the 1970s. The Japanese have basically given up the low-quality end of the U.S. import market to automakers in Korea, Yugoslavia, Mexico, and other newly industrializing countries. Consumers who prefer simple inexpensive models were hurt, at least temporarily, by the VERs.

Japan has recently entered into voluntary import expansion (VIE) programs on U.S. goods. U.S. computer chips, coal, beef, and construction have all benefitted from these recent VIE programs. Such programs discriminate against third countries. Japan buys fewer computer chips from Taiwan, less coal from Australia, and so on. VIEs, like VERs, distort overall trade.

Another popular form of NTB involves legal requirements that artificially favor domestic operations. Lawyers, doctors, and veterinarians from one nation are restricted from practicing in other nations, a policy existing to a limited extent between states in the United States. Health laws are often selectively and unfairly applied to foreign goods. Recent examples are fruits imported from South America that were banned when a random test haphazardly showed evidence of banned insecticides. No other imported fruits tested positive, and foreign exporters suspected a "plant" (contaminated fruits purposely placed in the samples). The telecommunications industry is completely protected from foreign competition in most nations, supposedly in the interest of national defense. Licensing of all sorts of activities serves to restrict competition. While some benefits may be associated with standards and licensing, these benefits should be weighed against the costs of misapplication. Constant monitoring is necessary to ensure fair application of standards. The practice of international law, which handles claims of unfair practice, is a growing field.

Other, more subtle forms of NTBs or discrimination against foreign products can play important protectionistic roles. U.S. firms complain that the transportation industry inside Japan does not deliver their goods. When shipments sit at the dock too long, business may become unprofitable. It may be difficult to determine who is at fault, but this sort of subtle discrimination against foreign products can severely curtail imports. The "Buy American" campaign sponsored by U.S. producers tries to prejudice U.S. consumers against foreign goods, presumably even when they are better and cheaper. This campaign promotes the inefficient allocation of scarce resources and asks consumers to waste their income.

> The bottom line on quotas and other nontariff barriers (NTBs) is that they are even less desirable than tariffs. NTBs create distortions that rob people of real income. A status quo of inefficient production is protected by a rigid wall of quantitative restriction.

EXAMPLE 4.5   Costs of the Japanese Voluntary Export Restraint on Autos

The current VER of Japan on autos shipped to the United States increases the cost of cars in the United States, passing gains along to other exporters to the United States, namely, Europe, Canada, and Mexico. Exporting firms in these countries are able to sell at the artificially increased price inside the United States. Dinopoulos and Kreinin (1988) examine this issue. In 1984, 18% of cars sold in the United States were from Japan, 10% were from Canada, and 5% were from Europe. The VER of Japan increased the price of an average European car sold in the United States by an estimated $6,562 or 53%! This figure discounts the quality upgrading of European cars that occurred and would have raised price on its own. The loss caused by the VER was about $27 per U.S. household to Japan, and about $38 per U.S. household to Europe. In 1982 the number of jobs saved in the United States by the VER was 22,358, but this was accomplished at an estimated cost of $180,785 per job. This amount is several times the yearly salary of automobile workers, pointing out the inefficiency of the VER.

A similar study by Bee Yan Aw and Mark Roberts (1986) examines U.S. footwear imports during 1977–1981. The United States had entered into an orderly marketing agreement with Korea and Taiwan that set a limit on the footwear exports to the United States. Quality upgrading occurred in the quota categories. The quota resulted in a 12% increase in the price of footwear in the United States.

EXAMPLE 4.6   Case Studies of Protection

Gary Hufbauer, Diane Berliner, and Kimberly Elliott (1986) put together a detailed study of the effects of protectionist legislation in the United States in a book, *Trade Protection in the United States: 31 Case Studies.* Tariffs, quotas, and nontariff barriers are included in their calculations, whose basis is the partial equilibrium supply-and-demand analysis presented in this chapter. The listed industries are currently protected. The date of the original protection is listed, along with the area of the world primarily hurt by the protection. It is worth remembering that protection that helps U.S. industry directly hurts the export industry of foreign countries. The column labeled $\%\Delta P$ is the estimated increase in the market's price over what the price would be without protection. The cost per job saved is an estimate of what consumers must pay to save a job in that industry. Firms in the industry also gain from the protection with increased profit. Since the cost/job ratio is much higher than the income created by the job, benefits of the protection are outweighed by costs. In some cases the price rise and cost/job ratio are startlingly high. Protectionism that hurts developing regions of the world is especially damaging from a global perspective.

Industry	Date	Region	$\%\Delta P$	Cost/Job
Books	1891	East Asia	40%	$100,000
Glassware	1922	West Europe	19%	$200,000
Rubber shoes	1930	Developing nations	42%	$30,000
Ceramics	1930	Japan, Korea	14%	$47,500
Ceramic tiles	1930	Brazil, Italy	21%	$135,000
Orange juice	1930	Brazil	44%	$240,000
Canned tuna	1951	Japan, Philippines	13%	$76,000
Textiles	1957	31 countries	30%	$42,000
Steel	1969	Argentina, Brazil	30%	$750,000
Autos	1981	Japan	11%	$105,000
Maritime	1789	Global	60%	$270,000
Sugar	1934	Global	30%	$60,000

Dairy	1953	Global	80%	$220,000
Peanuts	1953	Global	28%	$1,000/acre
Meat	1965	Australia, Canada	14%	$160,000
Fish	1977	Global	10%	$21,000

EXAMPLE 4.7   Are U.S. Consumers Biased against Foreign Goods?

A group of U.S. producers and retailers formed the "Crafted with Pride in the USA Council" in 1984 to promote U.S. products through advertising and special buying arrangements. Wal-Mart decreased its sales of imported goods from 25% to 5% by 1989. K-Mart conducted an experiment on identical jeans, one with a foreign label and the other "Made in USA." The two types of jeans were sold side by side. The domestic variety sold better. A *USA Today* survey also suggests the ad campaign may be effective. In 1985, 21% of U.S. consumers surveyed indicated they make conscious decisions not to buy goods if they are foreign in origin. By 1989 that figure had increased to 39%. Retailers realize it is more effective to appeal to quality than patriotism, which is the reason for their slogan "Crafted with Pride." Foreign producers also realize the potential of advertising, which means Toyota and Perrier ads can be expected to continue.

Problems for Section B

B1.   Calculate the deadweight and transfer loss resulting from the quota after the demand increase in Figure 4.3. Compare the situation with a quota to free trade at the world price of $5.

B2.   Compare the market adjustment with a quota versus a tariff when domestic supply decreases because of higher wages involved in a new labor contract.

B3.   Compare adjustment with a quota versus a tariff when the international price of the imported good falls.

C.   TARIFFS AND THE PATTERN OF PRODUCTION

Estimates of losses resulting from protection are lower bounds that do not include the efficiency losses in the pattern of production. The eventual issue that must be addressed concerns how much extra income the economy could produce if it specialized in producing what it does most efficiently. This section studies this issue with the production possibility frontier.

1. Free Trade versus Tariffs on the Production Possibilities Frontier

A PPF is drawn in Figure 4.4. Remember there is full employment of all resources and complete efficiency in production along the PPF. The slope of the PPF at any point is the marginal rate of transformation (MRT), which tells how many units of manufactures M must be given up to produce another unit of services S. If the relative price of services rises, the economy moves down along its PPF. A rising relative price of services creates higher profits in that industry, attracting new entrants and increasing the output of existing firms. A falling relative price of manufactures creates losses in that industry, causing firms to cut back their production or go out of business.

A hypothetical autarky production and consumption point is illustrated by point A in Figure 4.4. Without international trade, consumers in the economy pick the point along the economy's PPF that they most prefer. Consumers maximize their utility on an indifference curve subject to the constraint of the PPF. In autarky at point A, 400 units of each good are produced and consumed and there is no international trade.

Suppose the relative price of services on the international market is higher than the autarky price. In this example, $tt = M/S = 2$. If the economy opens itself to trade, specialization will move the economy down along the PPF to point P in Figure 4.4. Resources are shifted into the production of services S and out of the production of manufactures M. At point P the MRT equals the terms of trade. The terms of trade line is tangent to the PPF.

From point P the economy can trade at the world's relative price of

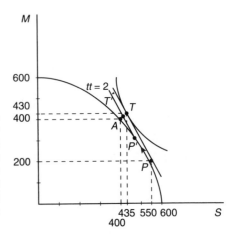

Figure 4.4. Specialization and Trade A relatively high price of services on the international market induces the economy to specialize from point A to point P. With specialization and trade, consumers pick a point T that maximizes their welfare along the terms of trade line $tt = 2$. The economy exports 115 units of S in exchange for 230 units of M. A tariff pushes the economy back up its PPF to point P'. Consumers are forced to consume along a lower tt line. Consumption falls from point T to point T'.

services, the terms of trade of 2 units of imported M per unit of exported S. The terms of trade line tt is steeper than the autarky price line. Each unit of exported services is traded for 2 units of manufacturers, providing a basis for the gains from trade. Consumers maximize utility subject to the consumption possibilities or terms of trade line. The consumer equilibrium in free trade is point T, where the tt line is tangent to the indifference curve. The slope of the indifference curve, the marginal rate of substitution (MRS), equals the terms of trade. With free trade, tt = MRT = MRS.

More of both goods are consumed at point T in Figure 4.4. Consumers in the economy are better off than they were at point A in that real income or the level of welfare will be higher. The community indifference curve tangent to point T lies above the autarky level at point A.

If a country has a low relative price of services in autarky, it gives up relatively few manufactures as it switches into service production. The country has a comparative advantage in services. Remember that comparative advantage relates inputs across countries and is expressed as a comparison of relative prices.

A tariff on imports of M distorts the globally efficient pattern of specialization. The relative price of services inside the country falls with a tariff. Production moves back up along the PPF from point P to a point like P' in Figure 4.4. The economy specializes less in services S, which is unfortunate because S has a relatively high value on the international market. This is called the *production distortion* of a tariff. Resources are wasted in the protected activity, which has output of a relatively low value in the world market.

The efficiency loss of this production distortion of a tariff is more difficult to estimate than are the static deadweight losses of Figure 4.1. It takes time for the nation to change its pattern of production. There are short-run costs of adjustment, moving and retraining, that must be paid by workers. Investment in the expanding industry takes times to realize. Moving along the PPF is costly and consumes time.

Once it arrives at point P', the economy trades up along the terms of trade line. Note that 2 units of M are still acquired for each unit of exported S, but the economy has reduced its consumption possibilities. The new tt' line or consumption possibilities line from point P' lies below the free trade tt line from point P. Note that MRT $< tt$ at point P'. Consumption falls to point T'. The community indifference curve tangent to tt' at T' lies below the one tangent at T. The tariff has reduced national welfare. Domestic consumers are hurt because their potential to consume both goods is lessened with a tariff. Real income, measured in terms of either good at the autarky price, falls from point T to point T'.

From a worldwide or global perspective, an inefficient pattern of production is produced by a tariff. Tariffs keep an economy from specializing according to comparative advantage and reduce the economy's consumption possibilities.

2.   An Introduction to Tariffs and the Terms of Trade

A tariff does, however, have the potential to improve the terms of trade for a nation that consumes a large portion of the world market for the good it imports. In the world market, demand for a good decreases when a large nation imposes a tariff on its imports. This decline in demand causes price of the imported good to fall and the relative price of imports for the large nation to fall. With better terms of trade, the nation imposing the tariff can potentially consume more of both goods.

In Figure 4.4, imagine the terms of trade improved enough with the tariff so the new consumption possibilities line tt' swings out beyond point T on the free trade tt line. Conditions for this *optimal tariff* are not easy to find in applications. The optimal tariff argument is not a generally accepted reason for tariffs.

Even if conditions for an optimal tariff are found, imposing one can lead to a tariff war. Other nations will retaliate with tariffs of their own, so the conditions that favored the optimal tariff are washed out. The most famous tariff war occurred during the 1930s, when the United States and other industrial nations raised tariffs to an average of 60%. The Smoot-Hawley Tariff Act enacted the high U.S. tariffs. More than 1,000 economists formally protested, inducing one senator to claim that these professors in the ivory towers do not make an honest living by sweating. International trade came to a virtual halt with the high levels of protection. The lack of international trade in no small part explains the Great Depression. The Federal Reserve Bank simultaneously carried out a tremendous contraction of the money supply. Although the heralded stock market crash receives much of the credit for the Great Depression, falling stock prices were more of a symptom of irrational economic policy than a cause of the Depression.

In the next chapter the mechanics of optimal tariffs and tariff wars will be studied in detail. Although tariffs have the potential of improving the terms of trade, for political reasons this use of a tariff should be avoided.

Protectionism inhibits an open economy's potential to provide goods and services to its consumers. Free trade offers a nation the potential to arrange production more efficiently and to provide its consumers with the potential of consuming more of every good. Protectionism takes away this potential.

EXAMPLE 4.8   An Appeal for Protection

Imagine you are a member of Congress and hear the following eloquent and passionate appeal for an increased tariff from a fellow member on the floor of the House:

Our industry is subjected to the intolerable competition of a foreign rival whose superior facilities for producing enable him to flood the market at so low a price as to take away all our customers the moment he appears, suddenly reducing an important branch of industry to stagnation. Our industry provides such valuable manufactures that our country cannot, without ingratitude, leave us now to struggle unprotected through so unequal a contest. Do you object that the consumer must pay the price of protecting us? You have always acted to encourage labor.

How would you vote on the issue of imposing this tariff? Would it matter if the orator had promised to vote in your favor on one of your pet projects? This appeal is actually an abridged version of a satire written in the early 1800s by the Frenchman Fredric Bastiat. The foreign rival was the sun. Bastiat's appeal was to pass a law shutting up all "windows, openings, and fissures through which sunlight penetrates" in order to encourage the domestic candle industry!

Problems for Section C

C1.   Explain the relationship between the relative price of S in autarky and with trade if the open economy of Figure 4.4 moves northwestward from point A up along its production possibility curve. Illustrate the effects of a tariff in this situation.

C2.   What will happen regarding international trade if the relative price of S in the world exactly equals the relative price in autarky in Figure 4.4? What would be the effect of a tariff?

D.   THE POLITICAL ECONOMY OF PROTECTIONISM

The arguments against protectionism seem overwhelming: inefficiency, lost income, and a misallocation of resources. Further, losses from protectionism multiply over time, since the economy fails to concentrate on its relatively efficient industries. William Brock, a U.S. trade representative, puts it this way: "Nations which protect their economies today will pay the costs of a decline in competitiveness tomorrow." Free trade also promotes a more equal distribution of income, as will be developed completely in later chapters. Economists have been making these points for 200 years, and people have realized and pursued the gains from trade since the dawn of history. Why then does protectionism persist?

1.   Protection as a Result of Rent Seeking

There are gains to be enjoyed in some industries through protection, so those firms and workers are willing to spend resources to acquire protected status. In the United States, Congress enacts all trade legislation. Congressional representatives are elected from relatively small districts, often having a single large firm or industry. Firms are willing to spend resources to get a sympathetic representative elected. Voters in the district naturally vote for a representative looking out for their narrow interests.

Industries hire lobbyists who live in Washington to put continual pressure on members of Congress to obtain protectionism. This *rent seeking* activity is inefficient in that these resources could be used to produce valued goods and services for the economy and international markets. Congressional representatives trade votes, or *logroll,* to gain enough support for the particular legislation they favor. Laws eventually passed often lump many individual tariffs and quotas together, indicating the trading of votes among representatives, each with narrow interests. A Congressional representative who does not support local industry, especially in hard economic times, will find it hard to appeal to global economic efficiency and typically would not be elected to office again. People may be global free traders, but they are typically local protectionists.

> Industries spend resources lobbying to acquire protected status. Consumers pay the cost of protection, but are disorganized and unable to influence the political process of protection.

The choice of tariffs is a political process. Industries lobby for protection, spending resources to obtain higher tariff rates. Lobbying creates benefits measurable by increased tariff rates. The marginal benefit of spending on lobbying determines the actual amount spent, as pictured in Figure 4.5. Every dollar spent on lobbying creates some benefit for the industry doing the lobbying. The optimal amount of lobbying occurs when the marginal cost (MC) of extra lobbying equals the marginal benefit (MB) to the industry from the extra lobbying. Industries can be expected to

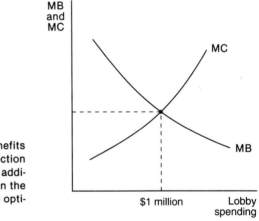

Figure 4.5. Optimal Lobby Spending The marginal benefits MB to the industry of lobbying come from the protection afforded by higher tariff rates. Marginal benefits from additional spending diminishes, so MB slopes down. Given the marginal costs MC of spending, an industry picks the optimal amount of lobby spending where MC = MB.

spend more on lobbying when MB > MC. In Figure 4.5, the industry will spend $1 million (per year) lobbying.

The political side of the imposition of tariffs can also be illustrated. Political parties gain voter support by imposing tariffs. Workers in a protected industry will support political candidates who promise or deliver protection for their jobs. Stockholders and local interests favor protection.

Figure 4.6 shows the marginal or additional benefits (MB) of increasing tariffs for a protectionistic political party. As the tariff rate increases, the level of MB decreases. The downward-sloping MB schedule reflects the fact that the most votes are gained by the first tariffs, and additional tariffs gain increasingly fewer votes. On the other hand, additional tariff protection creates distortions. Importing firms are disrupted, taxes increase, and national income falls, all of which cause lost votes. The distorting effects are summarized in Figure 4.6 by the marginal cost curve MC. As the tariff rate increases, the marginal cost in lost votes of an increase in the tariff rate increases. The optimal political tariff is the one that maximizes the votes gained by the protectionistic party. This occurs where MC = MB at a 10% tariff in Figure 4.6.

> The political economy model of protection explains why industries lobby and how political parties choose their target tariff rates.

2. Dumping: Unfair Competition

Industries in the United States can file claims of unfair trade competition with the Department of Commerce. If foreign firms are thought to be *dumping* their products (selling temporarily below cost to drive out the competi-

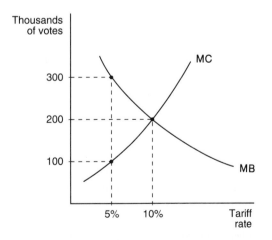

Thousands of votes

Figure 4.6. **Optimizing Votes with a Tariff** A tariff gains votes from those who benefit, while costing votes of those who suffer. If the tariff rate is 5%, the marginal cost MC of an increase in the tariff is only 100,000 lost votes while the marginal benefit MB is 300,000 votes gained. The political party seeking votes has an incentive to increase the tariff to its optimal level of 10%.

tion), a suit can be filed with the U.S. International Trade Commission (ITC). Subsidies by foreign governments to their export industries are also considered unfair, even though foreign taxpayers are effectively subsidizing domestic consumers.

Damages can be awarded by the president, and restrictive quotas can be put into place. The 1980s have witnessed a large increase in the volume of claims investigated and the value of awards granted by the ITC. This "new" protectionism tries to skirt GATT, which commits the United States to lower protectionism. The call for "fair trade" from industry has a good deal of popular appeal.

These suits with the ITC offer another political avenue for industries to pursue protection. Dumping allegations cannot in principle be proved unless cost data from the foreign firm are submitted. Typically the evidence is weak, but awards for dumping are made. Awards in the dumping claims have typically been based on the politics of protection rather than sound economic reasoning.

3. The Case for Free Trade

Protectionism introduces distortions in the pattern of international production. Inefficiency and waste of resources are promoted. Consumers lose through protectionism by having to pay higher prices and receiving fewer goods. Most consumers have little idea of the degree to which protectionism increases the price of goods and decreases their real income.

What are the marginal costs and benefits of an additional $1 of protection? The benefits of protectionism can be measured in saved jobs. Costs are measured in terms of lost goods and high-priced consumption. Ratios of costs to benefits in some industries have been estimated by Murray Weidenbaum and Tracy Munger (1983). In the case of autos the cost-to-benefit ratio has been estimated to be 4 to 1. It costs the nation $4 of deadweight loss for every $1 of job saved. Protectionism in other industries is even more inefficient: 9 to 1 in footwear, 6 to 1 in televisions, 5 to 1 in steel, 10 to 1 in CB radios, and 7 to 1 in apparel.

Even if consumers were completely aware of the costs imposed by protection, they would find it difficult to organize and lobby against it. Consumers are not organized, while firms, industries, and labor unions in a particular industry are organized by their nature. In addition, consumers tend to be local protectionists even if they are global free traders. Hardly anyone would favor opening a local protected industry to international competition if friends or family stand to lose their jobs and are forced to retrain or relocate. Free trade takes on a personal meaning when it hits close to home.

The only sure way to remove the inequities associated with protectionism is to phase it out slowly but completely. It is constitutionally illegal to tax exports in the United States, an activity other governments carry out.

The bias against export duties in the United States dates from colonial days, when the king of England heavily taxed exports from the colonies and kept the revenues. Outlawing tariffs, quotas, and NTBs would remove the waste and rent seeking associated with protectionism.

The temptation to pursue narrow local interests at odds with the national interest would be removed if protectionism were illegal. Pressures from key employers in their districts must often override what representatives may recognize as best in the national interest. While protection may offer short–run remedies for economic problems, it leads to long-run dependence and economic inefficiency. As one of the leading industrial nations, the United States must lead the way toward increased global efficiency through free trade.

EXAMPLE 4.9   Winners and Losers with U.S. Protection

Linda Hunter (1990) examines the industrial and regional pattern of winners and losers with current U.S. protectionism. The largest industrial winners are textiles, autos, and steel. Other winners are chemicals, mining, plastics, and utilities. The largest losers are furniture, fixtures, and construction. Regions that are coming out ahead with current protection are the Southeast and East, with losses spread across the Midwest and West. States enjoying the largest benefits are South Carolina, North Carolina, Georgia, Alabama, Tennessee, Missouri, Rhode Island, Mississippi, Kentucky, Virginia, Pennsylvania, and New York.

EXAMPLE 4.10   U.S. Farm Commodity Programs as Protection

Farm commodity programs are based on the idea of reducing the quantity supplied through "allotments" and keeping the price of the good high with supports. Lobbying during the 1920s and 1930s led to the support programs, which have persisted since. Milk, sugar, cotton, tobacco, wheat, rice, corn, grain, sorghum, barley, peanuts, and wool are currently supported. Bruce Gardner (1987) studies the causes of these support programs. Imported goods (wool, sugar, and beef) are more likely to receive the protection of a commodity program. Farmers appeal that they "need" protection from cheap foreign imports. A farm price support would act much like a tariff in the market for imported wool, sugar, or beef. If wool, for instance, cannot be sold below a certain price, the quantity demanded will be restricted, domestic production will be higher, and less will be imported. In the market for an exported agricultural good, an allotment program would reduce the quantity of exports.

EXAMPLE 4.11 The Pocketbook Issues

The AFL-CIO labor union actively pursues its political and economic objectives. A yearly pamphlet, *The Pocketbook Issues,* is prepared and circulated. Its policy recommendations for international trade and investment in 1990 provide a good summary of protectionist views:

(a) Negotiate bilateral trade deficit reductions
(b) Enforce the Omnibus Trade and Competitiveness Act of 1988 to address unfair trade practices
(c) Enact domestic content laws
(d) Implement policy to bring order and stability to trade in textiles, apparel, and shoes
(e) Extend Voluntary Export Restraints on steel imports
(f) Address inundation of U.S. telecommunications industry by foreign products
(g) Enact policy to reestablish domestic electronic and television industries
(h) Enact policy to ensure that U.S. raw materials (grains, logs, etc.) are processed before export
(i) Pass legislation to increase the portion of cargo carried on U.S. vessels
(j) Prohibit Alaskan crude oil exports
(k) Stem the export of office and service sector jobs
(l) Fully fund the Trade Adjustment Assistance program
(m) Discourage export of capital and technology
(n) Redirect U.S. international investments abroad and monitor foreign investment in the United States
(o) End tax loopholes and incentives for U.S. multinationals to move abroad
(p) Strengthen codes of conduct for multinationals operating in the United States, specifically rights of workers to organize and bargain collectively
(q) Repeal the Foreign (free) Trade Zone Act

EXAMPLE 4.12 Smuggling

Smuggling is illegal trade aimed at avoiding either protectionism or prohibition. The volume of smuggling worldwide is large, perhaps more than 10% of all trade (depending on what is included). A potential smuggler considers the benefits (profit) and costs (the penalty discounted by the probability of being caught). When illegal goods such as drugs are imported, users benefit but society as a whole may lose. Similarly, when illegal goods such as military hardware are exported, one industry gains but society as a whole may lose. In these cases the reason for the prohibition must be weighed. When goods are smuggled to avoid protectionist laws, the analysis is a bit simpler. Smuggled goods lower the relative price of the protected good inside the country and increase the amount of specialization and trade. The economy moves toward its free trade position, with the level of trade and welfare increasing. Free traders would perhaps not discourage smuggling aimed at avoiding protectionist laws. Promoting illegal activity may not be wise, however. Clearly it is best to eliminate the protectionist law. Additionally, smuggling may use more resources than legal trade in the import and distribution of the contraband. Generally, smuggling may lead to welfare gains or losses.

Problems for Section D

D1. Why are large firms and industries often more protected than small ones?

D2. Why might senators favor protectionism less than members of Congress? Presidents less than senators?

D3. Some industries claim they must be protected because they produce goods essential for national defense and could not otherwise compete with foreign firms. If you were president, which goods would you allow this strategic status?

CONCLUSION

Protectionism is the oldest issue in economics and one gaining much attention today. The free trade debate will rage as long as protectionism is legal and the potential benefits to protected industries outweigh the costs associated with lobbying to acquire protection. The next chapter examines the effects of a tariff in a large economy where international prices are affected by the drop in imports. The terms of trade for a large economy are altered by a tariff. The United States, Europe, and Japan are large economies in their imports of oil, automobiles, and other goods. Generally, the next chapter shows how the terms of trade are determined between large economies and continues the study of protection.

KEY TERMS

Deadweight loss	Fair trade
Dumping	ITC
Effective protection	Logrolling

Nontariff barrier (NTB)   Quotas
Production distortion   Rent seeking
Quality upgrading   Tariffs
Quota license   Voluntary export restraint (VER)

KEY POINTS

- Tariffs impose deadweight losses on an economy, benefiting narrow industrial interests at the expense of consumers.
- Quotas and other nontariff barriers to international trade have become popular in the wave of new protectionism arising in the face of lower tariffs and GATT.
- Tariffs shift production away from industries in which the economy has a comparative advantage, creating long-term efficiency losses.
- Protectionism arises when the benefits to the protected industry outweigh the cost of lobbying. Consumers benefit from free trade and are unaware of the taxation imposed by protection.

REVIEW PROBLEMS

1. Review problems 1 through 9 are based on the domestic demand for sports shoes given by $D = 100 - P$, and a domestic supply of $S = -10 + P$. Diagram this domestic market. Find the level of imports if the world price is $30.

2. Suppose a 50% tariff is put on sport shoe imports in the previous problem. The international price is $30. Find and diagram the change in imports.

3. Find the tariff revenue and the deadweight loss with the 50% tariff in the previous problem.

4. In the market for imported shoes in problem 1, find the *prohibitive tariff rate*, which would eliminate all imports of shoes.

5. With the domestic supply and demand for shoes in problem 1 and an international price of $30, suppose a quota of 10 units is imposed. Find the domestic price with the quota.

6. Find the total loss associated with the quota of 10 units of shoes compared with free trade.

7. Find the producer surplus of domestic shoe producers with the quota of 10 units in the previous problem compared with free trade.

8. Suppose foreign shoe producers voluntarily agree to limit their exports to the domestic market in problem 1 to 30 units. Find the domestic price with this VER. Compare total losses with the situation of a quota of 10 units.

9. With free trade, suppose all shoe imports come from two foreign countries: A and B. Each foreign country supplies half of shoe imports, using the demand and supply in problem 1. Under political pressure, foreign country A agrees to a VER of 15 units and country B agrees not to increase its level of exports. Find the price, level of imports, and the change in export revenue of both foreign countries with the VER.

10. Diagram the PPF of a closed economy where the relative price of manufactures is higher on the international market than at home. In which direction will the

economy specialize if it moves to free trade? Describe the direction of trade. Illustrate the effects of a tariff on the pattern of production.

11. Consider an economy producing three goods: services, manufactures, and agricultural goods. What does its PPF look like? What determines which goods are imported or exported? What are the effects of protection? Does the extra good make any fundamental difference in this analysis?

12. If all Congressional representatives were elected at the state level rather than from particular districts, would protectionist legislation be easier or more difficult to pass?

READINGS

Gary Clyde Hufbauer and Howard Rosen, *Trade Policy for Troubled Industries,* Institute for International Economics, Washington, DC, 1986. A detailed look at the potential of policy for U.S. industry facing stiff foreign competition.

William R. Cline, editor, *Trade Policy in the 1980s,* Institute for International Economics, Washington, DC, 1983. A fine collection of applied studies of protectionism and other trade policies.

I.M. Destler, *American Trade Politics: System Under Stress,* Institute for International Economics, Washington, DC, 1986. An analysis of the domestic politics of current U.S. trade policy.

Dominick Salvatore, editor, *The New Protectionist Threat to World Welfare,* North-Holland, Amsterdam, 1987. A collection of first-rate studies on current policy issues.

Inside U.S. Trade, Inside Washington Publishers, Washington, DC. A detailed weekly newsletter on U.S. government trade policy for those actively involved in trade.

Jagdish Bhagwati, *Protectionism,* Cambridge, MA, MIT Press, 1988. An entertaining, insightful look at the oldest issue in political economy.

Stephen P. Magee, William A. Brock, and Leslie Young, *Black Hole Tariffs and Endogenous Policy Theory,* Cambridge University Press, 1989. An advanced look into the politics of tariff formation.

Robert Baldwin, editor, *Trade Policy Issues and Empirical Analysis,* National Bureau of Economic Research, Washington, DC, 1988. A collection of articles on the empirical analysis of trade policy.

Ron Jones and Anne Krueger, editors, *The Political Economy of International Trade,* Basil Blackwell, London, 1990. A collection of advanced readings on the frontier of research in the economics of protection.

The World Economy, Basil Blackwell, London. An academic journal with articles of topical interest on international relations.

CHAPTER 5

The Terms of Trade

CHAPTER PREVIEW

A country's terms of trade measure the relative price of its imports in terms of its exports. A large country is able to affect the international market and international prices. Imagine two potential trading partners facing each other, each producing two types of goods. Either country might import or export either good. The terms of trade, the international relative price of one good in terms of the other, must be determined along with the direction and volume of trade. For each unit of a good exported, the terms of trade indicate how many units of imports the country acquires in exchange. Higher terms of trade are preferred, since the same amount of exports could be exchanged for more imports, or less in exports could be exchanged for the same amount of imports. This chapter:

  (a)   Develops *offer curves*, a tool used to examine and predict adjustments in the terms of trade
  (b)   Examines the attempt to improve the terms of trade through *optimal tariffs*
  (c)   Uses *tariff games* to study the ultimate effects of protectionism
  (d)   Studies the pricing of *exhaustible resources* in international trade

INTRODUCTION

When the effects of trade and protection are examined, it simplifies matters to assume that the terms of trade or the international prices of exported and imported goods and services are fixed. If the quantities exported or imported in a particular country are not large enough to affect international supply and demand noticeably, this small country assumption can be made with some realism. The effects of trade and protection inside a country can be examined with relative ease when the international price of traded goods is fixed in international markets. The terms of trade are unaffected as such a country opens to international trade and adjusts its pattern of production and consumption to international prices. The pattern of specialization, effects of protectionism, and gains from trade are determined with fixed terms of trade. Such a small country is called a price taker in the international market.

Industries in some nations, however, are large importers or exporters in particular world markets. Examples are South Africa exporting diamonds or gold, Australia exporting wool, the United States exporting soybeans and importing cars, Canada exporting lumber, Saudi Arabia exporting oil, Brazil exporting coffee or shoes, Greece exporting tourism or olive oil, Japan exporting electronics or autos and importing food, Germany exporting chemicals, and so on. Changes in these national markets affect the international prices. As pictured by excess supply and demand, a national market can affect the international price and level of trade in a particular good when the economy is large relative to the world market. The economy's terms of trade are variable if shifts in the nation's production or preferences are large enough to affect international prices. Such a large country is called a price maker in the international market.

A complete picture of how the terms of trade are determined between two economies would involve the interaction of excess supply and excess demand in the markets for every good traded between them. For simplicity, consider two economies that trade only with each other, and suppose they produce only two types of goods. The production possibilities frontier (PPF) and the pattern of preferences or tastes in each nation will determine the terms of trade and the level of trade. Changing technology, economic growth, or changes in consumer preferences can have an impact on the terms of trade and the level of trade. Offer curves are used in this chapter to illustrate this interplay between trading partners.

The international impact of protectionism between large countries can be traced with offer curves. Changes in an importing nation that buys a significant quantity on the world market will affect the international price. A tariff lowers the demand for the imported good. A tariff in a large country can lead to a fall in the international price of the import. In other words, a tariff has the potential to improve the terms of trade for a large country. Such potential gain, however, comes only with another country's loss.

If one large country imposes a tariff to improve its terms of trade (or for other protectionist reasons), the other country can be expected to retaliate. With each nation choosing its tariff level, a "game" can arise in which the outcome will depend on the opponent's strategy. Game theory has developed tools to predict what happens when nations face each other in such tariff games. Outcomes may be either stable or unstable, depending on the payoffs and strategies chosen by the playing nations. Free trade cannot be expected as a strategic outcome, even though it leads to higher world output and global efficiency.

Important international markets involve exhaustible resources like oil and other minerals. Ultimately only a certain amount of the exhaustible resource can be sold. How is the international value of an exhaustible resource determined? This question is critical for both oil-importing nations like the United States, Japan, and European countries, and oil-exporting nations like Saudi Arabia, the republics of the former Soviet Union, Iraq, and Mexico. How fast should Saudi Arabia deplete its vast stock of oil? How vigorously should the United States pursue alternative energy sources? What is the optimal rate of depletion of gold or platinum for South Africa? Offer curves provide background for studying the international markets for exhaustible resources, illustrating how the terms of trade involving an exhaustible resource evolve over time.

A. OFFER CURVES AND THE TERMS OF TRADE

This section shows how the terms of trade are worked out between two economies. Offer curves are based on the pattern of production and consumption familiar from the PPF and indifference curves. When two economies differ from each other, either in their PPFs or consumer preferences, gains from trade are possible.

1. Trade Triangles and Offer Curves

In Figure 5.1, imagine the economy starts at point A in autarky. Given this PPF, preference for the two goods is such that the economy would produce and consume 100 units of each good. Consumer welfare is maximized on the highest attainable community indifference curve (I) tangent to the

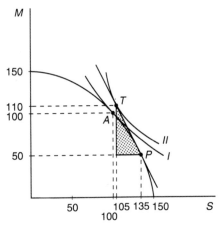

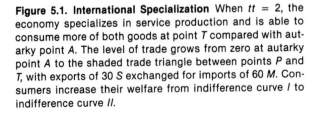

Figure 5.1. International Specialization When $tt = 2$, the economy specializes in service production and is able to consume more of both goods at point T compared with autarky point A. The level of trade grows from zero at autarky point A to the shaded trade triangle between points P and T, with exports of 30 S exchanged for imports of 60 M. Consumers increase their welfare from indifference curve I to indifference curve II.

PPF. The autarky relative price of S in terms of M would be given by the tangency at point A. The marginal rate of transformation (MRT) along the PPF equals the marginal rate of substitution (MRS) on the optimal indifference curve I.

If the international relative price of services is higher than the autarky price, production in the economy would shift toward more S. At the international relative price of services $M/S = 2$, the economy has moved down along its PPF to point P, where the terms of trade line $tt = 2$ is tangent to the PPF and production is $(M,S) = (50,135)$. The economy trades up along the terms of trade line to the highest indifference curve II at point T, where consumption is $(M,S) = (110,105)$. Exports of 30 S are traded for 60 M. In the optimal trading equilibrium, $tt = $ MRT $= $ MRS. The shaded trade triangle shows exports of 30 S on its base and imports of 60 M on its side. This is the picture of the small trading economy developed in the last chapter.

Consider what happens if the terms of trade were to increase to $tt = 3$. With this *improved* terms of trade, the value of exported services has increased on the international market. The economy would respond with increased specialization, producing more services and less manufactures. The economy shifts production so the MRT increases to 3. Production pushes to point P' in Figure 5.2 where $(M,S) = (25,145)$. The level of trade increases, as pictured by the larger trade triangle. Trade takes place up to the consumer equilibrium at point T' where $(M,S) = (130,110)$. Exports of 35 units of S are traded for 105 units of M. More is exported in exchange for increasing imports as the terms of trade improve. Consumers are better off in equilibrium on indifference curve III.

Note that the rising relative price of services in this example induces consumers to move to an increasing ratio of M to S. In the consumer equilibrium at point A, 100 units of each good are consumed and the ratio of M to S is 1. When the relative price of S rises to $M/S = 2$, consumption at

Figure 5.2. Increased International Specialization If tt rises to 3, the economy specializes more in service production and will be able to consume more of both goods at T' compared with point T in Figure 5.1. The level of trade grows, as indicated by the larger trade triangle compared to Figure 5.1. Exports of 35 S are traded for imports of 105 M at the improved terms of trade. Welfare increases to indifference curve III tangent to the tt line.

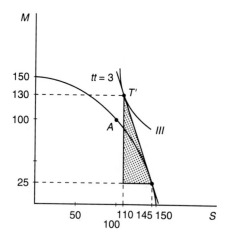

point T in Figure 5.1 is $(M,S) = (110,105)$ for a ratio of $110/105 = 1.05$. When the relative price $M/S = 3$, consumption at point T' in Figure 5.2 is $(M,S) = (130,110)$ for a ratio of $130/110 = 1.18$. Consumers switch toward a higher ratio of M to S when the relative price of M falls.

In Figure 5.3, a summary of this economy's response to varying terms of trade is presented. Imports of M and exports of S are plotted along either axis. A ray or line from the origin in this diagram represents the terms of trade, the number of imports per unit of export. This is a different way of picturing the terms of trade. In Figures 5.1 and 5.2 the slope of a tt line is (the negative of) the terms of trade. In Figure 5.3 the slope of a tt ray from the origin equals the terms of trade.

When $tt = 2$, 30 S are exported in exchange for 60 M. When $tt = 3$, 35 S are exported in exchange for 105 M. The trade triangles are the basis for Figure 5.3. The trade triangle grows with improved terms of trade. Connecting each of the levels of imports and exports as the terms of trade improve leads to the *offer curve* labeled H in Figure 5.3

An offer curve illustrates the levels of exports the country is willing to offer in exchange for imports at various terms of trade. Offer curves are powerful devices because they summarize the behavior of both producers and consumers in a trading economy. Improving terms of trade for the home country induces the economy to specialize more in services and increases the level of trade. The economy receives more gains from trade as it moves up its offer curve.

Every point along the offer curve H represents a potential international equilibrium for the home country. The country's willingness to ex-

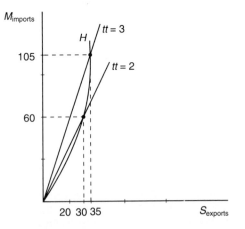

Figure 5.3. The Home Country's Offer Curve An offer curve shows the level of exports and imports for various terms of trade. At the autarky price, there is no trade. At $tt = 2$, 30 units of S are exported in exchange for 60 units of imported M. At $tt = 3$, 35 S are traded for 105 M. The home offer curve connects all the various levels of imports and exports for different terms of trade.

port in exchange for imports depends directly on the relative price of imports in terms of exports. Improving terms of trade creates the potential for larger gains from trade and expands the volume of trade up along the offer curve. For any potential terms of trade, the home country will offer a certain quantity of its exports in exchange for imports. The offer curve illustrates all of the potential trade triangles of the home country.

> Offer curves summarize how production and consumption in an open economy adjust to different international prices of traded goods.

Figure 5.4 illustrates a hypothetical foreign nation's offer curve. Without trade, suppose the autarky relative price of S in the foreign country is 3. If the terms of trade are 3 units of M for every S (1/3 S for every M), the foreign trade nation will not export manufactures. If the terms of trade are 2 units of M for every S (1/2 S for every unit of M), the foreign country will want to specialize in M and trade for S. Suppose at this price the foreign economy wants to export 60 units of M in exchange for 30 units of S. This point is plotted on the terms of trade line $tt = 2$. At $tt = 1$, each unit of exported manufactures brings in a whole unit of services to the foreign country. The foreign nation will then want to export 80 units of M in exchange for 80 units of S.

A higher price for M induces more specialization from the foreign nation and a higher level of trade. As the terms of trade line gets flatter, the foreign nation wants to export more. The foreign economy benefits as it

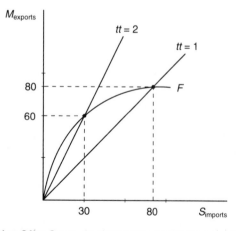

Figure 5.4. The Foreign Offer Curve As the terms of trade improve for the foreign country, the level of exported M increases as the foreign economy opens to trade. No trade is offered at the foreign autarky price. If the relative price of M rises from the autarky levels to 0.5, 60 units of M are exchanged for 30 units of S. At $tt = 1$, the foreign country offers 80 units of exports. The foreign offer curve connects the various levels of imports and exports.

moves out its offer curve. Underlying the foreign offer curve are the foreign PPF and indifference curves. Each point on the foreign offer curve represents an optimal trading equilibrium, with the terms of trade equal to the foreign MRT and the foreign MRS along their highest indifference curve. Note that the foreign offer curve bends toward its import axis. The home offer curve in Figure 5.3 also bends toward its import axis.

Each point along the foreign country's offer curve F represents a potential international equilibrium. As tt falls from 2 to 1, the relative price of the foreign country's exports rises and the terms of trade improve for the foreign country. For any tt line the foreign country locates its optimal level of exports (and imports) along its offer curve. The offer curve is a schedule of what the country is willing to offer and accept in trade at different terms of trade.

2.   International Equilibrium and the Terms of Trade

There are two trading nations in the examples of Figures 5.3 and 5.4. Foreign exports of M must equal home imports, and foreign imports of S must equal home exports. When the two countries trade, the international equilibrium determines the direction of trade, the quantities traded, and the terms of trade. At a terms of trade of $M/S = 3$, no trade is offered by the foreign nation because foreign exports would be too cheap. At an international price of $M/S = 1$, no trade is offered by the home nation, since its exports would be too cheap. The terms of trade must fall between these autarky prices, $M/S = 1$ and 3. Autarky prices in each country determine the *limits to the terms of trade*.

In the example of Figures 5.1 and 5.2, if the terms of trade M/S were equal to 2, 60 units of M would be traded internationally for 30 units of S. This is the only terms of trade for which the quantities offered by each country match. The terms of trade adjust so the quantity each nation is willing to export equals the quantity the other wants to import.

Home and foreign offer curves are combined in Figure 5.5, which illustrates how the terms of trade and the level of trade are determined in the *international equilibrium*. Where the two offer curves intersect, the level of S the home nation is willing to export exactly equals the level of S the foreign nation wants to import. The foreign nation wants to export exactly as much M as the home nation is willing to import. Each country would prefer better terms of trade for itself out along its own offer curve, but neither is able to induce its trading partner in that direction.

> Where the offer curves of two nations intersect, the terms of trade and the level of trade are determined.

To see the market forces at work, suppose the international relative price of services were a bit lower, say $M/S = 1.5$ as sketched in Figure 5.6.

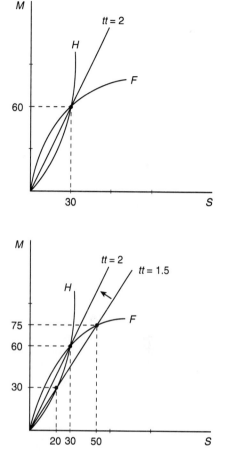

Figure 5.5. The International Equilibrium Where the home offer curve H meets the foreign offer curve F, the international terms of trade and the level of trade are determined. At tt = 2, the home country is willing to export 30 units of S in exchange for 60 units of M. The foreign country is willing to export 60 M in exchange for 30 S. At any other terms of trade, exports from one country do not match imports into the other country.

Figure 5.6. International Market Price Adjustment If the international price were M/S = 1.5, there would be a shortage of 30 units of S and a surplus of 45 units of M. These market conditions push the relative price of services up toward the international equilibrium. If tt were above 2, there would be a surplus of S and a shortage of M. The relative price of S would then fall back toward international equilibrium of M/S = 2. This international equilibrium is stable. The terms of trade tt = 2 is the only relative price consistent with a trading equilibrium for both economies.

There would then be a shortage of S in the international market. The level of exports of S supplied by the home country would be 20, while the foreign demand for imported S would be 50. This shortage of 30 units of S puts upward pressure on the price of services. Competitive buyers in the international market will bid up the price of services.

At M/S = 1.5, there would simultaneously be a surplus of M in the international market. Desired home imports of 30 would be less than the 75 the foreign nation offers. This surplus of 45 units of M puts downward pressure on the price of M. Foreign producers notice they are producing more M than they can sell, and lower their price. The relative price M/S rises from 1.5 toward 2.

The relative price of services would rise from 1.5 toward the international equilibrium terms of trade at 2. This international equilibrium is *stable*, which means the terms of trade and level of trade tend toward the equilibrium levels. Any other terms of trade lead the two trading nations back toward a relative price of 2. As an exercise, work through the economics of what happens when the international relative price is $M/S = 2.5$.

Offer curves illustrate how international markets clear between large trading economies. The terms of trade and the volume of trade are worked out through international competition. They can also be applied to trade involving groups of nations, as with world trade between the industrialized North and developing South, or between the Pacific Rim countries and North America.

3. Adjustments in the Terms of Trade

A nation's offer curve is affected by changes in its underlying PPF and consumption preferences. Changing technology in the supply of manufactures affects the home nation's term of trade and volume of trade. Suppose technology for manufactures declines because of reduced investment. Since manufactures would become more expensive to produce domestically, the country would be willing to sacrifice more exported services for each unit of imports. To get a unit of imported M, the home economy would be willing to give up more units of S.

Figure 5.7 pictures an expansion of the home offer curve to the right because of this declining technology in manufactured goods. The nation has become more open to international trade because it is now less efficient at producing the good it imports. The offer curve expands away from the import axis. For each level of imported M, the home nation is willing to sacrifice more exported S. For each unit of exported S, the nation would accept less M.

In Figure 5.7 before the shift, the home nation would have given up only 20 units of S for 30 units of imported M. After the expansion in its offer curve, the home nation would be willing to trade 30 units of S for the 30 units of M. Looked at another way, the home nation would accept less

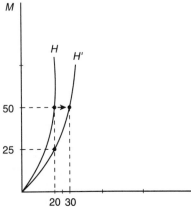

Figure 5.7. An Expanding Home Offer Curve When domestic technology for manufactures falls, the home nation's offer curve expands away from the import axis. For 50 units of M, the home country would be willing to export 30 units of S rather than the previous 20. In exchange for 20 units of exported S, the home country would accept 25 instead of 50 units of M. The economy has become more open to trade.

M in exchange for each unit of exported *S* after the shift, because the *S* has become relatively less valued. For 20 units of exported *S,* the home nation would accept 20 units of *M* instead of the previous 30.

A similar expansion in the home offer curve would result from:

(a) Increased demand for imported *M*
(b) Decreased demand for *S*
(c) Increased supply of *S*

When demand for *M* increases (because of changing consumer preferences or income) the economy places a higher value on consumption of *M* and becomes willing to sacrifice more *S* to obtain imports of *M*. A fall in the demand for *S* would have a similar effect, with *M* becoming relatively more valued in consumption. Finally, imagine that technology improves in *S* production and the home supply of services rises. Services have become cheaper to produce at home. The home country is now willing to accept less imported *M* for the same level of *S*. Manufactures become relatively more highly valued in the home country with each of these changes.

In the international market the expanded home offer curve will move the international equilibrium as in Figure 5.8. At *M/S* = 2, there would be a shortage for manufactures and a surplus of services in the international market after the shift from *H* to *H'*. The relative price of services, the slope of the *tt* line, falls. This means a higher international relative price for manufactured goods with the expanding home offer curve.

In the example of Figure 5.8, the terms of trade *tt* decline or worsen for the home nation. The relative price of services falls from *M/S* = 2 to 1.75. An expanding offer curve means falling terms of trade. Home exports rise to 40 units of services, while imports rise to 1.75 × 40 = 70 units of manufactures. Home consumers enjoy more manufactures, but each unit

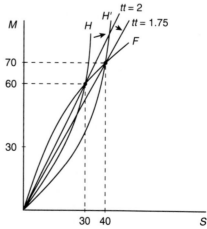

Figure 5.8. An Expanding Offer Curve and the Terms of Trade A large economy that wants to expand its international trade will see its terms of trade worsen. As this home offer curve expands from *H* to *H'*, the terms of trade for the home country fall from 2 to 1.75. The level of trade simultaneously increases. The expansion in the offer curve could be due to lower tariffs or increased efficiency in the export industry.

they consume costs more in domestically produced services. The trade triangle in each country corresponding to this shift has expanded. A good exercise is to sketch the corresponding new trade triangles in diagrams with each of the two nation's underlying PPFs and consumer indifference curves.

An expanding offer curve results in worse terms of trade and a higher level of trade.

It may pay domestic industry to advertise and establish a good reputation abroad. When foreign consumers increase their desire for your exported good, their preferences will move in its direction and its relative price will increase. It pays firms to advertise internationally for the same reasons it pays them to do so domestically. Increased demand means higher prices and more revenue. From a national perspective, increased demand abroad for home goods will mean higher income and potentially higher levels of consumption for all goods.

An expanding capability to produce exports has the same expansionary effect on the home offer curve. Since exports can be produced more cheaply, a lower level of imports would be accepted for any level of exports. In Figure 5.8, if 30 units of S were exported, the home country would be willing to accept in exchange only 30 M rather than the previous 60. With this growth or improved production technology, the economy becomes more open to trade. The volume of trade increases as the terms of trade decline, as in Figure 5.8.

Such a decline in the terms of trade may seem paradoxical, especially in light of the popular opinion that the United States needs to become "more competitive" in its export industry. Gains in efficiency in export industries can lead to worse terms of trade! A large country experiencing increased capability to produce exports, other things being equal, will see those exported goods become cheaper in international markets. This is similar to the effects of lower costs of production in a market, where expanding supply lowers price. Potential consumption of all goods inside the country can rise with increased efficiency. The new level of consumption can represent a higher value of real income or higher community welfare.

A contraction or reduction of the offer curve occurs with either a decreased desire to consume imported goods or a reduction in the supply of exports. Figure 5.9 illustrates a contracted or shrinking home offer curve. The terms of trade tt improve for the home country to 2.5, but only 20 units of S are exported. Decreased demand for imported goods is the desired effect of the "Buy American" campaign. Reduced supply of exports occurs through higher input costs or worsening technology. The terms of trade improve with the contracting offer curve, while the level of trade falls.

Suppose Japanese cars come to be viewed relatively less favorably in the United States, perhaps as the quality of U.S. cars improves. Since the United States is a major buyer of cars on the international market, a con-

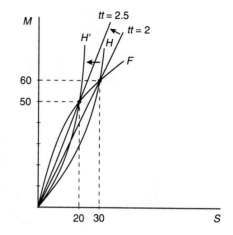

Figure 5.9. A Contracting Home Offer Curve A large economy withdrawing from international trade will see its terms of trade improving. As the home country's offer curve contracts from *H* to *H'*, its terms of trade rise from 2 to 2.5. The level of trade simultaneously decreases. The contraction in the offer curve could be due to increased tariffs, declining efficiency on exports, or a shift of consumers' tastes toward the exported good.

tracted offer curve of the United States would improve its terms of trade. As another example, suppose new technology made liquid petroleum gas (LPG) a very efficient fuel for automobiles, and carmakers began equipping cars for optional LPG use. Clearly, the U.S. offer curve depicting oil imports would contract as our demand for oil fell. The international relative price of oil would drop, as would the level of international trade in oil.

EXAMPLE 5.1   The U.S. Terms of Trade

The International Monetary Fund (IMF) reports every nation's total exports and imports, as well as its terms of trade, in *International Financial Statistics*. The terms of trade are calculated as price indexes or average prices, the value of a basket of exports in terms of the imports for which it trades. The U.S. terms of trade have undergone the pictured changes since 1970. The large decrease in the early 1970s was due to the Organization of Petroleum Exporting Countries (OPEC) oil embargo. Since 1980 the terms of trade have generally improved, but not back to the position of 1970. The improvement during the 1980s is due at least in part to the growth in manufacturing capacity of trading partners, mostly the newly industrializing countries like South Korea, Mexico, and Brazil. Additionally, the relative price of oil has generally fallen over the period.

1970 71 72 73 74 75 76 77 78 79 80 81 82 83 84 85 86 87 88 89

100   98 95 93 80 82 82 79 78 74 67 70 72 76 75 77 80 76 77 72

EXAMPLE 5.2   The Terms of Trade and the Balance of Trade

The overall terms of trade are the price of imported goods in terms of exported goods. The figures below are annual percentage changes in the terms of trade for industrial and developing nations since 1961, reported in *International Financial Statistics.* The large improvement in the developing nations' terms of trade during the years 1971–1975 was enjoyed exclusively by the oil exporters. Other exporting developing nations saw their terms of trade fall 2.5% during those years. The worsened terms of trade faced by the industrial nations during the 1970s was largely due to the higher price of oil imports. The balance of trade for all of the industrial nations fell dramatically from −$7 billion in 1970 to −$21.3 billion in 1975 and −$130 billion in 1980. Over this time period, import prices rose and import expenditure rose as well. Imports were inelastic. Since then, as industrial nations have moved toward more efficient oil consumption, their balance of trade has become more positive.

	1961–65	*1966–70*	*1971–75*	*1976–80*	*1981–85*
Industrial	0.5%	0.5%	−2.1%	−2.1%	0.6%
Developing	0%	−0.3%	10.0%	5.1%	0.2%

Problems for Section A

A1.   Sketch the production possibility frontier and community indifference curves that go with the offer curve in Figure 5.4. Illustrate the international equilibrium.

A2.   Using offer curves, illustrate two nations that would not trade at all. Explain why no trade occurs.

A3.   Explain why the equilibrium of the offer curves in Figure 5.6 is stable, starting with a relative price of 2.5.

A4.   Diagram the change in Figure 5.5 that would occur if foreign demand for services decreases. What happens to the terms of trade and the level of trade?

B.   TARIFFS AND THE TERMS OF TRADE

This section examines what happens when the government of a large country imposes a tariff. Demand falls on the international market for the imported good as a result of the tariff, resulting in a lower price. The terms of trade improve for the large country. The large country can achieve net gains as a result of the improved terms of trade, even though less international specialization occurs. This argument has been used in favor of a tariff on oil imports into the United States. If the international price of oil were to fall enough as a result of reduced U.S. imports, the United States could see net gains.

1. Potential Gains from a Tariff

Figure 5.10 illustrates the potential a large nation has to increase welfare and potentially consume more of both goods with a tariff. In autarky, consumption and production occur at point A. With free trade the nation specializes in services S, producing at point P and trading up along the terms of trade tt to point T. Consumers enjoy the welfare depicted by the indifference curve.

A tariff would protect the domestic manufacturing industry, pushing the economy away from specialization in services from point P to point P'. For this large country the reduction in the demand for M is sufficient to reduce the price of M on the international market. The terms of trade improve for the economy. Each unit of exported services commands more manufactures in trade.

In Figure 5.10 the terms of trade improve to tt'. The exports of this large country have become more expensive on the world market. Each unit of exported S brings more units of imported M. The economy trades up along the new terms of trade line tt', which springs out beyond the original tt line from point P. The potential to consume more of both goods arises. Consumers pick point T' on a higher indifference curve. Income evaluated at the domestic autarky price will be higher at point T' than at point T. Measured by community indifference curves, the level of community welfare is higher at point T' than at point T.

Note that the terms of trade line tt' is not tangent to the PPF at point P'. The reason is that the tariff drives a wedge between prices inside the country and outside the country. The tariff is applied to the imported good when it crosses the border. Thus the relative price of manufactures is higher inside the country than outside. Production moves to point P' with the increased relative price of M inside the country. The terms of trade become steeper at tt', indicating the increased international relative price of services.

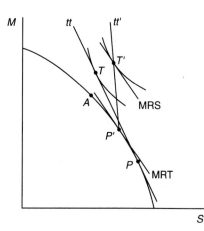

Figure 5.10. Improved Terms of Trade and Production with a Tariff Autarky production and consumption occur at point A. With free trade the economy produces at point P and consumes at point T with prices at the world level tt. A tariff protects the domestic import competing industry and pushes the economy to point P'. The relative price of exports for this large nation rise on the world market to tt'. From the production point at P', the economy trades up along tt' to consumption point T'. Note that at points P' and T', MRT = MRS ≠ tt'. The tariff drives a wedge between the domestic and international prices.

Also note that the terms of trade line tt' is not tangent to indifference curve *II*. The line labeled MRS is parallel to the line labeled MRT. These two lines indicate the relative price of manufactures inside the country. In absolute value, MRS = MRT < tt'. Manufactures are artificially cheap (services are artificially expensive) inside the country because of the tariff.

> A large country has the potential to improve its terms of trade with a tariff, leading to the potential to consume more of every good relative to free trade and to higher welfare.

In the case of U.S. imported oil, the international price of oil could fall enough with a U.S. tariff to lead to such gains. If the United States, Europe, and Japan together put tariffs on imported oil, their terms of trade would certainly improve. It is best to remember, however, that a major proponent of a tariff on oil imports is the domestic oil extraction industry. The main interest of this industry is not to improve the terms of trade for the country, but to see the United States move up along its production frontier toward more domestic oil production. It may not be wise in the long run to deplete domestic petroleum reserves in an artificially hasty fashion. The U.S. stockpiles oil in large underground salt domes in Louisiana and Texas and tapped these reserves during the war in Kuwait. It makes sense to buy oil when it is cheap and store it until it becomes expensive, but such foresight about oil prices is difficult to muster.

2. The Optimal Tariff

Protection restricts a nation's openness to trade. If a tariff is imposed by a large home country, its offer curve contracts toward its import axis. This creates improved terms of trade. The value of the large country's exports rises on the international market. Given free reign, the government of a large nation can search for the tariff that maximizes community welfare. Such a tariff is called the *optimal tariff*. Smaller nations have no such potential to gain from tariffs because they are unable to affect prices on international markets.

A tariff brings gains from the terms of trade improvement and losses because of decreased specialization and lost efficiency. Up to a certain tariff level the marginal benefits from improved terms of trade outweigh the marginal costs of lost efficiency. At higher tariff levels the marginal costs from decreased specialization outweigh the marginal benefits from improved terms of trade.

From the consumer's viewpoint, imports are an economic good and exports are an economic bad. Exports must be produced but are enjoyed by foreigners. Figure 5.11 pictures community indifference curves for imports and exports. Note that trade indifference curves slope away from exports, which are an economic bad. For consumers to remain as well off, increased exports have to be offset by increased imports. Trade indiffer-

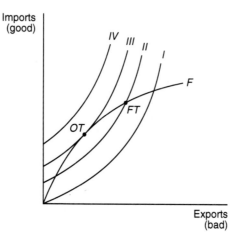

Figure 5.11. Trade Indifference Curves Imports are an economic good, while exports are an economic bad. Trade indifference curves *I* through *IV* represent consumer preferences between imports and exports. Along any one trade indifference curve, the community is equally well off. Curve *IV* is the most preferred, while *I* is the least preferred. An optimal tariff places the home offer curve (not drawn) through the foreign offer curve at optimal point *OT* (optimal tariff).

ence curves thus slope upward. Trade indifference curve *I* represents the level of welfare in autarky, since it goes through the origin of zero exports and imports. Indifference curve *II* is preferred to *I*, *III* is preferred to *II*, and *IV* is preferred to *III*.

If the foreign country's offer curve is fixed, the home country can maximize welfare subject to the foreign offer curve. Suppose the home offer curve (not drawn) goes through point *FT* (free trade). Optimizing welfare means finding the point along foreign offer curve *F* that is tangent to the highest trade indifference curve. This occurs at point *OT* (optimal tariff) in Figure 5.11 along indifference curve *III*. The optimal tariff will contract the home offer curve so that it goes through the foreign offer curve at point *OT*. Note that the highest level of welfare pictured, along indifference curve *IV*, is unattainable. The optimal tariff (*OT* on trade indifference curve *III*) is preferred to free trade (*FT* on trade indifference curve *II*), which is preferred to autarky (on trade indifference curve *I*).

> The optimal tariff maximizes community welfare subject to the constraint of the foreign offer curve. The home offer curve is manipulated to arrive at the optimal terms of trade and level of trade.

3. Quotas and the Terms of Trade

A quota can have the same effect on a large country's terms of trade as a tariff. A quota lowers the demand for a good on the international market and can lower its price.

In Figure 5.12 the home and foreign offer curves are drawn. Suppose

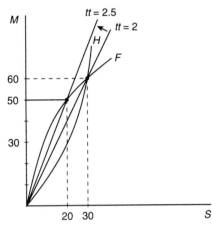

Figure 5.12. A Quota and the Terms of Trade A quota of 50 units of imported M will have the same effects on the terms of trade and the volume of trade as an equivalent tariff. The home country's offer curve is cut off at 50 units of M. No matter how cheap manufacturers become, no more than 50 units will be imported. The modified home offer curve intersects the foreign offer curve where $S = 20$. The home country exports 20 units of S in exchange for 50 units of M, with the terms of trade $M/S = 2.5$. Note the similarity with Figure 5.9, where the contracting offer curve could be due to a tariff.

the home country imposes a quota on imports of 50 units of M, limiting imports to that level. The home offer curve becomes horizontal at 50 units of M. This artificially restrained offer curve intersects the foreign offer curve at $(M,S) = (50,20)$ as occurs with the tariff in Figure 5.9

The terms of trade improve for the home country as a result of this quota. Distribution of income is not the same as with a tariff, but the same terms of trade and volume of trade are obtained.

4.   Retaliation and Tariff Wars

Suppose the home nation imposes its optimal tariff. The foreign nation notices this and can be expected to retaliate with an optimal tariff of its own. This would contract the foreign offer curve F, causing it to fall in toward the S axis, its imports. Foreign consumption of our export falls, reducing the international demand and price for home exports. The terms of trade turn back against the home country and community welfare is reduced. The story need not end here. A *tariff war* can ensue, the volume of trade shrinking with each round of tariff retaliation. Imposing an optimal tariff is sound practice only if trading partners can be counted on not to retaliate.

Figure 5.13 shows the first few steps in a tariff war. The home nation fires the opening shot, imposing an optimal tariff based on offer curve F and restricting its offer curve from H to H'. As the international equilibrium moves from A to B, the terms of trade improve for the home country and it is made better off at the expense of the foreign country. The foreign nation notices what has happened and imposes an optimal tariff of its own based on home offer curve H'. The foreign offer curve contracts from F to F', the international equilibrium moves down to C, and the terms of trade shift in favor of the foreign country to tt''. The foreign country gains, but the home country loses.

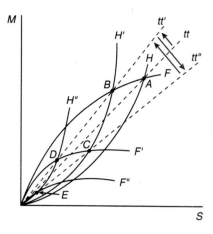

Figure 5.13. A Tariff War The home country opens the tariff war by imposing a tariff that shifts its offer curve from H to H'. This pushes the terms of trade in its favor from tt to tt' and reduces the level of trade from point A to point B. The foreign nation retaliates with a tariff of its own, improving its terms of trade from tt' to tt" but lowering the level of trade still further to point C. Subsequent rounds of retaliation swing the terms of trade between tt' and tt", while lowering the level of trade to point D and then point E.

In the next round the home country imposes an optimal tariff based on foreign offer curve F', restricting its offer curve to H". The terms of trade shift back in favor of the home country, but the volume of trade continues to fall to point D. A subsequent optimal tariff by the foreign country based on H" turns the terms of trade back in its favor, but reduces the volume of trade to point E. Followed to its conclusion, the tariff war results in little change in the terms of trade but falling levels of trade. Ultimately all trade can cease.

> Optimal tariffs create gains only at the expense of trading partners. Tariffs reduce the level of trade and invite tariff wars through retaliation by trading partners.

5. Optimal Tariffs in Practice

Given the current international political economy dominated by the General Agreement on Tariffs and Trade (GATT), the large industrial nations are unlikely to impose large new tariffs, even optimal ones. Participating nations are committed through GATT to a gradual reduction of tariffs and other forms of protection. Any country stepping out of line is noticed right away by competing industries around the world. These are institutional constraints on the imposition of optimal tariffs by large economies.

Another reason to discount the importance of optimal tariffs is the economic calculation and application of rational policy required to apply them. Conditions favoring an optimal tariff may not generally exist and may not be recognized when they do. The political process of protection is anything but scientific. Existing industries have the political incentive to perpetuate themselves through protection. What is best for a particular industry may not be best for the nation as a whole, even though local politicians lose sight of this fact. Tariffs are designed to benefit the protected industry. Typical protectionist legislation should not be promoted under the guise of an optimal or scientific tariff.

There is some sentiment that small developing nations should be allowed to impose their own tariffs without retaliation from the industrial nations. Developing nations are exempt from GATT and generally are allowed to set their own tariffs. Since individual developing nations are typically small in relation to the international markets for their imported goods, the optimal tariff argument does not apply. Tariffs simply promote what must be relatively inefficient industries inside the developing nations. Easily collected tariffs impose taxes on already poor consumers. Every economy should be free to develop in the direction of its own particular comparative advantage. In a world with thousands of types of goods and services, it makes more sense to search for those that have a comparative cost advantage than artificially to encourage those that do not.

> It is difficult to find a situation where it would be rational to apply an optimal tariff. The economy must be large relative to the international markets and must face no possibility of retaliation.

EXAMPLE 5.3   Britain's Move to Free Trade in the 1840s

Britain was the first country to go through an industrial revolution. During the early 1800s, Britain protected its agricultural sector through the Corn Laws. Classical economists debated whether Britain should move to free trade and enjoy the benefits of increased specialization and trade. A drawback to free trade, it was recognized, would be that the terms of trade for Britain could fall. Douglas Irwin (1988) examines this issue. In 1841 the average British tariff was 35%. "Free trade" was a reduction to 25% by 1841. Irwin estimates that a sudden unilateral reduction in tariffs of this magnitude would have worsened Britain's terms of trade by 3.5% and caused a loss of 0.4% of national income. The loss resulting from the fall in the terms of trade would have been greater in this instance than the gains from increased efficiency. By the 1880s British tariffs had dropped to an average of 14%. Other European nations followed suit. U.S. tariffs dropped from 33% to 24% with the Tariff Act of 1846. Britain gained from its move to free trade, since other nations reduced their tariffs.

EXAMPLE 5.4   Tariffs and the Great Depression

In popular folklore the Great Depression of the 1930s was caused by the stock market crash. The crash was actually an effect of the extremely pessimistic economic outlook at the time. Economists have isolated two

causes of the prolonged Great Depression: a very large and sudden reduction in the supply of money and the worldwide tariff war. The importance of a reliable growth rate in the supply of money cannot be overemphasized. As the medium of exchange and a primary store of value,
money has to be reliably supplied to an economy. The Smoot-Hawley
Tariff Act of 1930 raised average tariffs in the United States to nearly
60%. Other industrial nations replied with similar measures. The primary intent in each nation was to save domestic jobs, but international
trade came to a virtual halt. In the end our exports are someone else's
imports and our imports are someone else's exports. President Herbert
Hoover favored the act, but President Franklin Roosevelt pushed for
more liberal trade agreements when he was elected. The Democratic
Party can take credit for dismantling the harmful protectionistic law. Although President Ronald Reagan talked a free trade game, protectionism
actually increased slightly during the 1980s. Both political parties are
subject to the narrow forces of protectionism. Average tariffs have generally been declining since the 1930s and in the United States are now
about 4%. Nontariff protection, however, has recently been on the rise.

EXAMPLE 5.5   Estimated Global Effects of Tariff Elimination

Alan Deardorff and Robert Stern (1983) of the University of Michigan
have put together a large-scale computable model that estimates industrial changes and the economic adjustments that occur with protection.
They estimate exports would increase by 4% for industrial nations with
the elimination of all tariffs. They forecast small gains in income, less
than 1% for the United States. This assumes, however, that all quotas
and nontariff barriers would remain in place. Europe would suffer a decline in income, since the price of their imports would rise on world
markets with free trade. Europe's terms of trade, in other words, would
worsen with the elimination of tariffs. Developing countries as a whole
are estimated to face modest overall losses with tariff elimination. Japan,
Australia, and Canada would enjoy modest overall gains. Regarding industries in the United States, apparel, footwear, textiles, nonmetallic
mineral products, and rubber products would suffer the most through
tariff elimination. Agriculture, transportation equipment, chemicals,
mining, and electrical equipment would post the largest gains from
worldwide tariff elimination.

Problems for Section B

B1.   Illustrate the foreign nation's potential gains from a tariff with a
diagram similar to Figure 5.10.

B2.   Illustrate with offer curves how a tariff war could lead to the total
elimination of trade.

B3.   While the terms of trade may improve with a tariff, the volume of trade falls. Explain the analogy with a monopolist. What happens to the monopolist's revenue with a price increase? Where is the optimal price for the monopolist?

C.   TARIFF GAMES

Games are settings where players with conflicting goals face each other and have to make choices. The outcome of a game depends on the choice a player makes and the choice made by the opponent. This section looks at the setting of tariffs as a strategic game whose outcome depends on the choices made by opposing governments. Skill is typically at least as important as luck in strategic games. Popular board games, cards, and even most sports can be described as strategic games. This section applies game theory to the setting of tariffs.

1.   Tariffs as a Prisoner's Dilemma

Consider two countries that trade with each other. Each has the potential to levy tariffs on the other's imports. The countries can be described as being involved in a strategic game. It is a *two party game,* since there are only two players. The home and foreign nations (the two players) can gain through improved terms of trade, but only at the other's expense. If one player's gains are exactly offset by the other player's losses, the game is called a *zero sum game.* Tariff setting is a *negative sum game,* since overall losses must outweigh gains because of the lost worldwide efficiency.

To set up a hypothetical tariff game, suppose each government must decide on January 1st whether to impose a tariff that will last one year. To keep the story simple, suppose there are two choices: free trade or a 10% tariff. Choices must be announced simultaneously by both governments, and trade takes place accordingly for one year.

Table 5.1 pictures national incomes with and without the tariffs. Suppose both governments know the exact outcomes. The first number in the parentheses is foreign income and the second is home income.

The tariff game in Table 5.1 has four possible outcomes. Begin with free trade, where income is $100 in both countries. Each nation has the

TABLE 5.1. A Symmetric Negative Sum Tariff Game (foreign income, home income)

		Home Tariff	
		0%	10%
Foreign tariff	0%	($100, $100)	($60, $120)
	10%	($120, $60)	($80, $80)

potential to impose a 10% tariff and increase its own income by 20%, but only if the other nation imposes no tariff. A 10% home tariff with no tariff from the foreign country results in home income of $120 (billion) and foreign income of $60 (billion). The home country's gains are more than offset by the foreign country's 40% losses resulting from the lost global efficiency. The home country gains, but the foreign country loses more.

A symmetric outcome occurs if the foreign country imposes a tariff but the home country does not. In the southwest corner of the payoff matrix, the foreign country enjoys $120 in income while home income falls to $60.

If both nations simultaneously impose tariffs, they each lose 20% relative to free trade. The outcome with uniform 10% tariffs is an income of $80 for each country. Note that more global income is lost with uniform tariffs than with only one country imposing a tariff.

If this tariff game is repeated year after year, each nation will develop a *strategy*, a procedure to follow in deciding whether to impose a tariff for the year. Facing the game in Table 5.1, the nations would be better off if they both consistently chose free trade. The allure of quick gains, however, may induce the nations to impose tariffs. Once tariffs are established, it would cost a nation to unilaterally remove its tariffs (to remove its tariff while the other nation kept its tariff). The choice of tariffs in this situation is called a *prisoner's dilemma.*

In the classic example of a prisoner's dilemma, two suspected partners in a crime are separated by police, and each is offered reduced sentence for informing on the other. If they both keep quiet, each knows they will both go free. If found guilty, they face long prison terms. The police offer reduced sentence for a confession and try to convince each suspect that the partner will confess. A long jail term is in store for the suspect who keeps quiet but whose partner spills the beans. If they both confess, they both receive light jail terms. While it would be optimal to keep quiet, each prisoner may not trust the partner's willingness to do so.

Tariffs are the *dominant strategy* in the game in Table 5.1, since income with a tariff is larger regardless of the opponent's choice. A home tariff is the best choice whether the foreign nation chooses free trade or a tariff. If the foreign country sets no tariff, the home country enjoys $20 more income with a tariff ($120 opposed to $100). If the foreign country sets a tariff, the home country makes $80 with a tariff and only $60 without one.

Mutual tariffs are a *Nash equilibrium* in this game. John Nash defined a Nash equilibrium as occurring when each player makes the best choice, given a correct guess about the opponent's choice. The Nash equilibrium of mutual tariffs in this game will be stable because a penalty is imposed on each player for lifting the tariff. Even though free trade would benefit both nations relative to mutual tariffs, the nations are trapped by their circumstances and find it difficult to move toward free trade. The prisoner's dilemma in this tariff game may illustrate why the international negotiations of GATT have proved an important ingredient in moving toward free trade. Each country may be willing to lower its tariffs if it can be assured that the other country will do the same.

The reluctance of nations to relax tariffs can be understood as a prisoner's dilemma.

The home nation can signal a desire to move to free trade by *unilaterally* removing its tariff. This will mean a loss of income the first year if the foreign nation keeps its tariff in place. Since both nations realize the gains from free trade, the foreign nation might follow suit the next year by also moving to free trade. As long as each nation then resists the temptation of the short-run gain of a surprise tariff, free trade can persist. Free trade is, however, an unstable situation. It is not the best either nation can do given the other nation's choice of free trade.

2.   Tariff Reaction Functions

Each nation has an optimal tariff given the other nation's choice of a tariff. Suppose any tariff rate can be set. The process of arriving at a choice of tariffs can be pictured by the *reaction functions* in Figure 5.14.

The home nation's reaction function shows the optimal home tariff on the horizontal axis for any given foreign tariff on the vertical axis. If there is no foreign tariff, the optimal home tariff in Figure 5.14 is 2%. Given that the home nation is correct in its assessment that the foreign country will impose no tariff, a tariff of 2% optimally improves the home terms of trade

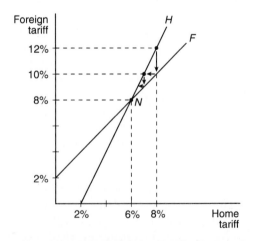

Figure 5.14. Reaction Functions and Equilibrium Tariffs Each nation reacts to a tariff from the other country with an optimal tariff of its own. Starting with a foreign tariff of 12%, the home nation sets its tariff at 8%. The foreign nation then responds to the 8% home tariff with a 10% tariff of its own. The adjustment process continues until the Nash equilibrium is reached at point *N*, with a home tariff of 6% and a foreign tariff of 8%.

and moves the home country to the highest trade indifference curve. Tariffs larger than 2% would not create as much gain, since the decline in the volume of trade would outweigh the benefit of improved terms of trade. If the foreign tariff is 12%, the optimal home tariff is 8%. Given a correct guess of 12% for the foreign tariff, a home tariff of less than 8% leaves untapped potential to improve the terms of trade.

The foreign reaction function shows the optimal foreign tariff for any given home tariff. If the home country has no tariff, the optimal foreign tariff is 2%. If the home tariff is 8%, the optimal foreign tariff would be 10%.

The home reaction function has a positive slope because a higher foreign tariff turns the terms of trade against the home country and requires a stronger response. The foreign reaction function has a positive slope for the same reason. There is no guarantee that the home reaction function H will be steeper than the foreign reaction function F. If the two reaction functions intersect, an international Nash tariff equilibrium is reached, as at point N in Figure 5.14.

Suppose the foreign tariff starts at 12%. The home nation will react with a tariff of 8%. The foreign nation will then respond with a tariff of 10%. The home nation reacts with a tariff of 7%, and so on until the Nash equilibrium at point N is reached. The home tariff is 6% and the foreign tariff is 8% in this Nash tariff equilibrium.

Reaction functions may shift with changing conditions in the economy. Suppose the home country becomes more efficient in producing its exported good. This increases excess supply on the world market and drives down the price of home exports. The falling terms of trade shift the home reaction function to the right as in Figure 5.15. The home country compensates for its weakened bargaining position by imposing higher tariffs, regardless of the level of foreign tariffs. The shift from H to H' drives home tariffs up from 6% to 8% and foreign tariffs up from 8% to 10% in the new Nash tariff equilibrium. Increased demand for imported goods in the home country would cause a similar shift in the home offer curve. Decreased supply of exports or decreased demand for imports would shift the home country's reaction function to the left.

An agreement to move to free trade will not be easy to come by because each nation would benefit by reimposing a tariff and rounds of reactions would follow. International negotiation and cooperation would be required in such a situation to maintain free trade.

3. Tariff Games with Small Countries

If the foreign nation is small, it cannot improve its terms of trade with a tariff. A foreign tariff would create losses for the foreign nation but would not affect the home nation. The situation of a small foreign country is pictured by the game in Table 5.2. The optimal strategy calls for no foreign tariff and a 10% home tariff. This is a stable Nash equilibrium, since nei-

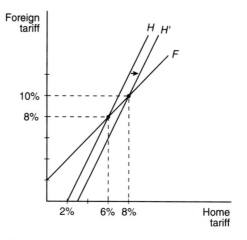

Figure 5.15. Shifting Reaction Functions If excess supply of exported goods or excess demand for imported goods rises in the home country, the home offer curve shifts from *H* to *H'*. To counteract the fall in its terms of trade, the home country will impose a higher tariff for any foreign tariff. The new Nash equilibrium tariffs are 10% for the foreign country and 8% for the home country.

ther country can do better given the choice of the opponent. While the home nation has no incentive to move to free trade, it may be induced to do so on grounds of fairness or equity.

The reaction function for a small foreign country lies flat on the horizontal axis. The optimal tariff for the small country is always zero, regardless of the tariff set by the large country. Given the home reaction function in Figure 5.14, the large home country will set a tariff of 2%.

Small countries are at a disadvantage in playing tariff games. With international prices beyond their influence, any tariff creates deadweight losses. Most small developing nations would be better off without tariffs.

4. Mixed Strategy Tariff Games

The payoffs in a tariff game may not lead to a Nash equilibrium. Consider the tariff game in Table 5.3. A tariff would help the home nation if the foreign nation has a tariff, with home income rising from $97 to $98. If the

TABLE 5.2. A Tariff Game with a Small Foreign Country (foreign income, home income)

		Home Tariff	
		0%	**10%**
Foreign tariff	0%	($100, $100)	($85, $102)
	10%	($ 90, $100)	($80, $102)

TABLE 5.3. A Mixed Strategy Tariff Game (foreign income, home income)

		Home Tariff	
		0%	10%
Foreign tariff	0%	($100, $100)	($95, $99)
	10%	($101, $97)	($93, $98)

foreign nation does not have a tariff, a home tariff would lower home income from $100 to $99. When there is a foreign tariff, a home tariff substantially improves the terms of trade for the home country. When there is no foreign tariff, a home tariff has little effect on the terms of trade.

For the foreign nation the situation is reversed. A tariff would hurt the foreign nation if the home nation has a tariff, with foreign income falling from $95 to $93. If the home nation does not have a tariff, a foreign tariff would raise foreign income from $100 to $101.

Such a game has no Nash equilibrium. If the foreign nation chooses free trade, the home nation would benefit by following suit. With the home nation picking free trade, the foreign nation would benefit through a 10% tariff. If the foreign nation then moves to this tariff, the home nation would benefit by imposing one of its own. With the imposition of a home tariff, the foreign nation benefits by moving to free trade.

The game in Table 5.3 is characterized by the name "chicken." The nations can be expected to vacillate between free trade and tariffs. In such a tariff game it would be optimal for either player to pick a *mixed strategy,* randomly choosing according to the roll of a die or flip of a coin. Each nation may realize the overall benefits of consistent free trade and enter into negotiations or agreements to ensure no tariffs.

> The outcome of a tariff game depends on the payoffs for the playing countries and the strategies they choose. A tariff game can be stable or unstable. Negotiations or agreements may be needed to move countries to free trade.

EXAMPLE 5.6   Nash Equilibrium Tariffs for the United States and Canada

James Markusen and Randall Wigle (1989) have applied tariff game theory to the free trade agreement between the United States and Canada. They use a large-scale computer model based on market descriptions of the U.S. and Canadian economies to evaluate the gains and losses caused by tariffs in both countries. Tariff levels are 5% for the United States and 13% for Canada. Since the United States is the large economy, it would benefit from tariffs more than relatively small Canada. Both na-

TABLE 5.4. A Tariff Game with Three Choices (foreign income, home income)

		Home Tariff		
		0%	5%	10%
Foreign tariff	0%	($100, $100)	($95, $102)	($90, $105)
	5%	($103, $96)	($97, $98)	($94, $99)
	10%	($102, $95)	($95, $96)	($90, $97)

tions would benefit from a move to free trade. Nash equilibrium tariffs are calculated to be 18% for the United States and 6% for Canada. Canada has relatively more to gain than the United States by moving into a free trade agreement because its terms of trade would improve. Free trade and Nash equilibrium tariffs result in essentially the same income for the United States. Canada, on the other hand, gains $4 billion with the move to free trade. The fact that the United States and Canada have been able to reach a free trade agreement indicates that negotiation and cooperation can pay off.

Problems for Section C

C1.   Find the Nash equilibrium outcome of the tariff game in Table 5.4. If you were a negotiator employed by GATT, what steps of tariff reduction would you recommend to move these two nations to free trade?

C2.   Explain the step by step adjustment process to the Nash equilibrium at point N in Figure 5.14 starting with a home tariff of 4%.

D.   THE TERMS OF TRADE
FOR EXHAUSTIBLE NATURAL RESOURCES

A very important allocation of resources occurs in international markets for exhaustible natural resources like oil, natural gas, coal, and minerals. A basic characteristic of markets for exhaustible resources is their limited available stock. When oil and other exhaustible resources are used in current consumption or investment, they cannot be used in the future. The opportunity cost of the present use of an exhaustible resource is lost in the future.

Nonexhaustible natural resources include the sun, wind power, geothermal heat, and hydroelectric power. These natural resources cannot be used up. Their supply is perpetual. Trees, most often grown and harvested like other agricultural crops, are sometimes called a renewable resource.

How should Saudi Arabia or the Soviet Union optimally price their oil? When and at what rate should Canada sell its silver on world markets?

What will happen to the price of oil or platinum over time? What are the total internationally available stocks of exhaustible resources like copper, iron, phosphorus, molybdenum, lead, zinc, sulfur, uranium, aluminum, and gold? The questions studied in this section take us into the economics of exhaustible (depletable) resources.

1.   The Pricing of Exhaustible Resources

The economics and pricing of exhaustible resources loom large in the future of international economics and international political relations. The economic upheavals of the 1970s and 1980s were caused in large part by the oil price increases, the subsequent international reorganization of production redistribution of income, and changing technology.

Owning the right to sell an exhaustible resource is much like owning any other asset. Examples of other assets are stocks (which represent ownership of private firms), government bonds, private bonds, real estate, precious metals, fine art, and rare coins. An asset produces a certain return per year. The *real rate of return* is the ratio of this return to the value of the asset:

$$Percent\ Return\ =\ Return/Value$$

For instance, imagine you have $1,000 in a bank account that pays 3% real interest. After inflation the purchasing power of every dollar kept in the bank for a year increases by 3%. Your real return to the $1,000 is $30. A perpetuity bond that pays a $50 return per year when the rate of return is 4% has a value of $50/.04 = $1,250. As another example, suppose you own an oil well whose current value is $1 million (mineral rights plus equipment). If the return from the oil you sell this year is $48,000, your rate of return is 4.8%.

A crucial issue in deciding how much oil to pump from your oil well this year is what you expect to happen to the price of oil over the coming years. You must compare the price of oil this year with the *expected price* next year. If the price this year is $20 per barrel and the real rate of return 5%, an expected price of $21 = $20 × 1.05 next year will leave you indifferent between selling oil this year and waiting to sell next year. Oil in the ground is worth exactly as much as other assets, since each will grow in value at 5% per year.

If you expect the price of oil to be $20 per barrel next year, it would be wise to sell oil now and receive the $20. Other assets whose value would rise by 5% could be purchased. With your expectations, oil in the ground is worth less than money in the bank. If you expect the price of oil to climb to $22 per barrel by next year, you would want to leave oil in the ground. Oil in the ground has a higher expected return than other assets.

In a large market with many buyers and sellers and many years' worth of oil, the price of oil will take the path defined by its generally perceived opportunity cost over time. Owners will deplete their oil assets at the rate that will push oil prices up by a percentage equal to the real return to other assets.

As the stock of oil is depleted, its price will rise. As the price of oil rises, its rate of depletion will fall. The price of an exhaustible resource will rise over time in an orderly fashion determined by the market real rate of return on assets in general.

With a 5% real rate of return, for instance, the real price of oil over a 10-year period starting from $20 will go $20, $21, $22.05, $23.15, $24.31, $25.53, $26.80, $28.14, $29.55, $31.03. Each year the price rises by 5% and is found by multiplying the previous year's price by 1.05. The *optimal depletion rate* involves selling just enough oil to create these real prices over time.

> The real rate of return determines the expected price path of an exhaustible resource. The value of the stock of the assets in a competitive market will increase at a return reflecting the interest rate.

2. Energy Substitutes and Backstop Resources

As the price of oil rises over the years, the incentive to find substitutes will increase. Ultimately the price will become so high that oil will no longer be used as a source of fuel. Doomsayers base their pessimistic predictions of fast-depleted resources on current prices and consumption rates, disregarding the natural conserving character of a competitive market. As a depletable resource becomes more scarce, its price rises and its consumption rate falls.

Backstop resources are close substitutes that can serve the purpose of an exhaustible resource. Solar, nuclear, wind, and geothermal power, natural gas, and coal are backstop resources for exhaustible oil. In this list, natural gas and coal are exhaustible resources as well, but their stocks are much larger relative to current consumption.

Over time, the technology to use these backstop resources for oil will improve. As the price of oil rises, these backstops resources become relatively cheaper. One implication for the Organization of Petroleum Exporting Countries (OPEC) is that an artificially high price resulting from supply restrictions will lead to improved backstop technology right away. Tremendous strides in energy technology were made in the 1970s and 1980s after the real price of crude oil increased because of the cartel.

3. Natural Resource Cartels and the Terms of Trade

Oil-producing nations formed OPEC to improve their terms of trade with the world. OPEC aims to restrict exports of oil and create a higher price for oil.

Figure 5.16 represents an idealized model of the trade between OPEC (an exporter of oil) and Europe (an exporter of manufactured goods). The terms of trade *tt* and volume of trade at point *A* are based on oil's competitive rate of extraction. At point *A*, oil in the ground is worth exactly as much as money in the bank. The return to owning oil is the same as the return to owning other assets.

Suppose OPEC imposes a restriction on oil output (a production quota) on its members. This restriction can be pictured as cutting off the OPEC offer curve at the cartel quantity. The offer curve becomes vertical at the cartel quota. The terms of trade move to *tt'*, an improvement for OPEC. The volume of trade falls to point *B*. The relative price of oil rises on the international market.

Revenues from oil exports might rise or fall with the higher oil price. With decreased quantity of oil sold, oil revenue (price times quantity) might rise or fall. There is evidence from the oil embargoes of the 1970s and 1980s that oil revenue rose in the short run with the cartel quotas but became about what it would have been over a period of eight years.

It is easy to understand why OPEC and other cartels have a difficult time agreeing on the quantities each member is allowed to sell. To keep the international relative price of oil at the desired high level, each nation in OPEC must sell only an agreed limited quantity, its cartel allocation or quota. A natural surplus of oil would occur in Figure 5.16 at *tt'*, the higher relative price of oil. At this artificially high price, OPEC exporters would want to sell more than importers want to buy. This surplus (glut) can be avoided only by restricting oil output to the cartel quota.

Over history, cartels in rubber, coffee, tea, and minerals have broken down because of the inability of members to stand by their cartel quotas. A member of a cartel has too much incentive to sell at the high international price. A lot can be gained by cheating and selling large quantities

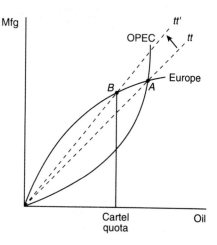

Figure 5.16. Oil Cartel Quotas and Prices A cartel agreement closes the resource exporter off from international trade at the cartel quota. The terms of trade improve for the oil exporting cartel, but the level of trade falls. Cartel export revenue (price times quantity) may rise or fall. The cartel must maintain restricted output to avoid a surplus (glut) of oil on the international market at the artificially high price of oil (*tt'*).

when the price is artificially high. The real price of oil in 1988 was not much higher than it was before the oil price increases of the 1970s, which means OPEC has had little lasting influence. Some commentators view the war between Iraq and Kuwait as stemming from disagreement over OPEC quotas and strategy.

4. Discount Rates and Depletion Rates

Rates of depletion vary across nations according to each nation's time preference. Developing countries and newly industrialized countries are more concerned with the present and the immediate future and want to acquire productive capital assets. This desire for immediate income creates a high *discount rate* for the future, a high real rate of return or real interest rate, and faster depletion of exhaustible resources. Rich developed economies discount the future at a lower rate, have a lower real interest rate, and have a more conservative approach to exhaustible resource depletion.

Figure 5.17 illustrates the depletion of an exhaustible resource in a nation with a low discount rate and a nation with a high discount rate. A nation with a low discount rate can be viewed as expecting higher prices for its assets in the future, and as willing to wait for it. A nation with a high discount rate can be viewed as unwilling to wait for the income from selling its asset. Starting with equal stocks, the nation with a relatively high discount rate will see its stock of the natural resource falling faster. Higher discount rates result in lower present prices but higher prices and more scarcity in the future.

> The discount rate of an exhaustible asset's owner determines how rapidly the resource will be depleted. Higher discounting of the future leads to faster depletion.

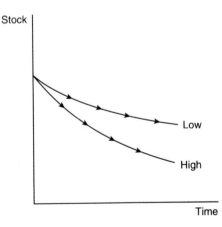

Figure 5.17. Depletable Stocks and Discount Rates A higher discount rate results in a quicker depletion of the stock of an exhaustible resource.

Game theory provides insights into cartel behavior. A cartel has a limited number of members. When an agreement succeeds in raising price, any nation can gain from cheating on the agreement. The other nations lose because price falls with higher supply. Incentives to cheat on a cartel agreement can be large.

Trade between oil-producing and oil-consuming nations can also be viewed as a game with a limited number of outcomes. The gains of one side are the losses of the other. If oil exporters form a cartel, importers may impose an optimal tariff. With the inefficiencies created by artificial restrictions, the gains of OPEC resulting from their restrictive behavior are less than the losses of oil importers. Cartel behavior creates an international misallocation of resources. The cartel is interested in maximizing its own wealth over time. Even that limited goal may not be reached if the quantity of imports of the exhaustible resource decline enough in the long run and cartel export revenue falls.

EXAMPLE 5.7   Real Oil Prices

Data from the U.S. Department of Commerce, *Survey of Current Business* (1988), shows that real oil prices (in constant dollars) have been fairly constant in the United States since the 1880s. A jump occurred in the 1970s because of the OPEC oil embargo, but since 1980 the real price of oil has been falling. The relative price of oil in terms of gold has remained about the same over all these years. Increases in demand over the years have been met with increases in supply because of improved drilling techniques and refining. The proven reserves of available oil increase with improved exploration and drilling techniques.

Problems for Section D

D1.   If the real rate of return is 4%, the present value of your oil well is estimated to be $800,000, and the current price of oil is $16 per barrel, how many barrels will you sell this year? How many barrels would you sell at a price of $20?

D2.   Find the pattern of real prices over the next 10 years if the present price of oil is $20 and the real rate of return is 6%. Compare this pattern with the example in the text of a 5% real rate of return, and explain the difference.

CONCLUSION

Production frontiers and offer curves summarize how entire economies adjust to various changes. However, the redistribution of income inside the economy resulting from trade policy, immigration, or foreign investment is often important. In the coming chapters, various structures of production enable the study of income redistribution among factors of production. Chapter 6 develops the factor proportions approach to production and trade. In the coming chapter a journey is taken behind the production possibility frontier.

KEY TERMS

Backstop resource	Optimal tariff
Cartel	Real rate of return
Discount rate	Repeated games
Dominant strategy	Smoot-Hawley Tariff Act
International equilibrium	Strategic games
Nash equilibrium	Tariff wars
Offer curve	Unilateral tariff removal
Optimal depletion rate	

KEY POINTS

- The terms of trade or the price of imports in terms of exports is determined between large nations through a process of specialization in production and bargaining through trade. Supply and demand in each of the trading nations play roles in determining the relative price of imports.
- Tariffs can improve the terms of trade for a large nation because they decrease the demand for imported goods and may lower those prices on international markets. Large nations can impose optimal tariffs that maximize welfare.
- If one nation imposes a tariff, its trading partners will typically follow suit and a tariff war ensues. Picking tariffs can be like playing a game where the outcome depends on choices made by all players.
- International prices of exhaustible resources like oil and minerals depend on how highly the resource owners discount the future.

REVIEW PROBLEMS

1. When the desire to consume imported manufactures increases in a large home country, show what happens to its trade triangle.
2. Show what happens when foreign consumers decrease their demand for home exported goods, using offer curves. Is the home country made better off or worse off? Do the home terms of trade improve or worsen?
3. Show what happens with offer curves when foreign PPF increases because of increased investment in their export industry. Could this growth in the foreign country possibly benefit the home country?
4. Explain what happens internationally when the foreign country's supply of its exported good falls because of higher input prices.
5. Evaluate what might happen if both the home and foreign nations increase the

TABLE 5.5. Charity in Tariffs and Trade (foreign income, home income)

		Home Tariff	
		0%	10%
Foreign tariff	0%	($100, $100)	($70, $90)
	10%	($90, $70)	($80, $80)

demands for their imported goods. Can you tell what happens to the terms of trade? What must happen to the volume of trade?

6. Explain the remark, "A tariff on oil imports amounts to a policy of Drain America First." Why is oil in the ground like money in the bank?

7. Suppose the terms of trade start at 1 and are improved by 10% for both the foreign and home economies through respective tariffs. If each country responds to the other's tariff with a tariff of its own after one year, describe what happens to the terms of trade over 5 years if the home tariff is imposed first. Do the same if a foreign tariff is imposed first. Under threat of a trade war, would you want to wait for the foreign nation to impose its tariff first?

8. Suppose the foreign nation has a policy of imposing a 4% tariff, regardless of what other nations do. Diagram its reaction function. Given the home reaction function in Figure 5.14, describe the adjustment process if the home nation enters with a tariff of 3%.

9. Illustrate the shift in the foreign country's reaction function starting with Figure 5.14 when foreign demand for the home exports falls. What happens to the Nash equilibrium tariff rates?

10. Illustrate a Nash equilibrium in tariffs with free trade (no tariffs in either country) using a payoff table.

11. Table 5.5 presents a tariff game. Describe it completely. Find the Nash equilibrium. Is there more than one Nash equilibrium? Why would such a game be called "charity"? How could this game characterize tariffs?

12. Show what happens in Figure 5.16 if OPEC imposes a tariff on manufactured imports. How is this different from the cartel quota? Would Europe or oil importing developing countries be more likely to impose a tariff on oil imports?

13. Why is it easier for cartels to form on primary products like oil, copper, minerals, coffee, and tea rather than on manufactured goods or traded services?

READINGS

International Financial Statistics, International Monetary Fund, Washington, DC, monthly periodicals. Contains the terms of trade of every member nation, detailed price data on many traded commodities, as well as detailed international financial data.

Alpha Chiang, *Fundamental Methods of Mathematical Economics,* 2nd ed., New York, McGraw-Hill, 1974. Chapter 21 is an introduction to game theory.

James A. Griffin and Henry G. Steele, *Energy Economics and Policy,* New York, Academic Press, 1986. A thorough text on the economies of exhaustible oil resources.

PART THREE

Modern Trade Theory

CHAPTER 6

Productive Factors and Trade

CHAPTER PREVIEW

Economics is largely the study of how scarce resources or factors of production are used to produce and allocate goods and services. This chapter presents simple models of production and trade, emphasizing the role of productive factors and the distribution of income among them. This chapter covers:

- (a) The *specific factors* model of trade
- (b) The structure of a *factor proportions economy* producing two goods with two productive factors
- (c) The *four basic propositions* of international trade theory
- (d) Various *extensions, applications,* and *tests* of the basic theory

INTRODUCTION

Microeconomics is based on the simple idea that firms minimize the cost of using various inputs to produce the output that maximizes their profit. Similarly, consumers choose the bundle of goods that maximizes their utility or welfare within their budget. Industries made up of firms generate the supply of goods or services in a market, while consumer choice determines demand. In markets for productive factors (labor, capital, natural resources), firms demand resources as inputs in productive processes, while people sell resources to derive income. Forces of supply and demand meet in the markets for goods and factors, which together form the economy's general equilibrium. This productive structure lies at the heart of international trade.

Partial equilibrium economics, pictured by supply and demand diagrams, holds things outside the market constant. This is called the *ceteris paribus* assumption and is often stated "other things equal." General equilibrium economics is the study of all markets in their interconnected network. Other markets in the economy are allowed to adjust in general equilibrium economics, which can be critical when the other things held constant in partial equilibrium economics change enough to alter conclusions or the desirability of some policy.

For instance, a tariff's deadweight loss is found in the partial equilibrium market for the imported good. In general equilibrium, production is distorted along the production possibilities frontier (PPF), and the economy's overall consumption possibilities are reduced. The PPF and the offer curve are simple ways to summarize an economy's general equilibrium. This chapter develops what goes on behind the scenes of these summary general equilibrium curves. A critical issue is the income redistribution resulting from tariffs and other trade policies. The payments to some productive factors will rise with a tariff, while the payments to some other factors must fall. This chapter develops the tools to find out exactly who wins and loses with a tariff.

A simple yet useful general equilibrium picture is provided by the specific factors model in the first section of this chapter. Each of the two sectors (services and manufactures) uses a type of capital specific to its production. This sector-specific capital machinery and equipment is not used to produce the other good. Both goods share a common input, labor. This specific factors model can be viewed as a short-run model, with the sector-specific capital unable to move between sectors. Adjustment across the entire economy to tariffs, international migration, and investment can be understood through examination of the market for shared labor.

In the fundamental version of a factor proportions model presented in the second section of this chapter, two goods are produced by two factors. This can be viewed as a long-run model, with both labor and capital mobile between sectors. Important ideas of factor abundance and factor intensity are introduced. The four basic propositions of international trade are derived from these important concepts. Issues of protection, migration, capital flow, and income redistribution are analyzed with the factor proportions model.

The final section of this chapter discusses various extensions and applications of factor proportions trade theory. The Ricardian factor endowment model is a simple version of the factor proportions model with unit inputs fixed. Production and trade with unemployment are also discussed in this chapter. When various sorts of inputs and outputs are included in applications of factor proportions theory, the behavior of actual economies can be understood and predicted. A realistic overall picture of the causes and effects of international trade can be developed with the factor proportions model.

A. SPECIFIC FACTORS AND TRADE

This section presents a simple, useful model of a productive economy, the specific factors model, which is commonly used by international economists in both theoretical and applied research. The specific factors model can be best understood by concentrating on the markets for its productive inputs.

1.   The Basic Structure of the Specific Factors Model

Figure 6.1 illustrates the input structure of a *specific factors* economy. For our purposes, labor (L) is a productive factor shared by both the manufacturing (M) and service (S) sectors. Each sector uses its own specific type of capital: K_M is used only in producing M, while K_S is used only in producing S. Think of services here as "business services," which includes telecommunication, banking, construction, consulting, entertainment, and so on. Each industry uses only two inputs, and one of those is not used in the other sector.

Manufacturing capital machinery and equipment (K_M) in Figure 6.1 is specific to manufacturing, and service capital machinery and equipment (K_S) is specific to the service sector. The specific factors model can alternatively be used to examine the situation with a single type of homogeneous capital shared between sectors and a specific type of labor in each sector.

2.   Factor Demand

In principle, each unit of an input will be hired only if it produces more revenue for the firm than the firm must pay to hire it. As the price of an input rises, *ceteris paribus,* the quantity demanded falls. This gives rise to the demand for productive factors. When all firms using a productive factor are summed together, the demand for the input or the *factor demand* is found.

Diminishing marginal productivity characterizes observed production processes. The principle of diminishing marginal productivity says that the *marginal product* of an input diminishes as the amount of the input used increases, holding constant the other inputs in the production process. Marginal product is the addition to output from an extra unit of input.

Suppose, for instance, the amount of capital is fixed in an industry. As the input of labor increases, the marginal product of labor will decrease. Extra units of labor input produce more output, but the amount of output added declines as more labor is hired.

Firms will want to hire a unit of labor only as long as its *marginal revenue product,* the value of the output produced when the extra unit of labor is hired, is at least as large as the payment to labor. Marginal revenue product is written

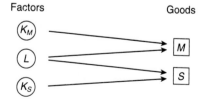

Figure 6.1. The Input Structure of a Specific Factors Economy
Each sector in a specific factors economy produces a good using an input that is sector specific. In this example, manufacturing M alone uses K_M, while services S is the sole employer of K_s. Both manufacturing and services share labor (L).

$$MRP = MR \times MP$$

where MR is the marginal revenue of the good sold by the firm and MP is labor's marginal product. The MRP slopes downward because of diminishing marginal productivity. As more L is used, with the K input constant, the marginal product of L declines. Extra units of L input add to output, but they add decreasing increments. MR is the extra revenue the firm gets from selling an added unit of output. MR is either constant (if the firm is a price taker) or decreasing (if the firm has some market power). The demand for labor is simply this MRP schedule, which tells how much L firms want to hire at different prices for the L input.

3.   The Market for the Shared Input

In Figure 6.2 the demand or MRP for labor in manufacturing is drawn. Labor input in manufacturing (L_M) is measured on the horizontal axis. The curve labeled $D_M = MRP_M$ is the demand or MRP curve for labor in manufacturing. If the wage of labor in manufacturing (w_M) is $20, firms will want to hire 30 units of L. The value of the manufactured output produced by the thirtieth unit of L hired is $20. If $w_M = $15, firms will want to hire 40 units of L. If w_M is $10, firms in the manufacturing sector will want to hire 50 units of labor.

The demand for L in services, $D_S = MRP_S$, is shown in Figure 6.3. The demand for labor in services is independent of its demand in manufacturing. The marginal revenue from selling service output comes from the demand for services. Labor has its own marginal productivity in the production of services. In Figure 6.3, 50 units of L would be hired in the service sector at a wage of $20. Quantity demanded increases to 60 units at a wage of $15, and 70 units when $w_S = $10.

At any time the economy will have a limited amount of labor to use in

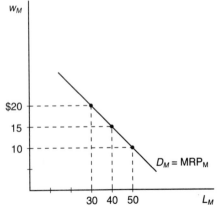

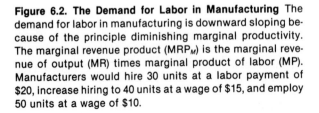

Figure 6.2. The Demand for Labor in Manufacturing The demand for labor in manufacturing is downward sloping because of the principle diminishing marginal productivity. The marginal revenue product (MRP_M) is the marginal revenue of output (MR) times marginal product of labor (MP). Manufacturers would hire 30 units at a labor payment of $20, increase hiring to 40 units at a wage of $15, and employ 50 units at a wage of $10.

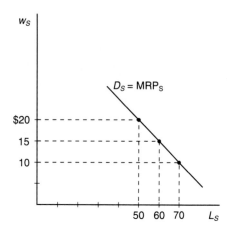

Figure 6.3. The Demand for Labor in the Service Sector The service sector would hire 50 units of labor at a wage of $20, 60 units at a wage of $15, and 70 units at a wage of $10. This labor demand is based on the marginal revenue of output in services and labor's marginal productivity in services.

its productive activities. Suppose the economy has 100 units of labor available for its two sectors. The length of the axis on the bottom of Figure 6.4 represents the total labor *endowment* of 100. There are 100 units of labor available for use in the entire economy.

Figure 6.4 combines the demands for labor in the two sectors into a single diagram. Labor in manufactures, L_M, is measured from the left. Demand for labor in manufactures, D_M, is also measured from the left. Labor in services, L_S, is measured from the right. Note that $L_M + L_S = 100$, the

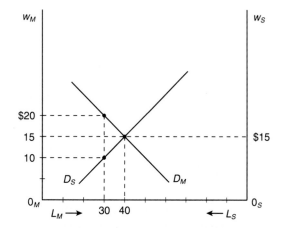

Figure 6.4. The Market for Shared Labor Input The demand for labor in manufacturing (L_M) is measured from the origin at the left, O_M. The demand for capital in M (D_M) slopes down to the right. The demand for labor in services (L_S) is measured from the origin at the right, O_S. The demand for labor in S (D_S) slopes down to the left. The total endowment of L is 100. In equilibrium, 40 units of L are employed in M and 60 units of L are employed in S, with a return of $15 in both sectors.

total labor endowment. Demand for labor in services, D_S, is measured from the right, flipping Figure 6.3 around.

Where the two demand schedules intersect in Figure 6.4, the wage equals $15 and the split of labor into the two sectors is accomplished. In this equilibrium, 40 units of labor are in manufacturing (measured from the left) and 60 units of labor are in services (measured from the right).

Since labor can move freely between sectors, its payment will be the same in both sectors. If the wage is higher in manufacturing, workers will move from the service sector to manufacturing. Labor supply will fall in services and rise in manufacturing. If only 30 units of L are in sector M, the wage of L will be $20 in M but only $10 in S. Workers in services would want the higher wage in manufacturing and would move to sector M. The increased supply in manufacturing would lower the wage in that sector, while the falling supply in services would raise the wage there. The wage would rise in services and fall in manufacturing until the two wages were equal.

> When a productive input is freely shared by different sectors in an economy, it will move between sectors to keep its return equalized across the economy.

Labor's demand or MRP in either sector depends on the demand for that good and labor's marginal product in that sector. An increase in the availability of the capital used in that sector would increase labor's MP, which is positively related with the amount of cooperating input. A higher demand or price of the output would also raise the demand for labor in that sector.

As an example, suppose the price of services rises. This could be due to the home economy's opening to free trade according to its comparative advantage in services, with the international relative price of services higher than the domestic price. The higher price of services increases the demand for labor in the service sector as pictured in Figure 6.5. A similar shift will occur if the endowment of capital in services increases.

As the original wage $w = 15, there is excess demand for labor across the economy. The original 40 units are demanded in manufacturing, while 80 are demanded in the expanding service sector. This sums to 120 units, but only 100 total units of labor endowment are available. There is an excess demand of 20 units of labor, the distance between points A and B. The payment to labor is competitively bid up to $20 as capital moves from manufacturing into services. After the full adjustment in w, there will be 30 units of L in M and 70 units of L in S at the equilibrium point C.

The economy adjusts to the higher relative price of services by shifting resources out of the manufacturing sector into the service sector. This process was summarized by a movement along the PPF in earlier chapters. The specific factors model takes us deeper into the workings of the economy.

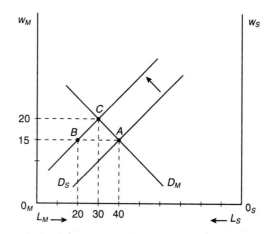

Figure 6.5. Increased Demand for Labor in Services At the current wage of $15, an increase in the demand for labor in services creates excess demand of 20 units of labor in that sector. The wage is bid up to $20 as 10 units of capital move from manufacturing to services. The equilibrium curves from point *A* to point *C*.

Figure 6.5 shows how the crucial market for the shared factor adjusts to the higher price of services and how the movement along the PPF is created.

4. Markets for Sector-specific Factors

When L moves into service production, the MP of capital in services (K_S) increases because K_S has more cooperating labor. This means a higher payment (r_K) to capital in the service sector. As L leaves sector M, the MP of manufacturing capital falls as does its payment r_M.

Figure 6.6 illustrates a market for one of the *sector specific factors*. This is the market for service sector capital (K_S). The vertical supply line reflects

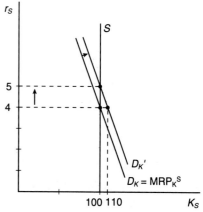

Figure 6.6. The Market for Service Sector Capital The supply of capital in the service sector is perfectly inelastic at the current endowment of 100. With capital demand at D_K, the capital payment is 4. When demand increases to D_K', excess demand for capital in services arises at payment of 4. The payment to capital in the service sector is bid up to the new equilibrium at $r_S = 5$.

the fact that the supply or endowment of capital (machinery and equipment) in the service sector is fixed. This capital remains employed and its payment is determined by demand. Capital owners do not vary the supply of capital they offer in the market according to its payment. If the capital used in the service sector is unique or if there is not enough time to alter the stock of capital, this assumption is realistic. Generally, factor supplies slope upward, but the assumption that factor supply is inelastic simplifies presentation. All of the available 100 units of capital will be used at a payment determined by capital demand.

With the increase in the price of services, the MR of service output increases. Additionally, the labor moving into the service sector raises the MP of capital in the sector. The demand for capital in services rises on both accounts, as does its payment r_S. In Figure 6.6 the demand for K_S rises from D_K to D_K'. This creates excess demand of 10 for capital at the original capital payment $r_K = 4$ in services. Firms want to hire more capital than is available, and they begin bidding up the price of capital. When r_K rises to \$5, the excess demand is eliminated.

In the market for capital in manufacturing, falling marginal productivity of capital means lower demand and creates a lower capital payment r_K. Figure 6.7 illustrates the market for manufacturing capital (K_M). When labor leaves manufacturing for the service sector, the marginal productivity of manufacturing capital falls. This lowers the MRP of capital, decreasing demand from D_K to D_K'. At the original capital payment of 4, there would be an excess supply of 20 units of capital. Firms will hire only the amount of capital on their demand curve. Capital owners want their capital gainfully employed, so competitive bidding drives the capital payment down to $r_M = 3$.

When the relative price of an output changes, markets for sector specific inputs adjust along with the market for the shared input as the economy moves along its PPF toward a new production pattern.

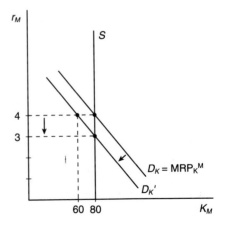

Figure 6.7. The Market for Manufacturing Capital With the supply of manufacturing capital at 80 units, demand at the level pictured by D_K creates an equilibrium capital payment of $r_M = 4$. When demand falls to D_K', the capital payment in manufacturing falls to $r_M = 3$.

5. Trade and Income Distribution with Specific Factors

This analysis goes behind the PPF to look at the important issue of *income distribution* caused by protection, subsidies, or changing prices in world markets. Protectionism raises the price of imports, causing increased production of import-competing goods and falling output in the rest of the economy along the PPF. With a tariff on manufactures, output of M rises as output of S falls along the PPF. With the nation importing manufactures M, a tariff on M raises the price of M and helps the capital that is specific to that sector.

One general lesson is that protection helps factors specific to the protected sector. The payment to the shared inputs also rises with the tariff, but the payment to the factors specific to the other sector falls. This general result illustrates why stockholders, management, and labor unions in a particular industry all agree that their industry should be protected from foreign competition.

Free trade is the opposite of protectionism. As a nation opens itself to free trade, demand for the good in which it has a comparative advantage rises. Suppose the home nation has relatively *abundant* capital in the service sector, but relatively *scarce* capital in manufacturing. The country has a higher ratio K_S/K_M than its potential trading partners. Its capital payment in services (r_S) would typically be low relative to its potential trading partners, while its capital payment in manufacturing (r_M) would typically be relatively high. A higher K_S/K_M typically leads to a lower r_S/r_M because of the difference in factor supply.

For simplicity, assume the demands for manufactures and services are identical across countries. Any differences in the autarky prices of M and S would then be due solely to supply. Since the home country has relatively cheap service sector capital that is used specifically to produce services, the autarky price of services in the home country should be lower than in its potential trading partners. The home nation then has a comparative advantage in services.

If international trade opens, the price of services in the home economy rises due to the increased demand from abroad. Demand for labor in services goes up, causing a movement of L to that sector. The wage rises as does the capital payment in services, while the capital payment in manufacturing falls. Free trade raises the payment to the relatively abundant and cheap factor, service sector capital in this example. The payment to relatively scarce and expensive, manufacturing capital in this example, factors falls with free trade.

> Free trade arising from cost differences distributes income more evenly across nations.

Some economists disagree with this basic viewpoint, pointing out that income is not very evenly distributed around the world. Trade, however, is not very free. Protectionism, foreign exchange controls, transport costs, and other influences inhibit free trade. The free trade argument stresses that increasing the level of free trade will create a more even distribution of income across nations.

In some circumstances free trade may not distribute income more evenly. For instance, if both sectors of the economy share three or more inputs, free trade could create wider differences in international factor payments. Imagine the expanding service sector increasing its inputs of labor and skilled labor rather than service sector capital. Demand for service sector capital could fall in the economy with free trade, depressing r_S, which is already cheap relative to the rest of the world. The possibility of factor prices being polarized by free trade has to be recognized. Still, there is substantial reason to favor free trade in principle and in practice.

Free trade based on comparative advantage generally creates a more even distribution of income throughout the world. Examples of steadily rising wages in open, freely trading economies are not hard to find. Japan, Korea, and Spain are recent examples of the benefits of free trade. While Japan and Korea are accused of being closed to imports, they have structured their economies on the production of exportables and are currently opening more to imports. Eastern Europe will rapidly begin to enjoy the benefits of free trade.

Nations with abundant and cheap unskilled labor will naturally want to produce goods that require much unskilled labor. If developed nations were to lower their protectionism on goods produced with unskilled labor (textiles, footwear, and other consumer goods), this would do more to stimulate growth in the less developed nations than any amount of foreign aid.

EXAMPLE 6.1   Do Tariffs Protect Specific Factors?

An article of mine (Henry Thompson, 1987) shows that a tariff can lower the payment to a specific factor when the sector shares more than one input with the rest of the economy. Similar outcomes are technically possible in economies with three or more common factors of production, as investigated in another article of mine (Henry Thompson, 1986). Tariffs and quotas on autos in the 1980s were associated with falling wages for U.S. autoworkers. Suppose there are two shared inputs, machinery and skilled labor, and autoworkers are the sector-specific input. A tariff on autos would increase output and the demand for both machinery and skilled labor in that sector. As machinery and skilled labor come into auto production, the marginal revenue product of sector-specific automobile labor may fall, even with higher auto prices. The incoming inputs take over much of the work previously done by labor. This raises the empirical question of whether tariffs really do protect sector-specific factors. Gene Grossman and Jim Levinshon (1989) examine this issue and find that protected industries on average do have a higher than normal return to sector-specific capital. Much research is needed to discover the actual patterns of income redistribution resulting from protectionism or increased free trade.

Problems for Section A

A1.   Suppose the price of a unit of services is $3. Given the fixed input of 10 units of capital, the outputs of S resulting from increasing inputs of L are:

L	0	1	2	3	4	5
S	0	2.5	4.5	6	7	7.5

Draw the MRP of L.

A2.   The marginal product of L in manufactures is 3.5 when $L = 1$, 3 when $L = 2$, 2.5 when $L = 3$, 2 when $L = 4$, and 1.5 when $L = 5$. If the price of M is $1.50, draw the demand for L in manufacturing.

A3.   Combine the two demands for L in the previous two problems to determine the equilibrium wage and the employment of L in each sector of the economy when the total labor endowment is 5.

B. PRODUCTION WITH TWO FACTORS AND TWO GOODS

This section introduces the factor proportions model of an economy with two productive factors and two outputs. Labor (L) and capital (K) are used to produce manufactures (M) and services (S). Imagine that the two types of sector-specific capital in the last section have become mobile between sectors. The model with two factors and two goods is sometimes called the Heckscher-Ohlin-Lerner-Samuelson model, after the two Swedish economists Eli Heckscher and Bertil Ohlin, who laid its foundations in the 1930s, and Abba Lerner and Paul Samuelson, who developed its structure in the 1950s. This simple production structure with two factors and two goods leads to the four fundamental theorems of international trade.

1. A Competitive Firm

The soundest approach to understanding how an industry operates is to study how individual firms in the industry behave. Figure 6.8 pictures a competitive *price-taking* firm. A competitive industry has many such firms, each taking the market price $p = 1 as given. A competitive firm can sell any amount it wants at this market price. A firm's *marginal revenue* (MR) is the extra revenue it gains from selling another unit of its output. For a

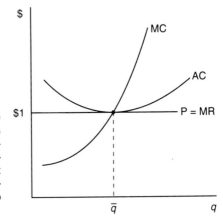

Figure 6.8. A Competitive Firm This competitive firm takes the market price of $1 and looks for the quantity that maximizes its profit. Marginal revenue (MR) from each unit sold is the market price for a competitive firm. Marginal cost (MC) is the additional cost of each extra unit of output. Where MR = MC, profit is maximized and output $q = \bar{q}$. With competitive entry, economic profit will be zero and average cost (AC) is driven to price.

competitive firm, MR = p. *Marginal cost* (MC) is the extra cost incurred by producing another unit of manufactures. Where MC for the firm equals MR, profit is maximized.

If MR > MC, profit is increased by raising output because revenue increases more than cost with the added output. If MR < MC, profit is increased by lowering output because cost falls more than revenue with decreased output. A firm adjusts output until its profit is maximized where MR = MC.

Entry and *exit* of firms drives prices to average cost (AC) in a competitive industry. Average cost is the total cost per unit of output. If economic profits are positive, firms enter the industry. Supply increases, lowing price and pushing up costs. If economic losses are typical, firms exit the market. Supply decreases, raising price and lowering costs. At the profit maximizing output level of $\bar{q}$ in Figure 6.8, AC is minimized.

Economic profits tend toward zero in the long run, which implies that all productive resources are paid a normal return and that no surplus or excess profit is left over after production. Remember from principles of economics that accounting and economic profit are different concepts. Accounting profit includes only explicit costs, those recorded by cash payments. Economic profit is a broader concept, including all implicit and opportunity costs. Accounting profits would be positive when economic profits are zero.

2. Production Isoquants

A ditch can be dug with tractors and little labor or with shovels and much labor. Naturally, the relative cost of labor and tractors determines which combination will be the most economical for the firm wanting to dig the ditch.

The firm has a choice to make in combining the productive factors K

and L to produce its profit-maximizing output. In Figure 6.9 the curve labeled $q = 1$ is the production *isoquant,* showing all the various combinations of labor (L) and capital (K) that can be combined to produce 1 unit of output.

Note that as more of one input is used, less of the other is required; the isoquant slopes downward. One input can be *substituted* for the other along the isoquant in the production process. For instance, this firm can produce 1 unit of output either with 0.1 unit of K and 0.05 unit of L or with 0.06 K and 0.1 L. Any other combination of K and L along the isoquant can be chosen. Firms learn through experience how their isoquants are shaped. Economic theory and empirical evidence point to isoquants shaped like the one in Figure 6.9, downward sloping and bowed toward the origin.

The slope of the isoquant is called the *marginal rate of technical substitution* (MRTS) of capital for labor. As capital input increases moving up along the isoquant, the MRTS of capital for labor increases. It takes increasing capital to substitute for labor as capital input increases. Similarly, the higher the labor input, the more labor would be needed to make up for any lost capital.

Each particular level of output has a different isoquant. Isoquants for more output are higher, representing more capital and labor input. Isoquants for less output lie lower, representing less inputs. The isoquants come from the *production function: $q = q$ (K,L).* The production function relates combinations of inputs to output. Along an isoquant, the change in q is zero.

3. The Isocost Line

The firm is assumed to be a price taker in the markets for its two inputs. The capital rent r and labor wage w are taken as given by the firm. Suppose $r = \$5$ and $w = \$10$. The cost of the inputs hired by the firm to produce

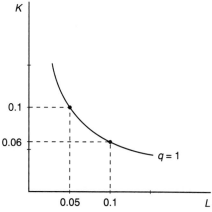

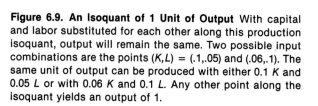

Figure 6.9. An Isoquant of 1 Unit of Output With capital and labor substituted for each other along this production isoquant, output will remain the same. Two possible input combinations are the points (K,L) = (.1,.05) and (.06,.1). The same unit of output can be produced with either 0.1 K and 0.05 L or with 0.06 K and 0.1 L. Any other point along the isoquant yields an output of 1.

one unit of output will be the sum of the products of the factor prices and the inputs hired. The cost (c) of producing output will be

$$c = rK + wL = \$5K + \$10L$$

The term $\$10L$ represents the labor bill or the total payment to all workers employed. Each of the workers is paid a wage of $\$10$. The term $\$5K$ similarly represents the capital bill or the total payment for capital employed.

The firm operates with zero economic profit in the long run, which implies that the price of each unit must equal the average cost AC. When the market price is $\$1$,

$$p = \$1 = AC = c/q$$

The total cost (c) of producing one unit of output must then be $\$1$.

Figure 6.10 shows all the combinations of inputs K and L that cost $\$1$. This is the firm's *isocost line*. The amount of labor that would cost $\$1$ if no capital were hired is $c/w = \$1/\$10 = 0.1$. The endpoint along the capital axis, $\$1/\$5 = 0.2$, represents the amount of capital the firm could hire for $\$1$ if $L = 0$. The isocost line connects these endpoints. The slope of the isocost line is its rise over its run: $-(c/r)/(c/w) = -w/r = -2$.

4. Cost Minimization

The firm must use a mix of both factors because of the shape of its production isoquant in Figure 6.9. The goal of the firm is to minimize the cost of producing the output that maximizes its profit. Each isoquant is assumed to be shaped like the unit isoquant in Figure 6.9. (The isoquants are concentric.)

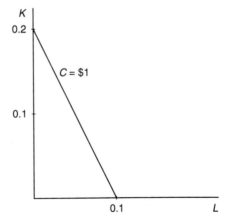

Figure 6.10. The $1 Isocost Line The isocost line shows all combinations of inputs of K and L that cost the same. In this example the wage of labor is $10 and the return to capital $4. If no K is employed, $1/$10 = 0.1 L can be hired for a cost of $1. If no L is employed, $1/$5 = 0.2 unit of K can be hired for $1. The isocost line connects these two endpoints. The absolute value of its slope $|-.2/.1| = 2$ equals the ratio of the wage ($10) to the capital payment ($5).

The firm looks for the lowest isocost line that will produce its desired output. The unit isoquant and the $1 isocost just touch each other in the *cost minimization* pictured in Figure 6.11. Since $p = \$1$, one unit of the good is defined as one dollar's worth. The isoquant depicting one unit can then be called the *unit value isoquant.*

The unit value isoquant represents the factors it takes to produce a unit (a dollar's worth) of output. The slope of the isocost line is given to the firm by the factor prices r and w. The firm chooses the point along its unit value isoquant that just touches the lowest possible isocost line. At this point the isoquant has the slope of the isocost line. The isoquant and isocost lines are tangent. The MRTS equals w/r.

If the firm were to produce output with any other combination of inputs along the unit value isoquant, the isocost line would cut through the isoquant, and cost would not be minimized. The isocost line would lie above the one in Figure 6.11 and c would be higher. Cost is minimized where the slope (the MRTS) of the unit value isoquant equals the slope (w/r) of the unit isocost line.

> Firms minimize the cost of producing a targeted output, which maximizes profit. The combination of inputs chosen depends on the prices firms must pay to hire them. Firms substitute away from an input whose price is rising.

Cost minimization leads to the inputs of labor and capital, $L = 0.05$ and $K = 0.1$, used to produce one unit of output. The *expansion path* labeled K/L in Figure 6.11 is the result of this cost-minimizing factor mix. The expansion path starts at the origin and goes through the cost-minimizing intersection of the unit isoquant and isocost line. The expansion path shows the optimal ratio of capital to labor for this firm, $K/L = 2$. Moving out the

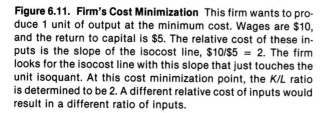

Figure 6.11. Firm's Cost Minimization This firm wants to produce 1 unit of output at the minimum cost. Wages are $10, and the return to capital is $5. The relative cost of these inputs is the slope of the isocost line, $10/$5 = 2. The firm looks for the isocost line with this slope that just touches the unit isoquant. At this cost minimization point, the K/L ratio is determined to be 2. A different relative cost of inputs would result in a different ratio of inputs.

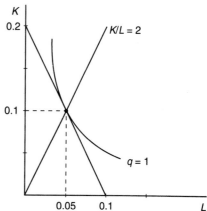

expansion path, inputs are proportionally increased and output expands to higher isoquants.

If the wage w of labor goes up, the slope of the isocost line will become steeper. The firm would substitute along its unit value isoquant toward more capital input. The expansion path rises to a higher ratio of capital to labor. If the rent r paid capital increases, the isocost line becomes flatter and the firm substitutes toward more labor input. The expansion path becomes flatter as the capital-to-labor ratio falls. This is the way the firm minimizes its cost of production, ending up at the bottom of its AC curve in Figure 6.8. Firms vary the input mix according to the prices of the inputs they hire.

5. The Lerner-Pearce Diagram

Both sectors are made up of cost-minimizing firms. There are service output isoquants based on the particular production process in services. These isoquants are different from those in manufacturing, since the products and processes are different. Each good requires a particular productive process. Capital and labor enter into each production process in different combinations, and opportunities for substitution are different. Service firms also hire capital and labor in a way that minimizes their cost of production. Suppose the service production diagram is the one in Figure 6.11. The manufacturing unit isoquant is located differently because producing manufactures is unlike producing services. Given the same costs of labor and capital, the resulting K/L ratio in services will be different from that in manufactures.

Capital and labor are assumed to be able to move freely between the manufacturing and services sectors in the economy. Jobs in the two sectors are assumed to be essentially the same. Managers, scientists, secretaries, clerks, production workers, salespeople, and janitors are hired in each sector. Each will naturally want to work in the sector where the wage for the particular job is the highest. Labor mobility between sectors equalizes the wage across sectors, and capital mobility equalizes the capital payment. The isocost line in services will have the same slope (w/r) as the isocost line in manufacturing. Since the two isoquants are different, cost minimization must lead to a different capital-to-labor ratio in each sector.

Combining the manufacturing and service sectors leads to the economy's *Lerner-Pearce* diagram illustrated in Figure 6.12. This production diagram is named after economists Abba Lerner and Ivor Pearce, who pioneered its development. Unit value isoquants are labeled $M = 1$ and $S = 1$. The price of a unit of each output is assumed to be \$1. Since wages and rents are uniform across sectors, the two industries must share the same isocost line developed in Figure 6.11. Cost minimization in each sector results in inputs of $(K/L) = (.1,.05)$ in services and $(K,L) = (.04,.08)$ in manufacturing.

Expansion paths for the two industries are drawn, with ratios $K/L = 2$

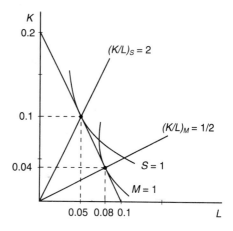

Figure 6.12. The Lerner-Pearce Diagram When two sectors are producing with the same two inputs, a general equilibrium in production occurs. Both industries face the same isocost line, since they both hire the same inputs K and L, which move freely between them. Cost minimization leads to a different K/L input ratio in each industry. Manufacturing in this example is labor intensive, while services is capital intensive.

in services and $K/L = .04/.08 = 1/2$ in manufacturing. Services are assumed to have a higher ratio of capital to labor than manufacturing. In the United States this is the case. Manufacturing uses a lot of labor in assembly operations and has a lower ratio of capital to labor. Agriculture has the highest K/L ratio. This Lerner-Pearce diagram is a compact picture of an entire productive economy. Its usefulness will be apparent in the next section, where the basic theorems of international trade are derived.

EXAMPLE 6.2   Input Ratios for Various Manufacturing Industries

Ed Leamer provides estimates of the ratio of capital to labor in numerous U.S. manufacturing industries in his book *Sources of International Comparative Advantage* (1984). The K/L figure reported here is the dollar value of plant and equipment per worker. Industries are listed from the most capital intensive to the most labor intensive. The ratio V/L of skilled workers (professional, technical, scientific) to unskilled workers is also reported. The more capital-intensive industries also generally use skilled labor more intensively. The United States has an abundance of skilled labor and relatively little unskilled labor and therefore has a comparative advantage in goods with low K/L and V/L ratios. Generally, these are the goods at the top of this list. Leamer's work is the most ambitious at testing the theory of factor proportions production and trade. These factor intensities provide a sound basis for predicting which goods a country will export and import.

Industry	*K/L*	*V/L*
Chemical elements	333	1/4
Plastic materials	250	1/4

Iron and steel	250	1/20
Fertilizers	167	1/4
Nonmetal mineral manufacturing	143	1/5
Pharmaceuticals	143	1/4
Rubber manufactures	91	1/17
Transport equipment	91	1/7
Nonelectric machinery	77	1/10
Metal manufactures	71	1/9
Instruments	67	1/5
Textiles	63	1/50
Electric machinery	56	1/6
Leather	53	1/50
Furniture	34	1/50
Footwear	14	1/100
Clothing	13	1/100

Problems for Section B

B1.   Diagram a competitive manufacturing firm's unit value isocost line if $w = \$2$, $r = \$3$, and $c = \$1$. Find the employment of capital if 0.2 unit of labor is employed along the isocost line.

B2.   Sketch the manufacturing firm's unit value isoquant in problem B1, picturing the cost minimization. Draw the expansion path. What is K/L in manufacturing?

C.   THE BASIC THEOREMS OF INTERNATIONAL TRADE

The theory of international trade has four fundamental theorems. The theorems are simple enough to be proved with the Lerner-Pearce production diagram developed in the last section. They describe the effects of protection, a move to free trade, international migration, and international investment or capital movements. Income distribution among the productive factors, the pattern of production, and the pattern of trade adjust with these changes.

The structure of production is an integral part of the story of international trade. While the overall story is summarized by production frontiers and offer curves, going into the production structure of the economy leads to a rich set of results. The basic propositions in this section are hardly the last word on international trade, but they do provide a solid foundation on which to build.

1. Cost Minimization and Full Employment

Figure 6.13 contains the expansion paths for manufacturing (M) and services (S) that occur as a result of the cost minimization process in each sector. For each unit of labor (L) employed in services, 2 units of capital (K) are employed. For each unit of L employed in manufacturing, 1/2 of a unit of K is employed. Manufacturing is said to be *labor intensive,* while services is *capital intensive* in this example. Manufacturing has a higher ratio of labor to capital: $L/K = 2$ in M and 1/2 in S. Geometrically, the vectors on the expansion paths to the output levels must sum to the endowment point. There is only one combination of outputs, as the following bit of algebra shows.

A nation at a particular time will have a certain amount of capital and labor, its *factor endowment.* The endowment point $(K,L) = (100,110)$ is labeled E in Figure 6.13. There are unique outputs of manufactures and services consistent with the *full employment* of both labor and capital and with the input ratios (K/L) that minimize cost in each sector. Paul Samuelson stressed the importance of factor intensities in developing the factor proportions

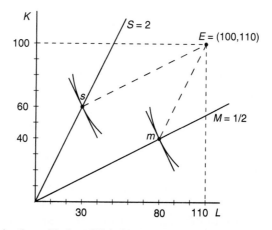

Figure 6.13. Production with Cost Minimization and Full Employment Cost minimizing firms hire inputs in the ratios $K/L = 1/2$ in manufacturing and $K/L = 2$ in services. The total endowment of K and L in the economy is given at point E: 100 units of K and 110 units of L. Completing the parallelogram from point E to the expansion paths for M and S yields the employments of K and L in each sector: 40 K and 80 L in manufacturing, and 60 K and 30 L in services. Outputs are given by the isoquants that pass through points m and s. Note that the slopes of the two cost lines at points m and s are the same.

model. While firms vary their input mix according to factor prices, the factor intensity ranking is assumed to hold regardless of factor prices.

Finding the equilibrium employment of factors in the two industries can be boiled down to an algebraic problem of solving two equations in two unknowns. Let L_M be labor employed in manufacturing and K_M capital employed in manufacturing. Along the manufacturing expansion path, $K_M = 1/2\ L_M$. Along the services expansion path, $K_S = 2\ L_S$. Capital is fully employed in the two sectors, so $K_M + K_S = K = 100$. Substituting, $1/2\ L_M + 2\ L_S = 100$. Labor is also fully employed in both sectors, so $L_M + L_S = 110$, which implies $L_S = 110 - L_M$. Substituting this into the equation above, $1/2\ L_M + 2(110 - L_M) = 100$, which implies $L_M = 80$. Then immediately $L_S = 110 - 80 = 30$, $K_S = 2 \times 30 = 60$, and $K_M = 1/2 \times 80 = 40$.

In manufacturing, the employment of L is 80 while the employment of K is 40, giving the cost-minimizing input ratio of $K/L = 40/80 = 1/2$. In services, the employment of L is 30, the employment of K is 60, and $K/L = 60/30 = 2$, the cost-minimizing input ratio in that sector.

The two points m and s are unique and represent a general equilibrium in production. They are located on the particular production isoquants pictured where output in each sector is consistent with cost minimization and full employment. Note that these two isoquants are tangent to parallel isocost lines. Remember that free mobility of K and L implies that w/r, the slope of the isocost line, will be the same in both sectors. The MRTS, the slope of the actual production isoquant, is the same in both sectors. These actual production isoquants represent equilibrium outputs of manufactures and services for the economy.

2.   The Rybczynski Theorem

If the endowment of capital increases, the endowment point E would move up to point E' as in Figure 6.14. The parallelogram shifts up, becoming taller and thinner. Output of services rises up its expansion path from s to s'. Output of manufactures falls down its expansion path from m to m'. Both factors leave the labor-intensive manufacturing sector and head for capital-intensive services. Remember that the capital used in manufacturing plus the capital used in services must sum to the total endowment of capital. The same can be said for labor. It is worthwhile at this point to convince yourself that if K increases from 100 to 112, $K_S = 76$, $K_M = 36$, $L_S = 38$, and $L_M = 72$. All of the new capital, plus 4 more units from manufacturing, goes into the expanding capital-intensive sector.

When the endowment of a factor increases with prices constant, output of the good using it intensively must increase. Output of the other good must fall. This is a fundamental result of international trade theory first stated by T.M. Rybczynski in the early 1950s:

The Rybczynski Theorem: With prices of goods constant in the factor proportions model, output of a good is positively related with the

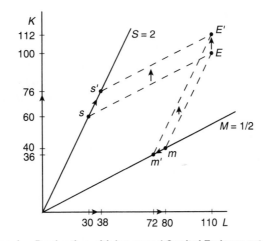

Figure 6.14. Changing Production with Increased Capital Endowment When the endowment ratio K/L rises, the economy switches away from labor-intensive production. In this example the K endowment rises from 100 to 112. The services sector gains 16 units of K and 8 units of L input. Output of manufactures falls from m to m' as output of services rises from s to s'. All of the new capital goes into the expanding capital-intensive sector, along with more from the declining labor-intensive sector. Convince yourself that when K rises to 112, $K_S = 76$, $K_M = 36$, $L_S = 38$, and $L_M = 72$.

endowment of the factor it uses intensively. Output of that good is negatively related with the other factor's endowment.

The Rybczynski theorem and the shifts in Figure 6.14 can be pictured on the economy's PPF. In Figure 6.15, international relative prices are given by the line p and production begins at point P. Output levels labeled m and s correspond to the points labeled m and s in Figure 6.14. When the endowment of capital increases, the PPF shifts out with a larger increase in

Figure 6.15. The Rybczynski Line for Capital An increase in the endowment of capital shifts the production possibilities frontier out, with a bias toward capital-intensive services. Production is determined by the international relative price lines p, which are parallel because prices are constant. Production moves from point P to point P'. The line connecting output points for capital endowment changes is labeled R, the Rybczynski line for capital. There is another Rybczynski line for labor endowment changes. It is good practice at this point to sketch the Rybczynski line for labor.

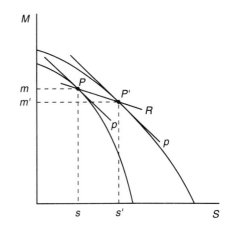

the potential to produce capital-intensive services. The added capital biases the PPF toward service production. The new production point P' is found where the new PPF is tangent to the price line p. Output levels m' and s' correspond to the points labeled m' and s' in Figure 6.14. The Rybczynski line for capital R connects these production points and shows how output adjusts with the capital endowment changing and prices constant.

3. The Heckscher-Ohlin Theorem

Factor abundance refers to a comparison of factor endowments across nations. Comparing the home and foreign (*) nations, the foreign nation is *labor abundant* if it has a higher labor to capital ratio:

$$L^*/K^* > L/K$$

The home nation would then be *capital abundant* because it has a higher relative endowment of capital. In Figure 6.14, let endowment point E represent the labor-abundant foreign country and E' the capital-abundant home country. The foreign nation is labor abundant and produces a higher ratio of labor-intensive manufactures. The home country is capital abundant and produces a higher ratio of capital-intensive services.

With these broad categories of manufactured goods and services, tastes and consumption patterns would be very similar across countries. If consumers in the two nations have similar demands, they will want to consume the same ratio of services to manufactured goods. The labor-abundant foreign nation must then export labor-intensive manufactures, while the capital-abundant home nation must export capital-intensive services.

Since the home nation is capital abundant, it is likely that $r < r^*$ for the two countries in autarky. Likewise, since the foreign nation is labor abundant, it is likely that $w^* < w$ before trade. Demand differences in autarky could alter this pattern of factor prices. Suppose, for instance, demand for services in the home country was relatively high. The price of services would then be higher, and the payment to capital, used intensively in services, would be bid high. If demand is similar across countries, it is reasonable to expect that $r < r^*$ and $w^* < w$ in autarky. This difference in factor prices accounts for the cheap capital-intensive services at home and the cheap labor-intensive manufactures abroad.

The following proposition was developed by Heckscher and Ohlin in the 1930s. It has become an important part of the fundamental intuition in international economics:

The Heckscher-Ohlin Theorem: Nations tend to export goods that use their abundant factors intensively.

The crucial difference between Ricardian and factor proportions trade theories is apparent. In Ricardian theory, different technology (unit labor inputs) is the cause of trade. In factor endowment theory, technology is the same across countries but different factor endowments lead to trade. Both theories find much support in the real world. Each theory makes a simplifying assumption in order to reach logical conclusions and testable hypotheses.

4.   The Factor Price Equalization Theorem

When the home and foreign nations in this example trade freely, the price of each good is equalized across nations. Arbitrage leads to equal prices between locations. The implication of equal prices of each good between two such economies is startling when production functions (isoquants) are the same in both nations.

In Figure 6.16 the isoquants represent $1 worth of the two outputs and are labeled $S = \$1$ and $M = \$1$. These are the same unit value isoquants as in Figure 6.12. The quantity of M along this isoquant indicates the amount of M valued at $1. Similarly, the service isoquant $S = \$1$ is the quantity of S valued at $1. These are the two *unit value isoquants*.

When prices are equalized between countries by free trade and production functions are the same in both countries, the unit value isoquants in Figure 6.16 will represent both nations. Production of one dollar's worth of either good is then carried out by the same cost-minimizing inputs in

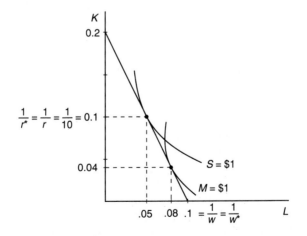

Figure 6.16. Factor Price Equalization This is a simple version of Figure 6.12, with $1 of output represented by the two unit value isoquants. With free trade and identical production functions, the unit value isoquants are the same in each country. The unit value isocost line is written $c = \$1 = 10L + 5K$. Wages are the same in both countries: $w = w^* = \$10$. Capital rents are also the same in both countries: $r = r^* = \$5$. The unit input mix in each sector is exactly the same as in Figure 6.12.

both countries. Since the unit value isoquants are the same in the two countries, the isocost line tangent to them also describes both countries.

Prices of the same factor are equalized between these two trading nation when trade is free. Remember the unit isocost line is described by the equation $\$1 = c = rK + wL$. Since the K and L unit inputs are the same in each country, the factor payments r and w must be the same across countries: $r = r^*$ and $w = w^*$. This result is stated as

> **The Factor Price Equalization Theorem:** Free trade between two factor proportions economies in which each produces two goods with two factors under the same production functions leads to equal factor prices.

More generally, freely trading economies will experience a tendency for prices of their similar factors to equalize. Note that factor endowments are irrelevant in determining factor payments once the prices of goods are equalized by free trade. Technically, all that is required for equal factor prices is that the endowment points for the two trading economies lie between the two expansion paths.

Factor price equalization, or the tendency toward it, depends on the structure of the economies involved in trade. The complete factor price equalization in Figure 6.16 may be best understood as a limiting proposition. This result of complete factor price equalization was discovered by Abba Lerner in the 1930s and then again by Paul Samuelson in the late 1940s.

The factor price equalization theorem continues to create a stir among economists. Some claim that it proves factor proportions theory useless, since observed wages vary so much across countries, especially between industrial and developing nations. Others use the factor price equalization theorem as a fundamental argument for free trade, which has the potential to equalize factor prices. Since nations will export goods that use their abundant (and likely cheap) factors, free trade will increase the demand for these abundant inputs. There is substantial empirical evidence that free trade generally brings prices for similar productive factors closer together internationally.

If labor were free to move between nations, it would seek a higher wage. This is the primary reason for Latin American immigration into the United States. Mexican workers wanting to come into the United States are seeking higher wages. This creates immigration control problems along the Mexican-U.S. border because only a limited number of immigrants are allowed each year. In the example of a labor-abundant foreign nation, foreign labor wants to migrate to the home nation in the absence of free trade.

Such immigration increases the home supply of labor and probably lowers the home wage in autarky. The wage of the labor left in the foreign nation would rise with its decreased supply.

If free to do so, capital owners would similarly want to move their re-source from the capital-abundant home nation (where r is lower) to the capital-scarce foreign nation (where r^* is higher). The owners of capital want their input to receive the highest payment available. Mexico limits the inflow of cars, trucks, machinery, and all sorts of investment at their border. By controlling the inflow of capital, Mexico compounds problems on the Mexican-U.S. border. Just as there is incentive for Mexican workers to enter the U.S. labor force, there is incentive for U.S. capital owners to place their capital in Mexico.

Free trade has the same ultimate effect on factor prices as does free international factor mobility. *Free trade is a substitute for free factor mobility.* To the extent that trade is free, after graduation you will not need to learn a new language and move to a foreign country to receive the highest wage.

5. The Stolper-Samuelson Theorem

Protectionism restricts free trade. With protectionism, factor prices are driven or kept apart across potential trading partners. While trade equal-izes prices to the same factors across nations, protectionism drives the prices for the same input farther apart.

The following result was proved by Wolfgang Stolper and Paul Samuel-son in the early 1950s:

> **The Stolper-Samuelson Theorem:** A tariff raises the payment to the input used intensively in the protected import competing industry and lowers the payment to the other factor.

Consider a home tariff that raises the domestic price of manufactures. The physical amount of the good that $1 can purchase falls. The amount of the inputs of K and L that is required to make $1 worth of the manufac-tured good falls.

In Figure 6.17 the original unit value isocost line and cost minimization are pictured at points m and s. With a tariff the manufacturing unit value isoquant falls toward the origin, forcing an adjustment in the isocost line and in the factor prices. The isocost line is pushed in and becomes steeper.

The new cost minimization occurs at points s' and m', as the isocost line rotates around the service unit value isoquant. The labor wage w rises as the capital rent r falls. On the labor axis the intercept $1/w$ of the isocost line falls to 0.08, which means $w = \$1/0.08 = \$12.50$ on the new isocost line. The wage rises from $10 to $12.50 with the tariff. The return to capital

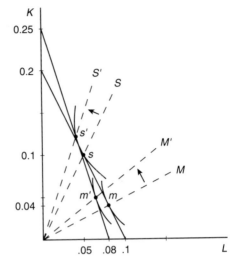

Figure 6.17. The Stolper-Samuelson Theorem An increase in the price of manufactures through a tariff lowers the isoquant depicting $1 of that good. With wages *w* and the return *r* to capital flexible, the isocost line must adjust to the new manufacturing isoquant. The new cost minimization occurs at points *m'* and *s'*. The wage rises and the return to capital falls in the economy. The tariff benefits the input used intensively in the protected sector. Both sectors switch to more capital-intensive techniques.

falls from $1/0.2 = \$5$ to $1/0.25 = \$4$. The price of scarce (and relatively expensive) labor goes up with the tariff as the price of abundant (and relatively cheap) capital falls. This tariff creates a more uneven distribution of income across countries.

It is worth noting that the induced increase in the relative price of labor causes firms in both industries to switch away from labor toward capital. The labor input per unit of output falls in both sectors as the capital input per unit of output rises. The ratio of capital to labor rises in Figure 6.17 in manufacturing from *M* to *M'* and in services from *S* to *S'*. Both industries become more capital intensive as the pattern of output changes. The protected sector, labor-intensive manufacturing, increases its output while capital-intensive services decline. With the tariff, the economy turns away from its comparative advantage and income is redistributed toward the factor with a high return relative to other countries.

A foreign tariff on services would raise the price of the foreign country's scarce (and relatively expensive) capital while lowering the price of its abundant (and relatively cheap) labor. With a foreign tariff on services, service output would increase as manufactured output falls. Protectionism creates a more uneven distribution of income all around. This is perhaps the primary reason economists almost universally favor free trade.

A 10% tariff increases the output of manufactures and the demand for labor, the input used intensively in manufacturing. Wages rise, but workers must pay higher prices for the manufactures they consume after the tariff. If wages rise by more than 10%, the real income of workers increases. But if wages rise by less than 10%, the real income of workers would fall, even though wages rose. It turns out that wages must rise in percentage terms by more than the tariff.

This result says that labor's real income will increase with the tariff, since the percentage gain in the wage is greater than the percentage rise in prices with the tariff. With any tariff, one productive factor always enjoys an increase in real income. This is the *magnification effect* of a tariff, discovered by Ron Jones.

Tariffs create overall losses, but the magnification effect tells us that some factor owners in the economy will gain with any tariff. Generally, these will be the factors used intensively in the protected sector. One factor clearly loses with the tariff in Figure 6.17. With the tariff on manufactures, capital owners are faced with lower income because of falling rent and must pay higher prices for the goods they consume.

Figure 6.18 illustrates the magnification effect. With a tariff on manufactures, the percentage change in the price of manufactures is positive ($\%\Delta p_M > 0$) while the price of services is constant ($\%\Delta p_S = 0$). Along this scale, $\%\Delta w > \%\Delta p_M$; wages rise by a larger percentage than the price of manufactures. Since $\%\Delta p_S = 0$, $\%\Delta r < 0$: the rent of capital falls.

The ranking in Figure 6.18 is based on factor intensity and runs up or down in either direction. A *ceteris paribus* increase in the price of services because of an increase in world demand results in this ranking: $\%\Delta r > \%\Delta p_S > \%\Delta p_M = 0 > \%\Delta w$. The payment to capital rises by a larger percentage than the price of services, while wages fall. Domestic consumers must pay the higher price of services when it rises on the international market. Capital owners enjoy gains in real income, while workers lose.

It is possible that a tariff on manufactures occurring simultaneously with a (smaller percentage) rise in service price would push the scale in Figure 6.18 up so that $\%\Delta r = 0 < \%\Delta p_S < \%\Delta p_M < \%\Delta w$. Capital owners then lose because prices are rising while their rent is constant; the real income of capital owners falls. Workers win because wages rise more than average prices.

A factor intensity link between productive factors and goods comes across in the Rybczynski and Stolper-Samuelson theorems. Between a good and its intensive factor, the effects are positive. Between a good and the other factor, the effects are negative.

For a one unit change in the labor endowment ($\Delta L = 1$) the Rybczynski theorem says that $\Delta M/\Delta L > 0$ (the change in the output of M resulting from the change in L is positive) and $\Delta S/\Delta L < 0$. The Stolper-Samuelson theorem

Figure 6.18. The Magnification Effect Changing prices affect factor payments in a magnified way according to factor intensities. In this example, services use capital intensively and manufacturing uses labor intensively. Percentage changes in wages and capital payments must flank percentage price changes. The scale can be read in both directions, and a zero can be placed anywhere. With a tariff the real income of one factor must rise while the real issue of another falls.

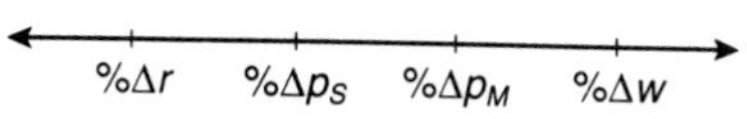

$$\longleftarrow \qquad \qquad \qquad \qquad \qquad \longrightarrow$$
$$\%\Delta r \qquad \%\Delta p_S \qquad \%\Delta p_M \qquad \%\Delta w$$

says that $\Delta w/\Delta p_M > 0$ and $\Delta w/\Delta p_S < 0$. These changes are based on the factor intensity.

Samuelson's reciprocity refers, for instance, to the further fact that $\Delta M/\Delta L$ actually equals $\Delta w/\Delta p_M$. The change in M output due to a one unit change in L equals the change in w due to a one unit change in p_M. The factor intensity link also concerns the strength of these general equilibrium effects. A stronger Rybczynski effect implies a stronger Stolper-Samuelson effect.

By Samuelson's reciprocity, it also follows that $\Delta S/\Delta L = \Delta w/\Delta p_S < 0$, reflecting the negative link between labor and services. Since capital is used intensively in services, $\Delta S/\Delta K = \Delta r/\Delta p_S$. Finally, $\Delta M/\Delta K = \Delta r/\Delta p_M < 0$.

6. The Foundation of the Theory of International Trade

The four theorems of this section form the basic intuition in the theory of international trade. The production structure of the factor proportions economy plays an important role in the theory of international trade. Together, these four theorems furnish a picture of what occurs along the PPF. Changing endowments cause the PPF itself to adjust. Changing international prices or protection cause adjustment along the PPF. The Rybczynski and Heckscher-Ohlin theorems are concerned with patterns of output and factor endowment differences. The factor price equalization theorem examines the returns to productive factors between freely trading countries. The Stolper-Samuelson theorem is concerned with the income redistribution due to protection. While international trade theory has developed in many directions, virtually all new results are compared with one or more of these four basic theorems.

EXAMPLE 6.3   Labor in U.S. Exports and Imports

Baldwin (1971) reports the distribution of different skill groups of labor between export industries and industries competing with imports. This table reports the percentage of seven types of labor in exports and imports in 1962. For instance, farm labor comprised 24% of the labor force involved in export activity and 17% of the labor force in import-competing activity. The export/import ratio for farm labor is 24/17 = 1.4. Farm labor was the group most highly involved in exports at the time, followed by professionals, crafts, and clerical. The United States was revealing its comparative advantage by exporting goods using these relatively abundant inputs intensively. Moving down the list, the factors become relatively more scarce (and expensive relative to other countries). Laborers and operatives were the groups involved the least with exports and competing most with imports. Similar studies have since upheld Baldwin's conclusions.

	% Exports	% Imports	Exports/Imports
Farm labor	24%	17%	1.4
Professionals	13%	12%	1.1
Craftsmen & foremen	15%	15%	1.0
Clerical & sales	15%	15%	1.0
Operatives	25%	30%	0.8
Laborers	8%	10%	0.8

Problems for Section C

C1. Let Figure 6.13 represent the home country. Suppose the foreign country has a factor endowment of $(K/L) = (80,70)$ and the two countries trade freely and have the same production functions. Find the different employments of K and L across sectors in the two countries.

C2. Compare the ratios of foreign outputs in Problem C1 with the ratio of outputs in home economy in Figure 6.13. Which country produces a higher ratio of M to S? Which will export M if consumers in both nations have similar tastes?

C3. How would the switch from autarky to free trade affect the payments to K and L for each country in the example of Problem C1?

D. TESTS AND EXTENSIONS OF FACTOR PROPORTIONS TRADE THEORY

The factor proportions, or Heckscher-Ohlin-Lerner-Samuelson (HOLS), model has become the basic building block in the theory of international trade. Conceptually, it captures how an entire economy adjusts to external influences. Like all scientific theories, it must be put to the test. This section reports on tests of the HOLS model. The HOLS model in simple form with only two factors and two goods has been extended in various ways. This section also reports on extensions of the simple theory.

1. Tests of Factor Proportions Theory

An attempt to test the factor proportions explanation of trade was made in the early 1950s by Wassily Leontief (1953). Examining the physical capital and labor content of goods exported from the United States and imported into the United States in 1947, Leontief found that U.S. exports were labor intensive. Since the United States is thought to be capital abundant, this finding created a bit of a stir among economists and was labeled the *Leontief paradox*. In dollars of capital input per person (per year), the *K/L* ratio was 141 in exported good production and 182 in the goods imported. The United States was importing goods that were capital intensive relative to its exports. World War II had just leveled much of the capital input of Europe and Japan, making this result even more paradoxical.

Robert Baldwin (1971) found the ratio of capital to labor of U.S. imports and exports in 1962 virtually identical when agriculture and natural resources were excluded. These *K/L* ratios were 116 in exports and 119 in imports. Once again the Leontief paradox arises, if only barely, with the United States exporting goods that were slightly labor intensive. Including agriculture and natural resources, the paradox is even more pronounced with *K/L* ratios of 143 in exports and 179 in imports. The argument for excluding agriculture and natural resources is that they depend on climate, land, and available minerals, all of which are unique to a nation and perhaps should not be considered "in proportion" to other countries. Baldwin also reported that the United States exported goods that use skilled labor intensively.

Robert Stern and Keith Maskus (1981) used Leontief's technique applied to 1972 data and found that the paradox disappeared. Maskus (1985) subsequently reported that the paradox is actually more of a commonplace, the United States being a net exporter of labor services frequently from year to year.

Ed Leamer (1980) argues that the goods actually consumed in the United States were much more labor intensive than exported goods. The *K/L* ratio in consumption at the time of Leontief's original study was 68, which means the goods exported from the United States (*K/L* = 141) were capital intensive relative to the goods kept for domestic consumption. Still, it seems odd that imports would be more capital intensive.

Some evidence indicates that Leontief's finding was a result of the large trade surplus in the United States during 1947. A country can be expected to be a net exporter of its abundant factor only if trade is balanced. Essentially the United States exported too much. Francisco Casas and Kwan Choi (1985) calculated what the pattern of trade would have been had it been balanced and found that the Leontief paradox disappeared. If trade had been balanced, the United States would have been a net exporter of capital embodied in exported goods and a net importer of labor embodied in imported goods.

In fact, the United States was a net exporter of both labor and capital. William Branson and Nikolaos Monoyios (1977) showed that the United States exported goods intensive in skilled labor while importing goods using unskilled labor intensively. This is similar to a result found earlier by Baldwin. Capital holds an intermediate position in the factor intensity ranking. Treating skilled labor (or for that matter natural resources) as separate inputs relaxes or eliminates the Leontief paradox. When various types of inputs are used to produce traded goods, the simple classification into labor and capital is misleading.

No truly comprehensive test of the factor proportions theory has been performed because data from different nations on production functions, factor abundance, and trade in various products have not been systematically assembled. Data on service production is exceptionally rare, even in the industrial countries. The United States exports services which use skilled labor and capital intensively relative to manufacturing, which uses unskilled labor intensively. Capital is difficult to conceptualize and measure without error. Labor, land, and mineral resources are each extremely varied across countries. Nevertheless, as a general proposition, nations can be expected to be net exporters of their abundant factors of production.

In his book *Sources of International Comparative Advantage,* Ed Leamer (1984) goes a long way toward developing scientific tests of the factor proportions theory. Leamer finds that the factor content of U.S. net exports is largest for these particular labor groups: scientists, engineers, technicians, and draftsmen. Robert Stern and Keith Maskus (1981) come to the similar conclusion that through trade the United States reveals itself as abundant in skilled labor and physical capital.

2. Extensions of the Heckscher-Ohlin-Lerner-Samuelson Model

The world of international trade is a complicated place. General theories are necessary to understand what is going on, but they can be misleading if applied in too simple a manner. The United States trades a wide variety of goods and services with many nations. Production processes involve many types of labor and capital input. The ideas of factor intensity and factor abundance become difficult to interpret when there are as few as three types of goods and three factors of production. Studies suggest that in fact many different factors of production exist. There are, of course, many types of goods and services, but the serious and largely unsettled issue is how best to aggregate or classify.

With the increasing importance of trade in services, reliable data and an understanding of service production are becoming more important. A wide variety of activity is classified as services. Skilled labor is used intensively in the production of business services. Since the United States has an abundance of skilled labor, the evolving pattern of U.S. trade toward specialization in services and import of manufactures is predicted by the factor proportions theory.

Large-scale *computable general equilibrium* (CGE) models of production and trade offer the chance to simulate real world economies more closely. Canada, Japan, the European Community, and the Arabian Gulf countries use CGE models to predict the effects of protectionism, export subsidies, oil price shocks, and so on. The Michigan model of Alan Deardorff and Robert Stern is a large-scale CGE model of production and trade for the U.S. economy.

CGE models contain many goods and have been expanded to include various inputs. Commercial models for personal computers can be used by firms or government planning agencies to simulate the effects of market changes or government policies. While CGE models are complex and sophisticated, the simple factor proportion model in this chapter provides their conceptual basis.

The future holds the promise of large-scale computer models that simulate the dynamic effects of tariffs, quotas, NTBs, migration, international capital flows, and changes in the terms of trade. These CGE models have been perhaps the major innovation in international economics during the 1980s.

3.   The Ricardian Factor Endowment Model

The factor proportions economy may seem quite a bit different from the simpler Ricardian economy. Roy Ruffin (1988) has shown how closely the two are related using the Ricardian factor endowment (RFE) model. The idea behind this approach to production and trade is that trade occurs between different types of labor that happen to reside in different nations. Certainly a lot of trade is interpersonal, occurring between people who have different skills and aptitudes.

The RFE model of production and trade has characteristics of both the Ricardian constant cost model and the factor proportions model. Ricardian labor inputs will determine the pattern of comparative advantage, as in the simpler Ricardian model with only one type of labor input. Relative endowments of the different types of labor will determine the observed trade pattern, as in the factor proportions model.

In the RFE model, services (S) and manufactures (M) can be produced by either unskilled (L) labor or skilled labor (H). The H stands for human capital, which skilled labor must acquire through education and training. Labor inputs are constant as in the Ricardian economy. Suppose the amount of L used per unit of M (L/M) equals 1, while the unit input of skilled labor is $H/M = 2$. In services, the two factor inputs are $L/S = 2$ and $H/S = 1$.

The home nation is assumed to have an abundance of skilled labor with an endowment of $(L,H) = (100,400)$ while the endowment of the foreign nation is assumed to be $(L^*,H^*) = (500,50)$.

If all the skilled labor at home produced M, $400/2 = 200$ units could be made. There are 400 skilled workers, and each unit of M requires 2 skilled workers. Home unskilled labor can produce an additional $100/1 = 100$ units of M. There are 100 workers, and each worker can produce 1 unit of M. With both skilled and unskilled labor producing manufactures, 300

M could be produced altogether in the home country. Alternatively, the *H* at home could produce 400/1 = 400 units of *S* and labor *L* another 100/2 = 50 units, for a total of 450 units of potential service output. The extremes on the home country's PPF are 300 *M* and 450 *S*. If all resources are put into *M* production, 300 units are produced. If all resources are put into *S* production, 450 units are produced.

The home PPF is started by plotting these two endpoints, as in Figure 6.19. From the endpoint *M* = 300, skilled labor is used to begin production of *S* according to the comparative advantage skilled labor has over unskilled labor in the production of *S*. If all of the available skilled labor is used to produce *S* and only unskilled labor produced *M*, output would move to the point (*M*,*S*) = (100,400). The 400 units of *H* produce 400 units of *S*, while the 100 units of *L* produce 100 units of *M*.

The home PPF connects this extreme point with the two endpoints. The PPF has straight segments because the unit factor inputs are fixed. There are constant costs of production. Consumers in the home country would have to pick a point along their PPF if there were no international trade. In Figure 6.19, home consumers maximize welfare by picking point *A*. Some skilled labor is involved in manufacturing production.

The foreign PPF connects endpoints *M* = 525 and *S* = 300 with the point (*M*,*S*) = (500,50). A good exercise is to derive the foreign PPF in Figure 6.20. Foreign consumers are constrained to consume along their PPF in autarky, maximizing welfare at point *A** in Figure 6.20. Some unskilled labor is involved in service production.

With free trade, production would move to the extreme point for each country. In Figure 6.21, production points shift to *P* and *P** with free trade. The terms of trade are then represented by the dotted line connecting the extreme points. With trade, each country's abundant factor specializes in the activity in which it has a comparative advantage. All of the skilled labor at home produces *S*, while all of the unskilled labor in the foreign country

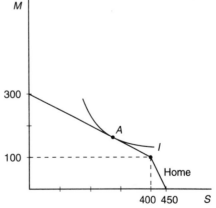

Figure 6.19. The Home Production Possibilities Frontier (PPF) in the Ricardian Factor Endowment Model This home country has 400 units of skilled labor and 100 units of labor. Unit inputs are *L*/*S* = *H*/*M* = 2 and *L*/*M* = *H*/*S* = 1. If all inputs go into *M* production, 300 *M* is produced. On the *S* axis, 450 *S* could be produced. With all skilled labor in services and all labor in manufactures, the extreme point (*M*,*S*) = (100,400) can be produced. Costs are constant along the two segments of the PPF. Consumers maximize welfare on indifference curve *I*.

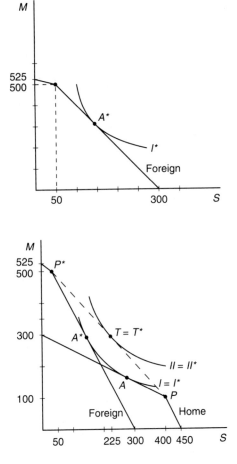

Figure 6.20. The Foreign Production Possibilities Frontier in the Ricardian Factor Endowment Model This foreign country is labor abundant, with an endowment of $(L^*, H^*) = (500,50)$. Input requirements are the same as those in the home country. The foreign economy can produce 525 units of M with all inputs in that sector, or 300 units of S with all inputs in services. With its 500 units of L^* in M, 500 units of M can be produced. Skilled labor in services then produces 50 units of S.

Figure 6.21. Specialization and Trade in the Ricardian Factor Endowment Model Each nation will specialize by producing the good that has low inputs of its abundant factor. In the home nation, abundant skilled labor is all attracted to the service sector, while in the foreign nation abundant unskilled labor is all attracted to the manufacturing sector. In this example the terms of trade $tt = M/S = 200/175 = 8/7$ and each nation consumes $(M,S) = (300,225)$ beyond its production possibilities frontier.

produces M. In this example the home nation exports 175 units of S in exchange for 200 units of M from the foreign country. Both nations consume 300 M and 225 S at point $T = T^*$, beyond each of their PPFs. In this example, tastes are identical across countries and autarky consumption points A and A^* are on the same indifference curve $(I = I^*)$. Free trade allows both countries to move to a higher level of welfare on indifference curve $II = II^*$.

International trade produces overall gains, with each country consuming beyond its PPF. Real income, measured in terms of either good, increases in each country. Both countries increase welfare with the move to free trade. Income is more evenly distributed as a result of trade. In the home country, trade increases the price of relatively cheap services. With all of skilled labor pulled into the service sector, the skilled wage rises. In the foreign country, trade increases the price of relatively cheap manufactures and the wage of labor.

Since the home nation has a relative abundance of skilled labor, relative wages before trade probably are characterized by $h/w < h^*/w^*$ where h is the wage of skilled labor and w is the labor wage. Labor is relatively cheap in the foreign country while skilled labor is relatively cheap at home. As a result, services are cheap at home and manufactures are cheap abroad. Trade increases the prices of services and skilled labor in the home country. In the foreign nation, trade increases the prices of relatively cheap manufactures and labor.

Trade in the RFE model essentially takes place between different types of workers who reside in different nations. Factor proportions are the cause of trade, while production is characterized by constant costs. The RFE, Ricardian, and factor proportions explanations of production and trade are closely related. It remains to be seen whether the RFE model offers a truer scientific explanation of observed international trade.

4. Unemployment and Trade

Unemployment arises for various reasons. It takes time and resources to match firms with workers. Searching for a job is costly. Most labor markets require training and experience. Industries expand and contract with the business cycle or the pressures of international competition. At any particular time, unemployment will be observed in an economy.

The pattern of outputs with unemployment will differ from the pattern with full employment. Suppose the minimum wage or a union-contracted wage is higher than the equilibrium market wage. Firms will only hire workers according to their marginal revenue product. Unemployment will be caused by the artificially high wage. With less labor employed, the output of labor-intensive goods will be relatively lower and the economy will operate below its PPF.

One general theory of persistent unemployment in urban areas, especially in developing countries, is provided by the Harris-Todaro model. Rural subsistence wages (w_r) are low, but everyone has a job in the rural area. Urban areas offer higher wages (w_u) but the probability π of finding a job is limited. Workers in rural areas who consider moving to the urban area discount the high urban wage by π. Suppose $\pi = 80\% = 0.8$ and $w_u = \$10$. The chance of finding a job paying $10 in the urban area is 80%. The discounted urban wage is $0.80 \times \$10 = \$8$. If $w_r \geq \$8$, rural workers will stay put. If w_r is less than $8, however, the expected urban wage of $8 is more attractive and workers will move to the urban area. Of course, workers face the possibility of being unemployed, but the expected wage is higher in the city. Other considerations (moving costs, tastes for urban versus rural life, etc.) may enter into the decision, but the Harris-Todaro model suggests how urban employment may persist.

The effects of international trade and migration in a Harris-Todaro model depend on which sector, rural or urban, produces exports and which sector produces imports. A typical policy issue is a proposed tariff on manufactured goods. Suppose the manufacturing sector is located in the urban sector. If the tariff on manufactures raises w_u, migration from rural areas will increase and the number of unemployed in the urban area will rise.

Given the generally low levels of unemployment typically observed in most industrial nations, the conclusions of trade theory are not affected very much by unemployment. The four fundamental theorems of trade (Rybczynski, Heckscher-Ohlin, factor price equalization, and Stolper-Samuelson) all continue to hold in the presence of commonly observed unemployment.

There is a level of normal unemployment associated with job searching, business cycles, and the society's unemployment benefits. Better unemployment benefits lower the cost of not having a job and raise the unemployment level. In the United States and other industrial nations with unemployment benefits, it is common practice to draw unemployment benefits while secretly working. Official statistics of unemployment can be misleading. Developing nations often report high rates of official unemployment, but everyone is constantly working at something. "Secondary" or "underground" economies are very active in most countries, producing valuable goods and services and providing income.

Economists almost universally oppose minimum wage legislation and long-term union contracts. In a dynamic economy, continuous change calls for flexibility. A reduction in the demand for labor must result in either lower wages or less employment. While neither is a desirable outcome, lower wages are less onerous. An increase in the demand for labor should be allowed to result in higher wages as well as more employment. An efficient labor contract would allow for flexibility in wages and hours worked on a job.

EXAMPLE 6.4   Testing the Heckscher-Ohlin Proposition

Economists studying international trade have subjected the Heckscher-Ohlin theory to empirical tests. The most ambitious effort to date is Ed Leamer's *Sources of International Comparative Advantage* (1984), which meticulously examines data from 47 nations. Resources are divided into capital, professional workers, unskilled workers, skilled workers, coal, minerals, oil, and four types of land. Manufactured output is classified into 10 categories: petroleum, raw materials, forest products, tropical agriculture, animal products, cereals, labor-intensive manufactures, capital-intensive manufactures, machinery, and chemicals. An examination of the many tables and charts in the book impresses the reader with the overall influence of factor proportions on comparative advantage and trade.

Leamer finds that the following developed nations are capital abundant and export machinery and chemicals: Belgium-Luxembourg, France, Germany, Italy, Japan, the Netherlands, Sweden, Switzerland, the

United Kingdom, and the United States. Chemicals are relatively inten-sive in both capital and skilled labor inputs. Machinery is relatively inten-sive in skilled labor inputs. These nations are especially abundant in cap-ital and typically abundant in skilled labor as well.

Another group of nations is identified as exporting capital-intensive manufactures: Austria, India, Korea, and Spain. Denmark, Hong Kong, Israel, Portugal, and Yugoslavia are consistent exporters of labor-inten-sive manufactures. Brazil, Colombia, Cyprus, Egypt, Finland, Greece, Malta, Sri Lanka, Thailand, and Turkey have begun to export labor-inten-sive manufactures. These nations are generally abundant in labor.

All remaining nations are importers of manufactures. Some of the relatively diversified economies in this group are Afghanistan, Australia, Canada, Mexico, Norway, Paraguay, Peru, and the Philippines. Less devel-oped countries (LDCs) export tropical agricultural goods, raw materials, cereals, or animal products.

Agricultural exports are consistently explained by the type of land abundant in a particular nation. These LDCs are scarce in capital. Min-eral and oil abundance naturally explain the instances of those exports.

EXAMPLE 6.5   Convergence of Manufacturing Labor Inputs

With free trade, factor payments tend to equalize over time across trad-ing economies in most situations. As factor payments become more simi-lar, so will unit labor inputs. David Dollar and Edward Wolff (1988) ex-amine the convergence of unit labor inputs in manufacturing among 12 industrial countries between 1963 and 1980. These figures show general convergence of L/M across industrial countries relative to the United States. Italy, for instance, used more than twice as much labor per unit of output as the United States in 1963, but only 1.1 times as much by 1982. The United Kingdom and Sweden showed similar convergence. Japan used 3.9 times as much labor per unit of output in 1963, but only 1.6 times as much in 1982. Dollar and Wolff find convergence in virtually every category of manufacturing. Among these industrial countries, this observed convergence of unit labor inputs and an implied convergence of wages can be attributed to increased trade, converging endowment ratios (resulting from international investment and labor migration), and international dispersion of technology.

	L/M Relative to the United States			
	1963	*1970*	*1976*	*1982*
U.S.	1	1	1	1
U.K.	1.9	1.7	1.1	1.1

Italy	2.2	2.0	1.7	1.1
Sweden	1.9	1.5	1.4	1.3
Canada	1.3	1.3	1.3	1.3
Germany	1.9	1.5	1.4	1.5
France	1.9	1.6	1.7	1.5
Japan	3.9	2.0	2.0	1.6
Australia	2.1	1.9	1.8	1.8
Norway	2.2	1.7	1.9	2.0

Problems for Section D

D1. Can you think of any explanations other than those in the text for the Leontief paradox?

D2. Using a Lerner-Pearce diagram, illustrate the effects of unemployment on the pattern of output.

CONCLUSION

The principles of the factor proportions model of international trade form the foundation of modern international economics. Firms are competitive price takers in the factor proportions model. The next chapter examines international trade when the firms involved have price searching or monopolistic power. The types of industrial structure included in the next chapter are monopoly, monopolistic competition, and oligopoly.

KEY TERMS

Computable general equilibrium models
Cost minimization
Diminishing marginal productivity
Exit and entry
Expansion path
Factor abundant and scarcity
Factor demand
Factor intensity
Factor price equalization theorem
Factor substitution
Harris-Todaro unemployment
Heckscher-Ohlin theorem
Isocost line

Isoquant
Leontief paradox
Lerner-Pearce diagram
Marginal cost (MC)
Marginal product (MP)
Marginal revenue (MR)
Marginal revenue product (MRP)
Price-taking firm
Ricardian factor endowment model
Rybczynski theorem
Specific factors
Stolper-Samuelson theorem
Unemployment

KEY POINTS

- Tariffs generally protect factors of production specific to an industry, while factors used specifically in other industries are hurt. Factors shared by industries may benefit through protection.
- In a competitive economy, firms choose the input mix that minimizes the cost of producing their profit-maximizing output. Input ratios are the result of a cost-minimizing process.
- Factor intensity and factor abundance are the key concepts leading to the fundamental theorems of international trade in the factor proportions model.
- Factor proportions theory does a reasonable job of explaining observed trade in empirical tests and applications.

REVIEW PROBLEMS

1. In the specific factors economy from the problems for Section A, suppose the price of imported M rises to $3 with a tariff. Describe what happens in the labor market. Where is a shortage for labor created? What happens to the wage?

2. Diagram what happens in the previous problem to the markets for sector-specific capital. What happens to the outputs in the two sectors?

3. Suppose nation A imposes a tariff on imported manufactures and its terms of trade with nation B improve. Describe what happens to income distribution in nation B using the specific factors model.

4. Sketch the cost minimization that occurs with $w = $2, r = $3, c = 1, and 0.2 unit of L used as input. Find the unit input of capital and sketch the unit value isoquant. Describe what happens in this cost minimization if r falls to $2.

5. Describe what happens to this cost minimization if w rises to $3 when $r = 3.

6. Given the factor prices in problem 4 ($w = $2 and $r = 3), suppose 0.35 units of labor are used in the manufacturing sector's cost minimization to produce $1 of output. Sketch the manufacturing sector's cost minimization and the expansion path. Find K/L in manufacturing.

7. Draw the Lerner-Pearce diagram of the economy with the service sector in problem 4 and the manufacturing sector in problem 6.

8. Imagine two economies with endowments $(K,L) = (100,200)$ and $(K^*,L^*) = (110,190)$. With the technology described in problem 7, predict and explain the pattern of trade between them. Explain which nation is labor abundant and labor cheap.

9. If the foreign nation described in problem 8 imposes a tariff, what happens to its w^* and r^*? Illustrate with a shift in its Lerner-Pearce diagram. What happens to the K/L ratios in manufacturing and services?

10. Complete Figure 6.17, showing the changed pattern of production resulting from the protection of manufactures for a given endowment.

11. Using expansion paths, illustrate an economy that is completely specialized in the production of manufactures.

12. Illustrate the factor price equalization result using a Lerner-Pearce diagram when the home country has twice as much capital and half as much labor as the foreign country.

13. Draw the home production frontier in the Ricardian factor endowment model if its endowment is $(L,H) = (400,500)$ with the unit inputs given in the text. Draw the foreign frontier with endowment $(L^*,H^*) = (300,600)$.

14. Find the terms of trade and the final consumption for the two economies in problem 13 if they trade with each other. Explain the pattern of trade.

15. With the three factors (capital, labor, and skilled labor) and two goods (manufactures and services) define factor intensity. Define factor abundance between the home and foreign nations in the same situation.

16. Given Leamer's division of inputs and outputs into 10 categories each, how can factor intensity and abundance be defined?

READINGS

Edward Leamer, *Sources of International Comparative Advantage*, MIT Press, Cambridge, MA, 1984. An excellent investigation of the quantitative basis of observed factor abundance and trade patterns.

Alan Deardorff and Robert Stern, *The Michigan Model of World Production and Trade: Theory and Applications*, MIT Press, Cambridge, MA, 1986. A presentation of one of the large-scale computable general equilibrium models of production and trade.

CHAPTER 7

Industrial Organization and Trade

CHAPTER PREVIEW

This chapter examines the influence of various sorts of industrial organization on the direction and volume of international trade. Industrial organization refers to the way in which firms fit together to make an industry. The four basic types of industrial organization are competition, monopoly, monopolistic competition, and oligopoly. There are examples of each type of industry in international trade. Up to this point in the text, industries have been competitive, with many firms producing a homogeneous product. Topics in this chapter include:

(a) Monopolistic or *price-searching* firms and their behavior in international markets
(b) *Intraindustry trade,* exporting and importing the same category of goods
(c) *Oligopolies,* industries with only a few firms, and their behavior in international trade
(d) Other causes of international trade: technology, product cycles, income differences, and increasing returns to scale

INTRODUCTION

The simplest type of industry is one composed of a single firm, a monopoly. An international monopoly occurs when a firm in a particular nation is the only supplier for an international market. Compared with competitive firms, an exporting monopolist produces less output, sells at a higher price and enjoys positive profit. Importing from a monopolistic firm in another nation means paying a higher price for less of the good. Examples of monopoly power abound in markets for minerals and primary commodities. International producer cartels like the Organization of Petroleum Exporting Countries (OPEC) and the coffee cartel are made up of members trying to join together to acquire monopoly power.

If buyers can be separated into distinct groups, it pays the international monopolist to discriminate by pricing according to the demand of each group. For a monopolist involved in exporting, buyers can easily be separated into two distinct groups: domestic and foreign. If foreign buyers have higher or more inelastic demand, they will have to pay a higher price.

A good deal of international trade occurs when only a few firms are in the market. This sort of industry is called an oligopoly. A firm in one nation may be competing with one or a few firms in other nations. The decisions made by a few foreign auto firms, for instance, affect U.S. auto firms. An oligopoly can turn out to be nearly as competitive as a market with many firms. On the other hand, firms may be able to collude and share monopolistic profits.

Monopolistic competition, as the name suggests, is an industry whose firms have monopoly power to set their price but are driven to zero profit in a competitive equilibrium in the long run. Many firms are in the industry, each selling its own particular brand or quality. Often a number of firms are foreign, and there is demand in foreign countries for home products. International trade within monopolistically competitive industries is common.

Various other theories contribute to an understanding of international trade. If nations have different production technologies, trade will benefit both. Some nations have a comparative advantage in coming up with new products, leading to international trade in what is called the product cycle. Different levels of income across nations can affect the demand for goods and international trade. Increasing returns to scale provide an additional reason to specialize because unit costs decline as output rises.

All of these industrial organizations and alternative theories of international trade contribute to the understanding of the tremendous variety of activity in international trade.

A. PRICE-SEARCHING FIRMS AND TRADE

A firm that faces a downward-sloping demand curve searches for the price and quantity that maximize its profit. This section examines the principles of international trade when firms are price searchers.

1. Price-searching Firms versus Price-taking Firms

When only one firm is in an industry, it is called a monopoly. The two general sorts of monopolies are natural monopolies and legal monopolies. *Natural monopolies* arise when average cost is declining for the single firm that produces enough output to meet demand in the market. Average cost declines because of economies of scale at the firm level. Since average cost is declining as the firm's output expands, one large firm is able to operate more efficiently than smaller firms. Any small firms are driven out of business. When the large firm captures the market, it has no competition. Positive profit persists because a small firm considering entry into the market would be discouraged by the high average cost at a low output level.

Legal monopolies arise from *property rights* that keep potential competitors from entering an industry even if profits are abnormally high. Patents, franchises, licensing, and ownership of resources are based on property rights and lead to legal monopolies. A newly developed production process can be patented in the United States for 16 years. Copyright laws ensure the property rights of authors, musicians, movie producers, and so on, and were a focus of the recent Uruguay Round of the General Agreement on Tariffs and Trade (GATT) negotiations. Utility companies are granted the sole right to sell their services inside a certain geographical area, which may include different nations. Licensing is similar in that it restricts competition, perhaps from foreign telecommunication firms or foreign doctors. A firm owning a titanium mine in Brazil has the sole legal right to sell the mineral from it. OPEC and other resource cartels have monopoly power based on the legal property rights of ownership.

When there is a single firm in an industry, demand for the firm's output is equivalent to the entire market demand for the product. A monopolist searches for the price and quantity combination along the demand curve that maximizes its profit. Instead of a supply curve, a monopolist has a supply point on the demand curve it faces. The *profit-maximizing* price and output are found by comparing the marginal revenue (MR) and marginal cost (MC) of an additional unit of output. If MR is greater than MC, profit rises if the monopolist produces an additional unit. If MC is greater than MR, profit rises if the monopolist reduces output.

Suppose all of the world's gold is owned by a single firm in South Africa. In Figure 7.1, the demand for gold in the entire world is labeled D. Even if only a single gold firm existed, it would be constrained in setting the price of gold by the demand it faces. There are substitutes for gold: silver in jewelry, titanium in industrial uses, stocks and bonds as assets, and so on. If the monopolist sets the price of gold at $1,000 per ounce, none will be bought (this year). To sell more gold, the monopolist must lower its price. Since the price on every ounce sold must be lowered, MR will be less than price. The monopolist's marginal revenue MR curve is drawn below its demand curve D.

The D and MR curves can be related algebraically. If demand is linear as in Figure 7.1, the inverse demand function can be written $P = a - bQ$, where a and b are positive numbers. Total revenue *(TR)* is price *(P)* times quantity *(Q)*: $TR = aQ - bQ^2$. MR is the change in TR for a one unit change in Q: $MR = a - 2bQ$. Students with calculus recognize MR as the derivative

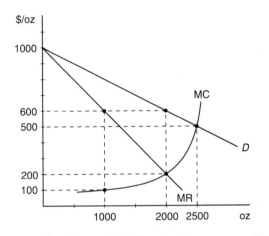

Figure 7.1. A Price-searching Monopolistic Exporter For a monopolist, marginal revenue (MR) lies below demand *D*. This monopolist produces where MR equals marginal cost (MC) at 2,000 ounces. Output is sold according to demand at $600.

of *TR*. Students without calculus can work through the example of the inverse demand function in Figure 7.1: $P = 5,000 - 5Q$. Marginal revenue in Figure 7.1 is $MR = 5,000 - 10Q$. MR is twice as steep as *D* when demand is linear.

Another basic fact constrains the monopolist's pricing and output of gold in Figure 7.1, namely the cost of digging the gold out of the ground. Each ounce of gold must be mined and processed. At any given time the firm has a certain amount of machinery and equipment to use along with the labor it hires. To produce more gold requires more labor and more wear and tear on the firm's machinery and equipment.

Economists have learned that marginal cost generally increases with output. The marginal cost curve MC in Figure 7.1 is drawn sloping upward. This is a short-run marginal cost curve, which holds the amount of capital input of the firm constant. Conceptually, MC slopes upward because of the law of diminishing marginal productivity. Holding capital input constant, additional workers add to total output, but beyond some point these additions become smaller. As marginal products for added workers fall, marginal cost of the extra output rises.

At outputs below 2,000 ounces (per day), the marginal revenue from selling an extra unit of output is larger than the marginal cost of producing it. Suppose for instance only 1,000 ounces are being produced; the MR of an extra ounce of output is $600 while it costs only $100 to produce. The monopolist would raise its profit by increasing output. This continues until $MR = MC = \$200$ at the *profit-maximizing output* of 2,000 ounces per day.

After finding the profit-maximizing output, the monopolist prices gold according to demand. All 2,000 ounces can be sold at a price of $600, which is found where the output of 2,000 meets the demand curve *D*. The monopolist produces where MR = MC and sells according to demand at the price that clears the market.

> Price-searching firms maximize profit at the output where MR = MC and price according to demand.

Gold buyers in the world would pay $600 per ounce when facing this monopolistic exporter. If the industry is made up of many small competitive firms around the world, each firm is a competitive *price taker* in the market. Such a price-taking firm, like the ones in previous chapters, is pictured in Figure 7.2. Each price-taking firm has no power to vary the lower international market price of $500. MR also equals $500 for each firm because every ounce can be sold for the same price. For competitive firms, D and MR are flat lines at the market price. Profit is maximized for this competitive firm where MR = MC at 2,500 ounces of output.

Imagine marginal revenue equal to demand D for the price searcher in Figure 9.1. The price searcher would then maximize profit where MR = MC, setting the price at $500 and output Q at 2,500, which is equivalent to the outcome pictured in Figure 7.2. A monopolistic firm prices higher and produces less output than a competitive firm with the same costs of production would.

2. Monopolistic Profits

When firms in a competitive industry are making profits, other firms enter the industry, pushing supply up and price down. In the long run, profit will be zero for a competitive firm. This is not the case, however, for a monopo-

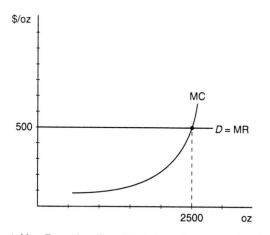

Figure 7.2. A Price-taking Exporting Firm The international price is taken to be $500 in this example. This price taker can sell any quantity it wants at this international price. Since each additional unit is sold at $500, marginal revenue (MR) = $500. This firm maximizes profit where MR = MC at 2,500 units of output.

list. By definition only one firm is in the market. Entry might be ruled out by the legal status of the monopoly or by cost advantages of the natural monopolist.

The level of monopolist profit can be found by looking at the difference between average cost (AC) and price *(P)* at the optimal output. In Figure 7.3, profit is maximized for the monopolist where MR = MC at Q = 100. Output is sold according to demand at a price of $15.

Consider first the lowest cost at AC_1 in Figure 7.3. At the optimal output of 100, AC_1 = $12, which means total cost TC = AC × Q = $12 × 100 = $1,200. Total revenue when P = $15 and Q = 100 is TR = $15 × 100 = $1,500. Price equals average revenue (total revenue divided by output). Profit (π) is the difference between total revenue and total costs: π = TR − TC = $1,500 − $1,200 = $300. Profit is the shaded area in Figure 7.3. Profit is positive if average revenue is greater than average cost.

At the highest average cost AC_3 in Figure 7.3, total cost TC = $18 × 100 = $1,800 is greater than total revenue TR = $1,500. Profit is π = $1,500 − $1,800 = −$300. This $300 loss is the dotted area in Figure 7.3. The monopolist may choose to operate with a loss if expected profit is positive for the future. The monopolist depicted by the high costs at AC_3 would *shut down* if fixed costs were less than losses. When a firm shuts down, it simply lays off its labor and ceases operation. Fixed costs (utilities, rent, and so on) must be paid whether or not the firm operates. A monopolist may decide to *sell out* (sell its capital machines and equipment and cease to exist) if it is suffering losses and does not expect a change in market conditions.

With costs at the level depicted by AC_2 in Figure 7.3, P = AC and π = 0. A price searcher has no guarantee of positive profit. Demand for the product and cost of production determine whether profit will be positive and indeed whether the firm should operate or even continue to exist.

Being a monopolist does not guarantee positive economic profit. Natu-

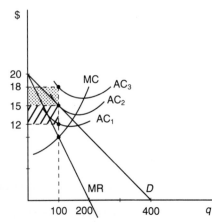

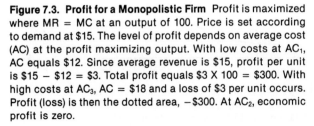

Figure 7.3. Profit for a Monopolistic Firm Profit is maximized where MR = MC at an output of 100. Price is set according to demand at $15. The level of profit depends on average cost (AC) at the profit maximizing output. With low costs at AC_1, AC equals $12. Since average revenue is $15, profit per unit is $15 − $12 = $3. Total profit equals $3 × 100 = $300. With high costs at AC_3, AC = $18 and a loss of $3 per unit occurs. Profit (loss) is then the dotted area, −$300. At AC_2, economic profit is zero.

ral monopolies arise because of cost advantages associated with large-scale operations and should generally be allowed to operate without regulation. If a natural monopolist tries to extract an exorbitant profit, other firms will be attracted to the industry. If entry costs are high, the government may prefer to tax away the profit of a natural monopolist but let it continue to operate.

A legal monopolist can enjoy positive profits as long as the legal restriction withholding competition remains in place. Legal monopolies like the phone and utility companies are typically *regulated* by local governments. Ideally, a legal monopoly can be forced into acting like a competitive firm.

3. International Monopolies

When a nation is importing from an *international monopolist,* a tariff is an attractive device.. While domestic consumers are forced by a tariff to pay a higher price for less of the good, the foreign monopolist loses some of its monopoly power and profit. The domestic government effectively taxes away some of the foreign monopolist's profit, and tax revenue can be redistributed to domestic consumers who suffer the higher price.

Suppose all of the consumers in a market are in the home country while the monopolist is foreign. Domestic demand is labeled D in Figure 7.4. Costs for the foreign monopolist are represented by MC* and AC*. The monopolist in Figure 7.4 would produce where MR = MC*, producing where quantity $Q = 100$ and pricing at $15. With AC at $12, profit would be $300.

Suppose a $2 per unit tariff is put on this imported good. The effective demand curve falls to D' for the monopolist, and marginal revenue falls to MR'. Output falls to 90 where the new MR' equals MC*. While price in the domestic market is $15.50, the monopolist receives $13.50 per unit. Profit

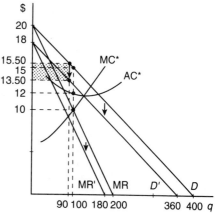

Figure 7.4. Taxing a Foreign Monopolist The foreign monopolist facing a tariff effectively suffers a fall in demand from D to D'. The profit-maximizing output falls from 100 to 90, and price falls from $15 to $13.50. The $2 per unit tax is collected by the importing country's government. Tariff revenue of $2 X 90 = $180 is created for the home government. Profit falls for the foreign monopolist. Domestic consumers must pay a higher price and reduce the level of consumption.

falls for the foreign monopolist with the tariff because average revenue is lower and average cost is higher (above $12).

The home government collects the tariff revenue, amounting to $2 × 90 = $180, the shaded area in Figure 7.4. This tariff revenue can be used to compensate consumers who must pay a higher price ($15.50 instead of $15) for less of the good (90 units instead of 100). Even if tariff revenues do not fully compensate consumers, the tax on a foreign monopolist may prove politically popular. Few consumers in the United States would be opposed to the idea of taxing some of OPEC's profits, although fewer still would enjoy the high fuel prices.

4. International Price Discrimination and Dumping

When a monopolist can distinguish among various groups of buyers, it can increase its profit by pricing according to the demand of each group. This activity is called *price discrimination.* An international monopolist can easily discriminate among buyers in different nations. Nations with higher, more inelastic demand for a good will pay higher prices. Nations whose consumers have lower or more elastic demand will pay lower prices.

Figure 7.5 pictures an international monopolist facing domestic demand D and foreign demand D^*. Each group of buyers has its own marginal revenue: MR and MR*. For simplicity, MC is assumed to be constant. Under

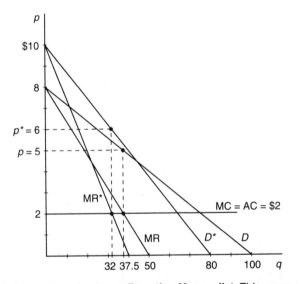

Figure 7.5. Price Discrimination by an Exporting Monopolist This monopolist can discriminate between home buyers along demand curve *D* and foreign buyers along demand curve *D**. The monopolist's MC is assumed to be constant at $2. Average cost (AC) is also $2. The monopolist will want to equate MC with both MR in the home market and MR* in the foreign market. In this example, 32 units of output are sold abroad for $6 and 37.5 units are sold in the home market at a price of $5.

this assumption, each additional unit of output costs the same to produce, which means AC must be constant as well. The monopolist produces where marginal cost MC equals MR for each group.

The profit-maximizing outputs for the exporting monopolist in Figure 7.5 are 37.5 units for the home market and 32 units for the foreign market. Foreign buyers in this example have higher and more inelastic demand and must pay $6, while domestic buyers pay only $5. Profit for the monopolist is higher than if the two demands were treated as one large demand. Selling to home buyers, the monopolist makes a profit of $3 per unit, which totals $3 × 37.5 = $112.50. Selling to foreign buyers creates a profit of $4 × 32 = $128.

Resale of products from the country with the low price to the country with the high price must be impossible for price discrimination to work. If traders in the low-priced home country in Figure 7.5 could resell to consumers in the high-priced foreign country, the price discrimination scheme would fall apart. The potential for resale across markets must discourage many monopolists from international price discrimination.

Cries of *dumping* are regularly heard from U.S. firms facing foreign competition. International dumping occurs when a foreign firm sells temporarily below its average cost to gain experience or run the competition out of business. Later the firm plans to enjoy positive profit. The International Trade Commission (ITC) hears complaints about dumping and can compensate industries and erect temporary barriers to imports. Japanese computer chip firms were found guilty of dumping in 1986, and antidumping duties were put into place. The steel industry has repeatedly charged European firms of dumping. Without detailed information from a violating firm it is impossible to determine accurately the costs of dumping. Needless to say, a guilty firm would be the last to open its books to foreign inspection. Even though foreign firms have provided data to the ITC, data reliability might be questioned. Determinations of dumping by the ITC are typically based on flimsy evidence.

Economists continue to debate whether trying to police dumping is worthwhile. Protection from dumping is certainly not a long-run problem. If foreign firms want to sell us goods for less than the goods cost to produce, it is not clear that we should be upset and rush to stop them. Protection from alleged dumping offers another type of nontariff barrier (NTB) to trade.

5. A Dominant and Fringe Import Market

Another application of price-searching behavior involves a market with a *dominant* firm that sets price and a number of competitive *fringe* firms. Suppose the domestic market for video players is characterized by a large foreign exporter and a number of small fringe domestic firms. The fringe domestic firms supply only according to the price set by the dominant foreign firm. A higher price results in more output by the domestic competitive fringe, whereas a lower price reduces domestic output.

In Figure 7.6, total domestic demand is represented by D. This domestic demand is broken down into two parts: demand for the product of foreign dominant firm (labeled DF*) and the residual domestic fringe supply (FS). In Figure 7.6, if the foreign dominant firm sets a price below $80, it captures the entire domestic demand and the domestic competitive fringe will supply zero. Domestic fringe suppliers cannot produce video players for less than $80. Imported components may play a large role in the costs of production of the domestic fringe.

At the other extreme, the domestic fringe would completely take over the market at a price of $140. While the dominant foreign firm sets price, the domestic competitive fringe is able to respond and sell its output in the domestic market. For any price in the range of $80 to $140, the domestic fringe firms share the market with the foreign dominant firm. As the foreign dominant firm raises price, it loses its share of the market to the domestic fringe firms.

Marginal revenue (MR*) for the foreign dominant firm is derived from its demand DF*. The dominant foreign firm maximizes profit by producing where MR* equals its marginal cost (MC*). In Figure 7.6 the dominant firm produces where MR* = MC* at 80 units of output. Price is set at $100 according to demand DF*. A price of $100 leaves a residual of 20 units for the domestic fringe firms on the fringe supply curve FS.

If the dominant foreign firm had higher costs of production, its MC*

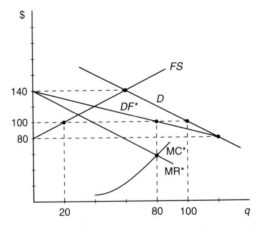

Figure 7.6. A Dominant-Fringe Import Market Domestic demand D is composed of the foreign dominant firm demand DF* and domestic supply FS from small domestic fringe firms. The dominant foreign firm produces where its MC* = MR*, and prices its output at $100. Domestic fringe suppliers produce a residual 20 units at this price. A tariff in this market taxes the dominant foreign firm and stimulates the domestic fringe firms, but creates overriding losses for domestic consumers.

would be higher. It would then be forced to produce less output and price higher, yielding more of the market to the competitive domestic fringe. If the dominant foreign firm had lower costs, its MC* would be lower, result-ing in higher output, lower price, and a smaller share of the market for the domestic fringe.

A tariff would reduce output by the dominant foreign firm, increasing the market share of the domestic fringe producers. Domestic consumers would have to pay a higher price for less of the good. A tariff would pro-duce revenue for the government and create gains in the domestic fringe industry, but would raise the cost to consumers. The argument for a tariff is somewhat stronger when a domestic fringe industry faces a dominant foreign monopolist. A tariff has the added benefit of taking away some of the foreign monopolist's market power and profit and increasing the share of the market for domestic fringe firms. Nevertheless, deadweight losses occur with the tariff: the loss in consumer surplus outweighs all potential gains.

EXAMPLE 7.1   Steel Trigger Prices

Ingo Walter (1983) has studied trigger prices in the international steel market. During the late 1960s and early 1970s the U.S. steel industry was having trouble meeting increased competition from Japan and Europe. The level of investment had been higher since World War II in Japan and Europe, resulting in more modern and efficient capital equipment in those countries. Wages were also lower abroad, perhaps 50% of the wage in the U.S. steel industry at the time. Unit costs of production were about 40% of the cost in the United States. These import penetration ratios (the percentage of total U.S. consumption from imports) are re-ported:

1960	1965	1970	1975	1980
5%	10%	18%	14%	16%

Using pressure from the State Department, the troubled U.S. steel indus-try was able to get Japan and Europe to agree to voluntary export re-straints (VERs) during the late 1960s and early 1970s. After repeated hearings on alleged dumping, the Carter administration instituted a *trig-ger price mechanism* (TPM) in 1978, based on cost data from Japanese firms. The TPM was designed to keep out imports when their price fell below a certain level, ideally the cost of production and shipping. How-ever, the TPM was difficult to administer and did not prove successful. After claiming that foreign governments were subsidizing their steel in-dustry unfairly, the U.S. steel industry received increased protection.

Currently, VERs reduce steel imports from Japan and Europe. The United States, Japan, and Europe are also having trouble meeting competition from newly industrializing nations such as South Korea, Taiwan, Spain, Mexico, Venezuela, and Brazil, where steel mills are modern and wages are low. The market share of steel imports from all developing nations in all of the industrialized nations increased from 3% in 1970 to 11% in 1985.

EXAMPLE 7.2   Pricing to Market and the Exchange Rate

When a currency depreciates, prices of the country's imports rise. From an exporting monopolist's viewpoint, a currency depreciation in the country buying its import means falling demand and falling marginal revenue. If the monopolist responds by lowering its price, the rise in the price of its goods is offset in the country with a depreciating currency. Lowering price in this fashion weakens the tendency for currency depreciation to increase the balance of trade. Michael Knetter (1989) presents evidence that German exporters to the United States are sensitive to exchange rate changes and adjust their prices so the dollar prices of German goods in the United States remain constant. This is called "pricing to market." U.S. exporters, on the other hand, do not generally adjust their dollar price to stabilize the foreign currency price in foreign markets. This may be because German importers enjoy more of a monopoly position in the particular industries involved. Without monopoly power, an exporting firm is not able to price to market. The dollar devaluation of the late 1980s did not in fact lead to a fall in the U.S. trade deficit. Knetter stresses that if foreign firms lowered the price in their appreciating currency to stabilize the dollar price in the United States, the devaluation will not lead to an increase in the trade deficit.

Problems for Section A

   A1.   Are legal monopolies more likely within a nation or internationally? How would this apply to natural monopolies?

   A2.   Why might an international monopolist operate temporarily at a loss?

   A3.   Should we be too concerned if foreign firms want to sell us goods for less than what it costs to produce them? What is this activity called?

   A4.   Illustrate a case of price discrimination with home buyers paying more. How might home consumers react to this situation? Could claims of dumping enter the story?

B. DIFFERENTIATED GOODS AND INTRAINDUSTRY TRADE

Imports are aggregated into categories to apply protectionist laws and to collect data. These categories are very broad: radio and television sets, computers, furniture, and plumbing fixtures are examples of the classifications. Within each category, some product differentiation (dispersion of quality) leads to price variation. When nations export and import the same category of goods, it is called intraindustry trade. Much of the trade between industrial nations is intraindustry trade. The theories of trade up to this point have suggested that nations will specialize and export some types of goods, while importing other types of goods. This section looks into intraindustry trade, exporting and importing within a given classification of goods.

1. The Principles of Product Differentiation

Markets ideally involve precisely defined goods with no quality variation. Basic commodities like wheat and silver are examples of goods that can be precisely graded. Buyers and sellers in such markets know exactly what they are trading. At the other extreme, the market for used cars contains little product consistency, even for a certain year's make and model (1987 custom Ford vans, for instance). Most goods fall between these examples, with some quality variation (production differentiation) in what is commonly regarded as a market. Defining a good and its market is one of the most difficult and fundamental problems in economics.

Within the common industrial classifications, a good deal of leeway typically remains for product variety. Economists distinguish between two related ideas: different (distinct) products and *product differentiation*. Within any class of a distinct good, some product differentiation resulting from quality variation will remain.

Grains, for instance, are clearly different from fruits, although they are both food. Rice is clearly different from barley, although they are both grains. Long grain rice is different from short grain rice, although they are both rice. Long grain Texas rice is different from long grain Indonesian rice, although they are both long grain rice. Long grain Texas brown rice is clearly different from long grain Texas white rice, although they are both long grain Texas rice. It is easy to see that some product differentiation will arise in any workable scheme of categorizing goods.

The problem faced by economists is a clear one. It is arbitrary to classify goods with rigid categories when gradings of characteristics are smooth and continuous. The key to designing a workable classification scheme is its purpose. If you are trying to predict what will happen in the aggregate international rice market next year so you can help domestic farmers make decisions, you can aggregate the various types of rice. If the issue is deciding whether to plant short grain rice or long grain rice or white rice or brown rice, each market should be treated as distinct.

Classifying goods is ultimately arbitrary and leaves scope for product differentiation within the categories.

Buyers and sellers in any market, no matter how narrowly defined, will certainly be familiar with their good. Firms competing internationally are the real experts in their particular markets. They know the goods better than anybody else because it is their business. Economists typically work with rough categories of goods designed by government officials and customs offices interested in applying tariffs and quotas. The working categories (yarn, glass, toys and games, medical products, alcoholic beverages, telecommunications apparatus, and so on) have plenty of room for different products and finer classifications. When goods are disaggregated by applying a finer classification scheme, the level of product differentiation within a category drops.

2. Intraindustry Trade

When goods in the same category are both imported and exported, intraindustry trade occurs. Intraindustry trade has numerous potential causes. Cost difference in producing different qualities of a good is one. A consumer buying a shirt is interested in the *service* the shirt provides. The service of this shirt amounts to so many days of dress, warmth, style, and so on. Higher quality is equivalent to better service. The market for shirts can be regarded as the market for shirt services. Increased quality costs more to produce, which means a higher marginal cost curve. Shirts with lower quality have a lower marginal cost curve.

Figure 7.7 illustrates the marginal costs of two qualities of shirt along with the demand (D) for shirt services. This monopolistic firm distinguishes between the two qualities of shirt just as consumers do. Profit is maximized for each type of shirt by producing where MR equals MC for each type of

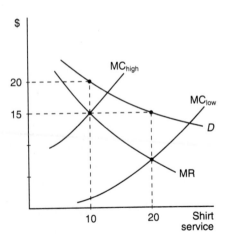

Figure 7.7. Quality Differentiation and Price When quality varies for a good, consumers can be regarded as demanding the services the good provides. This high-quality good has a higher cost of production than this low-quality good. This firm would produce a lower output and charge a higher price for the high-quality goods.

shirt. Output of 10 units of the high-quality shirt at a price of $20, and output of 20 units of the low-quality shirt at a price of $15 occurs in the market.

Production of the high-quality shirt is likely to be labor intensive. If so, the labor-abundant nation would specialize in manufacturing it. The low-quality shirt would then be capital intensive. The capital-abundant nation would specialize in its production. Since consumers in both nations want both types of shirt, *intraindustry trade* should develop between the labor-abundant nation and the capital-abundant nation.

Intraindustry trade is the simultaneous export and import of goods in the same category, in this example shirts. Given the finest current classification scheme, about one quarter of all observed international trade is intraindustry trade. Aggregating goods into broader classifications increases the amount of intraindustry trade. Disaggregating goods into finer classifications decreases the level of intraindustry trade, but some intraindustry trade is observed at any practical level of disaggregation.

Another cause of intraindustry trade is transport costs, both international and domestic. Often international shipping via the ocean is cheaper than crossing land within a country. In large nations, border regions are often closer for purposes of trade to other nations than to domestic regions along the other border. This gives rise to what is called border trade.

Considering transport costs, California is closer to Japan than it is to Virginia, and Texas is closer to Central America than it is to New York. The United States exports chemicals from California and imports them from Europe, partly because of the lower cost of shipping across the ocean as compared with shipping across land. Sending a tank truck all the way from California to New York is not feasible. The United States imports gravel from Mexico and exports gravel to Canada because of the high transport cost. Location and transport costs explain a good portion of intraindustry trade.

> Intraindustry trade occurs when the same type of good is imported and exported. Intraindustry trade has numerous causes.

Studies have isolated goods with high levels of intraindustry trade: envelopes, transformers, plumbing fixtures, machine tool accessories, synthetic rubber, fans, and sheet metal. Goods within each category have a high degree of price dispersion, which must reflect quality variation. Goods that are more narrowly defined have less price dispersion and intraindustry trade: women's handbags, soap, radios, TV sets, leather gloves, costume jewelry, refrigerators, and vacuum cleaners.

Manufactured goods are generally more differentiated than primary and agricultural goods. As nations develop, they produce a higher ratio of manufactured to agricultural goods. Theory correctly predicts that developed nations would have higher levels of intraindustry trade than less developed nations.

3. Monopolistic Competition and Trade

Firms selling differentiated goods have some monopolistic power and face downward sloping demand. If firms make positive economic profits, how-ever, other firms will enter the industry. Entry pushes up the cost of inputs because of competitive bidding and reduces the demand for each firm's output. The result in the long run is zero profit. An industry with monopoly power but zero long-run profits is said to have *monopolistic competition.*

Figure 7.8 illustrates a monopolistically competitive firm in the long run with zero profit. The firm maximizes its profit where MC = MR by producing 100 units of output, but the price of $10 equals average cost AC and profit is zero.

Monopolistic competition may be a common sort in industry. Many firms face downward sloping demand for their output because consumers recognize the product by its brand name. While these firms are price searchers, competition can drive profit to zero in the long run. As more firms enter an industry, consumers have more substitutes and the demand facing each firm falls and becomes more elastic.

When the firms are in different countries and consumers have similar tastes across countries, intraindustry trade will arise as international mo-nopolistic competition develops in the industry. If domestic monopolistic firms enjoy positive profit, entry by foreign firms can lower the demand facing domestic firms and drive their profit to zero. Increasing intraindus-try trade should lead to falling profits in the domestic industry.

4. Domestic Monopoly Power and Free Trade

When a nation opens itself to free trade, domestic firms are forced to com-pete with foreign firms. Suppose a protected domestic industry is a natural monopoly that makes a positive economic profit. With free trade, foreign

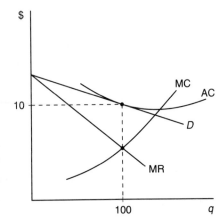

Figure 7.8. A Typical Firm in Monopolistic Competition A firm in a monopolistically competitive industry faces down-ward sloping demand and marginal revenue. This firm maxi-mizes its profit where MR = MC at an output of Q = 100 and prices its output at $10 according to demand. Competition pushes the firm to a position of zero economic profit, with price equal to AC.

firms will enter the industry and drive the domestic monopoly toward zero profit and the long-run equilibrium of monopolistic competition.

Allowing foreign firms to sell inside the economy freely makes a monopolistic domestic industry more competitive. The Federal Trade Commission (FTC) is charged with policing and limiting monopoly power in the United States. The competitive influence of free international markets has been increasingly recognized by the FTC.

Protectionism increases the monopoly power of domestic firms. Free trade widens the scope of competition, forcing domestic monopolistic firms to lower price and increase output.

EXAMPLE 7.3   Intraindustry Trade and Product Categorization

A look through the 1985 *International Trade Statistics Yearbook* of the United Nations shows the high incidence of intraindustry trade. In the international market for harvesting machines, the United States imported $386 million while exporting $594 million. Of the imports, $77 million was spent on combine harvester-threshers and $58 million on parts. Regarding exports, $122 million of combines and $94 million of parts were sold. In electrical transformers, the United States imported $286 million while exporting $134 million. The United States is the largest importer ($340 million in 1985) of basketwork and brooms, exporting very little ($28 million). These are the finest categories recorded.

The level of intraindustry trade falls as goods are categorized more finely. The *index of intraindustry trade* can be defined as

$$I = (\text{Exports} - \text{Imports})/(\text{Exports} + \text{Imports})$$

If a good is exported only, $I = 1$. If it is imported only, $I = -1$. If exports and imports are exactly equal, $I = 0$. The closer I gets to zero, the greater is the degree of intraindustry trade. In harvesting machines, $I = 0.21$. However, I in subcategories rises to 0.23 in combines and to 0.47 in parts. Similar examples can be found in many classifications.

Grubel and Lloyd (1975) show that the percentage of Australian intraindustry trade falls from 43% in the broadest classification scheme to 6% in the narrowest.

EXAMPLE 7.4   Testing the Theory of Intraindustry Trade

An empirical study by Elizabeth Wickam and myself (1989) in *Intra-Industry Trade: Theory, Evidence, and Extensions* finds support for the theory that intraindustry trade depends on observable national and industrial characteristics. Generally, larger and more capital abundant economies carry out more intraindustry trade. More product differentiation is found to increase the observed level of intraindustry trade in a consistent manner.

EXAMPLE 7.5   The International Beer Industry

The degree of international competition in the beer industry is increasing, as is intraindustry trade in beer. Jeffrey Karrenbrock (1990) examines the level of intraindustry trade and the degree of involvement in the international market. Trade in beer is discouraged by three factors: tariffs, a short shelf life (3 months), and high transport costs (beer is mostly water). Firms license foreign production, providing brewing techniques to a foreign firm, which produces the "foreign" beer. For instance, Miller brews Lowenbrau and Heileman brews Carlsberg in the United States. U.S. firms license foreign firms as well: Suntory brews Budweiser in Japan and Molson brews Coors in Canada. Generally, licensing plays a more important role than intraindustry trade in the international beer industry. Licensed U.S. beer production in Canada, for instance, is 17 times the level of exports to Canada. The countries below are those most involved in the international beer industry. The intraindustry trade index I is (Exports − Imports)/(Exports + Imports).

	I	Exports/ Output	Imports/ Consumption
France	0.57	3%	12%
Belgium	0.64	18%	5%
Ireland	0.67	42%	13%
Canada	0.69	11%	2%
Luxembourg	0.73	41%	10%
Netherlands	0.83	33%	4%
U.S.	0.85	22%	14%
Switzerland	0.86	1%	11%
Denmark	0.98	23%	0%
Czechoslovakia	1.00	12%	0%

Problems For Section B

B1.   The United States imports cars with a range of quality. VERs on Japanese imports have raised the quality of imported cars. Why? What will happen to the quality of domestically produced cars with the VER?

B2.   Suppose there are three types of goods: food, clothing, and household goods. What are the advantages of aggregating clothing and household goods into a new category called manufactured goods? What are the disadvantages? What probably happens to the level of intraindustry trade with this aggregation?

B3.   In a monopolistically competitive industry with profits below normal, what will happen over time to the number of firms and the profit of the typical firm? What difference does it make if the firms are foreign?

C. OLIGOPOLIES AND TRADE

When an industry has only a few firms, the situation is called an *oligopoly*. An oligopoly can create varying degrees of competition, with outcomes that range from pure monopoly power to pure competition. This section examines production and trade in oligopolistic markets.

1. Collusion

Firms in an industry have an incentive to *collude* and act like a single firm. When there are only a few firms in an oligopoly, collusion may be possible. Collusion raises price and reduces output. Acting like a monopoly maximizes total profit for all of the firms together, although the firms face the problem of splitting the monopoly profit. Cartels must agree on how to restrict output to attain a higher price.

Collusion across international borders may be more difficult because of distances and costs of communication, but it certainly occurs. A number of large international producer cartels exist, mainly in primary industries like oil, rubber, coffee, tea, and bananas. The various firms agree to produce and price their product as though they were a monopoly.

Antitrust laws in the United States recognize the incentive firms have to collude and are designed to encourage competition and discourage monopolistic behavior. A monopoly restricts output and charges a higher price, reducing the consumer surplus in the market. Governments in Europe and much of the rest of the world have a history of encouraging collusive monopolistic behavior because it is thought to create stability. No international antitrust laws restrict international collusion. Nations are becoming more integrated and dependent on one another, and such international laws and practices may begin to develop. Of course, nations forming such international agreements must agree on whether collusion is harmful or beneficial. *International law* is a growing field in the legal profession.

2. An Oligopolist Facing Kinked Demand

A possible dilemma of an oligopolist in its pricing strategy is pictured in Figure 7.9. Suppose the price charged by the oligopolist is $100. The oligopolist has the option of raising or lowering price to increase profit.

If the oligopolist raises price, consumers will buy cheaper substitutes, some of which may be foreign. Other firms in the industry, including foreign firms, enjoy increased demand for their products. The percentage fall in the quantity of the firm's product demanded is larger in absolute value than the percentage rise in price. Revenue (price times quantity) of the oligopolist falls with the price increase. Demand facing the oligopolist is elastic for prices above $100.

If the oligopolist in Figure 7.9 lowers its price, other firms have to do the same to keep from losing their customers. Foreign firms exporting to this market will also lower their price. The percentage rise in the quantity demanded of the firm's product is less than the absolute value of the percentage drop in price. Revenue of the oligopolist falls with the price reduction. Demand is inelastic for prices below $100.

The demand curve facing the firm in Figure 7.9 is *kinked,* steeper going down than going up. Revenue declines for the oligopolist whether price is raised or lowered. The kinked demand results in a split marginal revenue curve. Each section of the demand curve has its own corresponding MR curve. At the kink the oligopolist must switch from one MR curve to the other. If MC happens to come through this gap, the firm cannot equate MC with MR.

How a firm in this dilemma will act is hard to determine. Changing cost will not necessarily lead to price changes. If other firms lower their

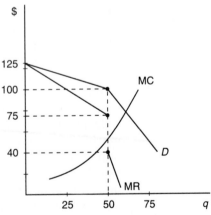

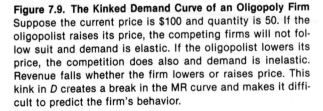

Figure 7.9. The Kinked Demand Curve of an Oligopoly Firm Suppose the current price is $100 and quantity is 50. If the oligopolist raises its price, the competing firms will not follow suit and demand is elastic. If the oligopolist lowers its price, the competition does also and demand is inelastic. Revenue falls whether the firm lowers or raises price. This kink in *D* creates a break in the MR curve and makes it difficult to predict the firm's behavior.

price, demand facing this firm will shift, but the firm cannot follow the simple rule of maximizing profit by equating MC and MR. Since each firm in the oligopolistic industry faces a similar dilemma, all firms (including foreign firms) may tend to keep price and output constant. This can occur with an explicit agreement or simply through informal implicit monitoring of one another's price and output. This theory is often criticized because it does not tell how the firm gets to the current price and quantity.

In international markets a domestic oligopolistic firm must contend with foreign firms selling locally as the domestic firm tries to penetrate foreign markets. The foreign firms may try to collude and act like a monopoly, and the domestic firm may join them. However, price and output may move erratically as firms jockey for profits. In international markets, such erratic price movements are more likely because the firms are separated by distance, culture, laws, and language, making collusion more difficult.

3.   An International Duopoly

The simplest sort of oligopoly is made up of two firms and is called a duopoly. Consider a duopoly made up of a home firm and a foreign firm. This simple industry is an *international duopoly*. To simplify matters further, suppose each of the two firms has the option of producing either a high or a low level of output. These are the only output choices available. Perhaps the capital machinery used in production is large and "chunky," and the firms use either one or two machines (low or high output). When capital equipment comes in large chunks, it is impossible to change output in a smooth incremental fashion. The profit of each firm depends on both the choice it makes to produce high or low output and the choice made by the other firm. This is a setting where *game theory* can be applied to describe how the two firms will behave.

Table 7.1 illustrates the outcomes that occur as the home and foreign firms choose either low or high output. In Table 7.1 the home firm's profits appear first in the parentheses. For instance, if the home firm produces a high output level while the foreign firm produces low output, profit for the home firm is $2 million while the foreign firm loses $1 million. If both firms produce high output, they both break even in a competitive outcome with zero economic profit. If the two firms collude and jointly restrict out-

TABLE 7.1. An International Duopoly Game (Home Profit, Foreign Profit)

		Foreign Output	
		Low	**High**
Home Output	**Low**	($1 mil, $1 mil)	(−$1 mil, $2 mil)
	High	($2 mil, −$1 mil)	(0,0)

put by producing low, they split a maximized monopolistic profit of $2 million.

Collusion and the resulting $1 million profit are clearly preferable to the competitive outcome of zero profit. A dilemma arises, though, in the temptation each firm has to cheat on any collusive arrangement. If the foreign firm decides to cheat by producing a high output, it grabs $2 million profit while forcing the home firm to suffer a loss of $1 million. But the home firm can also cheat, causing the foreign firm to suffer in a symmetric fashion.

If this game is repeated year after year, the two firms have an incentive to collude and agree to restrict output. An international cartel agreement between the two firms may be formed. The cartel restricts output of its members, resulting a higher international price of the product and profit for the two cartel members.

Game theory helps predict what eventually may happen in cartel agreements. Firms formulate a strategy for making choices. In the example of Table 7.1, regardless of the choice made by the foreign firm, the home firm will benefit by producing a high output. Since the game is symmetric, the same is true for the foreign firm: it will also benefit from producing high output. Given a correct guess about the opponent's behavior, each firm will produce high output. If both firms produce high outputs, however, they break even in the competitive equilibrium. Zero economic profit is exactly the outcome predicted for the long run in a competitive industry. A duopoly may be just as competitive as pure competition, depending on the structure of outcomes, the strategy adopted by the players, and their ability to enter into a restrictive cartel agreement.

The competitive cartel solution is a stable Nash equilibrium, since both firms will do better by producing high output regardless of the opponent's choice. To build an international cartel, the home firm could send a clear signal by restricting its own output one year. The foreign firm notices this behavior and realizes the home firm suffered a temporary loss while establishing credibility as a potential cartel member. The foreign firm may decide to restrict output as well in order to split higher industry profits. If the home firm continues to restrict output, an effective cartel arrangement has been established. This cartel behavior may fall short of an explicitly organized cartel. Notice that consistent restrictive behavior (not a meeting in Paris) is necessary to establish and maintain higher than normal profits for the cartel.

4. Sustainability of Cartels

Although the payoffs for collusion are sizeable, cartel arrangements generally break down. International cartels have an especially hard time holding together during periods of low demand and falling prices. Nevertheless, the oil cartel OPEC has enjoyed more success and lasted longer than experts predicted when it was formed. The recurring problem for OPEC is simply keeping its members from selling more than their allotted *cartel quota*. The war in Kuwait caused a split in OPEC as some members produced more to fill the vacuum left when Kuwaiti and Iraqi oil production stopped. Whether OPEC can hold together remains to be seen. As long as the cartel members are successful in limiting the quantity on the international market, the price of oil remains high.

International cartels easily break down into competition. Members often have too much to gain in the short term by breaking the agreement and selling to maximize profit. When OPEC speaks of wanting an orderly world market, it hopes to avoid increases in output by its members and subsequent falling prices. In an oligopolistic market, price may jump around as firms jockey for position and try to outguess their competition. Clearly consumers benefit from the competitive pricing of a cartel collapse. A giant sigh of relief can be heard from the industrial nations when negotiations in an OPEC meeting break down.

> In an international oligopoly the strategies chosen by firms determine the outcome. Given the wide range of possible outcomes and strategies, few general conclusions can be reached.

Oligopolies are made more competitive by the *threat of entry*. Firms that are potential entrants to an industry closely observe the existing industry. If profits are high, entry is encouraged. Existing firms may behave more competitively (produce more and sell at a lower price) to discourage entry. Existing firms can discourage potential entrants by making *credible threats* to engage in price cutting. To remain credible, threats of price cutting must be carried out. Oligopolists may keep prices near the competitive level to discourage entry.

Other sorts of *nonprice competition* such as advertising may also discourage entry. Freedom of entry creates a *contestable market,* where the threat of competition can be as forceful as the real thing.

5. Subsidies and International Duopolies

Paul Krugman (1987) examines the situation of an international duopoly where a government subsidy may lead to above normal profit. Suppose a U.S. firm (Boeing) and a European firm (Airbus) are deciding whether to produce and export a new type of passenger jet.

Table 7.2 presents profits with and without production of the new airliner. This is a one-time game. Suppose the decision about whether to produce must be made by January 1st. Boeing's profits appear first in the parentheses. If Boeing correctly guesses that Airbus will produce, Boeing will not produce, because zero profit is better than −5. But if Boeing correctly guesses that Airbus will not produce, Boeing will produce and make a profit

TABLE 7.2. A Duopoly Dilemma (Boeing's Profit, Airbus's Profit)

		Airbus	
		Produce	Don't Produce
Boeing	Produce	(−5, −5)	(100, 0)
	Don't produce	(0, 100)	(0, 0)

of 100. If Boeing produces and Airbus does not, Airbus is trapped. Subsequent production by Airbus would only create a loss of −5. Once Boeing is established, entry by Airbus is effectively deterred.

The European government may choose to subsidize Airbus, encouraging it to begin production before Boeing. Since this subsidy may actually be less than the ultimate profit enjoyed by Airbus if entry by Boeing is deterred, this strategic trade policy may seem rational.

Krugman and most economists, however, question whether governments can recognize and react to such situations in a timely and rational fashion. This sort of example makes hardly a dent in the arguments in favor of free trade. Generally it is wise to leave important risky business decisions to the experts in the industry, namely the firms competing with each other in the market.

EXAMPLE 7.6   International Cartel OPEC

By far the most famous cartel these days is OPEC. In the 1970s, world oil producers restricted output so much that price of a barrel of oil jumped from $3 to $35! Since industrial nations import oil, this price increase gained immediate attention. While the power of OPEC has declined, oil prices are evidently somewhat higher than they would be without OPEC. Higher oil prices have changed the structure of production and consumption since the 1970s, encouraging fuel efficiency and conservation. A comparison of the gas-guzzling U.S. cars of the 1970s with those made today is an example of the development of fuel technology. The distribution of income within economies has also been affected by higher oil prices. There is some evidence that a higher price for oil imports decreases output but increases the demand for labor. Labor may enjoy higher wages and increased income with an OPEC embargo. There is generally accepted evidence that the import elasticity for oil is between −1 and 0, which means that an increase in the price of oil leads to a smaller percentage decline in the quantity imported. We would see that oil export revenue for the OPEC countries would rise with price increases with this oil import inelasticity.

EXAMPLE 7.7   Economist Alfred Marshall and OPEC

Many of the principles of microeconomics presented in this text were developed by Alfred Marshall, an English economist at the turn of this century. He wrote on a wide range of economic matters. These remarks of Marshall (1926) are especially relevant today:

> ... before another century has passed the scene may have changed. There may then remain but a few small areas of fertile soil, and of rich mineral strata, which are not so well supplied with both population and capital as to be able to produce most of the manufactured products which they require, and to be able to turn to a tolerably good account most of their raw products for their own use. When that time comes, those who have surplus raw products to sell, will have the upper hand in all international bargains. Acting concurrently, whether by mutual agreement or not, they will be in the possession of unassailable monopoly; and any taxes, however oppressive, which they may choose to impose on the only products which densely peopled countries can offer to them, will be paid mainly by those countries. It is this consideration, rather than the prospect of any immediate danger, which makes me regard the future of England with grave anxiety.

Alfred would have rested much better had he known about the North Sea oil.

EXAMPLE 7.8   Bananas, Aircraft, and Export Taxes

It is unconstitutional to tax exports from the United States, a bias created at the time of the Revolution by England's heavy taxing of exports from the Colonies. Other countries, however, use export taxes as a means of creating government revenue and taxing foreign consumers. OPEC has a less famous cousin in the international banana market, UPEB (Unión de Paises Exportadores de Banáno). Less powerful than OPEC, UPEB is attempting to organize a cartel among the developing Central American and African banana exporters. Jessica Bailey and James Sood (1987) propose that an export tax of 50¢ per pound would maximize total revenue (sales revenue plus tax revenue) for the banana exporting countries. The tax would push the exporters into a monopoly position. Fewer bananas would be exported, however, which would mean a declining banana industry. The United States has a great deal of market power in the aircraft industry, with about 85% of the world market. Some economists have proposed that the United States begin taxing its aircraft exports. While this would create government revenue, it would ultimately erode the international competitive position of U.S. aircraft firms.

Problems for Section C

C1.   If costs rose for the firm in Figure 7.9 so that MC intersected MR at $100 and $q = 25$, what would be the price of the good? Explain how other firms in the industry react to this firm's higher price. Find and explain the change in revenue.

C2.   When OPEC's income skyrocketed in the 1970s, the OPEC countries did not spend it all. Considering international debt, what had to happen?

C3.   Given an estimated oil import elasticity of -0.6 and a price increase from $20 to $22, calculate the percentage change in the level of imports. What are the two sources of this decrease? If OPEC raises price to $40, find the reduction in imports. What happens to OPEC revenue with these price increases?

D.   TECHNOLOGY, THE PRODUCT CYCLE, INCREASING RETURNS, AND INCOME EFFECTS

Four possible causes of international trade that have not been discussed elsewhere are covered in this section. Three deal directly with the characteristics of producing goods. Differences in technology, the product cycle, and increasing returns involve the techniques of production and can be a cause of international trade. National income affects the demand for goods and the pattern of international trade.

1.   Technology and Trade

The production of goods depends on *technology,* the engineering put to use in combining the various inputs into outputs. Economists look for evidence of differing technologies by estimating the *production functions,* which describe the relationship between levels of input and output. Firms in different nations may employ the same amounts of labor, capital, and natural resource inputs but may get different outputs because of differences in technology.

Figure 7.10 shows the unit isoquants of two production functions for the same good with different technologies. The same amount of output, 1 unit, is produced along either isoquant, labeled t_1 and t_2.

When labor input is high, technology 1 can produce the same output with less of both inputs. For instance, at point A, 1.5 units of capital K and 4.5 units of labor L result in 1 unit of output with technology 1. With technology 2, 2 units of K and 5 units of L are required to produce the same unit of output.

If factor prices were the same, a different mix of inputs would be used according to technology. At points B and B', the cost-minimizing inputs

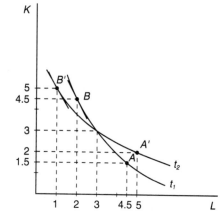

Figure 7.10. Productions with Different Technologies Isoquants t_1 and t_2 represent different ways to produce the same amount of output with different technologies. Less of both inputs may result in the same output, as illustrated by points A and A'. Cost-minimizing inputs will vary, as illustrated by points B and B'. Different technologies can be a cause of international trade.

for the same set of input prices (the same slope of the isocost line) are illustrated.

Imagine the extreme example of two nations that have identical factor endowments and the same number of consumers with identical preferences. They have no incentive to trade unless the nations have different technologies. If the home nation has better technology for producing services and the foreign nation has better technology for producing manufactures, total output in the world rises if the two nations specialize in producing the goods in which they have better technologies. Each nation can potentially consume more of both goods with gains from trade all around.

> Technology differences across nations are an added incentive for international specialization and trade.

Different input ratios by themselves thus give no indication of differing technology. When a firm minimizes cost, it picks the optimal mix of inputs depending on the costs of the inputs. Firms in different nations using the same technology are likely to use different quantities of inputs when the relative prices of inputs differ internationally. The firms produce with the same production functions, but they mix inputs differently according to local costs. This mixing of inputs makes it difficult to find empirical evidence to support the idea that technology varies from nation to nation.

Less developed countries (LDCs), which are labor abundant, economize by using labor intensively, even if they have the same production functions or technology as developed nations. As multinational firms become more prevalent, the same technology becomes more readily available around the world. LDCs send students abroad to become familiar with the latest technology taught in university engineering and agricultural schools. Knowledge quickly becomes a public good. Advantages in technology are difficult to maintain. Many economists argue that technology is a public good and essentially the same all over the world.

One commonly used proxy measure of technology is spending on research and development (R&D). Table 7.3 shows the shares of worldwide spending on R&D in 1983. Developed nations do almost all of the R&D in the world and must have some edge in new technology. Some of this R&D activity is aimed at labor-saving production techniques. In 1985, 27% of U.S. exports were goods using a high intensity of R&D, while only 9% used a low intensity of R&D. The United States will continue to develop and exploit its comparative advantage in high-technology goods. Exporting goods with high levels of R&D relates to another theory of international trade, the product cycle.

2. The Product Cycle and Trade

Many new products require a substantial amount of R&D. This R&D is costly for the firm, which must hope for future profit in selling the new product so the cost of R&D can be recovered. Nations with relatively large supplies of scientists and engineers (the United States, European countries, and Japan) have a comparative advantage in developing new products. Goods produced with established techniques require no R&D. Less developed countries have the comparative advantage in their production.

The pattern of production and trade that the *product cycle* predicts is the export of new products from the developed nations in exchange for old products from the LDCs. As time passes, the new products are picked up by the developing regions and production begins there. Products cycle from new to old and from production in developed countries to less developed countries.

The product cycle is illustrated in Figure 7.11, in which new products are unveiled at times 1 and 2. New goods are exported by the R&D country following the time of their development at time 1. The R&D country holds

TABLE 7.3. Shares of World Research and Development Expenditures

Region	Percentage
U.S.	33%
EEC	21%
USSR	18%
Japan	13%
Other developed nations	6%
Eastern bloc	6%
Developing nations	3%

SOURCE: From *Trade and Development Report* (p. 78), United Nation Conference on Trade and Development, 1987, New York: UN.

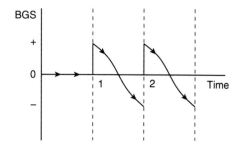

Figure 7.11. The Product Cycle and Trade The research and development (R&D) country is able to create innovations at times 1 and 2. Innovations result in trade surpluses as the new product is exported. R&D leads to new products or cheaper ways to make existing products. Over time, other nations copy the new technology. The R&D country loses its monopoly power and slips into deficit. Innovations lead to new products or cost savings that jump the R&D country back to a surplus.

a monopoly position in the new product and makes high export revenue. As time passes, developing countries learn to make these new products and begin low-cost manufacturing. Soon the developed country becomes a net importer of the good and moves to a trade deficit.

Firms that develop new products may actually plan on eventually being run out of the business but hope to make profits substantial enough to cover R&D costs just after the product is developed. By time 2, the R&D country has come up with another new good to export, net exports turn positive again, and the cycle continues.

> Products cycle from new to old, and their production shifts from innovative countries to copying countries. Nations that put resources into R&D should be net exporters of new products.

Data from the United Nations Committee on Trade and Development (UNCTAD) show that exports of manufactures from developing to developed nations have the largest market shares in the low R&D industries, just as the product cycle predicts. For low, medium, and high R&D industries, these market shares are 25%, 8%, and 12% respectively. In the low R&D category, the largest market shares are in textiles, clothing, footwear, and leather (38% of all low-tech exports together) and petroleum refineries (40% of low-tech exports). While some innovations may be made in the production of these goods, the techniques are well established and very familiar. In the medium R&D category, the largest market share is nonferrous metals (41%), while in the high R&D category the largest is electronic components (29%). Although classified as a high R&D industry, the production of electronic components is largely standardized and routine. Taken together, these figures provide some support for the product cycle.

Trade via the product cycle would perhaps be more prevalent if developed nations did not protect their domestic labor-intensive industries. According to data from GATT, the ratio of manufactured imports from LDCs to total consumption in the United States in 1983 was only 3%. Of the total consumption of manufactures in the United States, only 3% was imports from LDCs. Protection must keep the LDCs from adapting the routine manufacturing processes. U.S. policy gives preferential treatment to some developing nations, but protection of U.S. markets from imports from the LDCs should be gradually eliminated.

EXAMPLE 7.9   R&D and High-Technology Exports

According to a study of the National Science Foundation by John Mutti and Paul Morichi (1983), the United States employs slightly more than half of the world's R&D scientists. This certainly suggests that many new products would be produced in the United States. Since the 1960s, however, the growth rate of R&D scientists in Japan and Europe has been about 5%, while the United States has seen a 1% decline. As percentages of the world's total endowments, the following nations boast an abundance of R&D scientists and skilled labor:

	U.S.	Japan	Germany	U.K.	France	Canada	Other
R&D scientists	51%	13%	10%	9%	6%	2%	9%
Skilled labor	28%	9%	7%	5%	6%	3%	42%

The International Trade Commission (1983) reports that the United States experienced an export surplus of $26 billion in its high-tech industries. These high-tech industries are aircraft, computers, office equipment, electrical equipment, medical equipment, medicines, plastics, engines, chemicals, and scientific instruments. A good share of the products in these categories are new and innovative. An abundance of R&D scientists and trade via the product cycle may help to account for the U.S. trade surplus in these high-tech products.

3.   Returns to Scale and Trade

Returns to scale refer to the responsiveness of output to changing inputs in a firm's production process. Constant returns to scale (CRS) occur when the same proportional change in all inputs results in a proportionate change in output. For instance, if a firm with CRS doubles its inputs of capital and labor, output will double. With increasing returns to scale (IRS), output would more than double. With decreasing returns to scale (DRS), output would rise but by less than 100%.

There are two sorts of returns to scale: external to the firm and internal to the firm. As an industry expands, transportation, communication, and utility infrastructure tailored to the growing industry develop. Local suppliers become established, workers are trained, and so on. In this manner the *external* returns to scale increase. As output expands, labor and capital become more productive because of these improvements that develop external to the firm.

Internal increasing returns to scale may occur because of the character of the firm's capital equipment. As output rises from low levels, machines are used more efficiently with less stopping and starting. Proportional increases in inputs lead to more than proportionate increases in output with internal IRS. If labor and capital input rise by 50%, output may rise by 60% with internal IRS. Nothing outside the firm changes with internal IRS.

Average cost typically decreases up to a certain output level, the *minimum efficient scale* (MES). Declining average costs reflect internal returns to scale. Figure 7.12 illustrates a typical firm's long-run average cost curve. In the long run the firm chooses its optimal level of capital equipment. The long-run AC curve in Figure 7.12 illustrates the lowest cost of producing the range of outputs (*q*). When there are IRS, AC declines. In the region of CRS, AC is constant. With DRS, AC rises. As the firm expands into high output levels, DRS occurs, perhaps because of problems of organization or communication inside firm. Supervision may become a problem in large-scale firms. Workers may feel only remotely related to the success of a large impersonal organization. There are many reasons to expect DRS at high output levels.

For internal IRS to be important, the firm must be operating at an output that is less than its minimum efficient scale (MES). Any firm producing an output less than its MES could not compete with other firms in the industry at or above their MES. For this reason, firms are typically observed operating in the region of CRS where average costs are flat. Also, DRS has rarely been uncovered in practice.

Imagine two nations identical in every way, with IRS in their production. By itself, IRS would provide an incentive to begin specialization and

Figure 7.12. Internal Returns to Scale of the Firm Average cost (AC) is decreasing with increasing returns to scale (IRS) up to the minimum efficient scale (MES). AC is constant in the region of constant returns to scale (CRS). AC rises when the firm experiences decreasing returns to scale (DRS).

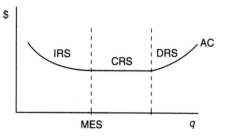

trade. The two nations need only specialize and increase production of their exports. With specialization, world output would be higher. Both nations would enjoy higher income and would potentially consume more of both goods.

It is certain that IRS occurs at low levels of output. When a firm enters an industry, it may be forced to produce low output and operate in the region of declining AC. Economists have estimated the MES of many industries. Firms considering entry into an industry know their MES and would not enter unless they could reach it and effectively compete with other firms in the industry.

While IRS and decreasing average cost may play a role for a particular firm, there is little evidence that they are fundamentally important in determining the overall pattern of trade. Firms tend to operate in the region of CRS.

4.   Income Effects on the Pattern of Trade

Income is one determinant of the sort of goods a nation wants to consume. Nations with higher income typically consume more luxury goods and services. Consumers in low-income nations spend their income on food, shelter, clothing, and other basics. While comparative advantage determines the pattern of production, income helps determine the pattern of consumption.

The *income elasticity* of a good is the percentage change (%Δ) in quantity demanded (Q) divided by the %Δ in income (Y):

$$\text{Income elasticity} = \%\Delta Q / \%\Delta Y$$

Goods with negative income elasticities are called *inferior* goods. Higher income leads to less consumption of inferior goods. Examples of inferior goods are public transport, used clothing, economy cars, and red beans.

Goods with positive income elasticities are called *normal* goods. When income rises, the quantity demanded of a normal good also rises. Most goods are normal.

A good with an income elasticity greater than one is called a *luxury* good. If income rises by 10%, consumption of luxury goods like steaks, foreign travel, imported cheese, and restaurant meals rises by more than 10%.

A positive income elasticity that is less than one makes a good a *necessity*. A 10% increase in income leads to an increase of less than 10% for necessities like food, transportation, housing, and clothing.

Nations with high income tend to import luxury goods while poor nations tend to import inferior goods and necessities.

Figure 7.13 predicts the pattern of trade between DCs and LDCs based on differences in income and income elasticities. If production of inferior goods, necessities, and luxury goods is uniform across nations, LDCs should be net importers of inferior goods and necessities and DCs should be net importers of luxury goods.

The *Linder hypothesis* states that income plays a predominant role in the pattern of international trade. Imports of the high-income industrialized nations do in fact include more luxury goods, while the developing nations do spend a greater portion on imports of necessities. Income and the composition of trade are linked. Nevertheless, income cannot be counted as the fundamental cause of international trade.

Linda Hunter and James Markusen (1988) have studied the effect of income on trade in 10 basic commodities. Their estimates of income elasticities are presented in Table 7.4. The data for these estimates came from 34 countries since 1975. Four of the 10 types of goods examined were found to be necessities: food, furniture, fuel, and education. A 10% increase in income would raise the quantity of food consumed by 4.5%, furniture by 7.6%, fuel and power by 8.1%, and education by 8.7%. Low-income countries should be net importers of these goods.

The rest of the goods were found to be luxuries. For instance, a 10% increase in income brings about a 19.1% increase in medical expenditures, which are not typically viewed as luxury goods. It may be that low-income countries simply rely more on folk medicine and home treatment. Recreation fits more naturally into the concept of a luxury good. The influence of income across nations on consumption patterns is significant. Since income varies across nations, income differences would influence interna-

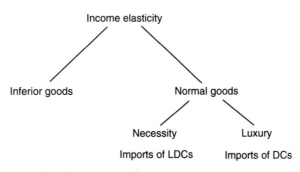

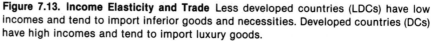

Figure 7.13. Income Elasticity and Trade Less developed countries (LDCs) have low incomes and tend to import inferior goods and necessities. Developed countries (DCs) have high incomes and tend to import luxury goods.

TABLE 7.4. Estimated Income Elasticities

	Income Elasticity
Food	0.45
Furniture	0.76
Fuel and power	0.81
Education	0.87
Clothing and shoes	1.00
Beverage and tobacco	1.23
Recreation	1.42
Transport and communication	1.72
Rent	1.74
Medical	1.91

SOURCE: From *Empirical Methods for International Trade*, (p. 96) by Robert Feenstra (Ed.), 1988, Cambridge, MA: MIT Press. Copyright 1988 by MIT Press. Reprinted by permission.

tional trade, but Hunter and Markusen find no empirical connection between income and international trade.

5. The Bottom Line on the Other Theories of Trade

The alternative theories in this section contribute to an overall understanding of international trade. In particular markets, one or the other of these other theories may explain some of the observed trade. Much has been learned by applying these different ideas to particular issues in international trade. Nevertheless, the factor proportions theory remains the fundamental tool for explaining international patterns of production and trade. The central importance of the factor proportions theory cannot be overemphasized. Relative abundance of labor, different skills of labor, productive capital, and resources is the fundamental cause of international trade.

Problems for Section D

D1. If the home nation has better technology for producing food and the foreign nation has better technology for producing clothing, draw their production possibilities frontiers. Suppose they are identical otherwise. Show the pattern of specialization and trade.

D2. Would it be wiser for the United States to spend resources protecting its automobile industry or developing new products?

D3. What do income elasticities predict regarding international trade in inferior goods? luxury goods? necessities? What must be assumed about production?

CONCLUSION

The industrial organization is this chapter adds depth to the basic explanations of international trade in the factor proportions model. In particular international markets, monopoly power and oligopolistic competition are important. International economics does not turn its back on any ideas that might help explain trade in particular circumstances. Still, the basics of factor proportions trade remain the heart of international economics. In the next section the important topics of international migration of labor, international flows of capital, and international economic integration are developed.

KEY TERMS

Cartel quota	Luxury good
Collusion	Minimum efficient scale (MES)
Contestable market	Monopolistic competition
Credible threat	Necessity
Dominant and fringe firms	Oligopoly
Income elasticity	Price discrimination and dumping
Inferior good	Price taker versus price searcher
International duopoly	Product cycle
International monopoly	Product differentiation
Intraindustry trade	Returns to scale
Kinked demand curve	Technology
Legal versus natural monopoly	Trigger price mechanism

KEY POINTS

- Price-searching monopolistic firms find the quantity and price that maximize their profit, restricting output and raising price relative to their competition. A tariff on imports from a foreign monopolist takes away some of the monopolist's profit.
- Product differentiation is a source of monopoly power and can lead to intraindustry trade in monopolistically competitive industries. The level of product differentiation and intraindustry trade increases as goods are aggregated into broader categories.
- Firms in an international oligopoly have an incentive to collude, forming a producer cartel to collect monopoly profit. Depending on the structure of payoffs and strategic behavior, oligopolies can be as competitive as industries with many firms.
- There are alternative theories of international trade, including different technologies, the product cycle, income differences, and increasing returns to scale. Factor proportions theory, however, remains the fundamental explanation of international trade.

REVIEW PROBLEMS

1. Complete Figure 7.1 with an average cost curve for a domestic firm showing total profit of $300,000. Illustrate zero profit for a foreign firm. Which firm has higher costs? Could the high-cost firm compete?

2. Suppose a new labor contract and rising energy costs raise the home firm's cost in Figure 7.1 so that output drops to 1,000. What is the price from the domestic firm in this situation? Predict the change in its profit. Is demand elastic? If all production is exported, what happens to export revenue?

3. Suppose a monopolist has two plants, one in the United States and one in Mexico. The Mexican plant has lower unit costs. Which plant will produce more? How does the monopolist determine the price of its total output?

4. Find the monopoly's profit in the example of price discrimination in Figure 7.5. Break profit down into profit from domestic sales and profit from foreign sales.

5. The following costs have been estimated from steel firms' operations in the United States and Japan by Peter Marcus in *Comparative Circumstances of Major Steel Mills in the US, European Community, and Japan* (1982). Numbers represent costs per ton of steel for labor, capital machinery, and material inputs:

	Labor	Capital	Inputs
U.S.	$209	$134	$330
Japan	$97	$171	$291

   Which country spends relatively more on labor input? What are two possible reasons? If it costs $100 per ton to ship steel to the United States, find the cost of Japanese steel in the United States if Japanese profit is zero. If Japanese producers make a 2% rate of profit, find the price of Japanese steel in the United States. Would U.S. producers want to allow less than 2% profit for the Japanese producers? Where will U.S. producers want the trigger price to be set?

6. Using the cost data in the previous problem, suppose the ratio of wages to capital rent *(w/r)* is 1 in Japan and 1.4 in the United States. Does the country with relatively expensive labor use labor-intensive production techniques?

7. Explain which category of good is likely to have more intraindustry trade: yarn or medical products; computers or IBM PC compatible computers? Which category of each will have less price dispersion?

8. In the international aircraft industry, suppose there is a dominant domestic firm and a competitive foreign fringe. At a price below $3 million, the foreign fringe cannot compete. At prices above $10 million, the fringe will take over the market. Diagram this market with an international price of $7 million. Show the effects on market shares of an increase in domestic costs resulting from a new labor contract.

9. Find the index *I* of intraindustry trade (see Example 7.3) for the following categories of goods. Figures are in million of dollars for 1985. Compare and explain the level of intraindustry trade in each good:

	Exports	Imports
Footwear	$128	$354
Cotton	$1671	$258

TABLE 7.5. An International Oil Game (Saudi Arabia's Profit, Libya's Profit)

		Libya	
		Low	High
Saudi Arabia	Low	(30,10)	(−20,40)
	High	(40,−30)	(0,0)

Leather	$287	$425
Leather goods	$121	$374
Toys and games	$271	$2968
Automotive electric equipment	$443	$568

10. Table 7.5 presents an duopoly game between Saudi Arabia and Libya in the international oil market. Figures are economic profits in million of dollars. The first figure in parentheses is Saudi Arabia's profit. Find the Nash equilibrium. Is the Nash equilibrium stable? Who has the greater incentive to cheat on a collusive cartel agreement where output is restricted? Can the other producer do anything to discourage cartel cheating?

11. Classify the following as internal or external returns to scale:
    (a) Labor in the firm becomes more experienced
    (b) A better port is built near the factory
    (c) Bigger imported machines result in lower unit costs
    (d) Public schools and education are improved
    (e) International phone system is improved

12. Show what happens over time to the production possibilities frontier as a nation specializes in manufactures when there are external increasing returns to scale. What happens to the level of trade with the external increasing returns to scale?

READINGS

Roger Blair and David Kaserman, *Antitrust Economics,* Irwin, Chicago, 1985. Develops the tools of modern industrial organization and regulation.

P.K.M. Tharakan and Jacob Kol, editors; *Intra-industry Trade: Theory, Evidence, and Extensions,* Macmillan, New York, 1989. A collection of articles on the frontier of thought in intraindustry trade.

Stefan Linder, *An Essay on Trade and Transformation,* Wiley, New York, 1961. Linder's own statement of the Linder hypothesis.

Paul Krugman, editor, *Strategic Trade Policy and the New International Economics,* MIT Press, Cambridge, MA, 1986. A collection of articles on topical issues in international economics.

Ryuzo Sato and Paul Wachtel, editors, *Trade Friction and Prospects for Japan and the United States,* Cambridge University Press, Cambridge, Eng, 1987. A collection of articles by leading economists on trade problems between the United States and Japan.

Yves Bourdet, *International Integration, Market Structure and Prices,* Routledge, London, 1988. A book on the wide range of issues raised through international industrial integration and different market structures.

Raymond Vernon, editor, *The Technology Factor in International Trade,* National Bureau of Economic Research, Washington, DC, 1970. An excellent collection of studies on the role of technology in trade.

PART FOUR

International Factor Movements and Economic Integration

CHAPTER 8

International Labor Migration and Capital Movement

CHAPTER PREVIEW

This chapter presents the principles of the theories of international migration of labor and capital movements. The important issue of income redistribution results from these international labor and capital movements is studied. International migration has shaped many of the nations of the world. International movement of productive capital equipment and machinery has stimulated most successful economic development. The main points of this chapter are:

(a) *International labor migration* is generally created by wage differences across nations

(b) *International capital movements* are similarly the result of international differences in the return to capital

(c) International movements of labor and capital *redistribute income* in both the source and the host countries

(d) International factor movements alter the international pattern of *production* and *trade*

INTRODUCTION

Relative to most other nations, the United States is populated by recent immigrants. There have been periods of massive immigration into the United States. From 1850 until World War I the rate of immigration averaged almost 1% of the population every year. If such a rate were to occur this year, a new city of almost 3 million could be filled. In the first part of this century, 1 million people per year immigrated, about the same as current estimates of legal and illegal immigration. The U.S. Census Bureau predicts San Antonio will become the second largest city in the United States, largely because of immigration.

When people leave their homes and emigrate to a land with strange language and customs, they typically are looking for higher wages and a better standard of living, although political repression and other considerations can play a role. When the wage in one nation is higher than the wage in another nation, workers have an incentive to migrate. For migration to occur, the international difference in wages has to be large enough to offset costs of relocation and readjustment.

Capital also moves between countries. Current international movements of productive capital input are large by historical standards. International markets for productive capital are very active. In the classical and factor proportions theories of international trade, it is assumed that the endowment of capital is fixed. This may be a reasonable place to start building an understanding of international trade, but international capital movement is a vital part of the trade and development of most economies.

International flows of productive capital are created by the potential to earn higher returns across national borders. If you own a turret lathe (or stock in a firm that does), you want it employed where it can earn the highest return. As its owner, you receive rent or return from its productive employment. If the return to this capital is higher in Mexico, the owner wants it located there. As with labor, the incentive to relocate capital internationally is based on differing returns across nations.

Since the turn of the century, the United States has typically held more than twice as much capital abroad as foreigners have held in the United States. In the 1980s this ratio declined. In 1985 the net U.S. international investment position turned negative. In 1985 the United States had a total of $952 billion worth of investment abroad, while foreigners had $1,060 billion worth of investment in the United States. The accounting process of the Department of Commerce, however, undervalues U.S. assets abroad, which are kept at their historical cost level. In 1987 the reported net debt was $368 billion, or about $4,000 per household. The United States holds net credit positions with Canada and Latin America, and net debit positions with Europe and Japan.

Nations restrict international movements of labor and capital. There are various incentives to erect legal barriers to the free flow of workers and foreign investment. Laws in one nation might keep immigrants out, while laws in another nation might keep international capital out. The border between the United States and Mexico is a fine example. U.S. laws keeps Mexicans from freely entering into the U.S. labor market, where the wage is substantially higher than in Mexico. Mexican law hinders U.S. investment in Mexico, where the return to capital is higher than in the United States. The primary economic consideration shaping policy on labor migration and international capital flows is the redistribution of income and the altered pattern of production these shifting factor supplies create.

When unskilled labor immigrates, the wage of unskilled workers in the nation falls because of the increase in supply. When productive capital leaves the nation, the return to the plant and equipment remaining in the nation rises because of the decrease in supply. These effects can be understood by looking at the markets for these particular factors of production. The marginal revenue product or demand for an input interacts with its supply. Across nations, an international pattern of factor returns evolves.

Prices of other productive factors are also influenced by international factor movements. Suppose, for instance, the immigration of doctors is stopped. Some productive inputs will benefit, while others will lose. Because of the decrease in competition, doctors inside the country see their wage rise or stay higher than it would be with the immigration. Nurses, on the other hand, become less productive and less valuable with the lower level of cooperating input. Capital equipment in the medical industry is also less productive than it would be with the immigrating doctors. This income redistribution occurs with restrictions on international movements of productive factors. The price of medical services increases with the higher wage of doctors. Since consumers spend more on medical care, demand and prices for other goods are affected. Outputs adjust all across the economy.

These issues can be understood through considering the interactions between markets for the various types of goods, services, and inputs (labor, capital, and natural resources). A workable complete picture of the economy, including the various input markets, is important for the study of international factor movements. One goal of microeconomics is a general equilibrium picture of how the entire economy works and hold together. This chapter continues the development of the general equilibrium approach to international production and trade.

A. INTERNATIONAL LABOR MIGRATION

This section examines the economic principles of international labor migration. A comparison of labor markets across nations provides a picture of the fundamental cause of migration. The market for a productive factor (labor, capital, or natural resources) is made up of its supply and demand. As in markets for goods and services, price or value is determined by the market equilibrium. Labor markets determine the wage of electrical engineers, school teachers, construction workers, and so on. Capital markets determine the return to investments in oil refining, the iron and steel industry, the computer industry, and so on.

1. Marginal Revenue Product and Marginal Factor Cost

Demand for a productive factor comes from its value to the firms that would hire it. A firm gains revenue by selling the output that productive factors contribute to producing. A firm's demand for a factor of production amounts to the value of what the input produces. A factor's *marginal revenue product* (MRP) is the marginal revenue (MR) of the good sold times the factor's marginal product (MP):

$$MRP = MR \times MP$$

The MRP of an input indicates the value to the firm of the last unit of that particular input hired. Suppose the MR of an extra unit of output is constant at the market price of $2. Each unit of output produced can be sold for $2, creating marginal or additional revenue of $2. If the MP of an extra worker is 5 units of output, the MRP of the added worker is MRP = $2 × 5 = $10. Hiring the extra worker brings $10 of revenue to the firm.

A firm would be willing to hire an extra unit of an input if the value of what it produces is greater than the cost to the firm of hiring it. In other words, the input's marginal revenue product must be greater than its *marginal factor cost* (MFC):

$$MRP > MFC$$

The MFC is what it costs the firm to hire an extra unit of the input. In a competitive labor market the firm can hire any number of workers it wants at the market wage. The market wage is then the MFC. If the MFC of an extra worker is $8/hour, while the MRP is $10/hour, the firm will increase its profit at a rate of $2/hour by hiring the worker.

2. Labor Supply and Demand

In Figure 8.1 the MRP of labor for a hypothetical firm is illustrated. This firm will hire 30 workers if the MFC = $5, 20 workers if MFC = $10, only 10 workers if MFC rises to $15, and no workers at all if MFC $20. The firm

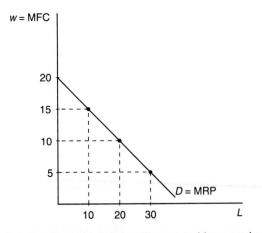

Figure 8.1. A Firm's Labor Demand A firm will want to hire a worker as long as the worker's marginal revenue product (MRP) is greater than the worker's marginal factor cost (MFC). Lower wages would induce the firm to hire more workers. Higher wages would cause the firm to hire fewer workers. The industry's demand for labor is the horizontal sum of every firm's demand.

in Figure 8.1 is assumed to be a price taker in the labor market, hiring the amount of labor it wants at the market wage.

Labor demand for an industry is the sum of the labor demands of all the firms in the industry. Labor demand in the economy is the sum of all industrial demands for labor and would slope downward like the individual firm's demand in Figure 8.1.

The economy's *labor market* is illustrated in Figure 8.2. Labor supply is pictured as a vertical line at 10 million workers. This labor supply is drawn as perfectly inelastic, meaning that workers in this market will accept any wage. Labor economics is concerned largely with examining the properties of labor supply. Some evidence indicates that labor supply slopes upward at low wages but bends back at higher wages. If wages become high enough, some workers choose to supply fewer hours of labor and enjoy more leisure. The vertical labor supply in Figure 8.2 is not crucial for the results that follow, but simplifies the market analysis.

This labor market clears where labor demand equals labor supply at a wage of $15. If the wage is above $15, there is a surplus of labor. Fewer than 10 million workers would be demanded at a wage of $18, and unemployment arises. Rather than remain unemployed, workers offer to work for less than $18, and the wage is bid down toward the equilibrium wage of $15. At any wage below $15, there will be a shortage of labor, with the quantity of labor demanded greater than the quantity of labor supplied. At a wage of $12, firms would compete for the available workers by bidding up the wage. Labor markets clear much like other markets. The equilibrium market wage equates quantity supplied with quantity demanded.

3.   International Wages: The Jevons Diagram

Figure 8.3 presents the picture of how international wages are determined in a *Jevons diagram*. British economist Stanley Jevons developed this technique over 100 years ago. For simplicity, assume there are only two nations.

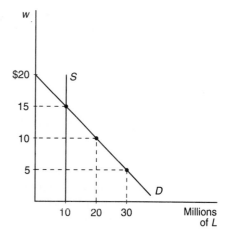

Figure 8.2. A Simple Labor Market Total labor demand is the sum of the demand or MRPs of every firm in the economy. Labor supply S is assumed to be inelastic or vertical for simplicity. This labor market (L) clears at the market wage (w) of $15.

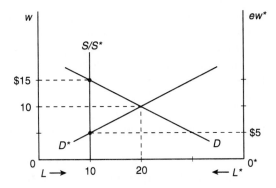

Figure 8.3. A Jevons Diagram of the International Labor Market The home labor market with demand *D* and wage *w* is measured from the left and origin 0. The foreign labor market with demand *D** and wage *ew** is measured from the right and origin 0*. There are 10 (million) workers in the home country and 30 (million) workers in the foreign country, as indicated by the relative supply line *S/S**. Wages are $15 at home and $5 abroad given the current relative supplies of labor.

Domestic demand for labor *D* is measured from the vertical axis labeled *w* on the left side. Foreign demand for labor *D** is measured from the vertical axis labelled *ew** on the right side. The foreign wage *w** is made comparable with the domestic wage *w* by the exchange rate *e*, which is assumed to be constant. The foreign wage in terms of the domestic currency is *ew**.

The length of the bottom axis represents the total endowment of labor in the two nations taken together. In this example, both nations taken together have a total of 40 million workers. The amount of home labor *L* is measured from the left, while the amount of foreign labor *L** is measured from the right.

The vertical supply line (*S/S**) drawn at *L* = 10 indicates that 10 million workers are located in the home nation and 30 million are located abroad. Demand for labor in the two nations is the same in this example, but the home supply of labor is relatively low. The home wage is found where home demand for labor intersects the supply line. The home wage is a relatively high $15. Foreign labor supply is relatively high, and the foreign wage is a relatively low $5.

If there are no migration laws, workers are free to come and go between the two countries as they please. This occurs in common markets like the European Community. Negotiations for a common market between the United States and Canada are proceeding.

To keep the story simple, imagine that only slight cultural differences and little distance separate the two hypothetical nations in Figure 8.3. Readjustment and relocation costs are assumed for the moment to be zero.

With free migration policy and zero costs of relocation, foreign workers have every reason to *emigrate* (leave their country) and go to the home country where the wage is higher. Emigration decreases the abundant supply of labor in the foreign country. Labor *immigration* into the home nation increases its scarce labor supply. The labor supply line S/S^* in Figure 8.3 shifts to the right with this labor migration.

With no costs of relocation or readjustment and no migration laws, migration would continue until the wage rates are equal internationally. This equilibrium occurs where $w = ew^* = \$10$ with 20 million workers located in each nation. With this migration, world output rises because labor is moving to a capital-abundant area where its marginal productivity is higher.

> A Jevons diagram shows how the distribution of a resource across nations affects the international pattern of resource prices. Relative abundance of labor means low wages, while relative scarcity results in high wages.

When migration occurs, the host country enjoys an expanding resource base, while the source country sees its resource base declining. In terms of overall production possibilities and national income, the host country gains and the source country loses. Migrant workers typically repatriate part of their earnings, which can compensate the source nation, especially if wages in the host country are much higher. More important for workers left in the source nation, the wage of relatively cheap labor begins to rise. Workers who remain in the source nation benefit through the higher wages that result from the emigration.

4. Trade as a Substitute for Migration

It is important to remember that free trade between the two nations also tends to lead to the international equalization of wages. This is the thrust of the factor price equalization result in the factor proportions model. Generally, trade increases the demand for cheap goods and the demand for the cheap inputs used intensively in their production. Trade thus serves as a substitute for factor migration. With free international trade, incentive for international migration decreases. With protectionism, incentive for international migration increases.

Consider the international labor market in Figure 8.4. If capital endowments are similar, the foreign country is labor abundant and labor cheap in autarky. The demands for labor in the two countries in autarky are labeled D_A and D_A^*. These are the same levels of labor demand pictured in Figure 8.3. Supplies or endowments of labor remain at $L = 10$ and $L^* = 30$.

If free trade begins between these two countries, the foreign country will export the labor-intensive good to the home country. The price of the labor-intensive good rises in the foreign country. The demand for labor rises in the foreign country, shifting from D_A^* to D_T^* in Figure 8.4. The demand for labor in the foreign country with free trade is D_T^*.

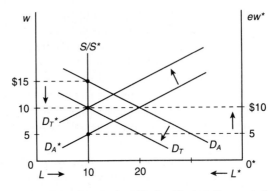

Figure 8.4. Free Trade and the International Labor Market Demands for labor in autarky are the same as those in Figure 8.3: D^*_A in the foreign country and D_A in the home country. With free trade, the labor-abundant foreign country increases its production of the labor intensive good, and D^*_A rises to D^*_T. In the home country, production of the labor-intensive good falls, as does the demand for labor (from D_A to D_T). With free trade, wages are equalized at $w = ew^* = \$10$.

Simultaneously, the home country lowers its production of the labor-intensive good. Price of the labor-intensive good falls in the home country. Demand for labor in the home country falls from D_A to D_T in Figure 8.4. In this example the equilibrium with free trade occurs where D_T intersects D_T^* at a common international wage of $w = ew^* = \$10$.

Free trade in this example raises the wage in the labor-abundant country and lowers the wage in the labor-scarce country through the shifting of factor demands. Factor demands shift because of changes in prices. Labor migration, on the other hand, shifts supplies to raise the wage in the labor-abundant country and lower the wage in the labor-scarce country.

> An important lesson is that international trade can act as a substitute for international factor migration.

This substitution of free trade for factor migration is a large part of the motivation for negotiations leading to the free trade agreement among the United States, Canada, and Mexico. With wages rising in Mexico owing to increased production of labor-intensive goods and higher demand for labor, the incentive for illegal emigration to the United States and Canada will be lowered.

Free trade is a politically acceptable alternative to immigration in the United States. The choice faced by the United States is whether freely to accept imported manufactured goods from Latin America and the Caribbean basin or to continue to invite immigration (both legal and illegal). An important result of free trade is the decrease in incentive for the migration it creates.

Labor migration creates more international efficiency as labor moves where its productivity and wage are higher. Free trade creates similar efficiency gains through specialization. Protectionism discourages free trade while encouraging labor migration. A labor-scare country like the United States can discourage immigration by trading freely. In a protected country, each of the two alternatives, free trade and free migration, creates hardships and the need for readjustment. Labor migration, workers leaving their home and culture, is the more costly way to gain international efficiency.

5. Legal Immigration into the United States

There are many different types of labor: physicians, laborers, engineers, butchers, machinists, accountants, bakers, college professors, fast food workers, migrant farm workers, and so on. Information would come from examining the markets for each type of labor individually. This is part of what you want to do in choosing a profession. Given that you would enjoy two careers equally, which promises higher wages? High demand and low supply are the two basic influences creating higher wages. Hakeem Olajawon of the National Basketball Association receives high wages for playing basketball because of his high marginal revenue product (high demand) and the limited supply of quick agile people who happen to be seven feet tall. Olajawon, who moved to the United States from Nigeria, also provides an example of profitable international labor migration. People who make the highest wages are the most productive in the most lucrative industries. People who make the lowest wages are the least productive in the industries producing goods with falling prices. Since every worker prefers higher wages to lower wages, it is important to understand what creates the difference.

The U.S. Census Bureau keeps records on various skilled groups of workers, listed in Table 8.1. The groups are listed from the highest paid (and most skilled) at the top to the lowest paid (and least skilled) at the bottom. Projections of future wages in more detailed occupations should interest college students faced with making career choices. It is discourag-

TABLE 8.1. U.S. Census Skilled Labor Groups

L1 = professionals
L2 = craft, repair workers
L3 = transportation workers
L4 = operatives (machine operators, etc.)
L5 = administrative support, sales personnel
L6 = handlers and laborers
L7 = agricultural, forestry, fishing workers
L8 = janitors, restaurant workers, etc.

SOURCE: From *Census of Population*, U.S. Census Bureau.

ing to spend the time and resources to train for a particular occupation only to find that wages have fallen because of increased labor supply (perhaps from immigration) or decreased demand (perhaps from an industry declining in the face of international competition).

Handlers and laborers, agricultural workers, and service workers are the lowest paid labor and the groups most Latin American immigrants to the United States enter. This immigration keeps the relative wages of these relatively unskilled workers low. Since many union members compete directly with the immigrants, it is no accident that the AFL-CIO has long favored strict enforcement of tight immigration laws. The unions suffer a weakened position for bargaining and lower wages with the higher labor supply produced by immigration. On the other hand, farmers and business people who hire the immigrant workers benefit directly through the increase in the supply of labor and lower wages. The wages of other groups of workers are affected indirectly along with the pattern of production.

The wage for incoming unskilled workers in the United States is typically much higher than the wage they would receive in their source nations. The United States has a relative scarcity of labor and large amounts of cooperating capital, skilled labor, and natural resources. The high levels of cooperating capital, skilled labor, and natural resources increase labor productivity.

The wage of each type of labor would be depressed by its immigration and raised by its emigration. When Congress cut off the immigration of foreign-trained physicians in the 1970s, the main beneficiaries were domestic physicians. It should come as no surprise that the American Medical Association (AMA) lobbied heavily for the cutoff, arguing that the quality of foreign doctors is low. The supply of doctors declined, and their wage was kept high. The AMA also restricts enrollment at medical schools to keep the supply of physicians low and the wages of those already in the profession high. Physicians in the United States are highly paid relative to physicians in other nations due largely to the restrictive monopolistic practices of the AMA. Relaxing the restrictive immigration policy would lead to an inflow of foreign doctors and lower medical bills.

The United States has attracted many skilled workers from around the world. The *brain drain* refers to an emigration of skilled workers from the source nation's viewpoint. Consider the resources spent by developing countries such as Taiwan, India, Korea, Nigeria, and others to train engineers, scientists, doctors, and other skilled workers who subsequently emigrate to a developed nation where they can earn better wages. Many students from less developed countries (LDCs) are sent to study in the United States or Europe and end up staying to work in the developed country. The brain drain must hinder development in the source nations. Since skilled labor is scarce in these developing countries, economic theory suggests their wage would be higher there. Often, however, there is not enough productive capital for the skilled workers. Industry in the developing country may not have progressed to the point where it can employ electronic engineers and neurosurgeons.

In the 1970s there was an influx of Vietnamese political refugees who were skilled and semiskilled workers into the United States. As they entered the United States, wages in their line of work were depressed. A lively example of this competition occurred along the Texas Gulf Coast when Vietnamese shrimpers entered what had been a closely knit local group. The price of shrimp fell considerably as did the wages of shrimpers, but not without some incidents of violence aimed at the new immigrants.

When workers immigrate, payments to other sorts of labor as well as capital and natural resources (land) are affected. Groups that are hurt by the immigration will call for stricter quotas. Groups that are helped by the immigration can be expected to favor letting the immigration continue. Without a doubt, immigration raises national income and generally stimulates economic development.

> Examining the income redistribution caused by international labor movements holds the key to understanding why some groups favor inflows and some groups do not.

6. Illegal Immigration into the United States

Immigration laws in the United States are selective in who will be admitted. Only a certain quota from any particular nation is admitted each year on economic grounds. There have been calls to institute a program similar to the Bracero Program, which lasted from 1942 to 1964 and allowed immigrant workers to legally work part of each year inside the United States. Temporary workers may now enter the United States for limited periods if employers verify their employment.

Many workers cross into the United States from Latin America as illegal immigrants. The risk of being detained must enter into the decision making of a potential illegal immigrant, but those costs are generally outweighed by the international difference in wages. Many farms, restaurants, and other small businesses depend entirely on immigrant workers.

For the potential migrant the gains from illegal immigration must be weighed against the costs. Part of this cost is the penalty when caught, which can be discounted by the probability of being caught. Current laws penalize firms that hire illegal immigrants, but enforcement is not proving workable. There is simply too much to gain through immigration, for the workers as well as the firms and locales employing them. *Illegal immigration* is likely to persist in the United States.

Illegal immigration can be reduced in two basic ways: by lowering its marginal benefits or by raising its marginal costs. Figure 8.5 illustrates the decision facing a potential illegal immigrant. The marginal benefit (MB) schedule illustrates the difference between wages in the host and source

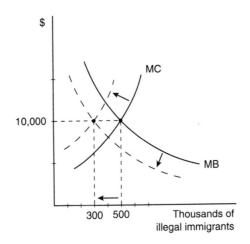

Figure 8.5. Controlling Illegal Immigration The marginal benefit MB schedule represents the perceived marginal benefits from migration for the potential migrant. Marginal cost (MC) is the cost of making the move. The quantity of illegal immigration can be controlled by lowering the MB of migrants and raising their MC.

and host countries. As more illegals enter, wages fall in the host country and rise in the source country, which means MB slopes down. The marginal cost (MC) schedule reflects the costs of relocation and adjustment. The MC curve also contains the costs of detainment and penalties if caught.

Currently about 500,000 illegals enter the United States per year. To reduce this quantity, MB can be lowered or MC can be raised. Making it harder for firms to hire illegals will reduce MB. Free trade between the two countries would reduce MB by lessening the wage difference. Increased patrolling of the border and stiffer penalties if caught raise the MC schedule.

> The main cause of illegal immigration is a large difference in wages between the source and host countries. Any solution to illegal immigration must take this inequity into account. Free trade, it should be remembered, will reduce the international difference in wages.

EXAMPLE 8.1   U.S. Immigration and Population

The United states has a history of allowing political refugees to immigrate. Currently, refugees from any totalitarian state are accepted: Chinese, Vietnamese, North Koreans, and so on. These data from the U.S. Immigration and Naturalization Service (1989) summarize historical levels of migration. Before 1940, most immigrants were European. Since 1960, immigrants have come mostly from politically troubled areas. The last column shows what the current population of the offspring of the immigrants would be, given a conservative 1% growth rate. As an example, the 750,000 immigrants mostly from Ireland, Britain, and Germany who entered between 1820 and 1840 would have 7.3 million offspring today. The sum of this last column is about equal to the current U.S. population, illustrating the point that the United States is a nation of recent immigrants. Almost 40% of this 248 million arises from immigration during the 1900s. The largest single group are those who entered during the first 20 years of this century. These immigrants make up about 30% of your generation's great-grandparents.

Years	Sources	Million	Growth to
1820–40	Ireland, Britain, Germany	0.75	7.3
1841–60	Ireland, Britain, Germany	4.31	36.8
1861–80	Germany, Scotland, China	5.13	37.6
1881–1900	Italy, Austria-Hungary, Russia, Turkey	8.93	54.5
1901–20	Austria-Hungary, Italy, Russia, Turkey, Japan, Mexico	14.53	70.9
1921–40	Italy, Germany, Poland, Canada	4.64	17.0
1941–60	Germany, Mexico	3.55	8.7
1961–80	Mexico, Cuba, Philippines, Vietnam, Korea	7.81	9.5
1981–88	Korea, China, Vietnam, Mexico, Central America	4.71	5.1
			248

EXAMPLE 8.2   International Labor Growth

These data from the World Bank's *World Development Report 1988* summarize labor growth trends since 1965 and project future growth. Growth rates are highest in the labor-abundant developing economies and lowest in the developed industrialized economies. The labor-abundant nations must be working hard to maintain their comparative advantage! International specialization and trade decrease the pressures caused by relatively low wages in the LDCs. The desire to emigrate to the developed nations can be expected to continue.

	1965–80	*1980–86*	*1986–2000*
Developing economies	2.3%	2.0%	2.0%
Oil exporters	2.7%	2.7%	2.5%

Manufacturing exporters	2.2%	1.6%	1.5%
Africa	2.7%	3.1%	3.2%
Developed economies	0.8%	0.6%	0.4%
U.S.	1.0%	1.0%	0.6%

EXAMPLE 8.3   A Profile of Current U.S. Immigration

These are some statistics on U.S. immigration from the *Census of Population* (1986). The population of foreign born indicates the current stocks of immigrants born in other countries. Of these, the estimated percentage of illegal residents from each area is listed. The legal immigration from each region in 1985, as reported by the Immigration and Naturalization Service, is also listed. The largest population of foreign-born residents comes from Europe, and very few are illegal. Only 11% of the legal immigrants in 1985 were from Europe. Asia accounts for about half as much foreign-born population as Europe, but currently has a higher level of immigration. More than half of the Mexican-born population in the United States is illegal. Similarly, a high percentage of Latin Americans from Central America, the Caribbean, and South America are illegals. Since wages in the United States and Canada are similar, Canadians have little economic incentive to migrate to the United States.

Origin	Current Foreign-Born Residents	Percent Illegal	1985 Immigration
Europe	5,153,000	3	63,000
Asia	2,534,000	8	264,000
Mexico	2,196,000	51	61,000
Central America and Caribbean	1,619,000	20	109,000
Canada	845,000	3	11,000
South America	563,000	23	39,000

EXAMPLE 8.4   International Differences in Wages

Production workers are relatively unskilled workers who are trained to work on assembly lines. Wages paid production workers vary tremendously worldwide. Firms considering setting up assembly line manufacturing operations must realize the international differences in wages. There are other considerations in the decision of where to locate a plant: local taxes, work habits of the locals, transport costs of different locations, familiarity with local customs, laws, and language, and so on. Nevertheless, international differences in wages are large enough to be overwhelming. Nations with the five highest and five lowest hourly production wages, according to *The World Competitiveness Report, 1990,* are listed below. Manufacturing production can generally be expected to locate in countries with lower production wages.

Norway	$18.92
Switzerland	$18.08
Germany	$18.03
Sweden	$16.82
Netherlands	$16.29
•	
•	
•	
Mexico	$1.57
Brazil	$1.50
Hungary	$1.22
India	$0.42
Turkey	$0.41

Problems for Section A

A1. Find the wages in each nation that would result from the immigration of 5 million workers to the home nation from the foreign country in Figure 8.3.

A2. Suppose the relocation and readjustment cost is $2/hour in Figure 8.3. In other words, if the wage rate at home is more than $2 greater at home than abroad, workers migrate. Find the equilibrium distribution of labor between the two nations when there is no immigration quota. How many workers emigrate from the foreign country?

A3. Name other ways to reduce the illegal immigration in Figure 8.5 by reducing MB and raising MC.

B. INTERNATIONAL MOVEMENT OF CAPITAL

This section presents the basic theory of international capital movement. Owners of productive capital input seek the highest return internationally. Capital owners want their input located where it earns the highest return. Capital may be more mobile internationally than labor because people do not have to move with the capital they own. Capital machinery and equipment can be "rented" across borders. The owner of capital can be in one country, while the capital is employed in another country.

1. Forms of International Capital Movement

When a firm based in one nation builds a branch plant in another nation and controls the branch plant operation, the activity is called foreign direct investment. When an individual or an investing firm buys a foreign firm's stock or bonds and no control is involved, it is called portfolio foreign investment. Both sorts of international investment are becoming increasingly important to the world's economy. The total stock of $952 billion of direct foreign investment by the United States abroad represents about $10,500 per U.S. household. This large figure reflects the importance of the transfer of productive capital across nations.

Capital, in the form of productive machinery and equipment, provides the means to produce more and better goods and services. Most developing economies rely heavily on foreign developed nations for this productive capital. A great deal of direct investment also occurs between developed nations. Foreign investment accounted for much of the recovery of the U.S. automobile industry in the 1980s. Much of this foreign investment was put in place to avoid the persistent protectionism of autos in the United States. Japanese and European firms producing cars inside the United States do not face protectionism against imports from their own country.

The international integration of investment activity is also reflected in *stock markets*, which have become internationally integrated. Stocks represent ownership of firms, either by other firms or by private investors. Major portfolios contain stocks and bonds from around the world. International diversification has become the buzzword of investment companies. Investment houses routinely offer connections with stock markets worldwide. The average person with a savings account at a local bank is involved in these international markets. In the long run, the return on a typical savings account relies in part of these foreign markets.

An important difference between international labor movement and international capital movement is that capital earnings are largely repatriated. In the host country, incoming capital raises the productivity and demand for labor and wages. The production possibilities frontier and the value of production both expand. Earnings on the foreign capital, however, are largely sent back to the source country. Labor migration is essentially different in that the owner of the productive resource must move with the resource. When capital comes into an economy, wages rise and the return to capital falls.

2. Jevons Diagram and International Capital Movements

Figure 8.6 presents the fundamental explanation of *international capital mobility*. It should seem familiar, since it is very much like the Jevons diagram for labor. The principles that explain international capital mobility are the same as those that explain labor mobility.

The domestic capital market is plotted from the left. The domestic demand or marginal revenue product of capital slopes downward. The marginal productivity of capital decreases, given a fixed amount of home labor and other resources. Foreign capital demand is plotted from right to left and slopes downward as well.

The payment to capital is expressed as a real percentage return, or the real interest rate. This is the expected percentage return on an investment after taking out expected inflation and expected depreciation of the capital stock. *Depreciation* is the wear and tear on the capital equipment. Suppose expected inflation is 3% and expected depreciation is 2%. A nominal return of 9% would reduce to a 4% real return: $9\% - 3\% - 2\% = 4\%$. For simplicity, it is assumed that there is no inflation and no depreciation in what follows.

The real rate of return can generally be found by dividing the net return to capital by the capital stock and is typically between 2% and 4% in the United States. A 3% return means that $1 invested in capital today will be worth $1.03 after one year. With a 3% real rate of return, $100,000 worth

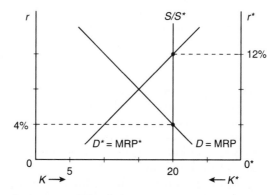

Figure 8.6. An International Capital Market The domestic capital market with demand *D* and return *r* originates from the left and origin 0. The foreign capital market with demand *D** and return *r** is measured from the right and origin 0*. With 20 units of capital at home and 10 units in the foreign country as indicated by the relative supply line *S/S**, the real returns to capital are 4% at home and 12% abroad.

of machinery, equipment, and buildings produces a net worth of $3,000 of output during a year. If additionally the machinery depreciated by $2,000 over the year, $5,000 of output would have to be produced to acquire the 3% real return. The 3% is called the real rate of return, the real interest rate, or the rental rate of capital.

The distribution of the capital endowment between the two nations in Figure 8.6 has 20 units at home and 10 units abroad, as represented by the supply line S/S*. There is a total of 30 units of capital endowment in the two countries taken together. The real return to capital is 4% at home, where the capital supply is high. The return to capital is 12% in the foreign nation, where supply is low. If labor supplies in the two countries are similar, the home country is capital abundant and the foreign country is capital scarce.

The difference in capital rental rates can persist if capital flows between the two nations are impeded. Some nations fear being "bought out" and controlled by foreign interest. Policy is instituted and laws are passed to limit the inflow of capital. There have been recent cries in the United States to keep foreigners from buying farmland and downtown skyscrapers. Mexico historically limited foreign investment, requiring majority ownership by Mexican firms or investors. Japan and Europe also have restrictive capital policies. Every government has some restrictions on the character and size of foreign investment it allows.

When capital is transferred to the foreign economy in Figure 8.6, the relative supply line S/S* shifts left. The real return to capital in the foreign country declines. In the home country the supply of capital falls and the capital rental rate rises. The returns to capital in the two countries move closer together with international capital movement.

Restrictions on foreign investment in the host foreign nation are typically due to efforts on the part of foreign capital owners to keep their input relatively scarce and its return high. Wealth holders can easily influence government policy. If capital is allowed to enter the foreign economy, r^* falls.

In the source home nation, labor wants to keep capital from going abroad because a decreased supply of capital will lower labor's marginal productivity and wage. Restrictions on the international flow of capital can come from both the potential host and the source countries.

Given the opportunity, the owners of home capital in Figure 8.6 will want to invest in the foreign nation. With completely free mobility, an international capital market equilibrium is attained after 5 units of capital have moved from the home to the foreign nation. Each nation then has a stock of 15 units, and the international return to capital settles at 8%. Restrictions on international capital flow would keep the supplies from adjusting all the way to this equilibrium.

International differences in the real return to capital arise because of demands for capital in each country and the given endowments or supplies of capital. If free to move internationally, capital will seek an international equilibrium with the real return to capital equal across countries.

3. Trade as a Substitute for Capital Movement

Free trade has the same effect on the international return to capital as does capital mobility. Just as trade substitutes for labor migration, trade can substitute for capital flows.

The United States is capital abundant and exports capital-intensive business services and high-tech manufactures. The increases in the price of these exports and the higher demand for capital that comes with free trade in the United States push up the return to capital. In the limiting case, free trade can lead to complete factor price equalization between nations and the loss of any motivation for international capital movement.

The return to capital falls in the capital-scarce foreign country with free trade. The return to capital rises in the capital-abundant home country with free trade. Capital-scarce countries are importing capital-intensive goods, and their relative demand for capital falls. Capital-abundant countries are exporting capital-intensive goods, and their relative demand for capital rises.

Free trade in Figure 8.6 would increase the demand for capital in the home country and decrease the demand for capital in the foreign country. Even without capital movement between the two countries, the return to capital can be equalized between them. The important lesson again is that free trade can substitute for free factor mobility.

> International mobility of capital tends to equalize the return to capital across countries. Free trade likewise has the effect of equalizing the return to capital across countries.

4. U.S. Foreign Investment

According to figures from the U.S. Department of Commerce, more than 3,000 U.S. firms have foreign direct investments. Most of the foreign affiliates (71%) are totally owned, while 83% are majority owned. These foreign assets are distributed in the industries in Table 8.2. The remaining 4% of U.S. foreign assets abroad are highly diversified, spread thinly among various industries.

The U.S. assets abroad are located primarily in the nations in Table 8.3. The remaining 8% are highly diversified. OPEC and Mexico, both interesting cases, each have 2% of the total. Investment levels in Mexico and Spain (also 2%) would be higher without their restrictions on foreign investment. Both Mexico and Spain are making moves to relax these restrictions. In Mexico, all firms must currently be majority owned (51%) by Mexican nationals. The Mexican government has worked to ensure that its

TABLE 8.2. Distribution of U.S. Assets in Foreign Industries

Manufacturing	42%
Finance	21%
Oil and coal	16%
Wholesale trade	10%
Banking	5%
Business services	2%
Other	4%

SOURCE: From *Survey of Current Business* (p. 86), U.S. Department of Commerce, August 1990, Washington, DC: U.S. Government Printing Office.

TABLE 8.3. Distribution of U.S. Foreign Assets by Country

Europe	47%
Canada	18%
Latin America	16%
Asia and Pacific	6%
Japan	5%
Other	8%

SOURCE: From *Survey of Current Business* (p. 86), U.S. Department of Commerce, August 1990, Washington, DC: U.S. Government Printing Office.

nation remains capital scarce! Many U.S. firms claim Japan is not receptive to foreign firms and their direct investments, although the Japanese government says it does not discriminate. Each nation presents its own legal and policy environment. Some nations are much more open to foreign investment than others.

The largest foreign investments inside the United States are from Canada, the Netherlands, the United Kingdom, Japan, Germany, France, and Switzerland. The following companies are foreign owned and hold foreign capital in the United States: Seagrams, Shell Oil, Standard Oil, Mitsui, A&P, American Motors, Mack Trucks, Carnation, Nestle, and Philips Petroleum. In 1987, 17% of all foreign assets in the United States were in direct investment. The remaining foreign assets are spread across U.S. stocks and bonds, real estate, and so on.

5. International Investment and Loanable Funds

Capital comes in many different types. Many sorts of equipment, machinery, and buildings exist. In an application to a particular industry, it makes sense to look at the market for a particular type of capital. There is a market for tractor trailers, a market for personal computers, a market for turret lathes, and so on. The capital market in Figure 8.6 represents an average or typical capital good.

The international loanable funds market is an important financial market. In practice, firms borrow to acquire capital equipment. International loanable funds markets work alongside the international market for capital goods. In the financial press the "capital market" refers to the market for loanable funds. It is important to keep the two senses of the word capital (productive capital versus financial capital) separate.

The link between international movements of productive capital and the international loanable funds market is important. When a U.S. real estate company wants to establish a branch operation in England, it can take funds directly out of its U.S. operations or it can borrow. It can borrow in the U.S. loanable funds market or it can go to the U.K. loanable funds market. The loanable funds market is becoming increasingly integrated internationally. The business of banking is adapting itself to the increased level of international trade and investment.

EXAMPLE 8.5   Foreign Direct Investment in the United States

International capital movements result in stocks of capital owned by wealth holders in foreign nations. When firms using foreign-owned capital goods make profits, stockholders abroad must be paid. Some idea of the level of foreign capital is represented by the stock of outstanding direct investment in the United States. These data come from the U.S. Department of Commerce *Survey of Current Business, 1986.* Assuming a 3% real return on this investment, $4.6 billion in net interest payments would have to be paid yearly on these stocks. This is about $18 per capita in the United States.

	Foreign Direct Investment Stock
U.K.	$51.4 bil
Netherlands	$42.9 bil
Japan	$23.4 bil
Canada	$18.3 bil
West Germany	$17.4 bil

EXAMPLE 8.6   U.S. and Japanese Patterns of Direct Investment

According to the *Survey of Current Business, 1986,* the following pattern of net stocks of direct investment exists between the United States and Japan. Figures are in billions of dollars of capital stock, plant, and equipment. The total net figure shows that Japan has a larger stock of capital in the United States than the United States has in Japan. The difference is due almost entirely to Japanese investment in wholesale activity in the United States. This can be taken as indirect evidence that Japanese firms have comparative advantage in wholesaling. Evidence suggests that Japan may now be slightly capital abundant relative to the United States.

	U.S. Capital Stock in Japan (billion)	Japanese Capital Stock in the U.S. (billion)	U.S. Net Capital Stock (billion)
Oil	$2.6	0	$2.6
Manufacturing	$5.3	$3.0	$2.3
Foodstuffs	$0.2	$0.2	0
Chemicals	$1.6	$0.3	$1.3
Metals	$0.1	$0.6	− $0.5
Wholesale	$2.3	$13.0	− $10.7
Banking	$0.2	$2.7	− $2.5
TOTAL	$11.3	$23.4	− $12.1

EXAMPLE 8.7   The Value of the Stock of Foreign Investment

Firms typically value their capital assets at historical cost (the price paid for the assets at the time of investment). Because of inflation and changing market conditions, the market value of a capital asset is typically higher than its historical cost. Using historical cost, the foreign capital stock of U.S. firms is understated relative to the stock of foreign capital in the United States. The market value approach estimates the current value of tangible assets (capital, land, and inventories) and intangible assets (patents and trademarks). *International Economic Conditions* (Federal Reserve Bank of St. Louis, 1991) recently reported a comparison of historical and market estimates of the stocks of foreign intestment. The figures are stated in billions of constant 1980 dollars. The stock of U.S. foreign capital abroad is labelled FK. The stock of foreign capital in the United States is labelled FK*. At historical value, the foreign capital stock in the United States has essentially caught up with the U.S. capital stock abroad. At market value, U.S. assets abroad remain ahead of foreign assets in the United States, although the ratio of U.S. to foreign capital stocks fell.

	1982	1983	1984	1985	1986	1987	1988	1989	1990
Historical									
FK	208	207	211	230	260	314	335	370	421
FK*	125	137	165	184	220	263	315	374	404
Market									
FK	228	273	268	381	519	578	678	808	714
FK*	133	158	178	228	283	316	391	533	530

Problems for Section B

B1. Illustrate and explain the effects of free trade in Figure 8.6 with a return to capital of 8% in each nation brought about by free trade in goods and services.

B2. Show and explain what would happen to the international pattern of the returns to capital in Figure 8.6 with an immigration of labor into the home nation from the foreign nation.

C. INTERNATIONAL FACTOR MOVEMENTS AND INCOME REDISTRIBUTION

When foreign labor or capital comes into an economy, adjustments must be made. Factor supplies change with the new workers or capital. Outputs across the economy adjust, as do levels traded. In the factor markets, supply and demand changes bring about different factor prices. The distribution of income in the economy is changed. This section examines the important issue of this income redistribution caused by international migration and capital flows.

1. Markets for Factors of Production

With an increase in the supply of a particular factor of production, its payment falls. National income, the total payment to all productive inputs, rises. The payments to some other factors of production rise because of their increased marginal productivity with the new inputs.

If an increased supply of one factor causes the payment to another to rise, the two are called *factor friends*. If payment to another factor falls, those two are called *factor enemies*. The pattern of income redistribution is an important aspect of international movements of labor or capital.

Figure 8.7 presents a picture of the market for a factor of production called *F*. Its payment is given by *f*. Migration of factor *F* itself will change its supply. Migration of other productive factors will alter *F*'s marginal productivity and thus shift the demand for *F*.

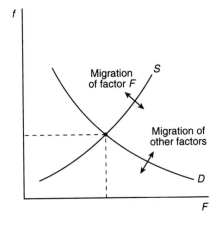

Figure 8.7. The Market for a Productive Factor The domestic market for a productive factor *F* is influenced in two ways when there are international factor movements. When the factor itself migrates, supply (*S*) shifts. When other factors migrate, its productivity and demand (*D*) shift. The adjusting pattern of outputs that occurs with the migration also affects factor demand.

Suppose factor *F* is a friend of immigrating unskilled labor. The marginal productivity and demand for *F* rise when unskilled labor immigrates. The payment *f* is pushed up. The market for *F* is adjusting in the economy's general equilibrium, with markets for outputs and markets for all other productive factors adjusting as well. If factor *F* is an enemy of immigrating professional labor, demand for *F* would fall in the general equilibrium, resulting in a lower payment *f*.

> The international inflow of a particular factor of production will increase the payment to its factor friends and decrease the payment to its factor enemies.

2. Unskilled versus Skilled Labor and Capital

The lowest paid types of labor (handlers, laborers, agricultural workers, and service workers) can be aggregated into a group called unskilled labor. The remaining higher paid groups (professionals, craft workers, transport workers, operators, and administrators) can be called skilled labor. The effects of labor migration on income distribution between these two types of labor and owners of capital depend on the ways in which the inputs are substituted for each other and the altered pattern of outputs.

Unskilled labor is generally thought to be a friend with the other two factors, skilled labor and capital. When unskilled Latin Americans immigrate to the United States, demands for skilled workers and capital increase. These inputs become more productive with the immigration of unskilled workers. Wages of skilled labor and payments to the owners of capital rise with unskilled labor immigration. The unskilled workers already inside the nation suffer lower wages because of an increase in their supply.

Labor unions represent the interests of unskilled labor and have long been opposed to immigration, favoring tighter restrictions and more active border patrol. Many if not most people in the United States benefit from the immigration of unskilled labor. This fact goes a long way toward explaining the reluctance to enforce immigration policy more actively. The recent sanctions on employers of illegal workers may signal a more sincere effort to reduce the immigration of relatively unskilled Latin Americans. Nevertheless, the overall benefits of immigration are likely to outweigh the concerns of those most directly hurt.

Local or regional effects of unskilled immigration can be startling. Construction wages in Houston are kept low by a supply of immigrants, most of them illegal. Farm workers in California face low wages for a similar reason. Wages of restaurant workers in most large cities are likewise kept low by the supply of unskilled immigrants. The Sun Belt bases much of its recent economic growth on lower wages, in part because of illegal immigration.

Changes are slow to take effect and may not be noticed right away, but the demographics of the United States in the 2050s will not be much like those of the 1950s. The population pattern across the United States is slowly changing. California has become the most populous state. Texas may become the second largest. Minority racial groups (blacks, Hispanics, and Asians) make up about half of the population. Both international migration and interstate migration are playing a role. As labor moves, the pattern of production and trade also changes.

Gains from the free international migration of productive factors, both labor and capital, outweigh losses in the same way that free trade improves on autarky. Migration of labor and capital result in higher output in the world and typically a more equitable distribution of income. Income for similar migrating productive factors approaches the same level across nations. Free trade and factor mobility are similar in the outcomes they produce.

> With free trade, a nation is effectively exporting its abundant and cheap factors of production. With free migration of labor and capital, a nation in fact exports its abundant and cheap factors of production. Regarding the distribution of income among capital and labor, free trade and free factor movement have similar effects.

3. Foreign Investment and Income Redistribution in the Specific Factors Model

Insight into the effects of foreign investment in a particular industry can be gained with the specific factors model. International capital flows are often aimed at particular industries, as when Japanese auto firms build plants in the United States or U.S. oil firms build refineries overseas.

Figure 8.8 shows the market for sector-specific capital in manufacturing. With the current supply of capital S in manufacturing, the return to capital is 4%.

Labor is the shared input in this model. The market for shared labor

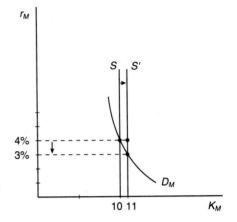

Figure 8.8. Foreign Investment in the Market for Manufacturing Capital This is the market for capital used specifically in manufacturing. When the supply of manufacturing capital (K_M) rises from S to S' with an inflow of foreign capital, the equilibrium return (r_M) to capital falls from 4% to 3% along curve D_M.

is drawn in Figure 8.9. The original equilibrium wage is $10, with 20 million workers in manufacturing and 30 million in services as indicated by the supply line S.

Suppose foreign capital now comes into the domestic manufacturing sector. The supply of capital in manufacturing rises to S' in Figure 8.8. At a return of 4%, excess supply of manufacturing capital arises. Capital owners are forced to accept a lower real rate of return. The return to capital in manufacturing falls to 3%.

In the labor market of Figure 8.9, demand rises in the manufacturing sector as labor's productivity increases with the incoming capital. With 20 million workers in manufacturing, the wage in manufacturing (w_M) jumps to $14 on the supply line S. The wage in services (w_S) remains at $10. Workers notice the difference and begin moving from the service sector to the

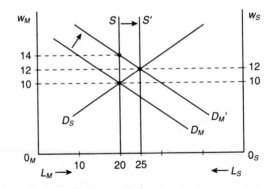

Figure 8.9. Foreign Investment and the Market for Shared Labor When the capital supply rises with foreign capital flowing into manufacturing, the productivity of labor rises in that sector. Demand for labor in manufacturing rises from D_M to D_M'. Wages (w_M and w_S) are pushed up from $10 to $12 across the economy, as labor leaves the other sector for manufacturing.

manufacturing sector. As workers move from services to manufacturing, w_S rises and w_M falls. In the final equilibrium the supply line has shifted to S', the wage of labor is a uniform \$12 in the economy, and 5 million workers have left services for manufacturing.

In the market for capital in the service sector (not drawn), demand falls because of falling productivity as labor leaves the sector. The return to capital in the service sector declines.

Capital inflows in a particular sector thus lower the return to capital in that sector and generally lower the return to sector-specific capital across the economy. Capital owners in the country will oppose incoming foreign investment, since it lowers the return to their capital. The wage of shared labor is bolstered by foreign investment. Workers in a country generally benefit from incoming foreign investment.

4. Computable General Equilibrium Models

It would be useful to have a large-scale computer model of the economy, including markets for all the various types of labor and capital inputs as well as markets for the many types of goods and services produced. Such a comprehensive approach could tell us, for instance, what would happen if 1,000 foreign physicians were allowed to immigrate this year by the U.S. Immigration and Naturalization Service. It would predict how much the wages of physicians would fall, how much medical costs would fall, how much new construction would result, how much the payment to agricultural workers might rise, how the output of electricity would be affected, and so on.

Such detailed computable general equilibrium (CGE) models are within the reach of current knowledge and technology. Robert Stern and Alan Deardorff of the University of Michigan have developed a CGE model of the U.S. economy with a good deal of industrial structure. The Canadian government uses a similar CGE model to examine the effects of immigration, which is closely monitored and controlled. The Japanese, European, and Arabian Gulf governments use such models to help shape economic policy. These models are useful for considering all sorts of changes, including the distributional effects of international factor movements.

Studies have estimated the elasticities of payments to various sorts of labor and capital with respect to changes in their supply resulting from international movements. Generally, these estimates show that migration and capital flows have relatively small long-run effects on income distribution. Both skilled labor and capital owners benefit when unskilled labor immigrates, which may explain why little persistent opposition to Latin American immigration can be mustered. Skilled labor and capital are weak enemies in the United States. This means that the net inflow of capital in recent years has reduced the payment to skilled labor and the return to capital as well. Unskilled labor, which benefits from the capital inflow, often works with expensive machines and equipment. This is especially true in agriculture and mining, the most capital-intensive industries in the United States. This same pattern of factor friendship is also found in Canada, as well as a number of developing nations.

Unskilled labor is generally a factor friend with both skilled labor and capital. Immigration of unskilled labor in the United States raises the income of both skilled labor and capital owners.

EXAMPLE 8.8   Estimates of Factor Friendship Elasticities

Using the general classification of skilled and unskilled workers in the United States, I have estimated elasticities in a CGE model (Henry Thompson, 1991). The elasticities below describe the long-run percentage change in the payments to capital, skilled labor, and labor resulting from 1% increase in one supply. The return to capital is r, the wage of skilled labor is w_S, and the wage of unskilled labor is w_U. Suppose the stock of capital increases 1%, a tremendously large inflow of foreign investment. The wage of unskilled workers would rise by only 0.15%. The capital payment would fall only 0.12%, and the wage of skilled labor would fall only 0.09%. These are very small adjustments to a very large capital inflow. These long-run estimates allow adjustment in all outputs and factor markets. Temporary and local effects can be much larger. Production of capital-intensive products would rise noticeably. Suppose the foreign investment was a foreign auto plant in a small town. Demand for labor and local wages would increase noticeably in the town. The United States is a large diversified economy, however, and average wages across the country would not be greatly affected. Immigration of unskilled workers that increased their supply by 10% would lower unskilled wages only 3%, while raising the price of capital 2.3% and of skilled labor 1.7%. Production of goods intensive in the use of unskilled labor would increase. On a national basis the current level of immigration of unskilled workers in the United States does not noticeably alter the overall long-run distribution of income. Local effects can be large in the short run. Global nationwide effects are very small in the long run.

1% Increase in Supply of:			
Capital	*Skilled Labor*	*Unskilled Labor*	
−0.12	−0.11	0.23	r
−0.09	−0.08	0.17	w_S
0.15	0.15	−0.30	w_U

EXAMPLE 8.9   The Mariel Immigration

A startling 7% increase in the labor force of Miami occurred between May and September of 1980. About 62,000 workers settled there after fleeing Cuba from the port of Mariel. David Card (1989) shows that there was essentially no effect on the Miami labor market. Wages did not fall, and no unemployment was created, even among unskilled labor groups that compete directly with the incoming unskilled workers. Mariel immigrants were less skilled and less educated than other Cubans in Miami and earned 18% less than the Cuban average. Card speculates that production of textiles, apparels, and other manufactures using unskilled labor increased in the Miami area to absorb the immigrants. Immigration has little effect on income distribution but does alter relative factor abundance and the pattern of production.

EXAMPLE 8.10   Effects of Decreased Immigration from Mexico

Clark Reynolds and Robert McClery (1988) have examined the effects of a decrease in immigration from Mexico that may come about with the immigration bill of 1986. The Simpson-Rodino bill imposes fines on employers who knowingly hire illegal workers and sets aside increased funds for border patrol. The minimum Mexican wage along the border was only $.55 in 1986, while across the border the minimum U.S. wage was $3.35. The incentive to cross illegally is substantial. The authors estimate the total effect up to the year 2000 in billions of U.S. dollars on high-wage workers, low-wage workers, and capitalists in both nations with the decrease in migration from Mexico to the United States. The figures below show that both nations are net losers. Low-wage workers are helped in the United States, while high-wage workers and capitalists are hurt. This is predicted by the pattern of factor friendship between unskilled workers, skilled workers, and capitalists. In Mexico the low-wage workers and the potential migrants are hurt. Mexican capitalists gain because more labor remains in Mexico, increasing capital's productivity. The United States has more to gain from free migration than does Mexico. Free trade can substitute for factor migration and would offset these estimated losses.

	U.S.	Mexico
High-wage workers	− $50 bil	$5 bil
Low-wage workers	$50 bil	− $12 bil

Capitalists	− $100 bil	$5 bil
Potential migrants	_____	− $8 bil
TOTAL	− $100 bil	− $10 bil

EXAMPLE 8.11   Immigration and Labor Markets in the United States

Further evidence that immigration has little effect on wages is presented by Kristin Butcher and David Card (1991). Recent immigrants have less education than the native population and must compete for jobs in the unskilled labor categories. Butcher and Card examine the wages of unskilled workers in the cities where most immigrants settle (New York, Los Angeles, Miami, and 21 others) and find no effect on unskilled wages. Cities that are growing rapidly (most of them in Texas, California, and Florida) attract both immigrants and natives relocating within the United States. Robert LaLonde and Robert Topel (1991) present evidence that immigrants are able to offset any disadvantage they have after 10 years in the workforce. Additionally, these authors find labor immigration has little empirical effect on wages in the U.S. labor market.

Problems for Section C

C1.   Illustrate the effect of an immigration of unskilled labor on U.S. markets for unskilled labor, skilled labor, and capital with diagrams similar to Figure 8.7.

C2.   Use the estimated factor friendship elasticities in Example 8.8 to predict the effects on the income of unskilled and skilled labor resulting from a 5% increase in the supply of skilled workers. Suppose the yearly skilled wage starts at $15,000 with the unskilled wage at $8,000.

D.   INTERNATIONAL FACTOR MOVEMENTS, PRODUCTION, AND TRADE

An economy's production and international trade are ultimately based on its productive factors: labor, capital, and natural resources. International movements of labor and capital change the underlying character of an economy. This section examines how international migration of labor and international capital movement alter the pattern of production and trade.

1.   Output Adjustment in the Factor Proportions Model

International factor movements affect the pattern of production and trade, as well as its income distribution. In the factor proportions model of production and trade, an increase in the supply of a factor increases output of the good that uses that factor intensively. This is the Rybczynski proposition.

Goods may be classified according to whether they are imported, exported, or not traded at all. If domestic supply of an imported good rises because of international factor movement, the level of imports falls. If domestic supply of an exported good rises with factor migration, so do exports. If domestic output of a nontraded good changes with factor migration, trade would not be affected directly. A theoretical link exists between international factor movements and international trade.

Figure 8.10 presents the expansion paths for business services and manufactures when there are two inputs, skilled labor (S) and unskilled labor (U). Services use skilled labor intensively, and manufacturing uses unskilled labor intensively. The ratios of skilled labor to labor input are built on a cost minimization in each sector, as pictured in a Lerner-Pearce diagram. Capital input is in the background and assumed not to vary or affect the outcome in this model. Point E represents the endowment or total supply of 100 units of each type of labor.

With both types of labor fully employed, outputs of S and M occur along the expansion paths for services and manufacturers. These outputs are represented by the isoquants labeled Srv and Mfg.

With immigration of unskilled labor the endowment point E moves right to E'. In this example a 10% increase in the endowment of labor up to 110 occurs. With the shift to E', output of manufactures rises to isoquant M' while output of services falls to isoquant S'.

Production shifts toward labor-intensive manufactures with labor im-

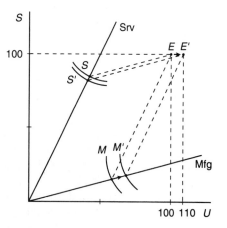

Figure 8.10. Unskilled Labor Immigration and Output Adjustments Immigration of unskilled workers (U) shifts the endowment point in this two-sector economy from point E to point E'. Production of the good that uses the immigrating workers intensively rises, while production of the other good must fall. If services are exported and manufactures imported, exports and imports fall. If manufactures are exported and services imported, exports and imports rise.

migration, as both inputs leave the service sector. All of the immigrating unskilled workers, as well as some unskilled workers originally in services, find jobs in manufacturing. Skilled labor also leaves services. Output of manufactures expands up the manufacturing expansion path, while output of services falls down its expansion path.

In this example, the expansion paths are held constant. If the immigration alters factor payments, firms will adjust their cost-minimizing mix of factors. Immigration of unskilled labor is expected to lower its own wage while raising the wage of skilled workers. Since these changes in factor prices are small, the adjustment in the input ratios should not be too great. The expansion paths are assumed to be constant in Figure 8.10, although they might adjust slightly with the immigration.

In a small open economy the prices of traded services and manufactures would not change. If services are exported and manufactures are imported, the level of trade must fall. The nation becomes relatively less abundant in skilled labor, the input used intensively in its exports. Immigration of unskilled labor causes the nation to lose some of its comparative advantage when imports use unskilled labor intensively. Factor mobility is substituting for free trade.

Suppose, on the other hand, that manufactures are exported. The level of trade will then increase when unskilled labor immigrates. The nation becomes more abundant in unskilled labor, the input used intensively in its exports. Immigration of unskilled labor causes the nation to gain in its comparative advantage when exports use unskilled labor intensively.

The effect of international factor movements on the pattern of trade depends on the factor intensity of traded goods.

2.   Output Adjustment in the Specific Factors Model

Consider again the specific factors model with a particular type of capital in each sector and shared labor. Figure 8.11 shows the structure of the specific factors economy, summarized by the expansion paths in each industry. Supplies of capital in sectors M and S are given by the vertical lines at $K_M = 10$ and $K_S = 10$.

Expansion paths adjust so that labor is fully employed in the two sectors taken together. With 10 units of capital in sector M, 20 million workers are employed in sector M with a K/L ratio of 1/2. With 50 million workers in the economy, 30 million are employed in services at a K/L ratio of 1/3.

Suppose foreign investment increases the supply of capital from 10 to 11 in the manufacturing sector. Output in sector M will rise. Labor will be attracted to sector M because of its increased productivity and higher wage. With labor leaving services, output in that sector falls. Output of the sector receiving the investment rises as other outputs across the economy fall.

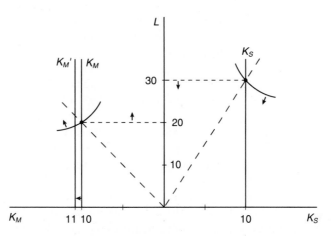

Figure 8.11. Foreign Investment in Manufacturing and Output Adjustment Foreign investment in manufacturing increases the supply of capital and draws labor from the rest of the economy. Output in manufacturing rises as output across the rest of the economy sags.

3. International Factor Movements and Intraindustry Trade

Interindustry trade and intraindustry trade adjust differently with international factor movements. Interindustry trade occurs when labor-abundant countries export labor-intensive goods in exchange for capital-intensive goods. Larger differences in relative factor endowments would increase the level of interindustry trade. Smaller differences in relative factor endowments would decrease the level of interindustry trade.

Intraindustry trade (export and import of goods within the same category) is known to be higher between countries with similar factor endowments. Capital- and skilled labor–abundant industrial countries trade similar goods with each other. For instance, high-quality television sets can be traded for low-quality television sets.

International labor migration between two countries brings their relative factor endowment closer together. Converging endowment ratios should decrease the level of interindustry trade between them and increase the level of intraindustry trade.

International factor movements can be expected to decrease interindustry trade between partners but increase intraindustry trade between partner countries.

4. Estimates of Output Adjustments in the United States

The three major industrial aggregates are services, manufacturing, and agriculture (which includes mining and raw materials). Splitting labor into the eight types reported by the U.S. Census leads to elasticities of output adjustment with respect to international factor movements. Table 8.4 presents estimated elasticities of outputs with respect to changing supplies of capital and each of the eight types of labor from a recent study.

Changes in the supply of inputs have the largest impact in industries where they are used intensively. Agriculture is very capital intensive in the United States, even though only 8% of the capital stock is used in agriculture. Capital in this model includes land. Capital (and land) owners receive 58% of all the income in agriculture. Capital inflows especially encourage agricultural output. A 1% increase in the capital stock resulting from incoming foreign investment would result in a 2.7% increase in agricultural output.

Immigration amounting to 10% of the present supply of agricultural workers (L7) would raise agricultural output by 9%. The United States exports many types of agricultural goods, while importing others. On net, the United States exports agricultural goods. The immigration of agricultural labor should increase our comparative advantage in agricultural production and with it our level of exports. Many migrant workers (legal and illegal) immigrate into the United States yearly to help with agricultural harvests. Farmers confess they would be hard pressed to meet the harvest without such workers.

Department of Agriculture programs are unfortunately aimed at restricting agricultural output and keeping agricultural prices artificially high. It is no exaggeration to say the U.S. Midwest is the breadbasket of the world. Without U.S. government programs that restrict output, the Midwest could keep the world in bread. Other agricultural regions in the United States are equally well endowed with productive agricultural land, experienced labor, and capital equipment. For the sake of global efficiency, agricultural programs discouraging output in the United States should be gradually dismantled.

Labor group L4 (operators) receives the largest share (29%) of manufacturing income. Most operators (54%) are used in manufacturing. Immigration of L4 workers would cause manufacturing output to rise, while outputs in the service sector and agricultural sector would drop. Output of

TABLE 8.4. Output Effects of International Migration and Capital Flows

			1% Increase in Supply of:						
L1	L2	L3	L4	L5	L6	L7	L8	K	
−1.4	0	0	−0.2	−1.0	0	0.9	−0.2	2.7	**A**
−0.5	0.7	0.1	1.8	−0.5	0	0	−0.1	−0.4	**M**
0.5	0	0	−0.3	0.5	0	0	0.1	0.3	**S**

SOURCE: From "Simulating a Multifactor General Equilibrium Model of Production and Trade," Henry Thompson, *International Economic Journal*, 1991, pp. 21–34.

manufacturing is elastic with respect to the supply of operators. Immigration of L4 amounting to a 10% increase would spur manufacturing output by 18%, while lowering agricultural output 2% and services output 3%. The United States currently has deficits in the trade of manufactures, meaning our comparative advantage lies in other areas. Immigration of workers in the L4 category would decrease the level of imports of manufactures into the United States. Again, international factor mobility would substitute for international trade.

Most of the labor groups L1, L3, and L5 (85%, 75%, and 86%, respectively) are used in the service sector. Skilled groups L1 and L5 receive 27% and 21% of the income in the service sector. The largest output effects on the service sector come from immigration of those skilled groups L1 and L5. Since the United States is a net exporter of services, immigration of skilled groups L1 and L5 would increase comparative advantage, the degree of specialization, and the level of exports.

> Output adjustments resulting from international factor migration are generally explained by factor intensities.

EXAMPLE 8.12   Exports, Imports, and Factor Movements

Kar-Yui Wong (1983) uses a model of production and trade to estimate the effects of international factor movements on U.S. exports and imports in *Empirical Methods for International Trade*. Responses of the exports of consumer durables, nondurables and services, and imports are measured relative to changes in the supplies of labor and capital. These elasticities show the estimated percentage change in trade resulting from a 1% change in the labor and capital endowments. Trade is apparently spurred more by labor immigration than by capital inflow. The export of labor-intensive nondurables and services is encouraged by immigration. Both immigration and capital inflow have positive net effects on the trade balance because the cumulative effect on exports outweighs the effect of imports.

		Percent Change in:		
		Durable Good Exports	*Nondurable and Service Exports*	*Imports*
1% change in:	*Labor*	1.5	2.2	1.5
	Capital	0.7	0.4	0.4

Problems for Section D

D1.   Show what happens in Figure 8.10 with an emigration of skilled labor. If services are exported, predict what will happen to the level of exports and imports.

D2.   Predict what will happen to the pattern of production and trade with an outflow of skilled labor from the United States.

CONCLUSION

International movements of labor and productive capital are vital forces in world economy. When a firm sets up a branch operation in another nation, it becomes a multinational firm. Nations can gradually integrate their economic activity by moving to free trade, open migration policy, and unrestricted international investment. The next chapter examines the process and politics of international economic integration.

KEY TERMS

Brain Drain
Depreciation of capital
Emigration and immigration
Factor endowment
Factor friends and enemies
Foreign investment

Host and source nation
International capital mobility
Jevons diagram
Marginal factor cost (MFC)
Marginal revenue product (MRP)
Restrictions on foreign investment

KEY POINTS

- Workers respond to international wage differences by migrating to high-wage nations. International labor migration leads to equalization of wages across nations. International trade substitutes for labor migration in that they both lead toward the equalization of wages.
- Capital also moves between nations, seeking a higher return. Free international capital flows lead to the same result as free trade, namely international factor price equalization.
- When a factor immigrates, national income rises, but the payment to that factor falls. Some other productive factors (friends) gain through higher income, while others (enemies) lose. International movement of factors redistributes income among the factors of production.
- International factor movements also affect the pattern of production and trade. Generally, international trade decreases as relative factor abundances are diminished through international labor migration and capital flows.

REVIEW PROBLEMS

1. Free trade between the two nations in Figure 8.3 would raise the price of the labor-intensive good in the labor-cheap foreign nation and lower the same price at home. Illustrate this adjustment with wages equalizing at $10 in each nation.

2. Do wages of the various census groups reflect only the skills and training needed to enter each group? What else could these wages reflect?

3. Explain how you think an inflow of foreign capital in the auto industry will affect wages of the various groups of labor in the census data. Consider also an inflow of foreign capital in agriculture.

4. Given the current trends in U.S. immigration, predict the evolving pattern of regional production and interregional trade inside the United States. What changes can be predicted in international trade?

5. If wealth holders in the United States traded evenly, at present value, their capital goods with wealth holders in Europe, what would be the net effect?

6. Look at the industries in Table 8.2 in which the United States has substantial foreign investments abroad and speculate on how this list compares with U.S. comparative advantage. Explain your conclusion.

7. Which group in an economy would most favor restricting the inflow of foreign capital? Which group would most oppose such restrictions? Predict what determines the political outcome.

8. The service industry includes categories like wholesale trade and banking, as in Example 8.6 of U.S. and Japanese investment. Assume the capital used in the industry is sector specific. What have been the effects on income redistribution and outputs of the observed pattern of investment?

9. Predict what will happen to the wages of the various types of labor in the census grouping with an emigration of professionals. Something like this would occur if U.S. firms expand their foreign branch operations.

10. Explain what happens to the income of the various types of labor and capital when the Japanese open a new factory in the United States. How are the local effects different from the national effects?

11. What happens to the long-run distribution of income when U.S. firms decide to open factories in Mexico rather than in Texas? What would be the difference if the plant was opened on the Texas border but Mexicans were allowed to come in and work?

12. Explain whether it is more likely that the United States would join a common market (with free trade and free movements of labor and capital) with Mexico or Canada. Consider the income redistribution in each case.

13. Given the birth rates in the United States are somewhat higher among unskilled labor groups in the West, South, and Southwest, predict what will happen to the pattern of production and trade between this region and the rest of the United States.

14. Free trade zones are set up partly to attract investment by foreign firms through the elimination of customs procedures. Explain whether they promote or inhibit trade through comparative advantage.

15. Describe the effects on the outputs of the three industrial sectors when there is an immigration of operators (machine operators, for instance). Predict the effects on imports and exports.

READINGS

Barry Chaswick, editor, *The Gateway: U.S. Immigration Issues and Policies,* American Policy Institute, Washington, DC, 1982. An insightful collection of studies on immigration.

International Migration Review, Center for Migration Studies, New York. A quarterly journal dedicated to the study of migration.

"The New Refugee," *U.S. News and World Report,* October 23, 1989. A startling look at current international migration.

"Applied General Equilibrium Models of Taxation and International Trade," John Shoven and John Whalley, *Journal of Economic Literature,* September 1984. Survey of research on computable general equilibrium models.

Julian Simon, *The Economic Consequences of Immigration,* Basil Blackwell, London, 1989. A thorough economic analysis of immigration, which comes to the conclusion that immigration quotas should be raised.

CHAPTER 9

International Economic Integration

CHAPTER PREVIEW

The process of international economic integration has accelerated with the formation of The European Community's common market, the free trade agreement between Canada and the United States, and similar steps around the world. From the viewpoint of global economic efficiency, national borders introduce various barriers or friction to efficient production, trade, and finance. Economic integration involves steps that can be taken to lessen these barriers. Topics covered in this chapter are:

(a) *Multinational firms,* which play an important role in international economic integration

(b) *International externalities* and market failures, which call for internationally coordinated policy

(c) *International political economy,* the influences shaping international agreements

(d) The stages of *economic integration,* which describe steps governments can take to make their economies increasingly interrelated

INTRODUCTION

The importance of multinational firms in international trade and investment continues to increase. Roughly a quarter of total world trade now consists of trade between branches of multinational firms. Direct investment by firms in foreign operations is becoming a more popular form of foreign investment.

Thousands of U.S. multinational firms have large investments abroad. According to figures from the U.S. Department of Commerce, more than 80% of these foreign branch firms are majority owned. Management from the U.S. parent firm must be an important input for the typical branch operation. One fifth of these U.S. multinational branches are in the business service industry, followed by 18% in oil and coal. Only a quarter of the branches are located in English-speaking nations. Foreign multinational firms in the United States employ about 2% of the U.S. workforce.

Multinational branch operations are formed when international transactions within a firm are more economical than they would be between firms. The firm "avoids the market" by internalizing transactions, a concept developed by Richard Coase. Often a multinational firm wants to use its own particular patent, process, or management technique in the foreign nation. An important theoretical issue is how a firm is defined or what limits a firm's size.

The multinational firm might be horizontally or vertically integrated. With horizontal integration, the firm operates similar plants in different nations. The amount of horizontal integration has increased in recent history. Vertical integration occurs traditionally in the extractive mineral industries. A domestic firm can buy intermediate or raw inputs from foreign suppliers, or it can begin a branch operation to produce the intermediate inputs itself. A copper wire manufacturer, for instance, may go upstream in the production process to operate a mine in a foreign nation.

Many nations have tight restrictions that keep the presence of multinational firms to a minimum. The stated reasons include control of the economy, mistrust of foreign motives, cultural purity, national pride, and so on. In fact, multinational firms bring in skilled management and new capital equipment and machinery. This inflow would lower the return to the host country's managers and capital owners, while increasing the demand for local labor.

In labor-abundant developing nations, multinational firms should be welcomed. Incoming multinational firms encourage specialization and efficient production but disrupt the local pattern of income distribution. Governments are supported by established industry and the wealthy, who do not want to see the traditional pattern of income distribution changed. In most Latin American countries, multinational firms are kept at bay.

One aspect of production that forces governments to cooperate is pollution, an important negative externality of many production processes. Neighbors of a polluting firm in effect pay part of the cost of production by having to suffer from living in a poorer environment. A pollution tax on the firm's output forces the firm to consider the costs of its pollution and to optimally restrict output. This economic solution to pollution of a tax is difficult to implement politically. International pollution is even more difficult to solve. What incentives does the U.S. government have to force reduction of the amount of acid rain produced by its industries but falling on Canada? Should U.S. farmers cut back on their use of fertilizers and pesticides that drain into the Colorado River and cause problems in Mexico? There are no internationally accepted laws or policies and few precedents for handling such international externalities.

Difficult issues lie at the heart of international political economy. As with domestic political economy, insight can be gained by considering the income redistribution resulting from a proposed policy. Every nation would like more income distributed its way. Policies that nominally may be aimed at promoting social welfare are often thinly disguised efforts to redistribute income.

Because of improved transportation and communication, the world is effectively shrinking. National economies are becoming more specialized and increasingly dependent on one another. International trade has increased and levels of international investment are higher, creating sizeable gains all around. Various stages of economic integration are being worked out between nations to facilitate this international economic integration.

Governments enjoy autonomy by their nature and have incentives to stand in the way of international economic integration. Each government wants to determine its own trade policy, designed in effect to enhance its power by protecting its most supportive industries. Governments also want to control their own money supplies. Through independent monetary policy a government can influence its price level and interest rates. The ability to print money also enables a government to spend more than its tax revenue. Economic integration can progress through various steps, as individual governments give up their ability to set trade policy, control migration and foreign investment, and finally print their own money.

The gains from international economic integration are large and should ultimately carry the day. The European integration is a prime example of the vitality that can be introduced by opening national borders to free trade, free migration, and free international investment. As the closed economies of Eastern Europe open themselves, dramatic improvements in their standards of living can be expected. The United States and Canada are moving toward more complete economic integration, and Mexico is being brought into the North American Free Trade Area. A free trade area has been proposed between Japan and the United States because of the high level of bilateral trade and investment. Various forms of international economic integration have arisen in the Caribbean, South America, the Arab countries, Southeast Asia, and Africa. Even sizeable political or ideological differences, as between the United States and China, can be ultimately outweighed by the incentive to gain through increased international trade and investment.

A. MULTINATIONAL FIRMS

A multinational firm (MNF) has its headquarters in one country and operates branch plants in different countries. This section looks into the causes of MNFs. It investigates the advantages of MNFs and their effect in the source and host countries. The potential role of policy in governing MNFs is explored.

1. International Marketing

A firm selling its product in another nation can use four basic techniques. Moving down the list, the four steps require more familiarity with the foreign country and how its markets operate:

(a) One technique is simply to produce the good at home and *export* it abroad. Foreign importing firms purchase and distribute the home export.

(b) A second technique is to enter into a *licensing agreement* with a foreign firm. Licensing gives the foreign firm the right or ability to reproduce the firm's product. The foreign firm typically agrees to pay the source firm a royalty.

(c) A third option is to form a *joint venture* with a foreign firm, in which the two firms join to develop and produce a product for the foreign market.

(d) A final choice is to set up a *branch plant* in the foreign nation and become a multinational firm. Branch plants are operated with management from the home plant.

The choice among these four options is based on familiarity with the foreign country, legal restrictions on MNFs in the foreign country, transportation costs to the foreign market, contacts among foreign firms, levels of protection in the foreign country, local economies of scale, the fixed costs of establishing a branch plant, the relative cost of foreign labor, and other influences. Japanese automakers have set up plants in the United States largely because of the high level of protection on Japanese auto exports to the United States. Some underlying cause of comparative advantage must make production in the foreign nation more profitable if an MNF is to set up a branch plant. Otherwise, the firm will remain an exporter.

Licensing with an existing foreign firm is clearly the easiest way for a domestic firm to move production to a foreign nation. Licensing lets the firm penetrate the foreign market when high levels of protection are faced. If the source firm has some special production process, licensing can transfer technology. The branch firm may attach its own label to the good, with the home firm receiving a royalty.

International joint ventures are another way to penetrate foreign markets. Agreements are made between firms in different nations to share management, production processes, information, and sources of raw materials or other inputs. The two firms become partners in the new joint venture. Joint ventures have become more popular in recent years. Improvements in telecommunications may largely explain their success. Prime examples are the agreements between General Motors and Toyota, National Intergroup and Japan's Nippon Kokan in steel, Corning Glass and Germany's Siemens in optical cable, and United Technologies and the United Kingdom's Rolls Royce in aircraft engines. By specializing between themselves in providing research and development, management, and marketing, firms enjoy lower costs and are able to carry out projects that might not be feasible if each operated on its own.

When a firm wants to protect a special process or relies on some *firm-specific input,* it wants either to export or to set up a branch plant. Licensing agreements and joint ventures are to be avoided. The firm-specific input or secret production process can be patented or a particular style of management can be maintained. With a firm-specific input, only the particular firm can make its good, and the only options are to export or to set up a branch operation.

No simple model or rule of thumb encompasses all of the considerations that a potential multinational firm faces. The four basic options of a firm wanting to market its product abroad are: export, license agreement, joint venture, and branch plant.

2. International Management

The United States has a relative abundance of entrepreneurial talent and specializes internationally in management. This comparative advantage is reflected by the fact that the United States is a net exporter of business services. In 1988 the United States exported $4.8 billion of business or professional services, while importing $1.6 billion. The United States is a global leader in the business services industry, which includes telecommunications, software, banking, finance, consulting, and information services. Also reflecting this comparative advantage is the $3.5 billion surplus in education. Many foreign students come to the United States to learn valued skills. In engineering, for instance, most Ph.D. students in the United States are foreigners. In economics the percentage of foreign graduate students is close to half.

Like other productive factors, management will migrate from nations where it is abundant and cheap to nations where it is scarce and expensive. This is the same sort of factor mobility that occurs with international labor migration or capital movements. Managers may not have to move themselves physically to the foreign country. Some managers may transfer abroad, or locals in the host country can be trained in the firm's management techniques. The speed of international telecommunication has made it easier for a manager in Des Moines, Iowa, for instance, to oversee production at a branch plant in Thessalonikki, Greece.

An increase in multinational activity is likely to lower the payment to management already inside the host nation. As a group, domestic management can be expected to oppose the unfettered influx of foreign MNFs and foreign management. Other domestic inputs, however, will generally benefit from the incoming management. Local labor and capital owners should see demand for their inputs increase as they become more productive.

> Increased international management involves costs and benefits. It is important to identify the winners and losers with incoming management from MNFs. Generally, MNFs will improve international efficiency.

Existing plants in an industry will have to compete with any new foreign branch plants. Local politicians come from districts where existing plants feel threatened by foreign MNFs. Political pressure from the domestic owners of existing plants to keep foreign competition out of the country will be constant. Entry into an industry will lower the profits of existing domestic firms.

The US automobile industry provides an example of the potential foreign MNFs have to increase productivity of the domestic industry. High levels of protection on autos have provided an incentive for foreign firms to locate branch plants inside the United States. Domestic automakers are on record as opposing new foreign-owned plants. The entry of foreign MNFs has forced the domestic firms to become more competitive. In fact, the difference in domestic value added between domestic cars and "foreign" models produced in the United States is small. The overall quality of cars in the United States increased dramatically during the 1980s, at least partly because of the innovations brought by the management of foreign MNFs.

Gains will outweigh losses with incoming foreign MNFs. Demand for domestic labor will increase, raising wages. If excess supply of labor exists, employment increases. This may not be true locally where the existing domestic plants are. With the foreign automobile plants being built across the United States, there was little increased demand for labor in Detroit where the traditional car plants had been located.

Viewing the nation as a whole, however, there is no doubt that labor benefits with foreign investment and management from MNFs. Foreign automakers have typically set up plants in states with right to work laws so union labor can be avoided. Japanese management techniques tie the wage of each worker to the profits of the plant, much like the incentives some white collar workers traditionally receive in U.S. industry. As with many governmental policies, protectionism for the U.S. auto industry resulted in something quite different from what it was designed to accomplish. The protectionist policy altered the structure of incentives and the behavior of U.S. auto firms, putting them at a disadvantage relative to the progressive and innovative foreign MNF branches.

EXAMPLE 9.1   Multinational Firm Activity in Services

Services is the industry in which most MNF growth occurred during the 1980s. Services includes construction, utilities, health, transportation, telecommunications, engineering, motion pictures, advertising, banking, finance, insurance, real estate, and others. The United Nations (1987) reports that 44% of U.S. foreign direct investment (FDI) and 52% of Japanese FDI was in services during 1985. For other industrial countries, between 30% and 40% of FDI is in services. Most of the investment coming into the United States is in the service sector. Japanese banks are making significant strides in that international industry. Regarding the MNFs of the United States, roughly half are in services. International Telephone and Telegraph (ITT) provides a case study. ITT has evolved from a domestic U.S. manufacturer of telephone equipment in the 1970s into a diversified multinational firm in the 1990s. It provides electronic mail, telecommunications software, data systems, insurance, and hotels, all of which accounted for 65% of its revenue in 1986. Almost half of ITT's revenue comes from its foreign branch operations.

3.   Horizontal Integration of Multinational Firms

A horizontally integrated multinational firm must decide how much to produce in each of its branch plants. A *multiplant* MNF is pictured in Figure 9.1. The firm in principle wants to produce where its marginal revenue (MR) equals marginal cost (MC) in order to maximize its profit. It must consider (MC) in both its domestic and foreign branch plants separately.

The demand (D) for the firm's product leads to the MR curve in Figure 9.1. The foreign branch plant has lower marginal costs than the domestic plant. MC* represents marginal cost in the foreign branch plant, and MC

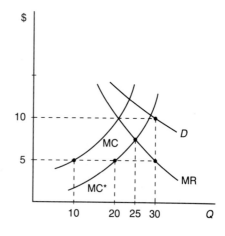

FIGURE 9.1. Horizontal Integration in a Multiplant Multinational Firm (MNF) This is an example of horizontal integration, with the MNF producing the same product in two countries. The MNF wants to equate *MR* and *MC* across plants, while producing a total that is priced according to demand. In this example the foreign plant has lower costs and produces 20 units while the higher cost home plant produces 10 units. The total output of 30 has a *MR* of $5 and a uniform *MC* of $5 across plants. Price is set according to demand at $10.

represents marginal cost in the domestic plant. In this example, both plants make the same product and the MNF is horizontally integrated.

> With international horizontal integration, an MNF produces the same product at different locations.

Finding the optimal output involves equalizing the level of each plant's MC and the firm's MR. Profit is maximized in Figure 9.1 where MR = MC = $5 at both plants. Domestic output of 10 plus foreign output of 20 adds up to a total output of 30. Over $5, the two quantities from the MC curves add to more than the quantity on the MR curve. Under $5, the two quantities from the MC curves add to less than the quantity on the MR curve. The output of 30 units is sold according to demand at a price of $10. Output will always be higher at the lower cost plant because the MC of the lower cost plant will be to the right for any level of MR.

If there is more than one foreign branch plant, profit maximization is carried out in a similar way. The firm looks for the level of output where *MR* equals *MC* at each branch plant and total output equals the sum of outputs from all of the branch plants. Higher outputs will occur at the plants with lower costs.

An important question is why the firm in Figure 9.1 would continue to operate the higher-cost plant. If the domestic plant has higher average costs, perhaps all production should be shifted to the foreign location. This would mean operating where MC from the foreign firm equals MR at $Q = 25$. Suppose that the firm would sell this output at a price of $11. Revenue from this level of output would be $11 × 25 = $275, less than the revenue from selling the output of both plants.

The important comparison, however, is in the two situations. The profit of each location is found by looking at each plant's average costs. Profit may be higher or lower from operating both plants than from operating the single low-cost plant.

Transport costs may be an incentive to keep both plants in Figure 12.1 operating. Some buyers may be closer to the home country firm, and output from the foreign plant would have higher transport costs to those buyers. Each plant may be located close to a particular source of natural resource, which has its own cost of transport. Costs of shutting down the domestic plant and expanding the foreign plant can also lead firms to operate parallel plants. Additionally, import protection in the home country may make shipments from the foreign branch operation back to the home country too expensive. If the firm's management is located in the home country, it might continue domestic production to train managers and keep them familiar with production techniques. The firm may additionally expect costs to fall at home or rise abroad. Multinational firms have many reasons to continue to operate plants with different costs.

4.   Vertical Integration of Multinational Firms

Multinational vertical integration occurs when an MNF produces one good in the foreign plant (such as electronic components) that is used in the home plant to produce another good (such as television sets). Natural resources or raw materials may be produced in one country to be shipped to another for refining, processing, or inclusion in manufactured products. Some degree of refining or processing may take place in the source country. With vertical integration the firm moves backward or forward in the line of production leading from raw materials to intermediate products to final products.

Figure 9.2 pictures an MNF that is vertically integrated. Demand and marginal revenue for the final good (television sets) appears in the left side of the diagram. The marginal cost of producing the TVs is also included. Part of the cost of producing TVs comes from the electronic components (ECs) produced in the foreign plant pictured on the right side of the diagram. The demand for electronic components is their marginal revenue product (MRP), which equals the marginal revenue of TVs times the marginal product of the electronic components. The marginal cost of producing the electronic components is also included.

Both of sides of Figure 9.2 are solved simultaneously by this profit-maximizing MNF. The demand for electronic components is derived from the demand for TVs since the marginal revenue of the ECs depends on the price of TVs. If the demand for TVs rises, the MRs of both TVs and ECs rise. Increasing MRs would increase the output of ECs and their price. The

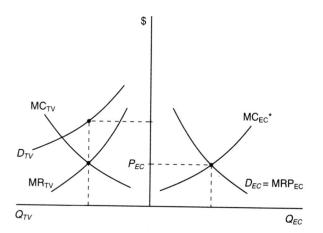

FIGURE 9.2. Vertical Integration in a Multinational Firm (MNF) This MNF producing televisions (TVs) has vertically integrated by producing the electronic components (ECs) for its TVs in a foreign country. Demand for ECs is derived from the upstream demand for TVs. An increase in the demand for TVs would raise their price and push up the marginal revenue product of ECs.

price of electronic components is called a *shadow price* because there actually is no market. The firm transfers the ECs from its foreign branch operation to the TV-assembling firm at home.

> An MNF can avoid the market through vertical integration by producing its own raw materials or components in foreign countries.

The MNF may use *transfer pricing* when it buys components from its own foreign branch operations. If the price of its imported component is understated, the foreign branch firm will appear less profitable and less tariff has to be paid. The stated price of the ECs in Figure 9.2 would then be less than its shadow price. If the price of the components is overstated, the branch firm will appear more profitable. The stated price of ECs would then be greater than its shadow price.

The firm may also manipulate the stated price to transfer profits to the location where taxes are lowest. If profit taxes are higher in the home nation, the price of components can be overstated, making the foreign branch operation appear more profitable and the home assembly operation appear less profitable. If profit taxes are higher in the foreign nation, the price of components can be understated, making the foreign branch operation appear less profitable and the home plant more profitable.

> Transfer pricing can be an added incentive to avoid the market and set up a foreign branch operation.

EXAMPLE 9.2   The Largest U.S. Multinational Firms

Ranked by total revenue, the six largest U.S. MNFs are listed in a special report ("The 100 Largest Multinationals") in *Forbes* magazine (July 28, 1986). As the numbers below indicate, large percentages of total revenue for these firms come from abroad. The firms also have large portions of their capital assets in foreign nations. Many other firms receive larger shares of their revenues from abroad and have larger shares of their capital stock invested abroad.

	Foreign Revenue	*Percent Foreign Revenue*	*Percent Foreign Assets*
Exxon	$59 bil	68	43
Mobil	$33 bil	57	45
IBM	$22 bil	43	41
GM	$16 bil	17	21

Ford	$16 bil	30	50
DuPont	$11 bil	36	30

EXAMPLE 9.3 Foreign Multinational Firm Branch Plants in the United States

According to 1986 U.S. Department of Commerce figures, the number of foreign multinational branch operations from these source nations operating inside the United States are:

Japan	351
U.K.	178
Canada	114
Germany	60
France	45

The Japanese External Trade Organization, or JETRO (1988), estimates that more than 200,000 workers are employed by Japanese branch operations in the United States. Many states of the United States keep offices in Tokyo to try to encourage Japanese firms to set up branch operations. The states with the most Japanese branch operations are:

California	163
Georgia	40
New Jersey	32
Illinois	28
Texas	26
Washington	23

EXAMPLE 9.4 Maquiladores

Maquiladores are U.S. MNF branch operations across the Mexican border producing goods for export to the United States. These plants hire Mexican labor at about $2 per hour, much less than the $14 per hour average in the United States. Labor unions in the United States claim that maquiladores steal U.S. jobs. The alternative to production in Mexico, however, is not production in the United States, but production around the Pacific Rim and in less developed countries (LDCs) where wages are close to those in Mexico. In 1970 the maquiladores had 20,000 employees. By 1989 employment had grown to 400,000, which comes from a fairly steady 4% annual growth. MNFs in the Unites States will continue to expand their maquiladores operations. If a free trade area is established between Mexico and the United States, increased growth of maquiladores operations can be expected.

EXAMPLE 9.5   A Breakdown of Foreign Direct Investment in the United States

Foreign direct investment (FDI) in new plants and equipment coming into the Untied States is concentrated in specific industries and comes almost exclusively from the EC, Japan, and Canada. Ed Ray (1991) presents a summary of manufacturing FDI in the United States between 1979 and 1987. FDI has occurred mostly in large firms in large U.S. industries that are intensive in both capital and skilled labor. Large industries may offer the promise of large profit. The foreign MNFs evidently have specific machinery or skilled labor techniques that they want to utilize. FDI was generally timed to take advantage of a depreciated dollar. Japanese FDI tends to avoid unionized labor. More FDI occurs in industries characterized by a smaller number of firms, which may be less competitive than industries with more firms. Tariffs and other nontariff barriers to trade do not generally influence FDI, so MNFs do not carry out FDI only to avoid protection. More FDI occurs in expanding industries. Only 10% of the foreign FDI coming into the United States went into new plant and equipment. Most went into buying shares or ownership in existing firms. Only 42% of the $211 billion of FDI from 1979 to 1987 went into manufacturing. The top 10 industries of FDI are:

Motor vehicles	$3.70 billion
Car parts and accessories	$1.30 billion
Semiconductors	$1.00 billion
Paper mills	$0.90 billion
Plastic materials	$0.90 billion
Petroleum refining	$0.80 billion
Pulp mills	$0.70 billion
Carbon and graphite	$0.51 billion
Rice milling	$0.50 billion
Steel pipes	$0.46 billion

Problems for Section A

A1.   Explain why the domestic automobile industry disagrees with the domestic steel and electronics industries on the desirability of the influx of foreign MNF car plants in the United States.

A2.   Explain whether a textile factory or an insurance company would be more likely to license a foreign operation. Which would be more likely to set up its own foreign branch operation?

B. INTERNATIONAL MARKET FAILURES

International economics is organized around the workings of international markets and the industrial organization in these markets. This section looks into situations where international markets fail in one way or another. Such market failures typically arise because of what are called externalities. Recognizing potential international market failures is important as governments shape international economic integration.

1. Negative Externalities: Pollution

A negative externality in production occurs when some part of the cost of the productive activity is not paid by the producing firm. The classic case of a negative externality is pollution, where residents close to a plant must pay part of the implicit costs of production. These implicit costs include breathing dirty air and subsequent diminished health, frequently painting houses and waxing cars, and so on.

The economic solution to pollution is illustrated in Figure. 9.3. Demand for the firm's good is represented by *D* and its marginal revenue by MR. The firm's *marginal private cost* (MPC) is the explicit costs actually paid by the firm. The MPC is based on the inputs of labor, capital, energy, intermediate inputs, and raw materials. Implicit costs associated with the plant's operation are due to pollution.

If the firm is completely insensitive to these implicit pollution costs, it produces where MR = MPC to maximize its profit. Output would be 12 units and price would be $20. If the firm is aware of the external social costs of its pollution, it might produce according to the higher *marginal social costs* (MSC). The firm would then produce where MR = MSC, restricting output to 10 units and raising price to $22. The difference between MSC and MPC in this example is $6, the vertical distance between MSC and MPC.

Firms that want good will and hope to remain in business may choose to operate along the MSC schedule. The firm could operate at MPC and allocate this $6 difference to community funds to offset the costs of pollution, although too much output would be produced. Alternatively, the $6

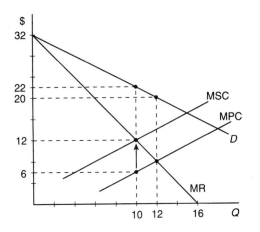

FIGURE 9.3. A Negative Production Externality The difference between marginal social costs (MSC) and marginal private costs (MPC) is the external pollution cost for each unit of output. In this example the external pollution cost is $6 per unit of output. A myopic profit maximizer disregards this external cost and produces where MPC = MR at Q = 10 and P = $20. A pollution tax of $6 per unit of output raises MPC to MSC, restricts output to 10, and raises price to $22. Pollution is reduced to its optimal level with this pollution tax.

difference could be spent on research and development to lower the level of pollution. While few firms in the United States took these strategies before the original pollution laws of the late 1960s, there was little general awareness of the widespread effects of pollution. Technology for controlling pollution did not begin to develop until that time. A firm that totally ignores its pollution these days may make higher profit in the short run, but bad publicity can make long-run profit lower.

> Negative externalities are the costs of production that are not explicit costs for the firm. Firms interested only in short-run profits may ignore the implicit costs their operations impose on society.

Suppose residents in the area could costlessly negotiate with the polluting firm. If the firm in Figure 9.3 is liable for the costs it imposes on others, it will cut output back to the socially optimal level of 10. If the firm is not liable, residents in the area could pay the firm the added costs that would come with the higher output and induce the firm to produce the optional amount of pollution.

The *Coase theorem* says that the socially optimal output will be reached if there is costless negotiation. Negotiation, however, is typically anything but costless. Those paying the external costs may not be fully aware of how much is being imposed on them. When negative externalities are international, negotiations will be even costlier. Given costly negotiations, a positive role emerges for the government to intervene and push the market toward the social optimum.

The government can force a firm to internalize its external costs. This is accomplished with a tax equal to the difference between MPC and MSC. In the example of Figure 9.3, the tax is $6 per unit of output. The firm's MPC is then forced up to the level MSC. The pollution tax forces the firm to consider explicitly the effects of its pollution. The firm then restricts output to 10 and prices output at $22. Tax revenues of $6 × 10 = $60 could be allocated by the government to those in the area actually paying the pollution costs. Revenue of the firm after the pollution tax is paid would be $160 = $220 − $60.

The optimal amount of pollution is produced with this pollution tax. This economic solution to pollution is unfortunately not practiced in the United States. The U.S. government through the Environmental Protection Agency (EPA) has imposed arbitrary limits of allowed pollution with little regard to costs. The EPA is not known for thorough scientific study of the pollutant's impact on the environment. Firms in the United States face fines when random and historically uneven sampling turns up levels of pollutants outside arbitrary guidelines. The EPA may have succeeded in slowing down polluting by some firms that have little regard for the environment. As a policing body, the EPA has a fairly good record. As a policymaker setting standards, the EPA has performed poorly.

A policy of pollution taxes has been consistently urged by economists since pollution become a political issue during the 1960s.

2. International Externalities

Negative externalities are enough of a problem inside a country, but more fundamental problems arise when the external costs are paid by those across national boundaries. The two governments involved may have different standards and policies for pollution.

When a steel plant in the United States produces sulfur dioxide that creates acid rain in Canada, the economic solution of a tax is impractical because the U.S. government would have to tax the domestic firm and transfer funds to Canadians. Similarly, when U.S. farmers use insecticides and fertilizers that drain into the Colorado River and cause problems along the river downstream in Mexico, tax revenues in the United States would have to be transferred to Mexicans.

There are few international legal practices or precedents that offer remedies for international externalities. Cooperation among governments, industries, and citizen groups across nations is the way to solve the international externalities. Awareness of negative externalities and the desire for good will and consistent long-run profitable operations are ultimately powerful forces.

International externalities pose special problems in that the economic solution of a pollution tax may not be workable.

Different standards for pollution control have recently been cited as an influence on the decision of where to locate new branch operations. Mexico has less strict environmental standards and enforcement than the United States. Those relaxed laws must attract some U.S. industry to Mexico. The Mexican government claims, however, that it will not allow pollution to get out of hand in Mexico.

Virtually all pollution can be technologically, but not economically, eliminated. The cost of pollution control must be weighed against its benefits. From the firm's private viewpoint, pollution control adds to the cost of production. Nations with less stringent pollution requirements may attract more industry but will have to pay high pollution costs. It is vital to reliably estimate the costs of pollution so that pollution taxes can be set at the proper level.

3. Positive International Externalities

Externalities also have a positive side. A very important positive externality is the learning that takes place with any productive activity. In LDCs, this positive externality can be vital.

Education itself is an activity with positive externalities. Through exposure to different ideas, students become more aware of their culture. A private market for education might only consider the technical training that has a definite market value and not take these external social benefits into account. If so, a private market would undersupply education.

The LDCs often send their brightest students abroad to study. This international exchange in education has positive externalities. Returning students take back more than their technical training. They return with impressions and habits from the host country that spill over into the developing country.

Another example of an international positive externality occurs around oil rigs in the sea. Built by firms of one nation, oil rigs supply excellent breeding grounds for fish that can be caught by boats of other nations. Other examples of goods with positive production externalities are electricity, roads, radio, television, and communication.

Figure 9.4 illustrates an example of a positive externality. Note that MSC lies below MPC. The spillover benefits of production make social costs lower than private costs. The firm that produces this good may not consider these positive spillover effects, producing only where MPC = MR at an output of 8 and a price of $24. If the external benefits are enjoyed directly by the firm, its costs fall to MSC, increasing output to 10 and lowering price to $22. There is an incentive for the government to subsidize firms produc-

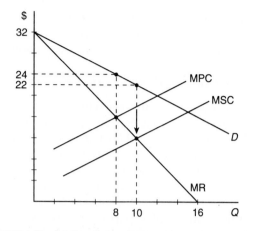

FIGURE 9.4. A Positive Production Externality When MSC < MPC because of a positive externality, benefits to the productive activity extend beyond the firm. A myopic firm would produce where MPC = MR at $Q = 8$ and $P = \$24$. A subsidy would induce the firm to produce the socially optimal higher output of $Q = 10$, and sell at $P = \$22$.

ing goods with positive externalities so they will increase their level of production. The aim again is to match MPC with MSC.

> Without compensation from those directly enjoying external social benefits resulting from positive externalities, a firm will underproduce and overprice.

4. International Public Goods

Public goods like police, parks, national defense, public health, open roads, and safe airways create positive externalities. These public goods suffer from the *free rider problem*. It is impossible to provide the public good exclusively for only part of the population. This nonexclusion property is characteristic of public goods. Free riders realize they can get by without paying and let others pay if the good is provided by the market. A free market might fail to provide these goods because some of those enjoying the good are not compensating the producing firm.

> Public goods provide a positive role for government to play in society. Because of the free rider problem, public goods are undersupplied by the private market.

Without public goods, the government may want to take over production entirely. When national boundaries are involved, government production is more difficult. Goods with positive externalities are generally undersupplied in the areas around national boundaries. Parks and highways close to a border will be used heavily by those from the foreign country. If governments do not want to subsidize consumers in other nations, they would tend to reduce the supply of public goods close to their border.

5.   Issues Involving International Market Failures

Numerous issues are raised by international externalities. Efforts have been made to integrate electricity generation and distribution along the U.S. borders with Canada and Mexico. International telecommunications, an industry with positive externalities, faces local protection as it develops and expands. Roads that span borders require international coordination. It has been proposed that Canada and Japan pay part of the U.S. defense bills because they are protected (and made a target) by U.S. defense policies. Other nations paid part of the cost of operating U.S. armed forces in the Kuwait war. Governments in LDCs often subsidize MNF branch operations because of the positive spillover effects as the locals become more involved in modern industry.

The solution to any international market failure must be political. National boundaries and different sets of laws and customs increase the cost of finding solutions, but the benefits can be substantial. The practice of international law is developing partly around the efforts to ease the solution of such problems.

Problems for Section B

B1.   Find the revenue of the firm in Figure 9.3 with and without the pollution tax. Find the amount of tax revenue and revenue of the firm after the tax is paid.

B2.   Suppose the EPA set pollution standards so that the firm in Figure 9.3 could produce only 10 units of output. Contrast this with the situation of a pollution tax.

B3.   Comment on the statement, "The idea of an optimal amount of pollution is ridiculous. Pollution is bad and should be totally eliminated."

C.   INTERNATIONAL POLITICAL ECONOMY AND PUBLIC CHOICE

This section looks into the realm of international politics and public choice. Political decisions that affect the nation's economy are made inside international economic organizations like the United Nations, International Monetary Fund (IMF), General Agreement on Trade and Tariffs (GATT), and the World Bank. Political agreements are also entered with trading partners and military allies. Income redistribution remains the connecting thread for studying the outcomes in these diverse political choices. The focus is on how a particular agreement or international policy affects the distribution of income among countries.

1. International Politics and Income Redistribution

A simple but effective way to view international political economy is the activity of nations trying to influence the international distribution of income. Groups of nations with high current income tend to support the status quo and are politically conservative. Poorer nations often try to use political arguments to improve their situation, sometimes favoring radical calls for a new international economic order.

Laws and customs inside a nation are typically well defined. Ownership of goods and resources is settled through the legal system. Damages are awarded if a firm or individual is negligent and damages another's property. Such everyday legal affairs are much more difficult to settle internationally. The main difficulty is the inability to collect judgments or fines across national borders. The laws, practices, and customs of international law are developing as the levels of international trade and investment increase. As international commerce grows in importance, so does the practice of international law.

> International political economy is concerned with the laws and practices between nations that affect international commerce and the international distribution of income.

An example of an international political agreement affecting economic activity was the Bretton Woods fixed exchange rate system of the 1950s and 1960s. The stable exchange rates of that period allowed international trade and finance to grow steadily. There was little or no risk from the fluctuating value of foreign exchange. The U.S. dollar was undervalued during the Bretton Woods period, meaning U.S. goods were too cheap abroad and foreign goods were too expensive in the United States. It may be difficult to believe in the light of recent history, but the United States had chronic trade surpluses during the 1950s. The desire for international political stability may explain why the Bretton Woods system lasted as long as it did.

A current example of an active international political agreement is GATT. Through GATT, member countries have agreed to negotiate multilaterally for lower protection levels worldwide. It is doubtful that individual governments would have been able to weather the constant forces of protectionism without the overriding international agreement of GATT.

The IMF is effective only because the individual nations support its policies. The IMF acts like a bank for government central banks, imposing constraints on government deficit spending and money creation around the world.

Protectionism, foreign exchange controls, limits on international investment, and labor migration laws are the main tools of international political economy. Protectionism is the most common policy tool of international political economy. Nations like to see income distributed their own way and may believe that protection improves their situation. There are conflicting goals across nations. The outcome in one nation typically depends on the actions of others.

> The bottom line of any international economic policy is the income redistribution it creates.

2.   Public Choice in International Policy

Most governments try to act on the principle of *majority rule,* in which policy is based on approval by more than half of the voters. Imagine a range of choice on protectionism, restrictions on foreign investment, and immigration restrictions. Voters can be expected to choose the policy that would distribute the most income their own particular way.

Voters may be inconsistent in their choices, as illustrated by the *paradox of voting.* Suppose there are three potential policy choices: protect industry competing with imports, restrict foreign investment, and restrict immigration. Suppose three voters rank their preferences as in Table 9.1. Each voter knows exactly how the potential tariff will redistribute income, and ranks the policies according to his or her advantage.

If there is a vote between protection and restricting foreign investment, voter B would choose to restrict foreign investment while both A and C would choose protectionism. If there is a vote between restricting foreign investment and immigration, voter C would choose to restrict immigration but both A and B would choose to restrict foreign investment. It would seem that protection would always be chosen by vote, since protection is preferred to restricting foreign investment, which is preferred to restricting immigration.

But consider what would happen if a vote were held between protectionism and restricting immigration. Voter A would choose protectionism,

TABLE 9.1. Tariff Preferences

	Voters		
	A	**B**	**C**
Protection	1	3	2
Restricted foreign investments	2	1	3
Restricted immigration	3	2	1

but voters B and C would opt for restricting immigration. This type of inconsistency in matters of public choice helps to explain why the world of politics often seems irrational.

Voters seem apathetic but may be politically inactive because of what is called *rational ignorance*. On issues like protectionism or restrictions on international finance or migration, becoming familiar with the issues takes a good deal of effort. Not everyone, after all, studies international economics. A bias remains in favor of protectionism, especially for local industry. It may be that the personal benefits that would come from an informed vote are outweighed by the costs of becoming informed. With most policies the benefits are concentrated and localized while the costs are spread out. The average voter may be rational to choose to remain ignorant on a particular issue.

The dilemma of rational ignorance is tied to the free rider problem. The average voter may assume that well-informed voters will make the right choice, so it is wasteful to spend the resources to make a wise vote. Actually, it can be assumed that voters will make choices in their own best interest. In the end, remaining generally ignorant on political issues cannot be rational.

The principles of public choice are perplexing but crucial for understanding political economy. Policy is open to the inequities created by special interest groups and logrolling. Lawmakers in Congress logroll by trading on issues of their own particular concern. A representative from Iowa, for instance, may agree to vote for a new dam in California if the California representative votes for new post offices in Iowa. Neither keeps the interests of the entire nation nor economic efficiency in mind. Negotiators in GATT or the other international agencies can enter into similar narrow deals without regard for international economic efficiency.

How are international policy choices to be made? What international systems will encourage rational decisions on policy? Certainly GATT is a step in the right direction. Through GATT, nations are committed to freer international trade. The IMF is a stabilizing influence, leading to more consistent monetary and fiscal policies around the world. The World Bank promotes development in the LDCs, encouraging the creation of public goods like dams and roads. Free international trade and investment remain elusive ideals worth pursuing.

3. International Political Economy and Economic Development

From the viewpoint of global economic development, the world has two basic regions. The developed North is abundant in capital and skilled labor, while the developing South is labor abundant. For global efficiency the North would specialize in services and high-tech manufactures, both of which are intensive in skilled labor. The North would also pursue capital-intensive agriculture. The South would specialize in labor-intensive manufacturing, attracting investment from the North. Agriculture in the South would remain labor intensive. Much can be gained through increased international specialization and trade. Extraction of exhaustible resources occurs wherever they are located and would be done in free markets. These are the fundamental lessons of international economics.

This pattern of international specialization will unfortunately be painful for the North's traditional manufacturing industries. But imagine how it looks to the developing economies in Africa and South America as they try to industrialize into labor-intensive manufacturing industries in the face of protectionism from the markets in the North. The industrial revolution is just beginning to dawn in many parts of the world. Industrial nations tax the activity of the poorest nations through protectionism. In the developing South, manufacturing operations could be set up to export low-tech manufactures to the North, but protection inhibits such activity.

The opening of world trade in manufactures remains a central issue in international political economy. The appeal to lower the protection of manufactures comes up regularly at GATT negotiations. The adjustment in nations of the North can be made less painful through a gradual dropping of protection. If a job is lost through international competition, compensation can be temporarily made and workers can be paid to retrain and relocate. These positive activities are less costly than misguided efforts at protectionism.

GATT continues to have a fundamental effect on international political economy. Through GATT, nations are committed to a systematic reduction in their barriers to free international trade. GATT has been successful in coordinating the lowering of tariff rates around the world. The United States and the other industrialized nations are committed to following the agreements of GATT, which represent the first systematic effort to coordinate trade policy internationally. Even though GATT talks often break down without apparent agreement, the process of negotiating continues.

The IMF acts as a bank for the central banks of nations and can loan funds to nations experiencing temporary deficits or foreign exchange shortages. The IMF has its own currency, the Special Drawing Right (SDR), which is accepted by national central banks. The SDR has the potential of becoming an international currency because it already forms part of every nation's monetary base. While forward and spot exchange markets eliminate some of the friction involved with international trade and investment, exchange transactions are costly. Imagine how complicated commerce in the United States would be if every state had its own uniquely defined currency. International trade and investment would be that much easier with a commonly accepted currency. In the foreseeable future, commercial banks will be keeping the private accounts of international traders and investors in SDRs.

International political economy raises clearly defined issues because nations differ in their economic circumstances. There will be winners and losers for any particular policy. The overall goal should be to choose international policy that creates a more equitable distribution of income and increased global efficiency. Some reflection will convince you that this way of thinking goes a long way toward coping with the world of international politics.

> Free international trade and investment remain the goal of rational international economic policy.

EXAMPLE 9.6   Escape Clauses in the GATT Agreement

Although the United States is committed to reduction of protectionism through GATT, legal ways exist for industries suffering from import competition to receive "temporary" help. The U.S. International Trade Commission (ITC) has offered temporary protection through the Escape Clause in the Trade Act of 1974 and Article 19 of the GATT agreement. As reported by Gary Hufbauer, Diane Berliner, and Kimberly Elliott (1986), the U.S. industries listed below received temporary protection from the ITC that exceeded the levels agreed to in GATT. The ITC regularly hears appeals and must make decisions based on the evidence presented. Foreign firms have supplied evidence about their costs of production at the hearings. Between 1954 and 1967, for instance, the U.S. watch industry enjoyed a tariff that kept out an estimated $55 million worth of imported watches. Reading down the list, reflect on the associated real deadweight losses.

Industry	Years	Trade Coverage	Protection
Watches	1954–67	$ 55 mil	Tariff
Bicycles	1955–68	$ 25 mil	Tariff
Carpets	1962–73	$ 30 mil	Tariff
Sheet glass	1962–74	$ 30 mil	Tariff
Ball bearings	1974–78	$ 60 mil	Tariff
Specialty steel	1976–80	$ 213 mil	Quota
	1983–87	$ 313 mil	Tariff, quota
Clothespins	1979–82	$ 2 mil	Quota
Televisions	1977–82	$ 412 mil	VER
Leather shoes	1977–81	$1,179 mil	VER
Ferrochromium	1978–82	$ 99 mil	Tariff

CB radios	1978–81	$ 61 mil	Tariff
Bolts and nuts	1979–82	$ 375 mil	Tariff
Motorcycles	1983–88	$ 229 mil	Tariff, quota

Problems for Section C

C1.   Minerals are fairly evenly distributed around the world. If all extractive minerals were in one nation, what difference would it make? Would the pattern of international mineral prices over time be any different? What difference would it make if the nation tried to maximize its profit for the present year or to maximize its profit over the next 100 years?

C2.   Illustrate the pattern of trade and the gains from trade between the North and South with the production possibilities frontier of each region. Show the effects of Northern protection of its tradition industries. Discuss the income redistribution in both regions that would occur with increased trade.

D.   STEPS TO INTERNATIONAL ECONOMIC INTEGRATION

This final section looks at the political process leading to international economic integration. As nations become more integrated economically, globally efficient production, trade, and investment increase. Measured political steps can be taken to encourage free international trade and investment. Through international economic integration, the political economy of a nation is altered and economic efficiency improves.

What exactly is a nation? We all have some rough ideas about what the word "nation" refers to: a central government, borders, territory, language, cultural differences, a common history, defense (against other nations), flags, currencies, and so on. Characteristics of nations stressed in international economics involve the right to erect artificial barriers to trade, migration, and investment. There is also the ability to print a national currency and conscript people into the military. These abilities differentiate nations from regions, provinces, or states and create the substance of international economics.

1.   Free Trade Areas

Protectionism is a costly activity, but it is difficult to persuade nations to quit the practice of protecting their existing industries. Nevertheless, free trade agreements are being made. The nations of the European Community (EC) are eliminating all of their protection with one another through the economic integration of 1992. Nations of South America, Africa, Southeast

Asia, the Arabian Gulf, the Caribbean, and other areas have entered into similar economic agreements. The United States, Canada, and Mexico are bilaterally eliminating tariffs. Nations that agree to eliminate barriers to free trade notice the overall gains, although costs of adjustment must be paid in some sectors.

> When nations enter into free trade with each other, a free trade area (FTA) is formed.

An FTA is the first step toward international economic integration. An FTA removes the temptation politicians have to chase votes by making international policy favorable to their own districts or regions but unfavorable to the nation as a whole. As the United States, Canada, and Mexico form an FTA, none of the potential tariffs or quotas that could have hindered trade among the three partners will be possible. Nations give up the right to tax imports and protect traditional industries, but gain in income and promote a fairer distribution of income. Economists favor FTAs because FTAs take control of trade out of the hands of shortsighted politicians.

2. Customs Unions

A further step toward international economic integration is a customs union (CU).

> A CU establishes a common policy of protection for the members with the outside world.

The EC is a CU as well as an FTA. The EC has common external tariffs and quotas. The step to a CU is much harder to take because each nation has its own industries that face international competition with the rest of the world. The industries may be willing to give up their chance at protection from a neighboring nation inside the FTA but still want protection from competing industries in the rest of the world (ROW).

A CU makes trade within an FTA much easier. It is difficult to maintain an FTA without an accompanying CU. Without the CU, goods coming in from member countries must be checked to make certain that imports from outside are not simply being reshipped. Otherwise, importers could buy a particular foreign good in the country with the lowest protection and ship it to other countries inside the FTA. For instance, if England has a 25% tariff on shoes while France has a 10% tariff, importers will buy Brazilian shoes in France and ship them across the channel to England. For an FTA to work smoothly, a CU becomes necessary.

An FTA is easier to form between two nations that have fewer common industries because there is little call for protection from the member's industries. A CU is easier to form if member nations have the same industries because they can agree on seeking protection from the ROW. The step from an FTA to a CU is typically difficult. There is little prospect of Canada, Mexico, and the United States moving to a CU.

It is no small thing for two governments to sacrifice power and to accept a common trade policy. This process involves compromise between two governments in setting common levels of protection. Given the political difficulties encountered in one nation, the job of agreeing to common protection levels across nations boggles the imagination. The European nations have struggled through years of political maneuvering and compromise, which will intensify with the formal customs union.

Ideally, all international protectionism would be eliminated. Imagine you are the dictator of a nation where tariffs, quotas, and other nontariff barriers to trade are illegal. Your imaginary economy trades freely with the world economy, efficiently carrying out activities according to its comparative advantage. Losses would occur if you started restricting trade. Relatively efficient industries would have to shut down and would be replaced by inefficient ones. Workers would have to be retrained in jobs that were relatively less productive. Average incomes would fall, with transfer going to the inefficient. The income redistribution would be from those with low income to those with high income. Industries would have to train professional lobbyists and spend revenues trying to influence you to protect their industry. This rent seeking is part of the cost of trying to obtain the increased monopoly power offered by the new potential protection. In your imaginary economy, protection is no less wasteful than it is in actual economies. Unfortunately, local legislators are unlikely to vote to make protectionism illegal because they would be eliminating one of their main avenues of support.

3.   Common Markets

A further step in international integration is the formation of a common market (CM), which is a customs union with no restrictions on the international movement of labor and investment.

The EC is an example of a CM, with people and firms free to move to any member country. Firms in one EC country are free to set up foreign operations anywhere inside the EC. Children in Europe learn at least one foreign language very well.

There is limited discussion of creating a CM between the United States and Canada. Both nations have restrictive immigration policies. Canada lets in restricted numbers of only certain types of skilled labor. The United States has a more open policy but is generally restrictive. It would not be too large a step for the two nations to open their borders to each other's workers and firms, while adopting common policies for international factor movement with the rest of the world.

The main international labor flows into the United States are occurring in the West and Southwest, with a steady instream of Latin Americans. Most people in the United States would oppose a CM with Latin America. Unskilled labor already in the United States would have to compete directly with the immigrants. Capital owners in Latin America would lose as labor becomes less abundant there. Historically, though, the United States has experienced its fastest economic growth during periods of intense immigration.

4. Economic Unions

A final stage of economic integration is an economic union (EU) with nations sharing a common currency.

The step to an EU is the most difficult to take because governments have a monopoly on money creation and are not apt to yield it easily. In effect, being able to print money gives a government a means to spend more than its current tax revenue.

An example of an operating EU is Belgium and Luxembourg. Europe is not a complete EU, but the value of most currencies moves closely with the German mark. Since World War II, Germany has had very low rates of money supply growth and low inflation. The Italians have a history of higher rates of money growth and higher inflation. In between, each nation of Europe has pursued its own monetary policy. Still, the exchange value of European currencies moves systematically together. Most European nations favor moving to a common currency, the European currency unit (ECU), which is currently used between European nations as a form of international payment and account. England has been opposed to an EU, apparently over misgivings about losing prestige as an international financial center.

Once an EU is formed on top of a CM, little is left of the nation from the viewpoint of economics. International economists would be out of their jobs if all nations of the world formed an EU, but everyone else would be better off. National boundaries are inhibiting in many ways. Stripping off the inhibitions one by one takes a nation through the various forms of economic integration, leading to gains at each step. From the standpoint of economics, the nation loses its identity when it forms an EU.

A political union would be a final stage of integration, with a commonly accepted legislative and judicial process. The states in the United States are joined into a political union. In a political union, nations lose their political identity.

Economic integration is proceeding at a dizzying pace. In South America, Central America, the Caribbean, the Pacific Rim, the Arabian Gulf, and

Asia, a dozen or so agreements are currently working. Nations in Africa so far have had little success in economic integration. Japan has not integrated at all with other economies. The move toward free international trade and investment in Eastern Europe will have dramatic effects.

The most powerful influences leading the world toward international economic integration are increasing foreign investment and improved communication. While international trade continues to grow in size and importance, direct investment puts MNFs into operation across borders. Everyone has an interest in increasing productivity and income. Most people in the world live in poverty, and many others live by standards well below those enjoyed in the industrialized countries. Getting all of the world into the mainstream of efficient economic activity is the greatest challenge facing political economy in the coming century.

EXAMPLE 9.7   Forming the European Community Common Market

The various steps of economic integration are typically slow. The EC has taken 40 years to move to its current stage. This is a brief description of key steps in the EC's formation:

1951   The European Coal and Steel Community is formed by France, Germany, Italy, Belgium, the Netherlands, and Luxembourg.

1957   These six countries establish the EC, signing the Treaty of Rome.

1968   All duties are removed for trade in the EC, and a common external tariff is set. The six members have a CU.

1972   Denmark, Ireland, and the United Kingdom join the EC. The "snake" exchange rate system links currency values.

1979   Greece joins the EC. The European Monetary System is formed.

1985   Spain and Portugal join the EC.

1986   The Single European Act is signed, leading to the Common Market of 1992.

Current problems of the EC include concern over crime, terrorism, and smuggling across borders. Migration policy varies for some EC countries. Laws regarding the health of plants and animals in trade are under debate. Workers' rights laws are different in Britain and the Continent. Differences in laws on ocean and air transport present some difficulties. Finally, tax systems vary across countries. These difficulties will slowly be resolved as the CM matures.

EXAMPLE 9.8   Projected Gains from the European Community

As the EC moves toward becoming a common market, gains are expected in most industries. Free trade within the EC will increase specialization. Also, firms will enjoy economies of scale as they expand operations. Evidence in favor of these views is presented by Alasdair Smith and Anthony Venables (1988). Some industries in some countries will lose with the move to a common market. In the electrical household appliance industry, Germany and Italy are projected to see their industry expand 7% and 10%, respectively. Average cost of production will fall, but only by 1%. The U.K. appliance industry will suffer a 9% decline in its output and France a 2% decline. The rest of the EC should see its appliance industry decline 5%. The largest industrial gains are projected to be in office machinery (16%), artificial and synthetic fibers (7%), motor vehicles (4%), and footwear (4%). Overall immediate gains from the integration are estimated to be in the range of 2% to 5%. Bela Belassa and Luc Baumens find, in the same issue, that interindustry trade within the EC depends on the ratios of capital and skilled labor to labor and the countries' relative factor abundances. Intraindustry trade is found to be higher between countries in the EC when their income per capita is closer together and when the countries themselves are closer together.

EXAMPLE 9.9   The European Community and the European Free Trade Association

The European Free Trade Association (EFTA) is a customs union that includes Austria, Finland, Iceland, Norway, Sweden, and Switzerland. Currently, there is a movement to include the EFTA along with the EC countries in a larger CU or possibly even CM. The 1984 Luxembourg Declaration called for the creation of a "European Economic Space." The EFTA is the EC's largest trading partner, followed closely by the United States, with Japan a distant third. The EC is by far the EFTA's largest trading partner, accounting for roughly 10 times the trade with the United States and Japan combined. Since the EFTA is smaller than the EC, it is projected to gain more through a free trade agreement because of improved terms of trade and access to the large EC markets. The political barriers to a common European Economic Space are more sizeable than within the EC, but it appears likely that such an agreement will come about.

EXAMPLE 9.10   The Special Drawing Right as an International Currency?

The International Monetary Fund acts as a bank for national central banks, lending to them to meet their temporary cash shortfalls. The Special Drawing Right (SDR) has developed as an accounting money among central banks, which keep SDR deposits at the IMF. The value of the SDR is defined by the IMF in terms of a basket of national currencies. As this table shows, central banks have switched to holding SDRs as an international money. Some experts suggest that the SDR could simply become the world's international currency. If all currencies were fixed to the SDR, monetary policy would be taken out of the hands of national governments, a single world inflation rate would exist, and foreign exchange markets would not be so critical. Such a proposal is, however, well beyond the scope of current international coordination. This table from the *Annual Report* (International Monetary Fund, 1987) of the IMF shows the evolution of reserves of central banks. As total reserves grew 52% over these years, SDR holdings grew by 164% to a total of $21.4 billion.

	1978	1980	1986
Gold	42%	58%	43%
Foreign exchange	53%	38%	51%
IMF reserves	3%	2%	3%
SDRs	2%	2%	3%

5.   Economic Systems and International Integration

The differences between the economic systems of *capitalism* and *socialism* are important. Economic systems differ primarily according to the ownership of resources. Capitalism is characterized by private ownership of productive factors and decentralized decision making. Socialism is characterized by public ownership of resources and centralized decision making. The nations of the world have various mixes of these two ideals.

The Soviet Union operated (and China operates) a predominantly planned socialist economy with a system of material balance planning. Priorities were set by the government for finished goods, and outputs of all intermediate goods had to be planned and allocated among these ends. Many agricultural goods and consumer products in the Soviet Union, however, were produced within a private market system. International trade and finance were planned by the government to meet certain goals. The evolution of the economy of the republics that were the Soviet Unions during the 1990s promises to be interesting.

The United States operates a predominantly capitalist economy with a market or price system. No overall government plan specifies which goods are to be produced. Markets determine outputs and prices. Production that is efficient and profitable continues. Production that is inefficient and unprofitable ceases. The United States has socialized postal service, as well as public housing and public medical care. International trade and finance are determined mostly by market forces.

> Every nation chooses an economic system along the spectrum from pure capitalism to pure socialism.

Eastern Block Communist countries have been closed to international trade and investment since World War II. As they begin to open, large gains will be realized quickly. Foreign investment and trade between the Western capitalist economies and Eastern Europe will increase. There are large markets to develop inside the former Soviet Union. China has similarly been a closed economy for most of this century. Signs are that China is slowly beginning to integrate itself back into the world economy.

LDCs and nonindustrialized countries (NICs) in South America, Africa, and Asia must choose an economic system. Free market economies readily lend themselves to free international trade and investment. Planned economies typically restrict international trade and investment and stress meeting targets with domestic means. Such restriction is unfortunate from a global perspective because economic planners are probably unaware of or insensitive to the potential gains from free international trade and investment. The LDCs and NICs would benefit from the choice of opening themselves to free enterprise and to free international trade and investment. The developed industrial nations should encourage this trend by dropping all protection of imports from the LDCs and NICs.

The desire for improving international economic relations and increasing international understanding is growing. The world is effectively becoming smaller and nations are growing more sensitive to one another, not through any common ideology but through the common and practical desire to develop international trade and investment.

EXAMPLE 9.11   Free Trade in the Americas

Canada and the United States are operating an FTA. Negotiations are under way to include Mexico in a North American FTA. In 1983 the United States started the Caribbean Basin Initiative, a program that exempts certain exports of the Caribbean countries from U.S. customs laws. The Andean Trade Preferences Act, which would give Colombia, Peru, Ecuador, and Bolivia exempt status, has been proposed. President Bush has started an "Enterprise for the Americas Initiative," which has the long-run goal of establishing an FTA in all of North, Central, and South America.

Problems for Section D

D1.   The Eastern Bloc nations were integrated closely with the Soviet Union. Will they benefit through disintegration? Apply the concepts in this section.

D2.   How l kely is it that two nations might agree to free international factor movements between them without an underlying FTA?

CONCLUSION

Free international trade and investment are goals worth pursuing and provide meaningful ideals in shaping international political agreements. The trend toward international economic integration will improve efficiency and raise standards of living around the world. The next section turns attention to important matters of international financial economics, namely the balance of payments, exchange rates, the international market for loanable funds, and international financial intermediation.

KEY TERMS

Branch plant	Horizontal and vertical integration
Common Market (CM)	Joint venture
Coase theorem	Licensing agreement
Customs union (CU)	Marginal social cost
Economic Union (EU)	Paradox of voting
European currency unit (ECU)	Public goods
Externalities	Rational ignorance
Free rider problem	Transfer pricing
Free trade area (FTA)	

KEY POINTS

- Multinational firms create a lasting form of economic integration and encourage international trade and investment.
- Externalities create market failures and the opportunity for rational economic policy. International externalities create the need for policy coordination between governments.
- International political economy is the study of the causes and effects of political choice across nations. Income redistribution remains the primary focus of the effects of political choice.
- Each nation operates with its own economic system, somewhere on the spectrum between pure capitalism and pure socialism. Nations can integrate themselves economically through various steps promoting free international trade and finance.

REVIEW PROBLEMS

1. Explain why the United States has many MNF branch operations involved in construction, business services, and oil and coal extraction.
2. Analyze what happens in a multiplant firm like the one in Figure 9.1 if the costs of operation are the same in each plant.
3. How could price discrimination between foreign and domestic markets lead a firm to establish an MNF branch plant?
4. Analyze what happens to the vertically integrated multinational firm in Figure 9.2 if costs rise in the foreign nation because of a new labor contract with the electronic component workers.
5. In an economical solution to acid rain on Canada, the U.S. government would tax domestic firms and transfer the funds to Canadian residents. Are there other ways the transfer could be handled?
6. How can a government that is host to a multinational firm encourage production and the positive externalities that come with MNF activity? How will domestic firms react?
7. Europe is a good example of how closely national governments can cooperate. In many ways Europe acts like a single nation and the separate countries in Europe act like states in the United States. What are the chances that this sort of international cooperation will spread?
8. Illustrate North and South trade with offer curves, including the protectionism of the North. What will happen to the volume and terms of trade when this protectionism is lifted?
9. Why has economic integration not been successful in Africa? Why has Japan not entered into any economic integration schemes?
10. What would be the economic effects of an FTA between the United States and Mexico? a CU? a CM? an EU? What are the political realities of such agreements?
11. Answer the same questions for the four stages of international economic integration between the United States and Japan.
12. What would be the consequences for the United States if an FTA was formed for all of North America? a CU? a CM? an EU?
13. What about those same steps for all of North, Central, and South America?

READINGS

James Cassing and Steve Husted, editors, *Capital, Technology, and Labor in the Global Economy,* The AEI Press, Washington, DC, 1988. Articles on the globalization of production and technology.

Jeffrey Arpan and David Ricks, editors, *Directory of Foreign Manufacturers in the United States,* Georgia State University Business Press, Atlanta, 1990. Detailed data on some 5,000 foreign MNFs in the United States.

John Carrol, editor, *International Environmental Diplomacy,* Cambridge University Press, Cambridge, Eng, 1988. A collection of articles on the international problems of acid rain, marine pollution, and other sorts of pollution.

Tom Tietenberg, *Environmental and Natural-Resource Economics,* Scott-Foresman,

Glenview, IL, 1984. Contains a good treatment of the fundamentals of negative production externalities.

James Buchanan and Gordon Tullock, *The Calculus of Consent,* University of Michigan Press, Ann Arbor, 1962. A classic in public choice economics.

Jeffry Frieden and David Lake, *International Political Economy: Perspectives on Global Wealth and Power,* St. Martin's Press, New York, 1987. A fine collection of articles on international political economy.

Stephen Easton, "Free Trade, Nationalism, and the Common Man: The Free Trade Agreement Between Canada and the United States," *Contemporary Policy Issues,* July 1989. A discussion of the free trade agreement from the Canadian viewpoint.

Harold Crookell, *Canadian-American Trade and Investment Under the Free Trade Agreement,* Quorum Books, New York, 1990. A nontechnical discussion of coming changes for the two countries.

Paul Gregory and Robert Stuart, *Comparative Economic Systems,* Houghton Mifflin, Boston, 1985. Offers perspective on the world's different economic systems.

Melvyn Kraus, editor, *The Economics of Integration,* George Allen and Unwin Ltd., London, 1973. A collection of readable articles on different aspects of economic integration.

The Likely Impact on the United States of a Free Trade Agreement with Mexico, U.S. International Trade Commission, Washington, DC, 1991, Publication 2353. One of a series of well-done studies of the ITC.

David Greenaway and John Whalley, editors, *The World Economy,* Basil Blackwell, London, various dates. A journal of descriptive studies of international trade policy.

PART FIVE

International Financial Economics

CHAPTER 10

Balance of Payments, Deficits, and Policy

CHAPTER PREVIEW

The goal of this chapter is to introduce the basic adjustment mechanisms of a country's international balance of payments. An important issue is exactly how a country can finance a balance of trade deficit, when spending on imports is greater than revenue from exports. Another issue of current concern is the effect of government deficits on the balance of payments. The role of government policy in influencing the balance of payments is examined. Specifically, this chapter examines:

(a) How *import and export elasticities* affect the balance of trade
(b) The components of the *balance of payments*
(c) The relationship between *government deficits* and *trade deficits*
(d) The international roles of the government's *monetary policy* and *fiscal policy*

INTRODUCTION

International excess supply and demand become useful tools when they are used to predict how international markets adjust. Adjustments occur continuously in both export and import markets. Agents in an international market participate today and want to predict what will happen tomorrow.

When the price of an imported good rises, the nation's expenditure on the import adjusts. As in all markets, the quantity demanded of the imported good will fall with the higher price. The higher price for the imported good increases production in the domestic industry competing with imports, causing further cuts in the level of imports. Import expenditure (price times quantity) may fall or rise. If quantity demanded falls enough, import expenditure will drop with the higher price of imports. A higher world price for an exported good will increase export revenue unless the quantity the country can sell of its export falls by a larger percentage than price rises.

For economies highly dependent on their export industries, international price changes can be crucial. Examples of countries highly dependent on particular goods are Colombia and Guatemala on coffee, Saudi Arabia on oil, and Costa Rica on bananas. Even for large diversified industrialized nations like the United States, changes in international prices can be important. When the price of imported oil rose because of the oil embargoes of the 1970s, shocks reverberated through the U.S. economy. Changes in international prices can be crucial at the industry or firm level, where competition from abroad must be met.

Given the thousands of international markets and continuous changes and adjustments taking place, no nation will spend on imports exactly what it earns in exports during any year. This chapter introduces the current account, which summarizes all the international cash flows connected with current transactions. The current account includes trade in goods and services plus international interest payments. If the current account is not balanced, international finance (borrowing and lending) must take place. A current account deficit can be financed through either international borrowing or spending accumulated wealth.

This chapter describes the fundamental mechanisms of balance of payments adjustment, building on the foundation of the balance of trade. The current and capital accounts of the balance of payments reflect this adjustment process.

An important issue is whether the government should use economic policy to influence the balance of trade. Fiscal policy refers to the policy of government spending and taxation. Monetary policy refers to the government's control of the money supply. Both types of economic policy are poor tools for influencing the balance of trade. The link between government deficits and trade deficits is explored.

A. PRICE ELASTICITIES AND THE BALANCE OF TRADE

This section examines the immediate effects of changing prices of internationally traded goods. Imagine you own a warehouse full of walking shoes and their demand rises because of news that wearing them might be good for posture. This is excellent because the demand for walking shoes increases. If you also operate a firm producing these shoes, you may want to plan on increasing production. This means hiring and training more labor, purchasing more supplies, and perhaps buying more capital equipment. Imagine that walking shoes are also imported and that your firm must compete with these imports. Having to compete with imports obviously makes a difference in your strategy. Will the international price of walking shoes rise? Will the level of imports rise?

1. Changing Export Prices

A nation that enjoys a higher price or increased demand for an exported good will increase production and enjoy higher export revenue, but domestic consumers would have to pay the higher price. Exported business services can be used as an example. In Figure 10.1, export volume equals 100 units of services at a world price of $10 per unit. Domestically, 200 units are produced but only 100 consumed. Suppose that exporters can sell as much as they want at the international price, which rises to $12. Domestic consumers cut their consumption from 100 to 75 units, while domestic producers increase output from 200 to 225. Excess supply grows to 225 − 75 = 150 at the higher international price.

Both suppliers and consumers respond to a change that is *exogenous,* or outside the domestic market and economy. There is no explanation of why the international price rises from $10 to $12 in Figure 10.1. The exogenous price change causes adjustments in the domestic market. The international market for services is large. This price could be increasing because of rising demand in the rest of the world for telecommunications, banking, or financial services.

Selling more services at a higher price creates higher export revenue. In this example the level of exports rises by 50 units and export revenue rises from $10 × 100 = $1,000 to $12 × 150 = $1,800. Total revenue of domestic service firms rises from $10 × 200 = $2,000 to 12 × 225 = $2,700. Total revenue includes export revenue and revenue from domestic sales. Producer surplus rises in the market. Domestic consumers pay a higher price and consume less of services, and consumer surplus falls. Consumers spend $12 × 75 = $900 on 75 units, instead of the previous $10 ×

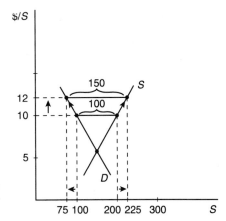

Figure 10.1. Rising Export Prices When the price of exported services rises from $10 to $12, the quantity demanded domestically *(D)* falls to 75 and the quantity supplied domestically *(S)* rises to 225. Exports rise from 100 to 150. Producer surplus rises, but consumer surplus falls.

100 = $1,000 on 100 units. The gain in producer surplus outweighs the loss in consumer surplus.

A higher export price can be caused by anything that increases demand among buyers or decreases supply among sellers in the rest of the world. This principle can be illustrated with an increase in the excess demand for services from the foreign nation in Figure 10.2. Canada might, for example, open its markets completely to U.S. banking and financial firms. In Figure 10.2, foreign excess demand shifts to the right and export revenue rises. Figures 10.1 and 10.2 are consistent with each other. The higher foreign excess demand in Figure 10.2 can be the cause of the higher price in Figure 10.1. In Figure 10.2 the price rise is *endogenous,* or explained by the model. In Figure 10.1 by itself, the price rise is exogenous.

2. Changing Import Prices

The level of imports is inversely related to the domestic currency price of imports. If the price of an imported good rises, the level of imports falls because of a decrease in the quantity demanded and an increase in the quantity supplied by the domestic industry, which competes with imports. Domestic consumers substitute away from the higher priced imported goods, while domestic firms increase their output. Consumers as a group are hurt by the higher price, while producers as a group benefit.

A classic example of increased import prices occurred when the Organization of Petroleum Exporting Countries (OPEC) was able to triple the price of oil in the early 1970s. Domestic consumers had to pay higher prices, while the domestic oil extraction industry boomed. As another example, bad weather in Colombia and Guatemala decreases the supply of coffee and drives up the international price of coffee. A depreciation of

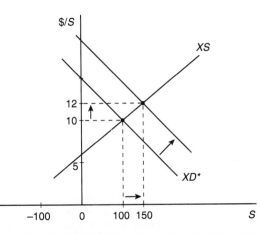

Figure 10.2. Increased Foreign Demand for Home Exports When foreign excess demand for home exports *(XD˙)* rises, the international price is pushed up from $10 to $12 and the quantity exported by the home country increases from 100 to 150.

the dollar on the foreign exchange market raises the dollar price of imports whose foreign currency price is stable. Many other examples occur regularly because of changing conditions in international markets.

Consider the rise in the price of imported manufactured goods from $5 to $7.50 in Figure 10.3. This is an exogenous increase in the price of manufactures. The domestic quantity demanded falls from 300 to 250 as consumers switch to substitutes and their real income falls. Spending by domestic consumers rises from $1,500 to $1,875. Consumer surplus falls more than producer surplus rises. The quantity supplied domestically rises from 100 to 150 as the domestic industry responds to the profit opportunity. New firms enter the industry or existing firms increase their capacity and output. Revenue of domestic firms rises from $500 to $1,125. Producer surplus rises, taking some of the previous consumer surplus. The domestic manufacturing industry benefits from the higher price of the exported good.

> Higher import prices help the domestic import-competing industry but hurt domestic consumers.

For the nation as a whole, the change in import expenditure with the higher import price alters the balance of trade (BOT). Import spending falls from $5 × 200 = $1,000 to $7.50 × 100 = $750. This particular increase in the price of imports, which could be due to a currency depreciation, lowers import expenditure and favors a BOT surplus.

3.   Import Elasticities and the Balance of Trade

If there is little time or opportunity for adjustment to a higher import price, demand for imports is likely to be *inelastic*. A price rise would then result in increased import spending, since the level of imports does not fall enough to offset the higher price.

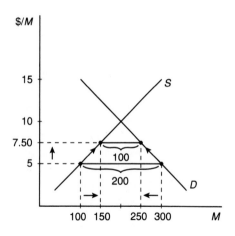

Figure 10.3. Rising Import Prices An increase in the price of imports from $5 to $7.50 increases the quantity supplied domestically from 100 to 150. The domestic quantity demanded *(D)* falls from 300 to 250. Imports, the difference between the domestic quantity demanded and the domestic quantity supplied, fall from 200 to 100. Import expenditure in this example falls. The loss in consumer surplus is greater than the gain in producer surplus.

If the price of imports and import spending are negatively related as in Figure 10.3, demand for imports is *elastic*. If consumers and firms have the time and opportunity to adjust the level of imports with a higher import price, spending on imports falls with the higher price of imports.

In the early 1970s at the time of the sudden increase in oil prices by OPEC, consumers were driving large inefficient cars and were not overly concerned with fuel conservation. There was little immediate opportunity for decreasing oil consumption with the higher prices. Oil imports were inelastic, and OPEC oil export revenue rose sharply. In the face of consistently high oil prices, cars became smaller and much more fuel efficient. Houses were soon being insulated, and heating and cooling technology improved. Over time, the quantity of oil consumed fell considerably. On the supply side, domestic drilling in the United States was taking place in remote areas and at tremendous depths. Government lands were opened to drilling, and offshore drilling expanded. The quantity of oil supplied domestically increased. OPEC learned the hard way about the effect of import elasticity on revenue. OPEC export revenue tapered as imports of oil became more elastic.

The *import elasticity* summarizes the relationship between import prices and import expenditure. The import elasticity is the percentage change in the quantity of imports divided by the percentage change in the price of imports, in absolute value:

$$\text{Import elasticity} = |(\%\Delta Q_{\text{imp}}) / (\%\Delta P_{\text{imp}})|.$$

The symbol Δ means "change in." Read "$\%\Delta Q$" as "the percentage change in Q." Quantity Q_{imp} and price P_{imp} are inversely related. Taking the absolute value makes the import elasticity positive, a practice that makes it easier to discuss the elasticity's value. To find percentage changes, subtract the original quantity of imports or price from the new one and divide by the average of the two.

In Figure 10.3, the $\%\Delta Q_{\text{imp}}$ is equal to $(100 - 200) / 150 = -0.667 = -66.7\%$ and the $\%\Delta P_{\text{imp}}$ is $(\$7.50 - \$5) / \$6.25 = 0.4 = 40\%$. The price elasticity of imports for the price change in Figure 10.3 is $|-66.7\% / 40\%| = 1.67$.

When the import elasticity is greater than one, demand for imports is *elastic*. Price and import spending will move in opposite directions when the demand for imports is elastic. Quantity is flexible or elastic relative to price.

When the import elasticity is less than one, the change in the level of imports is not large enough to offset the change in price. The quantity of imports is rigid or *inelastic* with respect to price. Higher import prices mean more import expenditure when demand for imports is inelastic and less import expenditure when demand for imports is elastic.

The effect of changing international prices on import expenditure depends on the import elasticity. When import demand is inelastic, price and import expenditure are positively related. When import demand is elastic, price and import expenditure are negatively related.

Whether a higher price for imported oil, coffee, bananas, automobiles, television sets, or tires increases or decreases import expenditure is an empirical issue that varies over time. Nations learn through experience about their particular import elasticities.

Higher elasticities occur for goods that

(a)   Have more available substitutes
(b)   Constitute a higher share of consumer budgets
(c)   Are luxuries

The more substitutes a particular good has, the more consumers can switch away from it when its price rises. When consumers spend a large share of their budget on a good, they will notice an increase in its price and search harder for substitutes. A 10% increase in the price of a new imported automobile, for instance, would be more noticeable than the same percentage increase in the price of imported tea. Purchases of a luxury item are easily put off when its price rises.

Higher import prices will generally increase the balance of trade at least in the long run when demand for imports is elastic.

4.   The Terms of Trade and the Balance of Trade

Considered as a whole, the nation of these figures exports business services in exchange for manufactured goods. Suppose the international price of manufactured goods M is $5, while the international price of services S is $10. Each unit of services is effectively being traded for 2 units of manufactured goods. The terms of trade or the relative price of exported services is 2.

With the increase in the international price of exported S to $12 in Figure 10.1, the terms of trade *(tt)* improve to $12/$5 = 2.4. Each unit of exported S brings in 2.4 units of M, an improvement of 20% in the *tt*.

This sort of adjustment in the relative price of traded goods takes place regularly. The International Monetary Fund (IMF) reports that since 1970

(a)   The terms of trade *(tt)* of industrial countries have fallen
(b)   Oil-exporting countries have seen their *tt* improve dramatically

(c) Developing countries that do not export oil have suffered a decline in their *tt*

These changes in the *tt* are estimated for a particular country by aggregating all goods that are exported or imported and examining the change in the average price of each group of goods. While a great deal can be learned by looking at each of the individual markets, lessons can also be learned from such aggregation. Changes in the terms of trade for a particular nation can be dramatic and affect everyone's standard of living.

Another illustration drives home the importance of import elasticities. Suppose the home country develops an improvement in the technology of producing its exported goods. With the same resources, a greater output can be produced. The home nation has become more "competitive," to use a currently popular term.

Improved technology in export production is illustrated with the increased excess supply in Figure 10.4. It is not immediately clear what will happen to export revenue. The nation certainly sells more services in the world market, as exports rise from 100 to 140. The price of services, however, falls from $10 to $8 in the process. The change in export revenue depends on the foreign import elasticity. In this example, export revenue rises from $10 × 100 = $1,000 to $8 × 140 = $1,120. Foreign import demand is elastic because price and domestic export revenue move in opposite directions.

If, however, foreign import demand is inelastic, becoming more "competitive" will lower export revenue. Improved technology in the production of exported goods would result in a decline in export revenue. If the new

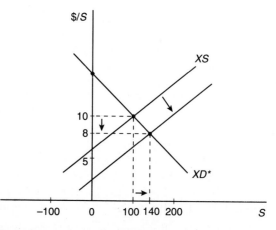

Figure 10.4. Improved Technology in Export Production Increased excess supply of services drives down the price of exports while increasing the level of exports. The direction of change in export revenue depends on foreign import elasticity.

level of exports in Figure 10.4 were less than 125, export revenue would decline. Suppose the level of exports rose to only 115 with the increase in *XS* and the same fall in price. Export revenue would then drop from $1,000 to $8 × 115 = $920. With inelastic foreign import demand, increased excess supply at home decreases export revenue and leads to a BOT deficit.

This seems paradoxical because improved technology and increased competitiveness are thought to be beneficial, as are lower trade deficits. Import elasticity is the rule, especially in the long run. The argument for *export optimism* (elastic foreign demand for imports) is strong. Export optimism implies that increasing the supply of exported goods through improved efficiency will ultimately favor a BOT surplus.

In the examples so far, prices in the foreign nation are stated in terms of dollars. In reality, every nation has its own currency and international trade involves the exchange of one currency for another. These transactions take place in the foreign exchange market, where exchange rates are determined. Changes in the foreign exchange value of currencies affect the price of imports and exports. The important influence of the foreign exchange rate on the trade balance is developed in the next chapter.

EXAMPLE 10.1   Changing Import Prices

In 1988 and 1989 the dollar appreciated against most currencies, lowering the price of imports and raising the price of U.S. exports abroad. These figures from the Federal Reserve Bank of Cleveland *(Economic Trends, September 1989)* show estimated percentage changes in the relative price of imports (how many units of exported goods must be given up for a unit of imported good). For instance, in 1989 the relative price of imported consumer goods fell 8%. Since imports are inelastic in the short run, import expenditure in these categories fell in 1989. If imports are elastic in the long run, import expenditure in the categories will ultimately rise.

	Relative Price of Imports	
	1988	*1989*
Industrial supplies	−4%	−2%
Capital goods	1%	−11%
Motor vehicles	3%	−11%
Consumer goods	0	−8%

EXAMPLE 10.2   The International Price of Oil and Oil Import Expenditures

The international price of oil is difficult to predict. OPEC tries to increase profits of its members through high oil prices. The oil embargo of 1973 caused oil prices to triple, and oil prices doubled again in 1979–1980. Oil prices sagged through the 1980s but are expected to continue a steady increase through the 1990s. The war in Kuwait disrupted supply and temporarily raised prices, although other OPEC members were quick to increase their production. Oil imports are generally estimated to be inelastic. James Griffin and David Teece (1982) estimate an oil import elasticity of 0.73 in the long run for all oil importers in their book *OPEC Behavior and World Oil Prices*. Other reported estimates are similar. With these oil import demand elasticities and gradually rising oil prices, oil importers can expect to increase their expenditures on oil over the coming decades.

Problems for Section A

A1. Start with Figure 10.1 and suppose the exogenous price of exports falls from $10 to $8, quantity demanded rises from 100 to 125, and quantity supplied falls from 200 to 175. Diagram this change in the export market and find the new export revenue.

A2. Similar to Figure 10.3, suppose quantity demanded falls from 300 to 270 and quantity supplied rises from 100 to 130 when the price of imports rises to $7.50. Find the import elasticity. What happens to the balance of trade with this increase in the price of imports?

B.   THE CURRENT AND CAPITAL ACCOUNTS

This section looks at the accounts in the balance of payments (BOP) and its two broad divisions:

(a)   The current account
(b)   The capital account

It is important to be familiar with the basic categories in the BOP because estimates regularly make the news and provide some insight into the economy's international performance.

1. Balance Sheets

Every year individual taxpayers in the United States are asked to produce an accounting balance sheet that serves as the basis for their income taxes. Firms must keep even more detailed records and produce balance sheets quarterly for both taxes and financial reports for stockholders. A balance sheet shows all current cash transactions for the time period. When cash comes in, a credit or positive number is entered. When cash goes out, a debit or negative number is entered. At the end of the accounting period the sum of these current transaction entries tells whether a net cash gain or loss occurred. This is the idea behind the current account in the BOP.

Borrowing is entered as a credit in the balance sheet because cash comes in, even though borrowing increases debt and implies future debt payments. Lending is entered as a debit because cash flows out, even though lending sets up future debt receipts. Wealth holders can accumulate assets other than cash. Suppose assets other than cash are increased during an accounting period. If these assets are bought with cash, a negative number or debit would be entered on the balance sheet. If assets other than cash are sold for cash during an accounting period, cash flows in and a positive number or credit is entered on the balance sheet. The capital account in the BOP is concerned with these changes in financial capital: borrowing and lending, or selling and buying assets.

2. The Balance of Payments

Much like firms and individuals, a nation keeps its books on international transactions on a balance sheet called the *balance of payments*. It is made up of two basic parts, the *current account* (CA) and the *capital account* (KA):

$$BOP = CA + KA$$

Transactions involving current goods and services are included in the CA. Investment transactions involving borrowing and lending are recorded in the KA.

The major components of the current account CA are the balance on goods and services (BGS) and net investment income (NII):

$$CA = BGS + NII$$

Net investment income includes all international payments on interest-earning assets such as stocks, bonds, and time deposits. All international interest payments on previous loans are included in NII. When interest payments come in, they are entered as credits. Outpayments are counted as debits. A positive NII indicates that the nation as a whole receives more payments on internationally held assets than it pays out. A negative NII indicates that the nation is in effect a net borrower internationally, paying more for foreign assets in the country than it receives from home assets abroad.

The BGS is composed of the BOT on merchandise plus net *trade in services* (TS):

$$BGS = BOT + TS$$

Trade in services includes transactions for transportation, travel, accounting, financial services, telecommunications, utilities, entertainment, and so on. This category is sometimes called true services or business services.

The capital account KA is the sum of direct investment (DI) and portfolio investment (PI):

$$KA = DI + PI$$

International investment spending by firms in the form of new plants and equipment is counted as DI. International portfolio investment by wealth holders is counted as PI. The conceptual difference between the two is that DI involves some control over branch firm operations, while PI would involve no control.

The distinction between DI and PI is difficult to draw. Suppose a U.S. oil firm wants to build a refinery in Poland. It first forms a corporation in Poland. Then it buys stock in the new corporation. Money is transferred to a Polish bank and construction begins. Other wealth holders may want to buy stock in the new refinery, and some of them may be Polish. Stockholders ultimately control the operation of the refinery, appointing a board of directors and manager. If stock in the refinery is offered to the public, it is difficult to say at what point the U.S. oil firm would lose control of the branch refinery. The U.S. oil firm may own only 10% of the stock and exercise complete effective control if there are many other stockholders, each holding small shares. The U.S. oil firm may own 49% of the stock and be excluded from management if a willful stockholder owns the other 51%. Ownership and management of foreign branch operations do not necessarily go hand in hand.

In practice, DI is recorded for the United States when 10% or more of the stock of the branch firm is held by the investing agent. Any investment in which less than 10% of the stock is held is counted as PI. This cutoff line is arbitrary. European nations use 25% as the standard cutoff, and data are kept in the United States for up to 50% cutoff. There is some incentive to eliminate the distinction between DI and PI.

A study by Roy Ruffin and Farhad Rassekh (1987) concludes that *DI* and *PI* are perfect substitutes in practice. This means that $1 more of portfolio investment results in $1 less of direct investment for U.S. firms. Clearly, the contribution to management of a branch firm is generally independent of the ownership of the firm's stock. Dropping the distinction between DI and PI would mean that the capital account would be made up of a single category, foreign investment.

The accounts in the balance of payments are summarized by Figure 10.5.

3. The Balance of Payments in the United States

Table 10.1 presents recent BOP data for the United States as reported by the Department of Commerce. A striking and much publicized trend is the growing balance of trade deficit of the 1980s. Domestic import-competing industries have used this BOT deficit as evidence that their firms need protection from foreign firms that pay lower wages to labor and are often subsidized. While the United States has specialized less in manufactured goods, it has increasingly specialized in exported services. A positive TS is reflected by the relationship between BOT and BGS over the period. In 1989, for instance, TS $= -91 - (-113 = 22$. The surplus in services does not seem to rate front page coverage in the local press.

The current account (CA) has historically been small in the United States relative to national income compared with countries. In the 1950s and 1960s the CA was generally in a surplus of less than 0.5% of national income. In the 1970s a deficit of 0.1% of gross domestic product (GDP) was the average. It is little wonder that the typical U.S. textbook on macroeconomics over these decades included little on international trade and finance. Trade imbalances and increasing international debt were unimaginable for the United States. The 1980s witnessed a fundamental change as the CA turned toward larger deficits. According to the International Monetary Fund's *International Financial Statistics*, 1988, the current account deficit of the United States was about 4% of GDP in 1987. Imports were 11% of GDP and exports 7% of GDP the same year, percentages that continue to grow steadily.

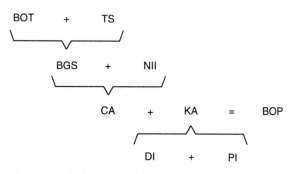

Figure 10.5. Elements of the Balance of Payments The balance of payments (BOP) is the sum of two basic elements, the current account (CA) and the capital account (KA). The CA is made up of the balance on goods and services (BGS) and net investment income (NII). The BGS equals the balance of trade (BOT) plus trade in services (TS). On the other side, KA is the sum of direct investment (DI) and portfolio investment (PI).

TABLE 10.1. U.S. Balance of Payments Data in Billions of Dollars

	1971	1973	1975	1977	1979	1981	1983	1985	1987	1989
BOT	−3	1	9	−31	−28	−28	−67	−122	−159	−113
BGS	6	14	25	−9	6	15	−30	−107	−148	−91
NII	7	12	13	18	30	31	27	16	5	−1
DI	−7	−8	−12	−8	−13	16	12	1	3	29
KA	11	−5	−24	17	−26	−28	29	102	156	88

SOURCE: From *Survey of Current Business* (various tables), U.S. Department of Commerce, 1991, Washington, DC: U.S. Government Printing Office.

The United States has traditionally posted high deficits in the DI account, which means that U.S. firms like to set up branch operations in foreign nations. A characteristic of U.S. direct investment is that management typically goes with it. When U.S. multinational firms establish branch plants abroad, they typically maintain a high level of ownership and visible control. By contrast, European firms rely more on portfolio investment to finance their multinational operations. The surpluses in DI during recent years have been due to an increase in the establishment of branch plants by foreign multinational firms in the United States.

There is no clear trend since the 1970s in PI, but the United States generally represents a secure haven for investment funds. The volatility and volume of PI in recent years reflects the increased interconnections in the world's financial markets. This competition has had a healthy effect. The New York Stock Exchange now must compete with equally strong financial centers worldwide for the attention of wealth holders in the United States. Wealth holders have diversified their portfolios internationally and hold stocks and bonds on various international exchanges. Foreign wealth holders, of course, hold a portion of the stocks traded on Wall Street.

A U.S. capital account surplus must be balanced by other countries with current account surpluses. In recent years, Taiwan, Japan, and Germany have been predominant among countries with current account surpluses. A component of the recent capital account surpluses in the United States has been net official inflow. Net official inflow summarizes investment transactions between central banks. It has been strongly positive in recent years, which means that foreign central banks have been buying U.S. government bonds. Net official inflow accounted for 28% of the capital account surplus in 1986, 40% in 1987, and 33% in 1988. Foreign central banks have been net buyers of U.S. dollars, U.S. bonds, and other dollar-denominated assets.

The BOP data are estimated by survey and include margins of error. Conclusive evidence shows that most nations, including the United States, underestimate export revenue. Actual BOT figures are more positive than reported. The statistical discrepancy in the estimating procedure is so large that in some years it cannot be determined whether the United States was a net international lender or borrower. When estimates of U.S. exports to Canada are compared with Canadian data on imports from the United States, it is clear that the U.S. Department of Commerce vastly underestimates U.S. exports. Governments keep more detailed records of imports because of tariff duties, quotas, nontariff barriers, health restrictions, and other protectionist devices. If the same margin of error realized with Canada is spread across all trading partners, the BOT deficit in the United States disappears for most of the 1980s.

EXAMPLE 10.3   Japanese Balance of Payments Data

These data from *International Financial Statistics* (IMF, 1990) present a recent history of the BOP for Japan. All figures are in billions of U.S. dollars, as in Table 10.1. Japan's BOT surplus has grown considerably during the 1980s. Japan is a net importer of services, as a comparison of the BOT and BGS indicates. Japan's current account surpluses are generally offset by increasing levels of direct and portfolio investment abroad. In some ways trends in the Japanese data are the mirror image of the U.S. BOP in Table 10.1.

	1971	1973	1975	1977	1979	1981	1983	1985	1987	1989
BOT	7.8	3.6	4.9	17.2	1.7	20.0	31.5	56.0	96.4	77.1
BGS	5.5	−0.4	−1.1	10.5	−9.9	3.2	19.3	47.5	83.3	52.5
CA	5.8	−0.1	−0.7	10.9	−8.7	4.8	20.8	49.2	87.0	56.8
DI	−0.1	−1.9	−1.5	−1.6	−2.7	−4.7	−3.2	−5.8	−18.6	−44.9
PI	0.8	−1.7	2.6	0.6	−1.2	7.7	−2.9	−41.8	−90.8	−32.6

EXAMPLE 10.4   The Japanese Dilemma

Naohiro Amaya (1988) discusses the future of the Japanese economy. Japan has developed into a leader in world trade with consistent trade surpluses. In international finance, Japan has been investing heavily abroad. Personal saving rates in Japan have been high but are beginning to fall as *shin-jinrui* (young wealthy) consumers spend more of their income. In the United States, by contrast, government budget deficits have reduced overall savings and consistent trade deficits have led to incoming foreign investment. The Japanese *keiretsu* system of business entails buying supplies from other firms in a loose group, a "buddy" system U.S. businesses have complained about. U.S. firms have only just begun to target Japanese markets, which had been traditionally seen as too small. For instance, driving in Japan is done on the left side of the road, and steering wheels should be on the right side of the car. U.S. automakers have never made this fundamental adjustment in their exports to Japan. Another example is U.S. refrigerators, which are too noisy for small Japanese houses and apartments. Education in Japan is famous for producing quick and efficient students, but there is a lack of creativity and independent direction and a fear of outside influence. Japanese business managers, traditionally loyal to one firm and underpaid, are finding themselves unable to deal with rapid changes and increasing international integration. Japan has become a world leader but that country is having some trouble accepting that role. Already Japan is the leading country in supplying foreign aid. Developing countries will turn more to Japan for help and guidance. Japan faces many challenges as it moves into the twenty-first century.

EXAMPLE 10.5   Will the United States Grow Out of Its Balance of Trade Deficits?

Michael Bryan and Susan Byrne (1990) make a convincing argument that the entrance of the baby boom generation into the workforce during in the 1980s led to BOT deficits. Baby boomers were born in the (evidently busy) years following World War II. The largest share of the U.S. population was born between 1945 and 1955. When these baby boomers entered the workforce, starting in the late 1970s, their current income was low but their lifetime earnings potential was high. People typically borrow when they are young, start saving when they are middle aged, and live off their assets when they retire. The baby boomers are pushing the entire country's spending and saving habits. As the baby boomers move into the middle of their working careers in the 1990s, they will save and so will the nation. BOT surpluses will probably become the rule as the 21st century approaches. About the BOT deficit, Bryan and Byrne say, "Don't worry, we'll grow out of it."

Problems for Section B

B1.   U.S. firms own and operate plants in Central America, producing tens of millions of brassieres annually for export to the United States. These firms produce, supply management, invest, and retain untaxed profits. Should these brassieres be counted as imports?

B2.   A Japanese carmaker that has been exporting to the United States decides to spend $10 million to build a plant in the United States to supply autos to the U.S. market and avoid protectionist tariffs and quotas. Predict subsequent changes that will occur in the U.S. BOP. Is NII affected?

B3. Calculate the following in 1989 for the United States using Table 10.1:

(a) TS

(b) CA

(c) PI

B4. Calculate the following in 1989 for Japan using the data in the example on the Japanese BOP:

(a) TS

(b) NII

(c) KA

C. INTERNATIONAL DEFICITS AND SURPLUSES

This section examines the workings of international deficits and surpluses. The loanable funds market makes it possible for individuals and firms to become borrowers and lenders. The nation as a whole may become a lender or borrower in the international loanable funds market. What exactly are the implications of a deficit in the current account, and how is such a deficit financed?

1. International Borrowing: Debt and Equity

As an individual consumer, you can spend either more or less than your income during a given year. As a student, you are probably spending more, either borrowing or spending family funds. In the process you are acquiring valuable human capital that will increase your income earning potential. With high wages after graduation, it will be relatively easy to pay off your debt. But this year, your (import) spending is greater than your (export) revenue. You have a (trade) deficit. In 20 years when you are earning $90,000 a year, you will find it relatively easy to have (trade) surpluses.

Firms behave exactly the same way when they are growing, spending to acquire capital goods and train labor. Typically firms assume *debt* by selling bonds and create *equity* by selling new stocks to raise the funds used to buy the capital equipment, machinery, and structures that increase productivity. A bond represents a promise to pay a certain amount of cash at some future date. The rate of return on a bond is fixed. A stock entitles the holder to a share of the firm's future profits. The rate of return depends on the firm's performance. A stock represents part ownership of the firm. During years of efficient and profitable production, the firm hopes to experience surpluses that will be used to pay off debts and pay dividends on stocks.

What is true for consumers and firms must be true for nations, which are collections of consumers and firms, plus the government. Deficits and surpluses in the current account are the rule rather than the exception. There is little reason why, during any period of time, a country should have balanced trade. When a nation spends more on imported goods and services than it receives from exported goods and services, it must be borrowing or spending some of its previously accumulated wealth.

Borrowing is typical for young and growing consumers, firms, and nations. In periods of low income when the potential exists for high income in the future, it is rational to borrow. Borrowing can be done to invest in capital goods or skills that will increase lifetime productivity and income. Lending and borrowing facilitate global stability and growth. Selling assets is another way wealthy consumers, firms, and nations can finance deficits.

2. The Loanable Funds Market

When an economic agent (individual, firm, or nation) makes more income than it spends, it saves and becomes a lender. A period of lending typically happens at the peak of individual careers, after the end of education and training and before the onset of retirement. Firms with positive profits must either invest in new capital or lend the funds to others. Nations with surpluses in their current account must find an outlet for the increased funds.

The market for *loanable funds* is the mechanism for this lending and borrowing. When a nation has a current account surplus, it must be accumulating assets. A current account surplus is not inherently good, and a current account deficit is not inherently bad; the same is true for borrowing and lending or selling and accumulating assets.

> It is natural for some individuals, firms, and nations at any given time to be borrowers while others are lenders. Managed debt with a purpose has the potential of increasing productivity and real income.

People have different habits and desires regarding wealth accumulation. Some are obsessed with accumulating wealth, while others seem content with less. Some firms are obsessed with growth, while some very successful firms maintain a stable level of production and size year after year. As collections of consumers and firms, nations vary in their desire for growth and accumulation of wealth. When it comes to financial planning for individuals, firms, or nations, there are no simple rules to follow. What is wanted and expected for the future is the key.

3. The Recent U.S. Trade Deficit

The popular press and news media have expressed great concern over recent U.S. balance of trade deficits. During the late 1980s, BOT deficits have been more than $100 billion, a number difficult to imagine. It is much easier to conceptualize that the BOT deficit has been in the range of $1,000 to $2,000 per household. The recent BOT deficits have been somewhat off-set by surpluses in service trade. Also, since exports are underestimated, the BOT deficits are overstated. Nevertheless, there is evidence that the United States has been borrowing internationally and selling assets interna-tionally in recent years.

Much of this borrowed cash is being spent on *capital goods* that will improve productivity and the standard of living in the future. Capital goods are the machinery and equipment used to produce other goods and ser-vices. Imports of capital goods, which have been high in the United States, are counted as debits in the BOT. There is little cause for immediate alarm when a nation is experiencing deficits by importing capital goods. The United States is a growing nation and should be expected to assume debt. Foreign investors must see the United States as a solid place for their funds. Just as consumers and firms borrow to invest in human and physical capital, so can the nation (a collection of these individuals, firms, and its govern-ment).

The main thrust of a current account deficit should be clear. A CA deficit means the nation is borrowing or selling assets. These assets can create either debt, as with newly printed bonds, or equity, as with new issues of stock. The direct sale of previously owned assets such as existing stocks, bonds, gold, or real estate also brings in cash to finance a current account deficit.

4. Increased Foreign Assets in the United States

Foreign-owned assets in the United States have been increasing alongside the recent current account deficits. Foreign investors have been net buyers of U.S. stocks, bonds, and other assets. Foreign investors must expect the United States to grow and prosper in the future. The perceived potential for growth in the United States makes the debt sustainable in the eyes of international investors. Investment opportunities in the United States have been relatively good. Rather than causing alarm, the current U.S. account deficit can be taken as a solid indicator of expected growth.

The popular press and special interest groups in the United States have fueled the fear that foreigners will buy up the country. This issue can be examined by looking at the net position of international stocks of wealth. In 1986 the *Survey of Current Business* estimated the stock of U.S. assets abroad to be $1.07 trillion, while foreign assets in the United States were $1.33 trillion. This makes the United States a net debtor of $260 billion, or about $3,000 per household. This figure, however, is overstated. The De-partment of Commerce values U.S. assets abroad on a historical, rather than current, basis. Suppose a U.S. firm built a foreign branch plant 15 years ago at a cost of $1 million. The current cost of building an identical plant might be $5 million because of rising costs and inflation. The current value of the plant would be its replacement cost, $5 million. The asset is valued on the books, however, at its historical cost of $1 million.

Even as reported, the level of net debt does not seem outlandish. Foreigners own about 8% of the gross capital stock in the United States. The United States has historically bought more into the rest of the world more than foreign investors have bought into the United States. There is little danger of an impending buyout. Multinational firms headquartered in the United States with operations abroad continue to expand as foreign firms and investors latch onto opportunities in the United States. International asset diversification has increased dramatically since the 1970s. The increase in foreign lending and borrowing is a healthy sign that the international economy is stabilizing.

These figures from the *Economic Report of the President* in 1990 on the capital account (KA) per household reinforce the notion that there is little impending danger of being bought out:

1971	1973	1975	1977	1979	1981	1983	1985	1987	1989
$264	−$101	−$450	$272	−$361	−$308	$297	$1020	$1509	$778

Figures have been converted to 1982 dollars to eliminate the influence of inflation. Positive numbers in the KA indicate net surpluses or cash inflows, meaning foreign investors are putting more into capital assets in the United States than U.S. investors are putting abroad. The numbers are not startling when viewed on a per household basis. Since the 1960s the capital account has been predominantly negative, meaning the United States has consistently invested more abroad than foreigners have invested in the United States. Over the past 30 years the net flow of investment has typically been negative.

Average U.S. investment abroad in the 1970s was $620 per U.S. household (again in 1982 dollars), while average foreign investment in the U.S. was $580. U.S. investment abroad continued a fairly steady climb, averaging $800 per U.S. household in the 1980's. During the 1980s, foreigners invested more in the United States than the United States invested abroad. Foreign investment in the United States averaged $1424 per household in the 1980s. As another gauge during the 1980s, payments on foreign assets in the United States grew by 200%, while receipts on U.S. assets abroad grew by 80%.

Journalists and the news media generally play into the hands of domestic industries that are forced to compete with the foreign firms entering the United States. When a Japanese carmaker builds a plant in the United States, the nation as a whole benefits through the free international investment, while certain *domestic competing groups* suffer. When foreign investment enters the nation, it is the current owners of capital in the competing industries who suffer the most. When the profitability of domestic firms falls, the value of their stocks falls. The owners of stock of the domestic competing firms are hurt through the foreign investment. Domestic automakers were hurt when Honda, Volkswagen, and others began establishing branch plants in the United States during the 1980s. Many new jobs were created, however, and consumers benefited from the increased supply of cars.

An interesting historical note that sheds light on the transitory nature of popular political concerns is the chronic BOT surpluses the United States experienced during the 1950s. There were constant calls for government policy intervention. With a wealthy nation like the United States running trade surpluses, the common perception was that we were spending too little. The rebuilding economies of Europe and Japan could not produce more if the United States refused to import more. Imagine a small town where the richest family was the most frugal. Everyone else would benefit if the rich family went out to eat more often, hired local service labor, and shopped more freely in local stores.

At the bottom line, deficits and surpluses in the international accounts are the rule rather than the exception. As a student of international economics, do not to fall into the trap of alarmism set by special interest groups. Deficits are not necessarily bad, nor are surpluses necessarily good. Those with special interests often want to use government policy for their own selfish motives. The next section looks into the role of rational governmental economic policy in an international context.

EXAMPLE 10.6   Components of the U.S. Gross National Product

These figures from *National Economic Trends* (Federal Reserve Bank of St. Louis, 1990) are shares of the categories of national income (Y) every 10 years since 1929. Consumption *(C)* has increased by 4 percentage points since 1969 through increased imports, although *C* is not a larger share of gross national product (GNP) than it has been historically. Investment spending *(I)* has remained relatively constant except for the Great Depression (1939). Government spending *(G)* displaced *I* between 1929 and 1939, then grew steadily as a percentage of Y until 1969. Since then, *G* has returned to its 1939 level (as a percentage of GNP). Both export revenue *(X)* and import expenditure *(M)* have grown, indicating the increasing openness of the U.S. economy. Surpluses in the early years have been replaced by recent deficits. Note that the recent trade deficits as a percentage of national income ($M/Y - X/Y$) are not historically very large, compared either with early surpluses or with the 1959 and 1969 deficits.

	1929	1939	1949	1959	1969	1979	1989
C/Y	67%	67%	63%	60%	60%	63%	64%
I/Y	19%	12%	16%	16%	16%	18%	17%

G/Y	13%	20%	20%	24%	25%	19%	20%
X/Y	6%	5%	6%	5%	7%	11%	14%
M/Y	5%	4%	4%	6%	8%	11%	15%

While the government deficit (*G* less tax revenue, not reported here) and the trade deficit have both grown recently, the link between them is not strong. Empirical studies have found little evidence of a systematic link between government deficits and trade deficits across industrial nations.

EXAMPLE 10.7   An International Comparison of Savings Rates

Savings come from the unspent income of firms, households, or the government. Mack Ott (1989) reports the following comparison. The percentage of each type of saving in total national income is reported. Household saving is consistently relatively high in Japan and France, while in the United Kingdom savings of firms switched from being relatively low before 1981 to relatively high since then. The United States has relatively low savings rates for both households and firms, as well as large negative government savings (government deficits).

	1975–1980			1981–1987		
	Firms	*Households*	*Government*	*Firms*	*Households*	*Government*
France	−8%	14%	3%	8%	11%	1%
Japan	−2%	15%	2%	3%	12%	3%
U.K.	−14%	8%	0%	13%	7%	−1%
U.S.	3%	5%	−1%	2%	4%	−3%

Problems for Section C

C1.   If the average age of a nation's population rises, anticipate what will happen to the:
  (a) BOT
  (b) KA
C2.   Explain whether South Korea or Austria would be more likely to have a BOT deficit.

D. THE INTERNATIONAL ROLES
OF FISCAL AND MONETARY POLICY

Economic policy refers to the actions government can take to influence the economy. International trade and finance are also affected by economic policy. The specific focus of this section is the influence of government fiscal and monetary policy on the economy's external balance.

The two types of economic policy examined in this section are:

(a) *fiscal policy*—government spending and taxation
(b) *monetary policy*—government control of the money supply

Both fiscal and monetary policy can indirectly influence international trade and investment. This section examines the issue of whether fiscal and monetary policy are rational tools to try to affect the balance of trade or international investment.

Economists differ widely in their opinions about the use and effectiveness of fiscal and monetary policies. Some economists favor *active* economic policy intervention to deal with publicized problems of unemployment, inflation, and recession, while other economists favor *passive* policy. The goal of this section is to become familiar with the potential international effects of fiscal and monetary policies.

1. Fiscal Policy

The government produces some goods and services. *Public goods* are consumed by the public at large and cannot be consumed by individuals exclusively. Examples are parks, police protection, national defense, clean air, health inspectors, sewers, fire departments, free highways and roads, and so on. Governments play a positive role in the economy by providing public goods that would not easily be provided by free markets. Market failures arise when free markets do not efficiently produce and distribute a good or service. Public goods create a market failure, since a free market cannot efficiently provide them. A free market fails to produce public goods because those who do not pay cannot easily be excluded from consuming the goods.

Taxes provide revenue the government uses to produce goods. The U.S. government has operated recently with deficits, spending more than its revenue in taxes. When this happens, the government creates national debt. The U.S. Treasury prints *government bonds,* which are sold to raise the funds the government needs to pay its bills. A bond is a promise to pay the face value on the bond to the bondholder at some future date. Government bonds are bought by lenders who are willing to forgo present consumption in favor of the interest premiums on the bonds and a higher level of consumption in the future. The bonds can be bought by consumers or firms in the private sector, by the Federal Reserve Bank (the Fed), by foreign investors, or by foreign central banks.

If a *public purchase* of the newly issued government bonds is made by the Fed, the central bank buys the new bonds with a new issue of its own, domestic money or credit. In this way a government deficit increases the supply of money. This change in the money supply amounts to monetary policy.

If a *private purchase* of the new bonds is made, funds are transferred from the private sector to the public sector. Government spending grows, with a fall in consumption spending and investment spending. Consumers and firms in the private sector have decided to spend resources on the new government bonds. The demand for loanable funds rises because of the government's increased desire to borrow. Interest rates, the price of loanable funds, are driven up. Bond prices fall with their higher supply.

The *governmental budget constraint* reflects the yearly cash flows of the government. Let B represent the stock of U.S. Treasury Bonds, the national debt, outstanding. The government must pay a certain percentage of these bonds off every year. Call r the annual return on these bonds. The government's yearly payment on the national debit is rB. Total government outlay for the year is $G + rB$. Subtract taxes to find the yearly budget deficit: $G + rB - T$.

A deficit must be financed by selling bonds (ΔB) or raising the money supply (ΔM_s). The government budget constraint is written

$$G + rB - T = \Delta B + \Delta M_s$$

EXAMPLE 10.8   Comparison of Government Taxes and Spending

Societies decide on the level of public services their government provides. Differences in tax receipts *(T)* and government spending *(G)* are found across countries. The following data from OECD's *Outlook* (1989) reflect these international differences. The figures are percentages of national income. *G* has generally risen worldwide over the past 25 years. When $G > T$, national debt is being created.

Country	1968		1987	
	T	G	T	G
Australia	26%	24%	35%	51%
Belgium	34%	36%	45%	52%
Canada	32%	32%	40%	46%

France	39%	40%	48%	52%
Greece	27%	24%	37%	43%
Italy	32%	35%	39%	51%
Japan	20%	19%	33%	33%
Norway	41%	38%	54%	52%
Spain	21%	21%	35%	42%
Sweden	46%	43%	63%	60%
Switzerland	25%	21%	34%	30%
U.K.	38%	42%	39%	46%
U.S.	29%	31%	32%	37%

2. Government Deficits and Trade Deficits

Activity in the domestic bond market has important implications for an economy open to international finance. Higher interest rates (cheaper bonds) attract investment from abroad. Foreign investors will want to buy some of the new cheap government bonds. The demand for dollars in the foreign exchange market increases, causing home currency or dollar appreciation. An appreciating home currency implies cheaper imports and more expensive exports, which may push the BOT toward deficit.

Some analysts believe this link between government deficits, interest rates, exchange rates, and the BOT is the fundamental cause of the trade deficits in the United States during the 1980s.

> Government deficit spending can lead to a trade deficit if higher interest rates attract foreign investment and cause a currency appreciation.

According to this argument, government deficits should be linked with trade deficits. Numerous empirical studies have shown, however, that the link is weak. The foreign exchange market is broad and vast, and influences other than incoming foreign investment can predominate. The induced effects on the trade balance from the foreign exchange market are small and slow to take effect.

By implication, increasing taxes to turn the government budget toward surplus would be a poor tool to combat a trade deficit. Decreasing government spending with the same goal in mind is also a poor way to combat a trade deficit. Fiscal policy, in other words, should not concern itself directly with the trade balance. Decisions on government spending and taxation should be based on the costs and benefits of the particular programs or projects.

Commercial trade policy (tariffs, quotas, nontariff barriers, subsidies, and so on) directly affects international trade and is more efficient in dealing with a trade deficit or in meeting other goals in foreign trade. The next chapter looks into exchange rate policy, active control or interference with the foreign exchange market, as a policy alternative for managing the BOT.

Figure 10.6 presents a summary of the channels of fiscal and monetary policy and their international effects. A foreign purchase of newly issued government bonds can create an appreciation. Inflation resulting from expansionary monetary policy lowers the value of the home currency relative to other currencies, leading to a depreciation in the foreign exchange market. The direct effect on the BOT of increased government spending and lower private spending depends on the composition of imports and domestic goods consumed by the government and the private sector.

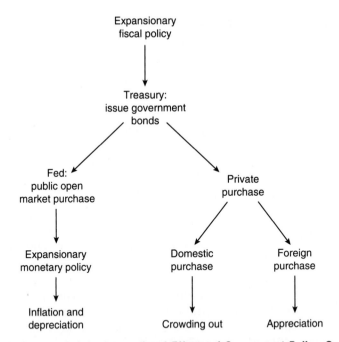

Figure 10.6. Summary of the International Effects of Government Policy Government debt created by expansionary fiscal policy is financed by the Treasury through the sale of U.S. bonds. If the Federal Revenue Bank (the Fed) makes a public purchase, the expansionary policy amounts to monetary policy. Private purchases can be domestic, which crowds out consumption or investment spending. Private purchases can also be foreign, which appreciates the home currency. Expansionary monetary policy can lead to inflation and depreciation if it is persistent and the growth rate of money exceeds the growth rate of output.

EXAMPLE 10.9   Budget Deficits and Ricardian Equivalence

Robert Barro (1989) examines the doctrine known as Ricardian equivalence, named after David Ricardo. In the standard view a government budget deficit creates an excess demand for loanable funds, which means borrowing from abroad and incoming foreign investment. The stock of national wealth will be lower in the future. A budget deficit, however, also implies higher taxes in the future to pay off the debt. If taxpayers realize they will be ultimately forced to pay more taxes, they save more now to have the funds for future taxes. This increased private saving eliminates the domestic excess demand for loanable funds, cutting off the potential borrowing from abroad and incoming foreign investment. Ricardian equivalence states that a budget deficit is equivalent to a tax increase. Empirical researchers have failed to find any significant relationships between government budget deficits and interest rates, national saving, or foreign investment. Evidence generally favors the doctrine of Ricardian equivalence. Taxpayers evidently perceive government budget deficits as taxes.

3. Monetary Policy

The effects of monetary policy on international trade and finance work through different channels. Inflation, which means generally rising prices, occurs when the supply of money grows faster than the supply of goods and services. Inflation and expected inflation can have real effects on the economy through the foreign exchange market and the loanable funds market.

Optimal monetary policy is perhaps the most important topic of macroeconomics. Macroeconomics is concerned with formulating simple rules for describing how the entire economy operates and for formulating economic policy. The level of inflation a nation chooses has little real effect as long as inflation is anticipated correctly by firms and consumers. Steady and reliable monetary policy results in steady growth in the money supply and steady and predictable prices.

Some monetary economists favor mechanical rules for controlling the money supply. Their argument is that money growth and inflation would be more predictable. Others favor some discretion on the part of the central bank, arguing that rules could be destabilizing. There are various schemes for monetary policy, but every scheme has the goal of a steady and reliable money supply. Unexpected or drastic increases or decreases in the money supply can harm consumers and firms. The large monetary contraction leading to the Great Depression and the large monetary expansions of the 1970s both had unsettling and undesirable real effects on the economy.

The theory of *business cycles* develops the notion that alternating periods of recession and boom are a natural part of a dynamic economy. Suppose, for instance, we start in a recession with a low level of economic activity and with firms selling off their inventories. Demand begins to grow (perhaps because of rising demand for our exports), and firms start building up their inventories. Investment spending expands, and an economic expansion takes place until inventories and capital are built up. Firms eventually cut back production to keep their inventories from overflowing. Perhaps demand for exports falls. A recession begins with declining output, and ultimately the story starts over again.

This is a vastly oversimplified account of a business cycle, but it gives a hint about the foundation of a business cycle theory. As pictured in Figure 10.7, the frequency of a business cycle can be measured from peak to peak. The United States has been through six business cycles since 1953. The average business cycle has lasted 54 months from peak to peak. The United States started an expansion in 1961 that lasted throughout the 1960s and started another expansion in 1982 that lasted throughout the 1980s. The early 1990s have been a mild recession and a slight recovery.

Some economists advise the government to manage the money supply actively and continuously to influence the business cycle. It has not, however, been demonstrated that active monetary policy can successfully guide an economy from periods of low output or recession into periods of high output or expansion. Monetary policy has not proved to be a consistent tool to fine tune an economy. It is much more important to establish steady and reliable money supply growth, leading to stable prices or low and steady inflation.

Monetary policy affects the inflation rate, the interest rate, and the exchange rate. Changes or expected changes in any of these economic vari-

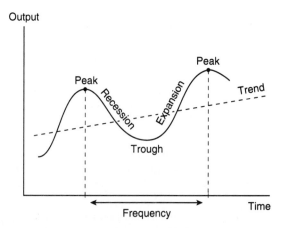

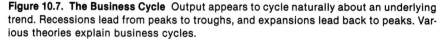

Figure 10.7. The Business Cycle Output appears to cycle naturally about an underlying trend. Recessions lead from peaks to troughs, and expansions lead back to peaks. Various theories explain business cycles.

ables can alter the international pattern of trade and finance. Monetary policy is, however, a poor tool for influencing an economy's international trade and finance.

Predictable and steady growth of the money supply is universally recommended by economists. A steady growth rate in the money supply leads to stable prices, a steady interest rate, and a reliable exchange rate. Businesses, traders, and investors are able to make better plans when currency growth and value are reliable. When it comes to influencing the international sector, there are more direct controls than the money supply.

4. Rational International Policy

Neither fiscal policy nor monetary policy is a viable control for international trade and investment. Governments have a range of international policy options, but domestic fiscal and monetary policy are not among them. Policies such as tariffs, quotas, nontariff barriers, voluntary export restraints, export subsidies, free trade areas, free trade zones, fixed or pegged exchange rates, foreign exchange controls, and foreign investment tax policy are best for controlling international trade and investment.

> Fiscal and monetary policy are poor tools to influence an economy's position in international trade and finance.

One recurring theme in this text is the income redistribution resulting from any policy action. Economics focuses on the costs and benefits of actions. Any policy that alters the incentives and behavior of economic agents will have both costs and benefits. There will be winners and losers associated with any economic policy. When it comes to a proposed government policy, the difficulty is to identify all of its costs and benefits. Often the secondary or side effects of a policy are as sizeable and important as the primary effects. It is important to try to uncover the ultimate winners and losers of a particular policy.

EXAMPLE 10.10   An Overview of U.S. Federal Government Finances

The following statistics are taken from *The Economic and Budget Outlook* published by the U.S. Congressional Budget Office (1988). Total government tax revenue *(T)* in 1987 was $854 billion, 19% of GNP. The composition of *T* was 46% from individual income taxes, 35% from Social Security taxes, 13% from corporate income taxes, 4% from sales taxes, and 2% from tariff revenues. Government spending (G) amounted to $1 trillion or 20% of GNP. Of this, 28% of *G* went to national defense, 20% to Social Security, 16% to discretionary spending, 14% to interest payment on the national debt, 8% to Medicare, and 2% to unemployment compensation. Since $G > T$, national debt rose. Interest payment on national debt grew from 6% of government outlays in 1962 to 8% in 1979, before rising to 14% during the 1980s. This interest payment is made to holders of the national debt. Of the total national debt, 27% is held by the Social Security Trust and the Federal Reserve Bank and 11% by state and local governments. Private U.S. banks hold 28%, while corporations and insurance companies hold 7% each. Individual U.S. bondholders account for 9% of the national debt. Foreign investors hold 11%, which means that less than 2% ($14\% \times 11\% = .14 \times .11 = .0154 = 1.54\%$) of government spending was used to pay interest to foreign debt holders.

EXAMPLE 10.11   Government Deficits as a Percentage of Gross National Product

U.S. government deficits relative to the economy's ability to produce goods and services is not overwhelming. As a percentage of GNP, U.S. government deficits have been declining since the early 1980s. Among the following industrial nations, the United States is outranked by Italy and Canada and is close to the United Kingdom, Japan, and France. Germany's government deficit has historically been among the lowest.

	1974–80	*1981–87*
Italy	11%	13%
Canada	3%	5%
U.S.	2%	4%
Japan	3%	3%
U.K.	5%	3%
France	1%	3%
Germany	2%	2%

Source: Federal Reserve Bank of St. Louis (1988) *International Economic Conditions*.

EXAMPLE 10.12   U.S. Macroeconomic Data and Deficits

These data from the *Economic Report of the President* (1988) show some macroeconomic variables along with the government budget deficit and the trade deficit as percentages of national income. For every $100 of output the government has produced an average of $3 of debt through the government deficit since the early 1970s. This does not sound as startling as the levels of national debt played up in the press. The budget and trade deficits move in the same direction only twice out of these seven observations. The link between the two deficits is empirically weak. There is little apparent regularity between inflation and unemployment, the postulated Phillips curve tradeoff of macroeconomics. Inflation is not apparently tied to budget deficits. Macroeconomic models relating these variables are difficult to formulate.

	Real Growth Rate	*Unemployment*	*Inflation*	*Budget Deficit/Y*	*Trade Deficit/Y*
1973	5.2%	4.9%	8.8%	1.1%	−0.0%
1975	−1.3%	8.5%	7.0%	2.8%	−0.6%
1977	4.7%	7.0%	6.8%	2.2%	1.6%
1979	2.5%	5.8%	13.3%	1.1%	1.1%
1981	1.9%	7.5%	10.2%	2.1%	0.9%
1983	3.5%	9.5%	3.6%	5.2%	1.9%
1985	2.3%	7.1%	3.6%	4.9%	3.0%
1987	2.9%	6.2%	3.8%	3.5%	3.4%

Problems for Section D

D1. If the U.S. government runs a deficit, describe how funds arrive from the two potential sources of funds: domestic and foreign.

D2. When the Treasury sells new bonds to a foreign resident, what are the effects on the balance of payments, present and future?

D3. Explain how government deficit spending, interest rates, exchange rates, and the BOT are related.

CONCLUSION

International markets for goods, services, and financial assets are extremely active. Historically, the United States has been relatively isolated from the rest of the world. While levels of international trade and finance remain low in the United States relative to other nations, they continue to grow. The world is becoming more integrated economically, in both trade and finance. Nations find themselves more dependent on one another with this international integration. In some countries a daily movement in the exchange rate can change consumers' minds about whether to buy groceries today or wait until tomorrow. Exchange rates are not so apparently crucial in the United States, but they regularly make the evening news, have impacts on profits in many industries, strongly affect the price of new cars and many other goods, and influence the level of foreign travel. In the next chapter the workings of the foreign exchange market are examined.

KEY TERMS

Active versus passive policy
Balance of payments (BOP)
Balance of trade (BOT)
Balance on goods and services (BGS)
Business cycles
Capital account (KA)
Current account (CA)
Debt and equity
Direct investment (DI)

Export pessimism and optimism
Fiscal and monetary policy
Government bonds
Import elasticity
Inflation
Net investment income (NII)
Optimal monetary policy
Portfolio investment (PI)
Trade in services (TS)

KEY POINTS

- International excess supply and demand are constantly changing, creating adjustments in prices and the levels of imports and exports. Elasticity determines how price changes affect expenditure.
- The balance of payments reflects international transactions for current expenditure (the current account) and investment (the capital account). A nation with a current account deficit must be depleting assets or experiencing a surplus in its capital account.
- Current account deficits or international borrowing is not a cause for immediate alarm. Growing nations typically assume debt to acquire capital goods that will produce higher income in the future.
- Government deficit spending either reduces private spending or creates inflation. Fiscal policy and monetary policy are not efficient tools to influence a nation's position in international trade and finance.

REVIEW PROBLEMS

1. Predict what will happen to foreign excess demand when lower prices are expected for home exports of business services because of improved technology in their production abroad. What will happen to international prices, the level of exports, and export revenue?

2. Explain what will happen in the international market for manufactured goods when domestic demand changes because of rising incomes. What happens to the international price, the level of imports, and import expenditures?

3. Explain the outcome if the increase in import price to $7.50 as in Figure 10.3

caused the quantity demanded to fall from 300 to 250 while domestic quantity supplied rose from 100 to 116 2/3.

4. If the price of M is $5 and the price of S is $12.50, find the relative price of exported M. Do the same if the price of S is $7.50. Find the relative price of S in terms of M (the terms of trade for the exporter of S) at both dollar prices for S.

5. Find the elasticity and explain what happens to export revenue when the quantity of exports rises from 100 to 125 with a fall in price from $10 to $8.

6. Given the 90 million households in the United States, find the 1989 BOP account figures per household using Table 10.1.

7. Explain the current and expected future changes in the BOP occurring when an investor in the United States buys stock on the Sydney stock exchange.

8. Suppose a U.S. firm wants to open a manufacturing plant in Costa Rica. It can take $1 million of its retained earnings, transfer it to a bank in Costa Rica, and build the plant. Another option is to offer stock worth $400,000 in Costa Rica to raise that part of the funds. Describe the current and future BOP entries for the United States and Costa Rica under each scenario. Contrast future NII for the United States and Costa Rica.

9. An old saying in business is that the only way to get ahead is by using "other people's money." Explain an analogy with the balance of payments accounts.

10. Why do wealth holders like to diversify internationally, buying assets from different nations?

11. Assume you were forced to live without borrowing or lending funds. How would your life be affected? What is the moral of your story for international economics?

12. During the expansion and recession phases of the business cycle, explain whether balance of trade surpluses or deficits would be likely.

13. Does the U.S. Congress rationally consider the marginal or additional costs and benefits of each newly proposed fiscal program? What laws would make this more likely?

14. An export tax is a tax put on a firm when it exports a good. What effect would reducing tariffs with raising export taxes have on the pattern of production in an economy?

15. Explain how the war in Kuwait affected the U.S. BOT.

READINGS

Robert Barro, *Macroeconomics*, McGraw-Hill, New York, 1990. A popular text on macroeconomics, carefully examining the effectiveness of monetary and fiscal policy.

Francisco Rivera-Batiz and Luis Rivera-Batiz, *International Finance and Open Economy Macroeconomics*, Macmillan, New York, 1985. A comprehensive textbook dealing with macroeconomic policy for an open economy.

Jürg Niehans, *International Monetary Economics*, Johns Hopkins University Press, Baltimore, 1984. An advanced text dealing with monetary policy for an open economy.

John Pool and Stephen Stamos, *International Economic Policy: Beyond the Trade and Debt Crisis*, Lexington Books, Lexington, MA, 1989. A sound little paperback filled with facts on government and international debt.

Federal Reserve Bank of New York, *Quarterly Review,* Winter/Spring 1989. A series of studies on U.S. external balances in trade and finance.

Fred Bergsten and William Cline, *The United States–Japan Economic Problem,* Institute for International Economics, Washington, DC, 1987. A deep look into trade and finance between the United States and Japan, stressing the potential gains from continued growth and stability.

James Rock (editor), *Debt and the Twin Deficits Debate,* Mayfield Publishing, Mountain View, CA, 1991. A collection of lively articles with different viewpoints on the effects of governments deficits and trade deficits.

World Economic Outlook, IMF, Washington, DC, published twice yearly. A fine reference for monetary developments, current and capital account balances, interest rates, exchange rates, the international oil market, and so on.

Rudiger Dornbusch and Jacob Trenkel, *International Economic Policy,* Johns Hopkins University Press, Baltimore, 1983. A collection of articles on the potential of policy aimed at affecting international trade and finance.

CHAPTER 11

Foreign Exchange

CHAPTER PREVIEW

This chapter presents a concise picture of the important operation of the foreign exchange market. Anyone involved in international trade, international investment, or foreign travel must use the foreign exchange market. The crucial role of the foreign exchange market in the smooth functioning of the world economy cannot be overemphasized. This chapter covers:

(a) Supply and demand in the foreign *exchange market*
(b) A comparison of *floating* and *fixed* exchange rates
(c) *Stability* and *arbitrage* of exchange rates
(d) The roles of *inflation* and *currency risk* in international transactions

INTRODUCTION

Currencies are bought and sold in the foreign exchange market, by far the largest market in the world. The exchange of goods, services, or assets among consumers, firms, or governments in different nations requires an exchange of one currency for another. The foreign exchange market is involved when U.S. tourists fly to Mexico for a weekend, Russia buys 10 million tons of U.S. wheat, an investor in New York buys 1,000 shares of Japanese stock on the Tokyo exchange, a French importer buys Italian olive oil, a California electronics firm buys components from Malaysia, or in any one of the millions of international transactions that occur daily. Each transaction at some point involves trading domestic currency for foreign currency, exchanging one medium of exchange for another.

Demand for foreign exchange comes from domestic buyers of foreign goods, services, intermediate inputs, capital goods, and financial assets (stocks, bonds, real estate, and so on). Supply of foreign exchange comes from foreign buyers of the same range of domestic economic goods. Supply and demand constantly work together in the foreign exchange market to determine the foreign exchange rate, the relative value or price of the traded currencies.

The setting for this currency trading is a huge electronic network linking private banks, foreign exchange brokers, traders, and central banks around the world. Figure 11.1 summarizes the basic structure of the foreign exchange market. Currencies can be traded at a very low cost per transaction. Almost any local bank can afford to open a foreign exchange desk. The worldwide foreign exchange market is continuously determining the value of floating currencies.

Although stock markets receive more publicity, their volume of activity, the potential speculative profits, and importance pale in comparison to the foreign exchange market. When the demand for a currency rises relative to its supply, its value or price in terms of other currencies rises. When the relative supply of a currency rises, its value will fall. Determinants of the supply and demand for a currency are examined in this chapter. Values of the three major currencies (U.S. dollar, German mark, and Japanese yen) are determined in free markets. These major currencies float in value relative to one another. The tools that exchange market professionals use to anticipate and predict exchange rate changes are examined in this chapter.

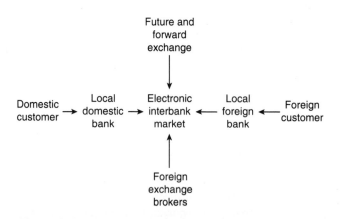

Figure 11.1. Electronic Interbank Foreign Exchange Market The major electronic market is the center for a vast amount of trading. Working through their local banks, international traders and investors buy and sell foreign exchange. Brokers act to bring buyers and sellers together in the central market, buying and selling foreign currencies themselves in search of profit. Future and forward exchange transactions moderate the risk and uncertainty of the exchange transactions.

Government central banks buy and sell currencies in attempts to influence or stabilize floating market exchange rates. For that reason the exchange rate system is often called a managed or dirty float. Many central banks have the policy of controlling their exchange rate, arbitrarily setting it to meet some desired goal and making unofficial transactions illegal.

A lower currency value would mean more expensive imports and cheaper exports. Governments may purposely devalue (decrease the value of their currency) to discourage imports in the hope of easing a trade deficit. Such control is a hidden tax on consumers, who must pay a higher price for any good or service involving an imported component. Some governments may want to revalue (keep the value of their currency high) to encourage foreign investment, which may be attracted to nations with strong currencies.

Fixed or managed exchange rate policies are inherently unstable and cannot be sustained long in the face of an underlying market disequilibrium without resort to the policing of transactions. Nevertheless, few governments seem willing to let exchange markets work completely freely. This chapter examines the ways in which a government influences and controls the market for its currency.

Relatively high growth rates in national money supplies generally lead to higher inflation and currency depreciation. A currency whose supply relative to other currencies is increasing will ultimately depreciate (lose value) on the foreign exchange market. In the long run, relative money supply differentials largely explain how currencies change in value relative to one another.

Any uncertainty about the future course of exchange rates introduces risk into international transactions. The mechanism for avoiding the risk of an unexpected depreciation is the forward exchange market, where a contract is signed to buy or sell foreign currency at some future date. The importance of the forward exchange market and its connection with the current or spot exchange market and international interest rates are also developed in this chapter.

A. THE FOREIGN EXCHANGE RATE AND TRADE

This section develops a picture of the foreign exchange market based on the supply and demand of foreign exchange. Some of the fundamental relationships involving exchange rates are:

- (a) The close connection between the foreign exchange value of a currency and both the domestic currency price of a nation's imports and the foreign currency price of its exports
- (b) The potential effect of a depreciation on the balance of trade
- (c) The dynamic response of trade to a depreciation

1. The Foreign Exchange Market Diagram

If a domestic importer wants to buy foreign manufactured goods, domestic currency must be traded for foreign currency on the *foreign exchange market*. Consider the situation of a U.S. importer buying manufactured goods from a Japanese manufacturer. The importer does business in dollars, while the foreign manufacturer does business in yen. In practice, the importer goes through a bank to buy the yen, typically wiring it to the Japanese exporter's bank. Some banks as well as import agencies specialize in currency transactions and dealing with import restrictions, customs paperwork, and so on.

The importer must check the domestic currency price of the goods to be imported. Suppose a U.S. importer is quoted a price of 625 yen per unit of the manufactured good. Right away the role of the exchange rate is apparent. Since the goods will be sold in the United States, their dollar cost is what matters to the importer.

The importer checks the foreign exchange rate listed in the daily newspaper and sees that the value of a yen in terms of dollars is $0.008. As with any commodity, value is expressed in terms of the home currency. Apples cost $1/pound, tuition costs $750/term, and the Japanese currency $0.008/yen. This means that one dollar equals $1/0.008 = 125$ yen. The price of the manufactured good M in dollars is then $625/125 = \$5$ per M. The decision of whether to import is made on the basis of this dollar price.

Suppose the value of the dollar rises on the exchange market, from yen/$ = 125$ to 200. The dollar price of a manufactured good M then falls to $625/200 = \$3.13$. An appreciating currency creates cheaper imports, increasing the quantity of imports demanded. The importer will want to buy more manufactured goods at a price of $3.13 than at the $5 price. If imports are elastic, import expenditure would rise as would the quantity of foreign currency demanded to pay for the imports.

This inverse relationship between $/yen and the quantity of yen demanded is illustrated by the demand for yen in the foreign exchange market in Figure 11.2. The rise in yen/$ from 125 to 200 is equivalent to a fall in the $/yen exchange rate on the vertical axis from 0.008 to 0.005. The quantity of yen demanded rises from 20 billion to 30 billion when $/yen falls from 0.008 to 0.005. The demand for yen, derived from domestic buyers of foreign goods, slopes downward.

On the supply side, when Japanese importers buy U.S. exports, they must sell yen in the foreign exchange market. Suppose the price of services is $10/S$ at home and the exchange rate is back at 125 yen per dollar ($/yen = 0.008). The yen price of a unit of services is then $125 \times 10 = 1,250$ yen. When the yen/$ rate rises to 200, the yen price of the services rises $200 \times 10 = 2,000$ yen. At this higher yen price the quantity demanded of imported services in Japan will be lower. If foreign imports of services are elastic, expenditure on services will fall as will the quantity of foreign currency supplied to buy the services. The quantity of yen supplied falls from

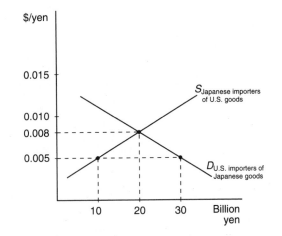

Figure 11.2. The Foreign Exchange Market The demand (*D*) for foreign exchange comes from buyers of foreign goods in the home country. The supply (*S*) of foreign exchange comes from buyers of home goods in the foreign country. These "goods" can be economic goods, services, or financial assets, including bonds and stocks.

20 billion to 10 billion when $/yen falls from 0.008 to 0.005. The result is an upward sloping supply curve of foreign exchange, which is also illustrated in Figure 11.2.

Where demand and supply of foreign exchange meet, a *market exchange rate* is determined and a certain volume of transactions is carried out. The market equilibrium exchange rate occurs where the quantity of yen supplied just equals the quantity of yen demanded by traders in the market, and the market clears. The foreign exchange market also includes financial trading of assets such as stocks and bonds. In Figure 11.2 the equilibrium exchange rate is $/yen = 0.008 and the equilibrium quantity of foreign exchange traded (per day) is 20 billion yen.

> Foreign exchange markets are characterized by demand and supply of foreign currencies. Prices of foreign exchange are exchange rates, or the value of the foreign currency in terms of the home currency.

EXAMPLE 11.1   Daily Foreign Exchange Rates

Exchange rate quotations appear daily in major newspapers. The first two columns show the exchange rate of the past two days for the various currencies in dollars per unit of the foreign currency. In the instance of Argentina at the top of the list, the price of the foreign currency is $/austral. The last two columns show the value of the dollar in terms of the foreign currency, austral/$, and so on. In countries with a great deal

EXCHANGE RATES

Wednesday, December 6, 1989

The New York foreign exchange selling rates below apply to trading among banks in amounts of $1 million and more, as quoted at 3 p.m. Eastern time by Bankers Trust Co. Retail transactions provide fewer units of foreign currency per dollar.

Country	U.S. $ equiv. Wed.	U.S. $ equiv. Tues.	Currency per U.S. $ Wed.	Currency per U.S. $ Tues.
Argentina (Austral)	.0015267	.0015267	655.00	655.00
Australia (Dollar)	.7837	.7825	1.2759	1.2779
Austria (Schilling)	.08051	.07995	12.41	12.50
Bahrain (Dinar)	2.6521	2.6521	.3770	.3770
Belgium (Franc)				
Commercial rate	.02699	.02610	37.04	38.31
Financial rate	.02698	.02609	37.06	38.32
Brazil (Cruzado)	.12654	.12892	7.9022	7.7567
Britain (Pound)	1.5760	1.5685	.6345	.6375
30-Day Forward	1.5675	1.5599	.6379	.6410
90-Day Forward	1.5512	1.5435	.6446	.6478
180-Day Forward	1.5269	1.5191	.6549	.6582
Canada (Dollar)	.8610	.8998	1.1614	1.1630
30-Day Forward	.8583	.8571	1.1650	1.1667
90-Day Forward	.8531	.8520	1.1721	1.1737
180-Day Forward	.8454	.8443	1.1828	1.1844
Chile (Official rate)	.0036016	.0036016	277.65	277.65
China (Yuan)	.268716	.268716	3.7214	3.7214
Colombia (Peso)	.002320	.002320	431.00	431.00
Denmark (Krone)	.1459	.1449	6.8537	6.8975
Ecuador (Sucre)				
Floating rate	.001497	.001497	668.00	668.00
Finland (Markka)	.2399	.2386	4.1675	4.1900
France (Franc)	.1657	.1648	6.0350	6.0667
30-Day Forward	.1654	.1646	6.0432	6.0750
90-Day Forward	.1648	.1639	6.0665	6.0989
180-Day Forward	.1637	.1629	6.1055	6.1372
Greece (Drachma)	.006188	.006277	161.60	159.30
Hong Kong (Dollar)	.1280	.1279	7.8130	7.8135
India (Rupee)	.05917	.05917	16.90	16.90
Indonesia (Rupiah)	.0005608	.0005608	1783.00	1783.00
Ireland (Punt)	1.4912	1.4790	.6706	.6761
Israel (Shekel)	.5244	.5244	1.9067	1.9067
Italy (Lira)	.0007668	.0007633	1304.00	1310.00
Japan (Yen)	.006946	.006958	143.95	143.70
30-Day Forward	.006959	.006971	143.69	143.44
90-Day Forward	.006981	.006990	143.24	143.05
180-Day Forward	.007007	.0070131	142.71	142.59
Jordan (Dinar)	1.5733	1.5733	.6356	.6356
Kuwait (Dinar)	3.3955	3.3955	.29450	.29450
Lebanon (Pound)	.002267	.002267	441.00	441.00
Malaysia (Ringgit)	.3697	.3695	2.7045	2.7060
Malta (Lira)	2.9027	2.9027	.3445	.3445
Mexico (Peso)				
Floating rate	.0003766	.0003766	2655.00	2655.00
Netherland (Guilder)	.5023	.4988	1.9905	2.0045
New Zealand (Dollar)	.5925	.5920	1.6877	1.6891
Norway (Krone)	.1477	.1467	6.7695	6.8125
Pakistan (Rupee)	.04716	.04716	21.20	21.20
Peru (Inti)	.0001122	.0001122	8905.00	8905.00
Philippines (Peso)	.04629	.04629	21.60	21.60
Portugal (Escudo)	.006439	.006439	155.30	155.30
Saudi Arabia (Riyal)	.26680	.26680	3.7480	3.7480
Singapore (Dollar)	.5154	.5138	1.9400	1.9460
South Africa (Rand)				
Commercial rate	.3862	.3847	2.5888	2.5993
Financial rate	.2512	.2512	3.9800	3.9800
South Korea (Won)	.0014836	.0014836	674.00	674.00
Spain (Peseta)	.008771	.008722	114.00	114.65
Sweden (Krona)	.15782	.15677	6.3360	6.3785
Switzerland (Franc)	.6297	.6287	1.5880	1.5908
30-Day Forward	.6299	.6290	1.5875	1.5897
90-Day Forward	.6301	.62920	1.5870	1.5893
180-Day Forward	.6302	.62924	1.5869	1.5892
Taiwan (Dollar)	.038461	.038476	26.00	25.99
Thailand (Baht)	.03878	.03878	25.78	25.78
Turkey (Lira)	.0004374	.0004374	2286.00	2286.00
United Arab (Dirham)	.2722	.2722	3.6725	3.6725
Uruguay (New Peso)				
Financial	.001311	.001311	762.50	762.50
Venezuela (Bolivar)				
Floating rate	.02252	.02252	44.40	44.40
W. Germany (Mark)	.5668	.5627	1.7640	1.7770
30-Day Forward	.5671	.5630	1.7634	1.7763
90-Day Forward	.5671	.5629	1.7634	1.7764
180-Day Forward	.5664	.5622	1.7655	1.7788
— — —				
SDR	1.28861	1.28670	0.776032	0.777181
ECU	1.14596	1.14064	...	...

Special Drawing Rights (SDR) are based on exchange rates for the U.S., West German, British, French and Japanese currencies. Source: International Monetary Fund.

European Currency Unit (ECU) is based on a basket of community currencies. Source: European Community Commission.

SOURCE: *Wall Street Journal*, Dec. 7, 1989.

of international trade and financial activity, exchange rates receive front page coverage and are publicized on the street outside banks and at trading windows. The quotations listed here are offer prices for transactions over $1 million. Rates at airports and small exchange shops are less favorable. With the United States becoming more involved in international trade and finance, the workings of the foreign exchange market assume more importance. In economies highly involved in international trade and finance, the general public is acutely aware of how the exchange market affects their daily lives. When you travel or do business abroad, you will find that the foreign exchange market plays an active role in many people's daily lives.

2. Currency Depreciation

A dollar depreciation occurs when the dollar loses value relative to foreign currencies. In the market for dollars and yen, a dollar depreciation occurs when $/yen rises. When the dollar depreciates, the purchasing power of U.S. consumers and firms over foreign goods and services declines. Simultaneously, U.S. exports become cheaper abroad. An appreciating dollar has more power to purchase foreign goods and services, but U.S. exports become more expensive abroad.

Causality can also run from changing demand or supply for traded goods to the exchange rate. Increased demand for imports of high-quality foreign automobiles, for instance, increases the demand for foreign currency and causes a depreciation of the dollar. A similar example comes from increased foreign travel, which leads to higher demand for foreign currency and a depreciating dollar. If a firm in the United States develops a new super-fast personal computer, foreign firms and consumers want to buy it, the supply of foreign currency rises, and the dollar appreciates. If the U.S. government issues new bonds that have a high and secure yield, foreign investors want to buy them, the supply of foreign currency rises, and the dollar appreciates. If stocks in Tokyo suddenly seem attractive because of a spurt in the growth of the Japanese economy, the demand for yen to buy Japanese stocks rises and the dollar depreciates.

The key to understanding the exchange market is think through both the markets for the traded goods or assets and the market for the currencies involved.

> The exchange rate is linked to international markets for goods, services, and financial assets.

Consider the example of an increase in the price of Colombian coffee. The higher price of coffee increases the demand for Colombian pesos to buy coffee already under contract. As illustrated in Figure 11.3, the demand

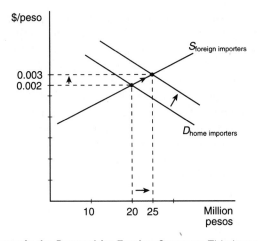

Figure 11.3. Increase in the Demand for Foreign Currency This increase in demand (*D*) drives the exchange up from $0.002/peso to $0.003/peso. The quantity of trading in the foreign exchange market also rises.

for Colombian pesos shifts to the right. The volume of activity on the foreign exchange market increases, and the dollar depreciates. Figure 11.3 shows the market for pesos, with the original exchange rate at $0.002/peso. With the increased demand for pesos, the value of the peso rises from $/peso = 0.002 to 0.003 in this example, meaning the dollar depreciates from 500 to 333 pesos.

As the dollar loses value, the domestic price of imported coffee rises further. Suppose coffee costs 750 pesos/pound at the time of the price hike. This peso price translates into 0.002 × 750 = $1.50 per pound at the original exchange rate. The dollar depreciation, however, increases the price to 0.003 × 750 = $2.25. The exchange market adjustment strengthens the underlying dollar price increase, further encouraging substitution away from Colombian coffee in the long run.

A dollar depreciation resulting from other factors also causes imports to become more expensive. Suppose the U.S. Federal Reserve Bank and other major central banks announce they plan to sell off dollars and buy other currencies in order to make the dollar lose value. The central banks want to depreciate the dollar. If traders, dealers, and investors across the world expect the dollar to lose value, the demand for other currencies increases and the dollar depreciates. Few want to hold dollars if their value is expected to fall relative to other currencies. Announced plans to devalue a currency purposely cause market participants to expect a depreciation. Another potential cause of a dollar depreciation would be foreign consumers and firms cutting back on their imports of U.S. goods because of perceived problems with quality. When the dollar depreciates for these or any other reasons, imports into the United States become more expensive.

Suppose imports are elastic all over the world. When the home currency depreciates and imports become more expensive, import expenditure falls. Simultaneously, exports become cheaper abroad and export revenue rises. A depreciation clearly leads to a positive move in the balance of trade (BOT) or the balance of goods and services (BGS).

Technically, imports around the world do not even have to be elastic for a depreciation to move the current account toward surplus. It is necessary only that home and foreign imports considered together be elastic, which makes sense because the effects of changing export revenue and import expenditure work together on the BGS. If import and export elasticities sum to more than 1, a depreciation leads toward trade surplus. This is called the *Marshall-Lerner (ML) condition,* after economists Alfred Marshall and Abba Lerner. Some empirical evidence indicates that the ML condition holds in the long run, which means a dollar depreciation will ultimately favor a trade surplus. Some experts, however, doubt that the ML condition has much practical significance.

3.   The Marshall-Lerner Condition

To examine the issue of whether a depreciation or devaluation will cause the BOT or BGS to move toward surplus, start with a statement of the balance (B) as export revenue less import expenditure:

$$B = p_X q_X - e p_M{}^* q_M$$

Exports (q_X) are aggregated into a single category with an average price (p_X). Imports (q_M) are priced in the foreign currency ($p_M{}^*$), which is converted to the domestic currency by the exchange rate (e). Both price indices are assumed to be constant. Assume also that B = 0.

A devaluation (a higher e) raises q_X and lowers q_M, which causes B to increase. Import expenditure is raised by the increase in e, however. A 1% devaluation raises import expenditure by 1% if q_M fails to adjust downward. If neither q_X nor q_M adjusts with the devaluation, B definitely falls.

Suppose q_X does not adjust but q_M falls by 1% with the 1% devaluation. The export elasticity ($\%\Delta q_X / \%\Delta p_X$) is zero, and the import elasticity $\%\Delta q_M / \%\Delta p_M$ is -1. Import expenditure and B do not change.

Suppose q_X rises 0.5% with the 1% devaluation and q_M falls 0.5%. The export elasticity is 1/2 and the import elasticity is $-1/2$. Export revenue then rises by 0.5%, and import expenditure rises on net by 1% $-$ 0.5% = 0.5% as well. If the export elasticity minus the import elasticity is equal to 1, B does not change with a devaluation.

Suppose the export elasticity is 1 and the import elasticity is -1. With a 1% devaluation, export revenue rises by 1%, since $\%\Delta q_X = 1$. Import expenditure ($e p_M{}^* q_M$) does not change because the 1% rise in e is offset by the 1% decline in q_M. B rises by 1%.

The ML condition states that if the export elasticity ($\%\Delta q_X/\%\Delta e > 0$) minus the import elasticity ($\%\Delta q_M/\%\Delta e < 0$) is greater than 1, B turns positive with a currency depreciation or devaluation.

If $B < 0$ to begin with, stronger elasticities are required for a devaluation to have a positive effect. In situations where a country has international market power, a devaluation increases the demand for exports, raising p_X and p_M^*. International market power strengthens the possibility that a devaluation would raise B.

The effect of a devaluation on B may not be easy to predict and certainly varies over time. Little consensus exists about the necessary effect of a depreciation or devaluation on B. Apparently more research is needed to determine the effects of a depreciation or devaluation on the BOT or BGS. The large exchange rate swings of the 1980s provide ample "experiments" of changes in currency values.

4. Timing and the J-Curve

A depreciation may require some time to have a positive effect on the BOT or BGS. Furthermore, a depreciation that ultimately leads toward surplus can temporarily create more of a deficit. This is called the *J-curve* effect because of the shape of the curve describing the course of the BOT or BGS over time following a depreciation.

Figure 11.4 illustrates the J-curve, with a one-time surprise depreciation of the currency at time d. Contracts for the delivery of traded goods and services are already written at time d, based on the expectation of a stable currency. The surprise devaluation lowers the price of exports and raises the price of imports under contract. During this *contract period*, the deficit in the BGS temporarily worsens. With the quantity of exports fixed and the price of exports falling, export revenue must fall. Simultaneously, import expenditure rises with the quantity of imports fixed and the price of imports rising. Over time, trade adjusts to the new prices, with the level of exports rising and the level of imports falling. The external balance increases during what is called the *pass-through* period.

Figure 11.4. The J-Curve Effect of a Depreciation A surprise depreciation of the currency at time d temporarily worsens the balance of goods and services (BGS) because contracts are set and goods and services must be delivered at agreed prices. The depreciation causes import prices to rise while export prices fall. Over time, substitution occurs, and the balance of trade (BOT) or BGS become more positive than they were before time d.

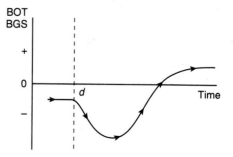

A currency depreciation may ultimately lead toward surplus or away from deficit in the BOT or BGS. The immediate effect of a surprise devaluation may, however, be a worsening in the external balance, as pictured by the J-curve.

5. Currency Appreciation

On the export side, increased international demand for U.S. exports (perhaps telecommunications services) would cause foreign buyers to increase the supply of their currencies on the foreign exchange market. As illustrated in Figure 11.5, an increase in the supply of foreign currency causes an appreciation of the dollar as the level of trading in the foreign exchange market increases. This dollar appreciation causes the foreign currency price of U.S. telecommunications exports to rise, strengthening the change in the market price. In Figure 11.5, the dollar increases in value from 1.667 to 1.818 marks. At a stable U.S. price of $12/unit of services, this appreciation causes a rise in the foreign price of telecommunications from $1.667 \times 12 = 20$ marks to $1.818 \times 12 = 21.82$ marks.

The accommodating and balancing effect of the foreign exchange market is an inherent and important reason that it should be allowed to operate freely. Induced movements in the exchange rate work in the same direction as the underlying price change, encouraging substitution by consumers and firms. The argument is often made, however, that foreign exchange traders create instability, which must be controlled by central bank intervention. Expectations of international investors can certainly cause a dollar appreci-

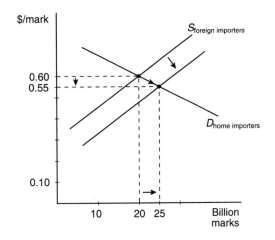

Figure 11.5. An Increase in the Supply of Foreign Currency This increase in the supply of marks comes from increased demand for U.S. exports. The value of the mark falls from $0.60/mark to $0.55/mark. The quantity of trading in the foreign exchange market rises.

ation. Much of the instability and volatility in the exchange market, however, is due to anticipation of central bank intervention.

EXAMPLE 11.2   Devaluation Episodes and the Balance of Trade

Daniel Himarios (1989) reports on the effects of a total of 60 episodes of exchange rate devaluation. A devaluation is an official decrease in the exchange value of the currency by the controlling central bank. Himarios first examines the era of fixed exchange rates under the Bretton Woods system up to 1973 and finds that devaluations improve the balance of trade in 80% of the cases. Effects are felt immediately during the year of the devaluation and lagged effects on the BOT last into the second and third years. Himarios extends his study to 15 countries with fixed exchange rates from 1975–1984 and again finds that 80% of the devaluing countries experienced an improved BOT. Full adjustment occurred within 2 years during this period. A J-curve effect occurred for Salvador, France, Greece, and Zambia.

EXAMPLE 11.3   The Exchange Rate and the U.S. Balance of Trade during the 1980s

Export revenue (X), import spending (M), and the exchange value of the dollar ($1/e$) during the 1980s are reported by the IMF in *International Financial Statistics*, 1990. Each is indexed to 100 in 1980. A clear trend is the appreciation of the dollar up to 1985 and its subsequent depreciation. Export revenue fell up to 1985, but the decline was sporadic and ultimately not very large. The industries that declined over this period were nonelectrical and electrical machinery, transportation equipment, apparel, and primary metal products. Overall, U.S. manufacturing prospered and increased its capacity during the 1980s. Import expenditure rose during the early 1980s, indicating elasticity because import prices fell with the dollar appreciation. With the dollar depreciation from 1985 to 1987, export prices fell while export revenue climbed, again indicating elasticity. The rise in import expenditure since 1985 indicates inelasticity and accounts for the recent trade deficits. Oil imports, specifically, remain insensitive to price.

	1980	1981	1982	1983	1984	1985	1986	1987	1988	1989
$1/e$	100	113	126	133	143	149	122	108	101	106
X	100	97	85	81	86	86	84	95	112	145
M	100	103	97	108	133	145	160	164	171	165

Problems for Section A

A1. Find the dollar prices of imported autos costing 880,000 yen when the yen/$ exchange rate is 110 and then rises to 125.

A2. Illustrate the exchange market for German marks with an equilibrium exchange rate of 1.6 DM/$. Suppose the United States announces a lifting of all restrictions on German imports after a one-month wait. Consumers and firms in the United States will expect cheaper German goods after one month. Diagram how this affects the current exchange rate. What happens to the current price of German goods in the United States?

A3. Suppose a U.S. petrochemical company discovers a cheap way to produce chlorine, which is exported to Germany. Illustrate the effect on the exchange market in its original position at 1.6 marks/$ in the previous problem.

A4. Diagram and explain the effect of an official revaluation or appreciation of the currency on the balance of trade, similar but opposite to the J-curve effect of a devaluation or depreciation.

B. MANAGED EXCHANGE RATES

Governments resort to various methods in order to control foreign trade and investment. Managed exchange rates offer a relatively simple way to control the price of traded goods, services, and investments. This section looks at:

(a) The workings of a fixed exchange rate
(b) Foreign exchange licensing
(c) Black markets, which arise with exchange market controls
(d) The pros and cons of managed exchange rates

1. Fixed Exchange Rates

Governments often have the apparent goal of keeping the value of their currency high. One motivation is the feeling that foreign investors will keep their funds in or put their funds into a country whose currency has a high or stable value. A highly valued currency also keeps down the price of imported goods, which may be intermediate inputs or capital goods in vital domestic industries. If a country is paying off debt, an overvalued currency makes the task easier. Managed exchange rate policy takes place in many nations.

In Figure 11.6 the market exchange rate between dollars and pesos would be $0.00050/peso, but suppose the Mexican government wants to keep the value of its peso at $0.00055. The target overvalued rate is 1,818 pesos/$, and the market rate is 2,000 pesos/$. The fixed exchange rate of

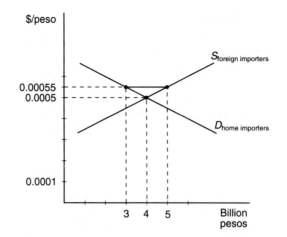

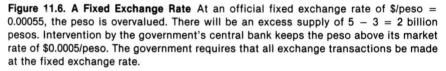

Figure 11.6. A Fixed Exchange Rate At an official fixed exchange rate of $/peso = 0.00055, the peso is overvalued. There will be an excess supply of $5 - 3 = 2$ billion pesos. Intervention by the government's central bank keeps the peso above its market rate of $0.0005/peso. The government requires that all exchange transactions be made at the fixed exchange rate.

$0.00055/peso would create an excess supply of $5 - 3 = 2$ billion pesos per market period, for example, every day.

At the fixed exchange rate the excess supply of pesos is equivalent to an excess demand for dollars of $1.1 million. The central bank would have to sell the $1.1 million every day out of its *foreign exchange reserves*. Foreign exchange reserves are depleted at the taxpayers' expense. Supporting a currency's value by depleting foreign exchange reserves can be expensive, especially when the currency ultimately depreciates. The central bank has been selling off its assets of foreign exchange at a discount.

Suppose the Mexican central bank supports the peso as in Figure 11.6 for five days. Mexican foreign exchange reserves of $5.5 million must be sold off in exchange for $1818.18 \times \$5.5$ million $= 10$ billion pesos. Perhaps the Mexican central bank is forced to stop because of declining foreign exchange reserves: The exchange rate jumps to the market rate of $/peso $= 0.0005$, and the 10 billion newly bought pesos are worth only $5 million. An implicit tax of $500,000 has been imposed by the Mexican central bank. This is a popular form of taxation because citizens do not typically keep up with the level of foreign exchange reserves and are influenced to believe that an appreciating or highly valued currency is somehow desirable.

2. Foreign Exchange Licensing

A way exists to sustain the value of a currency without spending valuable foreign exchange reserves. A government can limit the quantity of imports to the level that occurs at an artificially high exchange rate by issuing *foreign exchange licenses.*

In Figure 11.7 only 15 billion pesos are supplied to prospective importers. The supply of pesos is perfectly inelastic at 15 billion pesos. Importers are unable to buy more foreign currency (or imports) than is available through selling of 15 billion pesos. If the demand for pesos falls, the government will have to decrease import licenses to keep the value of the peso at the target level of $0.00055. Governments can also curtail tourism of their citizens and prohibit the purchase of foreign stocks and bonds for the same effect.

> By fixing the exchange rate or licensing foreign exchange, a government can support the value of its currency.

Greece is a nation with strict foreign exchange controls. Greek citizens are allowed to travel freely but cannot leave the country with more than about $800 worth of cash. This diminishes the quantity of foreign travel and foreign currency demanded, helping to support the value of the Greek drachma. Greek investors are not allowed to invest freely abroad, again curtailing the supply of drachma on the foreign exchange market. These controls will have to be dismantled as Greece integrates into the European Community after 1992.

3. Foreign Exchange Black Markets

Invariably a *black market* for foreign exchange will arise if the fixed or managed official rate is too much at odds with the underlying market rate. When this happens, the black market rate can be taken as a reliable indication of what the market rate would be. In the example of an overvalued

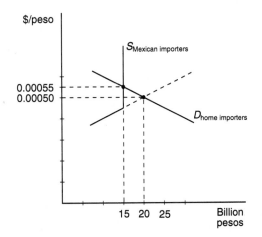

Figure 11.7. Foreign Exchange License The foreign government can support its peso by licensing importers to sell no more than 15 billion pesos per period. The peso can be kept above its market rate of $0.0005/peso by this effective restriction on imports.

Mexican peso, U.S. tourists, importers, and investors holding dollars would be tempted by black market rates on the street closer to the underlying market rate. If permitted, Mexicans would buy dollars that are artificially cheap at the official exchange rate.

An artificially supported peso would be expected to devalue sooner or later. Nobody would expect the peso to appreciate against the dollar. Such expectations keep the value of the peso low. Suppose the official exchange rate is 1,818 pesos per dollar, while a black market operates at 2,000 pesos per dollar. Nobody would expect the official rate to move to 1,800. Everyone would anticipate an official devaluation of the peso toward the black market rate. U.S. exporters would not discourage black market trading because their goods are cheaper at the unofficial rate.

Turkey provides an example of a nation where merchants dealing with tourists are happy to accept foreign (hard) currency at a rate more favorable to the tourists than the official rate. Such trading is strictly illegal, as an official with armed guards informs tourists at border crossing.

Some governments allow unofficial transactions in what is called a *parallel exchange market*. The official markets then work openly alongside the black market.

4. Fixed versus Floating Exchange Rates

Governments have learned that it is impossible to sustain indefinitely a currency value far out of line with the underlying market value. Some economists, however, believe that some central bank control or intervention is desirable to ensure an orderly foreign exchange market. The typical argument is that speculators feed on instability and want to create wild exchange rate movements. Speculators are pictured as scoundrels bent on profit who can cause the collapse of a currency's value if they are left unchecked.

The real experts, however, are the banks, dealers, traders, and speculators who make their living off the foreign exchange market. Central bank intervention destabilizes exchange rates by changing these traders' expectations. There are sound practical reasons that governments should not try to influence the value of their currency.

A prime historical example is the Mexican peso, whose value has been typically kept above its market level. Unquestionably the Mexican central bank support will ultimately collapse and a sharp depreciation of the peso will occur. The only question is when. Episodes of support and sudden depreciation have repeated themselves over and over again. This unstable situation results in consistent speculation that the peso will fall in value. Note that all of the speculation is on one side of the market, in favor of a devalued peso. Everyone expects the peso to lose value. Nobody will want to hold pesos. This depresses the inherent value of the peso and forces it to sell at a discount.

There is some disagreement over how well floating exchange rates work. Some experts think a more regulated foreign exchange market with stable exchange rates would better serve economic efficiency. The Bretton Woods fixed exchange rate system enforced through international agreement and cooperation was in effect from the end of World War II until the Organization of Petroleum Exporting Countries (OPEC) price hikes in the early 1970s. The United States was the dominant economic power of the world during this period, and the U.S. dollar was the standard for other currencies. The Bretton Woods system is looked upon by some experts as having been reliable and encouraging economic stability and steady growth. Others yearn for a return to the gold standard of the late 1800s, or some other common standard or definition for the value of each currency.

Any such fixed exchange rate arrangement would have collapsed under the economic upheavals of the 1970s and 1980s. The Bretton Woods system succeeded because the United States was the dominant economy at that time. Europe and Japan had been devastated by World War II and were trying to rebuild during the 1950s and 1960s. Conservative U.S. monetary policy led to stable prices and a reliable international currency standard, the U.S. dollar. Other central banks defined the value of their currencies in terms of U.S. dollars.

The 1970s and 1980s were vastly different. Oil price increases, the Latin American debt problem, the emergence of Japan as a world economic leader, European economic integration, the successes of the newly industrializing countries, high levels of migration and international investment, the emergency of Eastern Europe, and large inflation rate differentials all have made a fixed exchange rate system unworkable. The level and intensity of international transactions continue to grow dramatically. The possibility of formulating a workable fixed exchange rate system during the 1990s is remote.

Individual governments do not seem likely to give up their ability to print their own money. A government can increase its spending without raising taxes through the creation of debt and printing money. Each nation chooses its own particular inflation rate through a political and economic process. If inflation rates vary across nations, exchange rates must be able to adjust. An alternative to fixed exchange rates would be a single world currency, with the money supply beyond the control of any single government.

> The current floating exchange rate system has proved generally workable. Given the propensity governments have to create different rates of inflation, floating exchange rates are necessary.

It is crucial to recognize that a fundamental foreign exchange market is at work. Forces determining the supply and demand of foreign exchange are not altered by central bank management of the exchange rate. Furthermore, active exchange rate policy, if anticipated, has a tendency to exacerbate or worsen the trends that it tries to manage. The issue of whether and how much to manage exchange rates creates disagreement among economists. Given the increasing openness of the U.S. economy to international trade and finance, exchange rate policy promises to be a forum for important debate during the 1990s.

EXAMPLE 11.4   Fixed and Managed Exchange Rates

Most governments do not allow a free exchange market to operate, although forces of the market ultimately surface. Below are totals of fixed and managed exchange rates from *International Finance Statistics* (1990) of the IMF. A total of 148 currencies do not float freely. The major currencies float relative to one another, with occasional central bank intervention. The current exchange rate system is called a dirty or managed float.

Currencies fixed to:

Currency composites	44
U.S. dollar	31
French franc	14
Other currency	5

Rates adjusted according to:

Cooperative arrangements	8
Set of economic indicators	5
Something else	41

EXAMPLE 11.5   The Fed's Transactions in the Exchange Market

Total official foreign exchange reserves of $140 billion held by the Federal Reserve Bank of the United States (the Fed) would cover three months of imports into the United States. This may sound like a large amount of foreign currency, but it represents only $156 per U.S. household and only 30% of the estimated daily volume in the foreign exchange market. The Federal Reserve Bank of New York regularly summarizes the foreign exchange intervention of the Fed in its *Quarterly Review.* It reports that in 1989:

As the dollar moved up in January, the U.S. monetary authorities intervened to counter the rise. From January 6 to January 27, the U.S. authorities intervened on 12 days to sell a total of $1.88 billion against marks in coordination with the [German] Bundesbank and other foreign central banks.

For those 12 days the total volume of transactions on the foreign exchange market would have been about $6,000 billion. Official U.S. intervention of $1.88 billion amounted to about 0.03% of the total market transactions. Even if the Bundesbank and other major central banks had doubled this effort, not much of a lasting effect could have been expected. Between May and July of 1989, the value of the dollar rose in spite of the Fed's selling $6.84 billion against yen and about $5 billion against marks. This was less than 1% of the total market. Analysts agree that the foreign exchange market is so large that it shrugs off official efforts at intervention. Government central banks simply cannot buy or sell enough currency to have a true influence on the equilibrium exchange rate. Emergencies can arise, however, that require central bank action. On the day President Reagan was shot, the dollar began to plummet and the Fed responded by buying $10 billion in one day. The Fed's purchases were only about 2% of a typical day's volume.

EXAMPLE 11.6   Different Views on Exchange Rate Policy

Economists in the United States have an annual meeting of the American Economic Association around New Year's to present new research findings and policy viewpoints. The International Monetary Fund (*IMF Survey*, December 2, 1991) reports on the topic of exchange rate intervention discussed at the 1989 meeting. Differences of opinion were apparent. Paul Krugman of the Massachusetts Institute of Technology thinks that the depreciation of the dollar in the late 1980s was no cause for alarm or intervention. Ronald McKinnon of Stanford University disagrees, arguing out that the dollar should be revalued (increased in value) to its 1985 level. Martin Feldstein of Harvard University argues against attempts to stabilize or influence the value of the dollar because flexible exchange rates make the international economic system operate more smoothly. Peter Kenen of Princeton strongly encourages governments to intervene and stabilize to offset exchange rate movements created by international investment. John Williamson of the Institute for International Economics also favors active intervention, concluding that joint central back activity has been successful in influencing expectations and stabilizing exchange rates. Jacob Frankel of the International Monetary Fund (IMF) observes that the key issue is whether intervention would contribute to better fiscal and monetary policies. Regarding the foreign exchange market, experts disagree over the proper role of policy.

EXAMPLE 11.7   Effectiveness of Central Banks in Influencing Major Exchange Rates

Although central bank intervention by the United States, Germany, and Japan may not account for a large share of daily foreign exchange transactions, it does receive publicity and may influence exchange rates. Kathryn Dominguez (1992) puts forth evidence that coordinated efforts by the three large central banks to influence the value of a currency can be interpreted as a signal of a change in monetary policy. If the central banks buy dollars in the foreign exchange market, they are attempting to support the dollar. In the long run, tight monetary policy will increase the value of the dollar. Market participants may view central bank purchases of the dollar as a credible signal that the Fed will reduce the growth in the supply of dollars, which certainly would lead to dollar appreciation. Following the Plaza Agreement of September 1985, the Fed, the German Bundesbank, and the Bank of Japan publicized their plan to sell dollars through coordinated intervention. Foreign exchange market participants believed that the Fed had agreed in principle to increase the growth of the U.S. money supply, expected dollar depreciation, and began selling dollars. The Plaza Agreement worked by influencing expectations. Germany and Japan tried to resist continued dollar depreciation with the Louvre Agreement of June 1987, but the Fed did not immediately join in the buying of dollars. Market participants did not give the central bank efforts credibility, and, because of that, the dollar depreciation continued.

Problems for Section B

B1.   Suppose Germany tries to undervalue its currency. Diagram the market for marks, and illustrate an artificially low value. Using foreign exchange reserves, how could the central bank of Germany sustain this value below the market? Why would it want to?

B2.   How could the German government use exchange controls to keep the mark below its market value?

C.   TRADING FOREIGN EXCHANGE

This section looks deeper into the workings of the foreign exchange market, examining:

(a)   the role expectations play in influencing the exchange rate

(b) the frequently made claim that foreign exchange markets are un-
     stable
(c) triangular arbitrage across currencies

1. Expectations and Exchange Rates

If enough international investors and foreign exchange traders expect the
dollar to rise in value relative to other currencies, they supply any foreign
currencies they hold and demand dollars in the foreign exchange market.
As a result of the expectation that the dollar will rise in value, the dollar
does just that. Expectations have the ability to make themselves come true
in efficient markets. Much of the hourly or daily movement in exchange
rates is due to foreign exchange traders looking for short-term gains from
trading currencies. If a currency is expected to appreciate, traders will want
to buy it, increasing its demand and value in the foreign exchange market.

Other investors are looking for longer-term securities and want to hold
investments denominated in currencies that are expected to maintain or
improve their purchasing power over time. This is the motivation for someone with cash in high-inflation countries like Mexico, Brazil, or Israel to buy
real estate in Houston or Berlin, stock in IBM or Mitsubishi, or government
savings bonds from the United States or Great Britain. The dollar, mark,
and yen are expected to hold their value relative to currencies with high
inflation over long periods, say for 2, 5, 10, or even 20 years.

Expectations of what will happen to a currency's value influence the
current or spot exchange market. This is the best explanation of the dollar
depreciation that started in 1985. The major central banks of Germany,
France, Britain, Japan, and the United States (the Group of Five or G5)
announced in September 1985 that they would act together to depreciate
the dollar. This plan, called the Plaza Agreement, was announced after a
meeting of the G5 at the Plaza Hotel in New York.

Traders and investors paid attention to the Plaza Agreement and expected the dollar to begin losing value. The volume of central bank purchases of other currencies was not nearly enough actually to depreciate the
dollar, but the altered expectations of foreign exchange traders and investors were. Market participants realize that central bank intervention is small
relative to the market. Between May and July of 1989 the dollar appreciated
in spite of the concentrated selling of dollars by major central banks. Ultimately, the expectation of a depreciating dollar caused the demand for dollars to fall and the dollar depreciated.

Expectations and "market psychology" affect the foreign exchange
market. Central bank intervention is more often the cause of volatile
exchange rate movements than the cure for any imbalance in the
exchange market.

Foreign exchange markets arise where a lot of international trading and financial activity takes place, in busy ports and international commercial centers. Some nations are small, and the amount of currency trading may not support a competitive exchange market. If the volume of transactions is small in a thin market, a monopolistic trader could make excess profit. The monopolistic foreign exchange trader could sell foreign exchange at a high price to domestic importers, taking profit from domestic importing firms and consumer surplus from domestic consumers. When the foreign exchange market is very thin, the government may want to control the market and eliminate the monopoly profit of the foreign exchange trader.

Overwhelming evidence demonstrates that central banks should not interfere with the foreign exchange market in broad exchange markets with lots of activity where competitive conditions prevail. Exchange markets complement the price movements in international markets for goods, services, and financial instruments. Central bank intervention alters the expectations of foreign exchange traders and probably leads to wider fluctuations in exchange rates than would occur without official intervention.

2. Exchange Rate Speculation

A debate continues about the effects of speculation on the foreign exchange rate. Milton Friedman has argued since the 1950s that profitable speculation would result in less exchange rate fluctuation over time.

Figure 11.8 presents a picture of the market for yen at two times. On

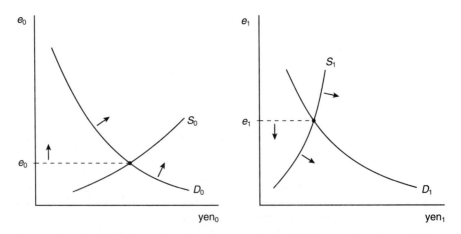

Figure 11.8. The Stabilizing Influence of Profitable Speculation The supply and demand for yen at time 0 is pictured on the left, and at a later time 1 on the right. Note that the supply yen at time 1 (S_1) is less than supply at line 0 (S_0). Speculators who anticipate the reduced supply and higher e at time 1 will buy yen now (increasing D_0 and e_0) and sell yen later (increasing S_1 and lowering e_1). Profitable speculation lessens the fluctuation in e over time.

the left the exchange rate at time 0 is determined. On the right at a later time, e_1 is determined. Note that the supply of yen at time 1 (S_1) is less than the supply of yen at time 0 (S_0). Perhaps Japanese investors at time 1 have shifted to keeping more of their assets in Japan because of change in Japanese tax laws or expected high stock returns in Japan.

Speculators at time 0 (the present) who correctly anticipate the coming change in the market and the higher value of the yen at time 1 (the future) will want to buy yen now (at time 0) and sell them at time 1. Buying yen low now at e_0 and selling them high later at e_1 results in a speculative profit.

Inadvertently, speculators dampen the variation in e over time. Increased D_0 raises e_0, and increased S_1 lowers e_1. The variation in e over time will be reduced with profitable speculation.

Unprofitable speculation would result in larger variation of e over time, but unprofitable speculators would quickly be out of the market. Only profitable speculators, on average, can persist. Speculation is likely to lessen the changes in e from period to period, transferring yen from time 0 when the yen is plentiful to time 1 when the yen is scarce.

Detractors of this theory of speculation argue that speculators may jump on the bandwagon of a trend in the exchange rate and create speculative bubbles that widen the variation in e over time. If the yen is appreciating, for instance, speculators will buy yen on the expectation that the current trend will continue. This speculative buying pushes the yen up faster and further. If the yen starts to fall, speculators rush to sell off their yen, pushing the value of the yen down faster and further. Speculators may make a profit and at the same time worsen or exacerbate swings in e.

Both theories of the effects of exchange rate speculation may contain hints of truth. Extensive testing of the current vigorous exchange trading continues. Financial economic experts disagree regarding the net effects of speculation in foreign exchange.

Even if exchange rate speculation is definitely linked with more variability in the exchange rate, no way to improve on the current market system has appeared. Any scheme of fixed exchange rates or central bank intervention would create speculation on one side of the market only. Free exchange markets, although far from perfect, are the best option available.

EXAMPLE 11.8   Chartists versus Fundamentalists in Foreign Exchange Trading

A chartist looks at recent trends in the exchange rate and projects that the trend will continue for at least a short time. The chartist then jumps on the bandwagon, buying the currency whose value is trending upward. The speculating chartist plans to sell the currency after a short time, before it begins to fall. Jeffrey Frenkel and Kenneth Froot (1990) report that chartists have become more prevalent among the firms predicting exchange rates, replacing market "fundamentalists," who examine factors that would shift the underlying supply or demand of foreign exchange. About 95% of all foreign exchange trading in New York City takes place among financial firms (banks, exchange brokers, and traders). Suppose an upward trend starts in the dollar. Expectations of an appreciating dollar cause demand for the dollar to rise. Chartists jump on the bandwagon, creating a speculative bubble. Eventually the bubble bursts and the value of the dollar falls sharply. The large swings in the value of the dollar during the 1980s lend support to the theory that speculative bubbles may play a role. Whether speculators ultimately stabilize or destabilize foreign exchange markets remains a topic of dispute among financial economists.

3. Stability of Exchange Markets

Demand for foreign exchange slopes downward and supply slopes upward if imports are elastic in the nations of both currencies involved. There is empirical evidence that supply and demand for foreign exchange look like those pictured in Figure 11.2, at least in the long run. Some financial economists, however, feel that a free foreign exchange market is inherently unstable.

The market equilibrium in Figure 11.2 is stable. An exchange rate above the equilibrium $/yen = 0.008 means excess supply of yen and a falling exchange rate. The adjustment process is identical to that in any market. If $/yen = 0.009, more yen will be supplied on the market than foreign exchange buyers want to purchase. Banks and foreign exchange dealers see their inventories of yen increasing as dollar inventories decline, and they respond by discounting the price of yen in the market. If the exchange rate is below the equilibrium at $/yen = 0.007, buyers clamor for yen but too few will be offered to meet their demand. Yen are then scarce, and their price is bid up.

An unstable foreign exchange market results if imports are inelastic, causing supply to have a negative slope or demand to have a positive slope. Suppose foreign imports are inelastic and supply slopes downward, as in Figure 11.9. Remember that a higher export price caused by an appreciation leads to increased export revenue when exports (foreign imports) are inelastic. In Figure 11.9 a lower $/yen exchange rate leads to an increase in the quantity of yen supplied along the supply curve. The supply of yen might slope downward, at least in the short term on the contract period.

At an exchange rate of $/yen = 0.009, an excess demand for yen develops and $/yen is bid up. At $/yen = 0.007, an excess supply of yen is available and the yen falls in value. Figure 11.9 presents the picture of an unstable explosive equilibrium. The exchange rate would move explosively if market supply and demand were in positions like the one in Figure 11.9.

Very large swings in the dollar's value have occurred during the 1980s.

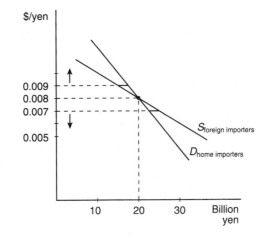

Figure 11.9. An Unstable Foreign Exchange Market At any price above the equilibrium exchange rate, excess demand occurs and the exchange rate is pushed upward. At any price below the equilibrium exchange rate, excess supply occurs and the exchange rate is pushed downward. Instead of stabilizing at the equilibrium, the exchange rate in this figure would rise and fall without bound.

The dollar appreciated 87% from July 1980 to February 1985, then depreciated 42% to December 1988. These large swings in the dollar's value have strong price effects on international transactions. The long-run swings in the dollar's value during the 1980s are best understood as increases in demand up to 1985, resulting from the inflow of foreign investment, and increases in supply since 1985, resulting from consistent U.S. trade deficits and the expectations of market participants formed by continued central bank efforts to depreciate the dollar.

On an hourly, daily, weekly, or monthly basis, exchange rate movements can be substantial. These short-term fluctuations are best understood as the result of foreign exchange market participants' looking for a longer-run equilibrium exchange rate. Some evidence indicates that immediate supply and demand may create explosive situations. With short-term movements in the exchange rate, some banks and dealers profit while others lose. Such high risk and high return are attractive to many investors, keeping the foreign exchange market a busier place than it would be if exchange rates were more stable.

A popular Public Television program follows three exchange rate dealers, one at a bank in Hong Kong, another who is a private trader in New York, and a third at a bank in London. During one day in June 1986 the three dealers exchange a total $1 billion. After a day of ups and downs the New York dealer makes $30,000 in an explosive few minutes of active trading. The dealer happily closes shop and sends his staff home early.

With the large appreciation of the U.S. dollar in the early 1980s, import expenditure rose. Imports include merchandise, capital goods, and inputs or supplies for industry. Export revenue in the United States simultaneously dwindled. These changes indicate import elasticity and downward-sloping long-run demand in the foreign exchange market. The early 1980s witnessed an unexpectedly strong recession in the United States that can be attributed in part to lagging production of exports and increased consumption of relatively cheap foreign goods. As the dollar depreciated after 1985, import prices rose and export revenues climbed. Import expenditure continued to climb, primarily because of inelasticity in U.S. oil imports. Imports of most other types of goods are elastic with respect to the exchange rate. Export revenue accelerated in the late 1980s, and the United States experienced trade surpluses early in 1991.

Exchange rates have been more volatile than proponents of a floating exchange rates in the 1960s predicted. Financial economists hold a consensus, not unanimous, that foreign exchange market is generally stable and should be allowed to operate freely.

4. Triangular Arbitrage

The tens of thousands of banks, brokers, and traders involved in the foreign exchange market instantaneously know the market equilibrium exchange rate because of their electronic links. All the banks, brokers, and traders in fact make the market, continuously trying to match buyers and sellers of foreign exchange. The slightest difference in exchange rates between dealers results in a profitable opportunity for *triangular arbitrage,* which occurs continuously and keeps the relative values of currencies in line.

Suppose current exchange rates are posted at mark/\$ = 2 and yen/mark = 62 while yen/\$ = 125. Exchange traders could take yen, buy marks, and then buy dollars at 62 × 2 = 124 yen/\$. This *cross rate* is lower than the market rate of 125. Dollars are cheap at the cross rate and expensive at the market rate. Arbitragers will want to buy dollars at the cross rate and sell dollars at the market rate for a profit of 1 yen for every dollar traded. This arbitrage decreases the demand for the overvalued dollar, pushing the cross rate and the market rate together. When the dollar is even slightly overvalued, its supply rises and its value will fall immediately. The undervalued yen will see its demand and value rising.

Billions of dollars worth of currency are involved in continuous triangular arbitrage. Arbitrage keeps the value of currencies in line with one another. Among the three currencies in the example, there are only two independent exchange rates. Cross rates between any two currencies determine the value of the other currency through triangular arbitrage. Because of triangular arbitrage, among any number n of currencies there are only $n-1$ independent exchange rates.

The largest traders in the U.S. foreign exchange market are Citibank, Chemical, Barclay's, Chase, Morgan Guaranty, and Bank of America. The foreign exchange market is highly competitive. The top twenty banks compose only about one third of the total market. Thousands of brokers and traders operate profitably on volumes that are minuscule relative to the market. The foreign exchange market, broadly defined, is the world's largest market. Worldwide volume exceeds $500 billion per day. Daily transactions in New York City alone were estimated by Chemical Bank in 1989 to be $350 billion, far surpassing the stock market in volume. In only 13 working days, the foreign exchange transactions in New York City alone match the volume of transactions in the yearly gross national product (GNP) of the United States.

> The foreign exchange market is a vast competitive market made up of thousands of banks, dealers, and traders profitably trading currencies with one another.

In many places you can witness and take part in the worldwide foreign exchange market. Most large banks have a foreign exchange desk, which may be involved in continuous trading or may only serve customers. In large cities, foreign exchange trading businesses specialize in quick service. This is true near the Canadian and Mexican borders of the United States, where the foreign currency is often used alongside the domestic currency. Even cities as far north of the Mexican border as Houston and Dallas have foreign exchange businesses. Travelers in Europe and most other nations notice an abundance of foreign exchange businesses. Major airports have foreign exchange windows where travelers can buy and sell foreign currencies. Watching foreign exchange transactions take place drives home the point that currencies are economic commodities whose ultimate value is based on scarcity.

EXAMPLE 11.9   Predicting Exchange Rates

Economists are often called on to do the impossible and will gladly do so for a fee. Predicting short-run changes in exchange rates is impossible. The *Economist* magazine analyzed economists' predictions of the dollar's value ("Every Which Way But Down," 20 May 1989). During 1989 the dollar's value increased in spite of predictions of its decline. Strong output growth was often cited in the first quarter of the year as a reason for the strong dollar. Production in the United States increased, and foreigners wanted to buy dollars in order to buy U.S. exports. When growth apparently slowed in the second quarter, that was also seen as a reason for a strengthening dollar. Slower growth meant less inflationary pressure, which is "bullish" for the dollar. The international market for dollars is huge and complicated, generally defying efforts to understand it and central bank intervention. Hundreds of thousands of participants buy and sell foreign exchange for all sorts of reasons. An economist who could predict what the dollar will do would certainly not want to tell anyone else.

EXAMPLE 11.10   The Exchange Rate's Effect on Particular Markets

Every market has its own production processes and buyers. Production takes planning and investing. Buyers may be anything from final consumers with many available substitutes to firms wanting a particular intermediate input in their production. A changing exchange rate will affect some markets more than others. The destination of trade makes some difference if exchange controls exist. In a study of U.S. agricultural exports, Nathan Childs and Michael Hammig (1987) trace the regional pattern of U.S. exports of corn, wheat, soybeans, and rice from 1968 to 1984. Soybean exports are found to be sensitive to the exchange rate, while corn exports are not. Rice and wheat exports are sensitive going into some regions of the world. Exports of rice and wheat to Europe and Asia depend on the exchange rate, while exports to Latin America do not. For these agricultural products the effects of changing exchange rates are felt the strongest after two to three years. Participants in international markets learn through experience how their particular market works. When talking in broad terms about export markets and import markets, we should remember that the market for each particular good is different. The real experts are out there making a living through their production and trading.

Problems for Section C

C1.   If the lira/$ exchange rate is 1,050, the peso/$ rate is 175, and the lira/peso rate is 5.95, describe a way to make profit through triangular arbitrage. Start with $1,000. Find the profit when there are no transactions costs.

C2.   Suppose the demand for yen slopes upward because of the current inelasticity of demand for Japanese bonds. Diagram an unstable exchange market with upward-sloping demand. Describe its explosive behavior.

D.   INFLATION AND FOREIGN EXCHANGE RISK

Over years or decades, exchange rates reflect relative inflation or loss of purchasing power across different currencies. Unexpected exchange rate changes add a degree of risk to international trade and finance. This section describes how the foreign exchange market attempts to deal with such risk.

1. Expected Inflation and Exchange Rates

Inflation occurs when the general price level or the average price of all goods is rising. The foreign price level is written P^*, which can be expressed in units as pesos/good. The inverse of P^*, $1/P^*$, is then goods/peso, which represents the purchasing power of the foreign currency (the peso). If P^* is rising, the purchasing power of the peso $1/P^*$ is falling. If P^* rises from 100 to 125, the purchasing power of the peso falls from $1/100 = 0.01$ to $1/125 = 0.008$. An index of the goods that can be purchased with a peso has then fallen from 0.01 to 0.008. Inflating currencies lose their value in terms of the goods they can purchase.

All currencies have been generally inflating since World War II, but some have inflated much more rapidly than others. Periods of currency *deflation,* when the general price level falls, have occurred throughout history. Changes in the value of a particular currency do not matter greatly, as long as the changes are predictable and the currency's exchange rate is free to float. Residents and firms in a country readily adjust to any degree of inflation, as long as it is steady and predictable.

If one currency is expected to inflate more rapidly than another, international interest rates will reflect this expected inflation differential. The *real interest rate* is the return on an investment after the eroding influence of inflation has been removed. The real interest rate typically does not vary greatly over time or between countries. The *nominal interest rate,* which does vary across countries, contains an inflation premium added onto the real interest rate.

Suppose the interest rate on your savings account is 6%. If $1,000 stays in the account for a year, it will contain $1.06 \times \$1,000 = \$1,060$ at the end of the year. Suppose expected inflation for the year is 5%. The purchasing power of the $1,060 must be discounted by the expected 5% inflation to arrive at the real interest rate for your savings. The net between nominal interest and expected inflation is $6\% - 5\% = 1\%$. There is an expected 1% increase in the purchasing power of the $1,000 savings. The $1,060 next year is expected to be able to purchase $1,010 worth of current goods and services.

The *Fischer equation,* named after economist Irvin Fischer, is expressed

$$i = r + \pi$$

where i is the normal interest rate, r is the real interest rate, and π is the expected rate of inflation.

Suppose the expected inflation rate for pesos is 25%, while the expected inflation for the dollar is 5%. Expectations are based on the history of inflation in each country as well as any news or information about monetary policy over the coming year. A 28% nominal interest rate in pesos amounts to a real interest rate of 3%. An equivalent in real terms would be an 8% nominal interest rate in dollars. Investing at the nominal interest rate in either nation would yield the same purchasing power at the end of a year if actual inflation turns out to be what was expected in each country, 5% in the United States and 25% in Mexico. The increase in purchasing power from investments in either country would then turn out to be 3%. Since it is easy to be fooled about the future of inflation, choosing among international investments based on nominal interest rates differences is a real challenge. International differences in the real rate of interest are effectively veiled.

> The nominal interest rate discounted by expected inflation gives the real interest rate. Choosing between international investments is more difficult because of unexpected inflation differences across currencies.

Suppose the spot exchange rate is 125 pesos/$ and inflation turns out to be 30% for pesos and 3% for dollars over the year. What should have happened to the exchange rate during the year? Clearly the peso has lost value relative to the dollar. In fact it will have lost 27% = 30% − 3% of its value, so the exchange rate should be 1.27 × 125 = 158.75 pesos/$ at the end of the year. This calculation assumes a floating exchange rate that is free to adjust in the foreign exchange market.

The trick is that *expected inflation* is not observed directly. Nominal interest rates are quoted everywhere by banks, firms, and government bond traders competing for funds. Since much of this competition is international, a comparison of expected rates of inflation becomes necessary. An effort at an international comparison of two real interest rates involves the double risk of two expected inflation rates.

The difference between the nominal interest rates in two countries with free exchange and financial markets is the market's overall expectation of the future of the two inflation rates. This difference between nominal interest rates is called the weaker currency's *discount*. If the nominal interest rates are 28% for pesos and 8% for dollars, the peso would have a 28% − 8% = 20% discount against the dollar. The dollar in this example would have a 20% premium against the peso.

> Nominal interest rates denominated in currencies with higher expected inflation must be discounted. An international comparison of nominal interest rates reveals which currencies have future discounts or premiums.

2.   Foreign Exchange Risk: The Forward and Future Exchange Markets

Currencies sporting high inflation rates will lose value relative to those with low inflation rates. The Italian lira, Mexican peso, and Brazilian cruzado lose value year after year relative to the German mark, the U.S. dollar, and the Kuwaiti dinar. Foreign exchange markets systematically discount inflating currencies. However, a great deal of risk remains in international transactions because of unexpected changes in inflation and the exchange rate. Most contracts in international trade are written for future delivery, sometimes six months to two years in advance. International investors are often committed to leaving their wealth in assets denominated in the foreign currency for some time.

Consider the example of a firm assembling personal computers in the United States. The firm orders computer chips from a Japanese firm, with delivery spread out over the next six months and bills to be paid on delivery. The current exchange rate (perhaps $/yen = $0.006958) is known from the newspaper or the local bank, but nobody knows what the exchange rate will be after one, three, or six months, when the bills will have to be paid. The U.S. firm can assume the *foreign exchange risk,* buying the yen when needed in the *spot* or current exchange market. International investors face the same exchange risk when they buy a foreign bond that matures after some time, perhaps one year.

To avoid this foreign exchange risk, trading firms and international investors can hedge in the *forward exchange market.* A contract can be signed to buy or sell foreign currency at a date in the future for a price agreed on today. The supply and demand for forward exchange are derived from international traders and investors who want to make certain of the value of their foreign purchases, sales, or interest earnings in terms of their own currency.

Forward exchange rates for 30, 60, and 180 days appear daily in the financial pages of major newspapers. The importing firm can use forward contracts to pin down a dollar price for the chips from Japan that will be shipped and paid for in the future. Suppose the U.S. importer knows a bill for 5 million yen will have to be paid in 30 days, and the forward exchange rate for 30 days is 0.0069. The importer can sign a contract to buy the yen for 5 million × 0.0069 = $34,500. Similar forward contracts can be signed for the yen wanted after 60 and 180 days.

The forward market reflects what market participants think the exchange rate will become over time. The forward exchange rate has proved an unbiased predictor of the exchange rate, meaning it will overestimate and underestimate the future exchange rate with equal frequency. Rapidly inflating currencies like the lira, peso, and cruzado are systematically discounted in the forward market. Their forward rates are less than their spot rates. Currencies with relatively low inflation rates like the mark, dollar, and dinar have a premium in the forward market relative to currencies with high inflation. If market participants come to expect the Mexican peso to suffer less inflation because of economic growth, the demand for pesos in the forward market rises and the peso will be discounted less heavily.

Another sort of agent buys and sells forward or future currency contracts to make a profit. Speculators make contracts in foreign exchange when they believe the exchange rate will turn out to be different from the forward rate. *Future contracts* for standard quantities of foreign exchange and standard time periods have developed for those wanting to speculate in foreign currencies. The transaction costs of future contracts are low. The market for currency futures was established in 1972 by the Chicago Mercantile Exchange. International traders and investors can also use the futures market, whose main advantage is the low transaction cost created by the use of standard contracts. Its disadvantages are the standard quantities of foreign currency that must be bought (£25,000, for instance) and the specified trading dates. In the forward exchange market, traders can make contracts for any amount and any date, but transaction costs are higher.

Suppose the current spot rate for South Korean won is 760 won/$ and the future rate is 780 won/$. The won is selling at a discount, but the speculator thinks the won will go all the way down to 800 won/$. She will want to sign a contract to sell won at the forward rate of 780 and will plan on buying won in the spot market a year later. Note that this speculation is totally unleveraged, since no current down payment is required to make the contract. This speculation is risky because the spot rate can turn out to be lower than 780 won/$ after one year. Such foreign exchange speculation in the futures market can be very profitable.

> Forward and future foreign exchange markets offer hedgers a way to avoid risk and speculators a way to gain from assuming risk in exchange rate movements.

It is striking how forward and future foreign exchange markets have developed to meet the desires of international traders in goods, services, and assets. Whether in business or foreign travel, most of you will be exposed to the foreign exchange market. Understanding how it works will give you a definite advantage.

EXAMPLE 11.11   Future Exchange Rates

Future exchange rates are listed in many daily newspapers. Future contracts are for standard quantities (12.5 million yen, for instance) and specified dates (the third Wednesdays of September, December, March, and June). Firms and investors can readily enter into hedging contracts at these rates. Investors and speculators can match their wits against the

FUTURES

	Open	High	Low	Settle	Change	Lifetime High	Low	Open Interest
JAPANESE YEN (IMM) 12.5 million yen; $ per yen (.00)								
Dec	.6962	.6964	.9646	.6952	– .0012	.8635	.6705	50.505
Mr90	.6993	.6997	.6980	.6987	– .0006	.8357	.6780	12,793
June	.7018	.7020	.7012	.7014	– .0002	.7530	.6850	503
Est vol 24,068; vol Tues 19,669; open int 63,803, + 877.								
W. GERMAN MARK (IMM)—125,000 marks; $ per mark								
Dec	.5632	.5674	.5626	.5670	+ .0042	.5895	.4925	90,968
Mr90	.5632	.5675	.5626	.5671	+ .0043	.5675	.5000	17,854
June	.5630	.5670	.5622	.5666	+ .0044	.5670	.5057	3,035
Est vol 47,000; vol Tues 40,808; open int 111,862, + 2,970.								
CANADIAN DOLLAR (IMM)—100,000 dlrs; $ per Can $								
Dec	.8591	.8607	.8590	.8603	+ .0016	.8607	.7990	23,373
Mr90	.8511	.8527	.8511	.8525	+ .0017	.8527	.7890	4,854
June	.8447	.8455	.8447	.8456	+ .0018	.8455	.8107	2,411
Sept	....	....		.8387	+ .0019	.8375	.8100	158
Dec	.8345	.8345	.8345	.8318	+ .0020	.8345	.8120	108
Est vol 6,459; vol Tues 3,828; open int 30,930, + 424.								
BRITISH POUND (IMM)—62,500 pds.; $ per pound								
Dec	1.5716	1.5764	1.5696	1.5736	+ .0082	1.7450	1.4550	20,321
Mr90	1.5472	1.5518	1.5452	1.5490	+ .0086	1.6180	1.4600	3.020
June	1.5242	1.5270	1.5230	1.5252	+ .0082	1.6950	1.4400	363
Est vol 12,689; vol Tues 9,458; open int 23,704, +640.								
SWISS FRANC (IMM)—125,000 francs-$ per franc								
Dec	.6284	.6316	.6277	.6298	+ .0012	.6653	.5600	36,218
Mr90	.6285	.6317	.6281	.6302	+ .0014	.6355	.5740	13,632
June	.6290	.6315	.6285	.6302	+ .0014	.6350	.5850	799
Est vol 28,974; vol Tues 31,329; open int 50,658, + 1,935.								
AUSTRALIAN DOLLAR (IMM)—100,00 dlrs.; per A.$								
Dec	.7800	.7816	.7798	.7812	+ .0008	.7835	.7080	1,418
Mr90	.7620	.7643	.7620	.7639	+ .0005	.7660	.7055	331
Est vol 80; vol Tues 66; open int 1,752, – 1.								
U.S. DOLLAR INDEX (FINEX) 500 times USDX								
Dec	96.23	96.32	95.72	95,80	–	.46	106.55 95.05	4,812
Mr90	96.80	96.85	96.25	96.31	–	.48	105.65 96.25	2,350
Est vol 1,855; vol Tues 1,798; open int 7,210, –56.								
The Index: High 96.24; Low 95.75; Close 95.82 –.43								

—OTHER CURRENCY FUTURES—

Settlement prices of selected contracts. Volume and open interest of all contract months.

British Pound (MCE) 12,500 pounds; $ per pound
   Mar 1.5490 +.0086; Est. vol. 100; Open Int. 293
Japanese Yen (MCE) 6.25 million yen; $ per yen (.00)
   Mar .6952 –.0012; Est. vol. 200; Open Int. 549
Swiss France (MCE) 62,500 francs; $ per franc
   Mar .6302 +.0014; Est. vol. 250; Open Int. 406
West German Mark (MCE) 62,500 marks; $ per mark
   Mar .5671 +.0043; Est. vol. 200; Open Int. 739
   FINEX—Financial Instrument Exchange, a division of the New York Cotton Exchange. IMM—International Monetary Market at the Chicago Mercantile Exchange. MCE—MidAmerica Commodity Exchange.
SOURCE: *Wall Street Journal,* Dec. 7, 1989.

market. Banks list future rates to attract foreign exchange business. Investment houses also offer standard future contracts in smaller amounts for the investor who wants high risk and high returns.

EXAMPLE 11.12   Disagreement over Exchange Rate Reform

Conflicting views of three economists regarding a proposal for actively stabilizing exchange rates with exchange rate policy and controls were recently published in the *Journal of Economic Perspectives* (Winter 1988). The past 20 years have witnessed large parallel fluctuations in the $/yen and $/mark exchange rates, pointing to unstable U.S. monetary policy. Ronald McKinnon of Stanford University favors a fixed exchange rate system managed by the central banks of the United States, Japan, and Germany. If the three major currencies stabilize, McKinnon argues, others will follow suit. Rudiger Dornbusch of the Massachusetts Institute of Technology counters that the current floating system has worked reasonably well and that no "correct" level at which to fix the three currencies exists. John Williamson of the Institute for International Economics agrees with McKinnon that the costs imposed by the large swings in exchange rates over the past 10 years have been substantial. Rather than a fixed system, Williamson favors target zones for exchange rates and international cooperation to keep exchange rates within these zones. The views of these three hardly exhaust the range of opinions of economists on the exchange rate system. All reformers concede that the current market system has seen the international economy through adjustments during which virtually any fixed scheme would have collapsed.

Problems for Section D

D1.   Suppose current price levels are $P = \$/\text{good} = 100$ in the United States and $P^* = \text{DM}/\text{good} = 150$ in Germany. If the same goods are consumed in each country, what must the current exchange rate $/DM be? Five years later, the U.S. price level has risen to $P = 120$, while Germany's has become $P^* = 160$. What should the exchange rate have become? Which currency has probably depreciated?

D2.   Suppose the nominal interest rate is 12%, while inflation has been running at about 9%. Find the real interest rate. Starting with $100, express the nominal and real return to saving. If the expected inflation rate rises to 15% but the real interest rate is unchanged, find the nominal rate and the nominal and real returns to $100.

CONCLUSION

The foreign exchange market is a vast, lively, and important market. Firms and consumers in the United States are becoming increasingly familiar with the foreign exchange market. As the United States integrates more completely into the world economy, familiarity with the exchange market becomes more important. The exchange market both affects the economy and is affected by it. This chapter has presented the basics of the foreign exchange market. The influence of the exchange rate on international trade and finance are fundamentally important. The following chapter turns attention to issues of international finance and the important roles of money.

KEY TERMS

Black exchange market	Import license
Cross rate	J-curve
Currency discount	Market exchange rate
Expected inflation	Marshall-Lerner condition
Fischer equation	Parallel exchange markets
Fixed exchange rate	Real and nominal interest rates
Forward exchange rate	Speculation
Foreign exchange reserves	Spot exchange rate
Foreign exchange risk	Triangular arbitrage
Future and forward contracts	

KEY POINTS

- The demand for foreign exchange comes from domestic buyers of foreign goods, services, and financial assets. The supply of foreign exchange comes from foreign buyers of domestic goods, services, and financial assets.
- Foreign exchange markets are very large, very active, electronic, efficient, and vital to the world economy. They are influenced by the economy and influence the economy in return. For most economies the foreign exchange market is the single most important market.
- A depreciating currency raises the domestic price of foreign goods and lowers the foreign price of domestic goods, favoring an increase in the BOT or BGS. An appreciating currency lowers the domestic price of foreign goods and raises the foreign price of domestic goods, favoring a decrease in the BOT or BGS.
- Governments often artificially fix or manage their exchange rate to meet some policy goal, even though theory and experience recommend that exchange rates float freely.
- High inflation rates are associated with high nominal interest rates and depreciating currencies. Currencies that are expected to depreciate are systematically discounted in the forward exchange market.

REVIEW PROBLEMS

1. Suppose the domestic demand for the Japanese autos is given as $Q = 10,000 - P$, where P is the dollar price. Find the quantity of Japanese cars costing 880,000 yen that would be demanded at the two exchange rates: yen/$ = 110 and 125. Find and plot the quantity demanded of yen to buy the Japanese autos at these two exchange rates.

2. Find the yen prices of U.S. rice costing $4.50 per bushel when the yen/$ exchange rate is 110 and then 125. Demand for wheat in Japan is $Q = 9,000,000 - 10,000 P^*$, where P^* is the yen price. Find the quantity of U.S. rice demanded in Japan and the quantity of yen supplied at both exchange rates. Plot this supply of yen.

3. Start with $1,000 and find a way to make a profit if the lira/peso exchange rate is 6.05, lira/$ = 1,050, and $/peso = 0.00571.

4. Suppose the Europeans launch a number of high-grade communications satellites, improving their telecommunications industry relative to that of the United States. Given that the United States exports telecommunications services, diagram what happens in the foreign exchange market. Predict the subsequent effects on the BGS.

5. Find the short-run percentage change in import expenditure and export revenue with a 5% depreciation of the currency when the short-run import elasticity is 0.3 and the short-run export elasticity is 0.4. Describe what must happen to the BOT in the short run.

6. If the long-run import elasticity is 1.5 and the long-run export elasticity 1.2, find the long-run percentage change in the export revenue and import expenditure with a 5% depreciation of the home currency. Does the BOT rise or fall in the long run?

7. Illustrate the effect on the exchange market of a limit on cash for foreign travel.

8. Explain why a central bank supporting its currency by buying a surplus of its own currency is taxing its citizens. What other sort of explicit tax would have the same effect?

9. Which group of economic agents demands pesos in the forward market? What happens to the quantity of pesos demanded when the forward price of pesos rises? Who supplies pesos forward in the market?

10. The *Foreign Exchange Review* of the First Wachovia Bank reported in its March 12, 1990, issue: "Despite repeated central bank intervention last week, the U.S. dollar rallied to highs of 1.7095 marks, 151.35 yen, and $1.6155/pound." Were the central banks buying or selling dollars? Illustrate with a relevant exchange market diagram.

11. Suppose the spot exchange rate for Kuwaiti dinar is $/dinar = 3.60, and the six-month forward rate is 3.65. Does the dinar have a forward premium or discount? If the inflation rate in dollars is expected to be 4%, would it be more or less in Kuwait?

12. In the example of a speculator in Korean won in the text, calculate her profit if she signs a contract to sell 10 million won and the spot rate turns out to be exactly what she expected. Find her profit in dollars if the spot rate instead falls to 750 won/$.

13. Start with $1 million and keep an imaginary record of buying and selling spot exchange. Compete with your friends to see who can create the largest profit. Assume zero transaction costs.

READINGS

Mike Melvin, *International Money and Finance,* Harper & Row, New York, 1989. A short and lively text with excellent coverage of the foreign exchange market.

Federal Reserve Bank Economic Bulletins. Published by each of the Federal Reserve Banks, these monthly bulletins contain analyses of the current situation in the foreign exchange market.

Longman is committed to publishing only the finest texts in your field and your comments are invaluable to us. After you have examined this text, please take a few moments to complete this form. Thank you.

Author _____

Title of Text _____

Name _____

Department _____

Institution _____

Telephone ( ) _____ Office Hrs. _____

Name of course _____ Enrollment _____

Present text _____

Is the Longman text applicable to the course you teach?
☐ Yes   ☐ No

How would it be used?
☐ Main Text   ☐ Supp. Text   ☐ Recommended

Do you plan to adopt this text?
☐ Yes   When? _____   ☐ No   ☐ Undecided

Comments _____
_____
_____
_____
_____
_____

May we quote you?
☐ Yes   ☐ No

BUSINESS REPLY MAIL

FIRST CLASS   Permit No. 3679 White Plains, NY

POSTAGE WILL BE PAID BY ADDRESSEE

College Marketing Manager
Longman Inc.
95 Church Street
White Plains, N.Y. 10601-1505

Longman

John Williamson, *The Exchange Rate System,* Institute for International Economics, Washington, DC, 1985. One of a series on international policy analysis.

The Economist, The Economist Newspaper Limited, Winterthur. A first-class weekly magazine with readable economic analysis, including insightful articles on foreign exchange and international finance.

Roger Kubarych, *Foreign Exchange Markets in the U.S.,* Federal Reserve Bank of New York, 1983. A practical discussion of the structure of the foreign exchange market.

Paul Einzig, *The History of Foreign Exchange,* St. Martin's, New York, 1962. An excellent history of foreign exchange dating back to ancient history.

CHAPTER 12

International Finance and Money

CHAPTER PREVIEW

This final chapter turns attention toward international financial markets and the crucial international role of money. The essence of finance is borrowing and lending, the transfer of liquidity. International finance refers to borrowing and leading across nations and the international pricing of financial assets. International trade and finance require money and an exchange of different monies. The important link between money and international prices is explored. This chapter covers:

(a) The international *loanable funds* market
(b) The relationship between the exchange rate and the international loanable funds market
(c) Money and its international impact on prices
(d) How relative money supplies affect international finance

INTRODUCTION

Money functions mainly as a medium of exchange, facilitating trade between consumers and firms. We all trade our labor for food and housing, using the medium of money in the form of paychecks, bank deposits, checks, and cash. We all know how it feels to have less of the medium at our disposal than we would like. This scarcity of money reflects the world's scarcity of resources and the unavoidable necessity of making choices.

Income for an individual consumer or firm may be greater during a particular year than the desire to spend. Markets for loanable funds develop through the interaction of potential lenders and borrowers. The interest rate is the price or return of a loan. Banks and other financial intermediaries bring together those who currently have either more or less cash than they want to spend.

A nation is composed of individual consumers and firms and may as a whole have more or less income than it wants to spend during a given year. One nation can become a net lender and the other a net borrower, with loans flowing internationally. International banks are the mechanisms through which these international loanable funds flow. Each nation would have its own loanable funds market in autarky, but both nations benefit through an international loanable funds market. International interest rates are established when free international lending and borrowing exist.

Besides its role as a medium of exchange, money functions as a unit of account for the goods and services an economy produces. Currencies effectively serve as a unit of account for each other in the foreign exchange market. International price comparisons must be made through the exchange rate. Money also serves as a store of value. An inflating currency loses value and is a poor store of value. Currencies with relative high inflation rates depreciate in the foreign exchange market. A large amount of currency trading takes place as investors look for the currency that will be the best store of value.

International financial flows are reported in the capital account of the balance of payments. Interest payments on previously made international loans are reported in net investment income of the current account because the funds are available for current transactions. Borrowing nations experience cash inflow and capital account surpluses but are committed to future investment income and current account deficits. Lenders experience cash outflows and capital account deficits but enjoy future investment income and current account surpluses. International loans are used to purchase productive machinery and equipment or consumer goods and are associated with balance of trade (BOT) deficits.

While often interpreted as bad news, a trade deficit and international debt may be a signal that a nation is expected to grow. Developing nations should be expected to incur debt in order to acquire needed capital goods. Investors will want to have interest in an economy that is expanding because ownership of a growing enterprise can create sizeable gains. As output expands, a growing country can repay its debt more easily.

Students similarly take out loans (a capital account surplus) and spend more than they make (a current account deficit). Later, with a good education and high-paying employment, paying off the loan causes relatively little strain. Income is higher over the person's lifetime because the debt was assumed.

There is an optimal amount of debt that a nation should acquire for growth. Debt is harmful only if it is not managed well. Some commentators argue that recent U.S. borrowing is harmful, since it has been carried out to finance current consumption rather than investment for growth. The issue of concern is whether the United States can manage its debt.

Stocks, bonds, certificates of deposit, and overnight paper are some of the financial instruments involved in international finance. If a firm in the United States wants to raise money for a new building, it can offer new stock or bonds on the market. Investors buy this paper to receive returns over time. Investors give up cash in hand for more cash later in the form of dividends on stocks or premiums on bonds. When such transactions occur internationally, they typically clear the foreign exchange market and affect exchange rates.

On the other hand, the exchange rate influences international financial flows. Suppose the home currency depreciates. Foreign lenders may then want to buy more home stocks and bonds because they have become cheaper in terms of the foreign currency. The appreciating foreign currency makes home assets cheaper in the foreign country. A depreciation immediately encourages a nation to become more of a borrower. An appreciation causes foreign financial instruments to become cheaper and immediately encourages the nation to become a lender.

The international market for loanable funds and the foreign exchange market are closely related. A tremendous amount of arbitrage trading occurs internationally among financial intermediaries (banks, investment houses, and brokers). The primary positive role governments should play in these international financial markets is to control their money supplies. A government central bank has the job of controlling its country's money supply. A nation whose money supply is growing relative to the rest of the world will experience currency depreciation. Both domestic and international markets for loanable funds, as well as the foreign exchange markets, are affected by central bank action.

International financial markets are very active and are becoming more important. There are constant calls for the international integration of monetary policy, which would stabilize exchange rates. European nations are attempting to move toward a common currency. The debt crisis among the developing nations has fundamentally reshaped international economic relations since the 1970s. International financial and monetary relations are vital forces in the everyday life of the world economy.

A.   CAPITAL AND INTERNATIONAL LOANABLE FUNDS

This section examines how markets for loanable funds develop, considers the international market for loanable funds, and describes the scheme of international financial accounting.

1.   The Two Senses of "Capital"

Capital has different meanings in microeconomics and finance. In microeconomics, capital is a factor of production, namely the machinery and equipment combined in production processes along with labor and natural resources. In finance, capital refers to loanable funds. When you read a newspaper or magazine that refers to international capital flows, it is referring to international lending and borrowing. The word "capital" is most commonly used in this financial sense.

The two uses of the word are closely connected. When a firm borrows from a bank, it is likely to invest in productive capital equipment in order to increase future production. A firm could try to borrow to pay current labor or material expenses, but this would indicate losses. A firm could not do this for long because banks will not make loans to firms with current losses. To receive a loan, a firm must convince a bank that the loan will be repaid. By investing in new capital equipment, a firm increases its earning potential. Since loans are most often used to purchase new machinery and equipment, the two senses of "capital" go hand in hand.

Economic agents are faced with the dilemma of choosing between current and future spending. This applies to consumers, who can put off current consumption by saving out of their current income or increase current consumption beyond current income by borrowing. Governments can also increase their current spending beyond tax revenues by borrowing and selling new bonds. Government bond sales bring cash into the government's coffers but represent obligations for future payments. A government can also save by spending less than its tax revenue. Firms can use a portion of current cash profit for their own investment spending, or they can become lenders in the market for loanable funds. If a firm lacks cash to fund a worthwhile investment project, it can borrow in the loanable funds market.

A firm deciding whether to invest in a project looks at the project's *rate of return.* This is found by first estimating the profit created by the project over its lifetime. Suppose a new machine is expected to create added revenue of $100,000 per year. Labor to run the machine costs $40,000 per year, maintenance $5,000, and material $15,000. The net cash profit from the machine would be $40,000 per year. For simplicity, suppose the machine has an indefinitely long lifetime and there is no inflation. The net benefit of the machine is the $40,000 per year it adds to profits indefinitely. The machine costs $1 million, and its rate of return is 4%.

To determine whether installing the machine is worthwhile, we must consider the opportunity cost of $1 million. Suppose the current interest rate is 3% in the loanable funds market. With no inflation, this is a real rate of return. If our firm has $1 million cash on hand, it can become a lender and earn $30,000 per year, which is less than the machine would add to revenue. The benefit of buying the machine outweighs the cost, and the firm will buy the machine. If the market interest rate were 5%, the firm could earn $50,000 yearly through becoming a lender and would not buy the machine.

If the firm has no cash in hand, it could borrow to carry out the project. Suppose the interest rate is 2% and it costs $35,000 per year to pay back the principal and interest on a loan of $1 million over the estimated lifetime of the machine. Benefits from the project ($40,000 per year) outweigh the costs ($35,000 per year), and the machine should be added. If the interest rate were higher and it cost $45,000 per year to pay back the principal and interest, the project would no longer be worthwhile.

A general principle is that investment spending varies inversely with the interest rate. Firms examine the rate of return on potential investment projects and compare it with the market interest rate. Any firm is a potential lender or borrower, depending on the rates of return of its potential projects and the interest rate.

When there is inflation, investors calculate the real interest rate, which discounts the expected effect of inflation. Demand in the loanable funds market comes largely from the investment opportunities of firms. Financial capital is translated directly into productive capital by firms borrowing to invest in new projects. This is the link between the two senses of the word capital.

EXAMPLE 12.1   Emerging International Stock Markets

Financial capital is transformed into productive capital when firms sell stocks and bonds to raise funds for investment projects. The major international stock markets in New York, Tokyo, and London are in the news daily. The World Bank's *Emerging Stock Markets Factbook 1989* presents information on smaller but quickly growing stock markets. These emerging stock markets offer high returns with high risk. The largest of these emerging stock markets, with their total market value or capitalization and percentage returns (in U.S. dollars in 1988), are listed below. In 30 developing countries monitored by the International Monetary Fund (IMF), the value of stocks traded increased by 500% between 1984 and 1989. Similar growth is projected through the year 2000.

	Capitalization	*1988 Return*
Taiwan	$120 bil	60%
Korea	$ 94 bil	76%
Brazil	$ 32 bil	83%
Mexico	$ 24 bil	−10%
India	$ 24 bil	22%
Malaysia	$ 23 bil	7%
Thailand	$ 9 bil	46%
Portugal	$ 7 bil	−24%

| Chile | $ 7 bil | 22% |
| Greece | $ 4 bil | −3% |

2. The Loanable Funds Market

If the real interest rate is 2%, more money will be borrowed than if the rate is 5%. As the cost of borrowing increases, the quantity of loanable funds demanded decreases. On the other hand, at higher real interest rates more people are willing to save their income and forgo current spending for future spending. The quantity of loanable funds supplied increases with the return to saving.

These two market forces of demand and supply in the loanable funds market are illustrated in Figure 12.1. The *real interest rate r* represents the price of borrowing to demanders and the return on a loan to lenders. The real interest rate equals the nominal interest rate minus expected inflation.

The *Fischer equation* tells us the real interest rate r is the difference between the nominal interest rate and expected inflation. When $r = 5\%$, saving $100 today results in $105 of purchasing power after one year. The nominal interest rate might be 11%, with an expected inflation rate of 6%. From the borrower's viewpoint, it costs $5 worth of current goods and services to borrow $100 for a year. From the lender's viewpoint, $5 worth of goods and services can be gained by giving up $100 for a year.

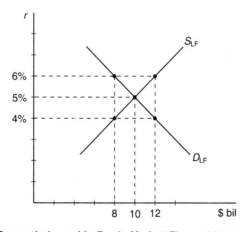

Figure 12.1. The Domestic Loanable Funds Market The real interest rate *r* represents the expected return of an investment after inflation. The demand for loanable funds (LF) is based on the marginal efficiency of various investment projects, which can be lined up in order of decreasing expected returns. When higher real interest rates must be paid, the quantity of LF demanded falls. The supply of LF comes from those with liquidity who must sacrifice current spending to make a loan. With higher real interest rates, the quantity of LF supplied rises. Equilibrium occurs where the demand for LF equals the supply of LF, at *r* = 5% with $10 billion of loans.

Note that in Figure 12.1, at a real interest rate of $r = 4\%$, the quantity of loans demanded ($12 billion) is greater than the quantity supplied ($8 billion). Banks and other financial intermediaries perceive this excess demand of $4 billion for loans. They respond to this excess demand or shortage by rationing their loanable funds and raising the interest rate from 4% toward 5%.

If the interest rate were 6%, there would be an excess supply or surplus of loanable funds amounting to $4 billion. Banks would not be able to loan out their reserves. Idle excess reserves would spur banks to lower interest rates to encourage potential borrowers. The market equilibrium interest rate in Figure 12.1 is 5%, the rate at which the quantity supplied of loanable funds just equals the quantity demanded and $10 billion worth of loans are made.

EXAMPLE 12.2   International Comparison of Effective Real Interest Rates

Real interest rates reflect the difference between nominal interest rates and expected inflation. After the fact, actual inflation can be subtracted from nominal interest rates to derive the *effective* real rate of interest. According to data from the IMF's *International Financial Statistics* (1989), the following wide range of real effective interest rates prevailed during 1988:

Indonesia	8%
Thailand	6%
Chile	5%
U.S.	3%
Malaysia	3%
Philippines	1%
Greece	0%
Korea	0%
India	0%
Nigeria	−2%
Colombia	−7%
Turkey	−9%
Venezuela	−19%
Mexico	−38%

3. The International Loanable Funds Market

Financial intermediation is becoming an international activity. Lenders and borrowers in different nations increase their interaction as banks become more integrated internationally. In most nations it is possible to hold bank accounts in foreign currencies. The United States quietly began this prac-tice in the summer of 1989. The central issue in the international loanable funds market is a comparison of the level of real interest across nations.

If the interest rate in the rest of the world is 4% and the nation in Figure 12.1 can acquire as many loans as it wants at that rate, an inflow of $12 billion − $8 billion = $4 billion will occur. This inflow is recorded as a capital account surplus. The nation as a whole would be borrowing internationally. If the world interest rate is 6%, a national excess supply of $4 billion of loanable funds will be exported. This outflow is recorded as a capital account deficit, with the nation lending internationally.

> A small economy open to international financial flows takes the inter-national interest rate. The economy will be a borrower (lender) if the international interest rate is below (above) the domestic autarky interest rate.

Many small developing economies have strong potential for growth but a low supply of loanable funds. Such developing countries should borrow internationally, running capital account surpluses. A rich developed econ-omy with average potential for growth is likely to become an international lender, with an excess supply of loanable funds at the going international interest rate and capital account deficits. Any economy that is small relative to the international capital market is a price (interest rate) taker in the world loanable funds market. The amount of borrowing or lending by such small economies is too small to affect the international interest rate.

Determination of the international interest rate between two large economies is pictured in Figure 12.2. This is exactly analogous to the inter-national excess supply and demand of goods and services. The home na-tion's excess demand (XD) for loanable funds (LF) is derived directly from Figure 12.1.

The foreign nation has a different set of lenders and borrowers with their own plans and perceptions of the future. The foreign excess supply curve (XS^*) is derived from the foreign loanable funds market. Note that the foreign autarky interest rate of $r^* = 3\%$ is less than the home autarky interest rate of $r = 5\%$. Loans are valued more in the home country, and a flow of loanable funds to the home country can be expected. In the for-eign nation, loans have less value and an outflow of funds can be expected.

At $r = 4\%$, the excess demand for loanable funds at home equals ex-cess supply from the foreign nation: $XD = XS^*$. Loans of $4 billion are made to the home nation from the foreign nation. Borrowers will be better

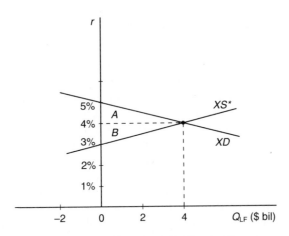

Figure 12.2. The International Market for Loanable Funds The excess demand XD for loanable funds from the home country slopes down to the right. When there is no international finance, the home autarky return to capital is 5%. The excess supply XS^* from the foreign country slopes upward to the right. The foreign autarky return to capital is 3%. An international equilibrium is found at $r = 4\%$ with $4 billion of loanable funds going from the foreign to the home country.

off at home because loans can be taken at a lower rate. Lenders will be better off in the foreign nation because they receive a higher interest payment. On the other hand, lenders at home suffer lower returns because they must compete with foreign lenders. Borrowers abroad must pay a higher return than they would in autarky because they have to compete with borrowers in the home nation.

Net international gains are represented by the triangles A and B in Figure 12.2. Net gains in the home country are represented by the area between domestic demand and supply from the autarky interest rate of 5% down to the international rate of 4%. This is area A, which equals 1/2(.01 × $4 bil) = $20 million.

In the foreign nation, lenders gain and borrowers lose. The foreign net gain is the area between foreign supply and demand from the foreign interest rate of 3% up to the international rate of 4%. This is area B, equal to 1/2(.02 × $4 bil) = $20 million. The international gains are the sum of the gain to each country, $40 million. Each nation gains a net $20 million from this international loanable funds market.

Gains in the international loanable funds market are assessed through the surpluses of suppliers and demanders, exactly as in the international markets for goods and services.

The United States was an international borrower during the 1980s, like the home country in Figure 12.2. This may seem unusual, since the United

States is a developed nation with high per capita income. Nevertheless, the demand for loanable funds in the United States is relatively high. This is a signal of the desire and potential for economic growth. Foreign investors view the United States as having solid investment and growth potential. Population in the United States continues to grow, in large part because of immigration.

EXAMPLE 12.3   Loans to Less Developed Countries

The international loanable funds market has seen sizeable loans to less developed countries (LDCs), especially in the early 1970s when the Organization of Petroleum Exporting Countries (OPEC) enjoyed large profits. Oil embargoes at that time created high oil revenues and a huge excess supply of loanable funds from the OPEC countries. These funds were filtered through the big banks of the industrial nations as loans to developing nations. The LDC debt problem arose when the LDCs sagged during the worldwide recession of the late 1970s and early 1980s. As these data from the International Monetary Fund (IMF) suggest, paying off the debt is no easy task for the LDCs, given their current levels of production. Major borrowers would have to spend 49% of their export earnings to make timely payments on their outstanding debt. The major borrowers are Latin American middle-income economies, particularly Brazil and Mexico. One sensible proposal to ease the debt burden was put forth by Rudiger Dornbusch and Franco Modigliani (*Wall Street Journal*, January 3, 1989). They propose that the debt be paid in nonredeemable local currency so that it would have to be spent in the local economy.

Total LDC Debt (in 1980 $billion)

1973	1977	1980	1984
$290	$413	$475	$769

Debt Service in 1983 (paying back the principal)

	Low-Income Nations	Major Borrowers
Percent of Exports	13	30

Interest Payments

	Low-Income Nations	Major Borrowers
Percent of Exports	5	19

EXAMPLE 12.4   The International Debt Crisis Revisited

The international economy has evolved through numerous debt crises, as surveyed by Barry Eichengreen (1991). Latin American countries defaulted on their loans in the 1820s, followed by the states in the United States in the 1830s and 1840s. Latin America again defaulted in the 1880s along with Egypt, Turkey, and Greece. International lending between 1880 and 1914 was three times as large as in the 1980s (scaled to world output). In the worldwide depression of the 1930s, virtually all debtor countries defaulted. Lenders continue to make loans to governments with a history of default because of the higher potential returns. When a nation defaults, other countries may penalize defaulters with trade restrictions and loans will be hard to come by for a period of time. Eichengreen finds historical evidence that defaulting countries tend to perform better than those that continue to struggle to pay back the interest and principal on (typically bad) international loans.

4.   International Financial Accounting

Yearly estimates of the international flow of loanable funds are made by governments and by international agencies like the United Nations, the IMF, and the World Bank. These financial flows enter into the capital account of the balance of payments as foreign investment. For borrowing nations, the capital account reports a surplus (a positive number in the balance of payments). Lending nations report a deficit in their capital account because cash is flowing out.

Net investment income on foreign investment also enters into the balance of payments. When a Japanese investor buys stock in General Motors, a yearly return is expected. These dividend payments enter as a negative amount in U.S. net interest payments. When someone in the United States holds a German government bond, interest payments enter as a surplus for the United States. Payments on international loans enter into net interest payments in the current account.

Suppose consumers and firms at home have a stock of $2,200 billion invested abroad, while foreigners have $1,675 billion invested at home. If the international interest rate is 4%, then 0.04 × $2,200 billion = $88 billion is received as investment income. Given the 4% interest rate, 0.04 × $1,675 billion = $67 billion is paid out. Net investment income (NII) is then ($88 billion − $67 billion) = $21 billion. There is a surplus or net cash inflow in NII, in fact approximately that recorded for the United States in 1986. (See Example 12.5.)

If the stock of home-owned investment abroad increases from $2,200 billion to $2,296 billion, $96 billion of investment will have left the nation. This investment outflow could be in the form of firms building branch plants abroad with retained earnings, private investors buying foreign stocks or bonds, a domestic bank buying a foreign bank, and so on. Suppose during the same year the foreign-owned capital stock at home increases by $213 billion from $1,675 billion to $1,888 billion. The capital account should then report a surplus of ($213 billion − $96 billion) = $117 billion. There is a net cash inflow in the capital account, approximately that recorded for the United States in 1986. Future increased cash outflows in net investment income will occur as these international loans are repaid.

Estimates of the capital account and net investment income are based on data from surveys and have historically come under criticism for a lack of reliability. For instance, it is not known for certain whether the United States was a net international debtor or creditor in some years during the 1980s. The statistical discrepancy has outweighed the reported net capital account balance. The array of financial activity is expanding so quickly that government surveys have a difficult time keeping abreast of all transactions. The *Wall Street Journal* (Oct. 31, 1989) carried a story that U.S. exports are vastly underreported because of omissions in the data. Since exports are not taxed, there is little incentive to keep a complete account of them. The volume and variety of international financial transactions are not accounted for well.

The practice of international accounting is due for a major overhaul. Multinational firms account for an increasing portion of international trade and finance. If the United States imports goods or services from branches of U.S. firms abroad, how much of these imports should be counted is not clear. After all, U.S. management and investment make up a large part of the value of the imports. If imports from U.S. multinational firms abroad are taken away from our import expenditures during the 1980s, the United States has experienced BOT surpluses rather than deficits. The increasing development of international banking and financial markets makes an analogous story true for the capital accounts.

Imagine the following story. A branch of a U.S. bank operating in Laredo, Mexico, buys $1 million of new stock in an industrial plant being built in a free trade zone in McAllen, Texas, which plans to employ 50% Mexican nationals. Which way is investment flowing? Further, suppose 49% of the stock of the Mexican bank is owned by a bank in Los Angeles, and 60% of the deposits in the Mexican bank originate in the United States. Machinery in the assembly line might be put together by a firm based in Michigan, which imports components from Mexico. When the machinery is actually put into place in the new plant, is this an international flow of productive capital? How should wages soon to be earned and spent by the Mexican national in Texas be recorded?

Such international activity presents a quagmire for accountants trying to sort out national income. From a global perspective, however, there are no accounting dilemmas. Imagine the difficulties if every city and town in the United States tried to estimate its capital and current accounts! International financial accounting faces a difficult chore. Although balance of payments figures are not very reliable, they offer a rough notion of the pattern of international investment.

EXAMPLE 12.5   U.S. Capital Account and Net Investment Income

The following is a summary report of U.S. international financial transactions from the U.S. Department of Commerce, *Survey of Current Business* (1987). All numbers are net cash flows in $ billion. With U.S. assets abroad, a net increase would mean a cash outflow and is reported as a negative number. With foreign assets in the United States, a net increase would mean a cash inflow and is reported as a positive number. Total U.S. investment abroad has not kept pace with incoming foreign investment, although U.S. direct investment abroad consistently outweighs incoming foreign direct investment. When receipts from U.S. assets abroad are larger than payments on foreign assets in the United States, the United States has a larger stock of direct investment abroad than foreigners have in the United States. In 1989, net investment income became negative in the United States for the first time since World War II. In 1980 the balance on the capital account of ($-$\$86.1 billion $+$ \$58.1 billion) $= -\$28$ billion was almost matched in magnitude by the statistical discrepancy of \$25 billion. These estimates are compiled by survey but give some indication of international financial flows. By 1989, payments on foreign assets in the United States had grown to $-\$128.4$ billion, while receipts on U.S. assets abroad had grown to only \$127.5 billion. Net interest payments fell to \$900 million in 1989, indicating that the stock of foreign-owned assets in the United States is greater than the stock of U.S. assets abroad.

	1970	1980	1986
U.S. ASSETS ABROAD	$-$\$9.3 bil	$-$\$86.2 bil	$-$\$96.0 bil
U.S. official reserves	2.5	-8.2	0.3
Special Drawing Rights	-0.9	-0.0	-0.3
IMF reserves	0.4	-1.7	1.5
Foreign currencies	2.2	-6.5	-0.9
U.S. government assets	-1.6	-5.2	-1.9
Long-term assets	-3.3	-9.9	-8.9
Repayments	1.7	4.5	6.1
Foreign currency	-0.0	0.2	0.9
U.S. private assets	-10.2	-72.8	-94.4

Direct investment	−7.5	−19.2	−28.0
Foreign securities	−1.1	−3.6	−3.3
Claims of nonbanks	−0.6	−3.2	−4.0
Claims of U.S. banks	−1.0	−46.8	−59.0
FOREIGN ASSETS IN U.S.	6.4	58.1	213.4
Foreign official assets	6.9	15.5	34.7
U.S. government bonds	9.4	11.9	33.3
Other U.S. liabilities	−2.5	3.6	1.4
Other foreign assets	−0.6	42.6	178.7
Direct investment	1.5	−16.9	25.1
U.S. government bonds	0.1	2.6	8.3
U.S. securities	2.2	5.5	70.8
Nonbank liabilities	2.0	6.9	−2.8
Bank liabilities	−6.3	10.7	77.4
BALANCE ON CAPITAL ACCOUNT	−2.9	−28.0	117.4
Receipts, U.S. assets abroad	11.8	72.5	88.2
Direct investment	8.2	37.1	36.7
Portfolio receipts	2.7	32.8	45.2
U.S. government receipts	0.9	2.6	6.3
Payments, foreign assets in U.S.	−5.5	−42.1	−67.3
Direct investment	−0.9	−8.6	−5.8
Portfolio payments	−3.6	−20.9	−38.9
U.S. government payments	−1.0	−12.6	−22.6
Net investment income	6.3	30.4	20.9
Statistical discrepancy	−0.2	25.0	23.9

5.   The Role of Policy in International Finance

An issue of political concern is whether economic policy should be designed to affect the capital account or net interest payments. Rather than providing a basis for rational policy, balance of payments data provide some indication of the international flows of goods, services, loanable funds, and net interest payments. Loanable funds will flow from nations with excess supply where the real interest rate is relatively low to nations with excess demand where the real interest rate is relatively high. Most international loans are made to finance the expansion of productive capital input. Governments generally should not be allowed to control or try to influence international financial flow.

An understanding of what is occurring in the extremely active and specialized international financial markets is beyond the scope of governments. Nevertheless, most governments try to influence the financial markets in one direction or the other. Many governments place direct controls on international investment. Most developing nations strictly control the outflow of investment to force domestic investors to keep their funds at home. At the same time, many governments are reluctant to see inflows of foreign funds for fear of being bought out and controlled by foreign interests. There are calls for such limiting policies even in the developed industrial nations. Recent concern in the United States finds expression in popular magazines in stories of how the Japanese are buying U.S. farmland, downtown sky-scrapers, golf courses, and so on.

A concern typically voiced is the increasing percentage of gross national product (*GNP*) that is paid abroad as investment income to foreigners. In his presidential campaign, Michael Dukakis pointed out that an increasing percentage (currently about 4%) of U.S. *GNP* is paid out yearly as interest to foreign countries. U.S. investment income from abroad, however, is increasing as well. The United States has historically enjoyed positive net investment income internationally, although the figure turned slightly negative in 1989. Receipts on U.S. assets abroad have grown steadily since the 1950s, although payments on foreign assets in the United States have grown at a faster rate. If a country were to borrow to finance current consumption, it would soon lose the ability to repay its debt and loans would stop. Financial markets, not politicians or bureaucrats, should allocate international financial flows. There will always be political pressure for controls on international investment, just as there is for protectionism.

Controls on free international investment are typically counterproductive. Through international competition, domestic banks are forced to become more competitive. Foreign banks are beginning to offer competition to U.S. banks inside the United States. Financial intermediation, like other industries, becomes more efficient in the face of competition. Efficiency results in lower costs and better service for customers.

An example of a nation that has isolated its financial industry and suffers from inefficiency is Greece. Foreign investment and foreign competition have been strictly outlawed. In the 1980s a trip to a bank in Greece was a step back in time. Most transactions were done by hand. Workers had to take their paychecks to a particular bank, which often meant a wait of hours just to cash or deposit a check! Tellers were extremely slow and took long coffee and cigarette breaks in front of customers waiting in line. There were no automatic tellers, no drive-in windows, no conveniences of any sort. Nominal interest rates were so slow that savers could not keep up with inflation, suffering negative real interest earnings. In short, there was no competition. As Greece enters completely into the European common market of 1992, its banks will certainly feel the force of international competition.

> There are sound reasons for open international finance. Loanable funds markets allow economic agents to plan, increase productivity, and grow wealthier. International financial interaction widens the scope of global gains.

EXAMPLE 12.6   U.S. Investment Income in the Balance of Payments

International investment income has steadily increased in the United States over the past 40 years. Signs are that the trend is accelerating. Figures on U.S. foreign investment income in constant 1982 dollars are listed below from the *Economic Report of the President* (1990). Receipts on U.S. investments abroad increased dramatically in the 1970s. Payments on foreign assets in the United States doubled in the 1960s and almost tripled in the 1970s. Growth rates for each decade are listed. In 1950, U.S. income from assets abroad was almost 4 times payments on foreign assets in the United States. In 1989, payments on foreign assets in the United States were larger than receipts on U.S. assets abroad for the first time since World War II. While income from assets abroad grew almost 12 times over these four decades, payments on foreign assets in the United States grew 44 times.

	Receipts on U.S. Assets Abroad	Percent of Increase	Payments on Foreign Assets in U.S.	Percent of Increase
1950	$8.7 bil		$2.3 bil	
1960	$14.9 bil	73	$4.0 bil	71
1970	$28.0 bil	87	$13.1 bil	228
1980	$83.3 bil	198	$49.6 bil	278
1989	$102.9 bil	23	$103.6 bil	109

Problems for Section A

A1.   Draw a foreign market for loanable funds consistent with the foreign excess supply *XS* in Figure 12.2.

A2.   Find the amount of investment income that will be due on the international loans in Figure 12.2. Which country makes, and which country receives, the payment?

A3.   Find net investment income given a 5% interest rate at home and a 6% interest rate abroad, with a home-owned investment stock abroad of $1,470 billion and a foreign-owned stock at home of $1,346 billion. Is there a surplus or deficit on NII?

A4.   If there is a 5% increase in the home-owned stock abroad in the previous problem, while the foreign-owned capital stock at home increases by 39%, find the capital account. Is it in surplus or deficit? Find the new net investment income.

B.   INTERNATIONAL FINANCE AND THE FOREIGN EXCHANGE MARKET

International financial transactions involve the exchange of currencies through the foreign exchange market. Exchange rates both affect and are affected by international financial transactions. When the exchange rate changes, the prices of foreign financial assets change. On the other hand, if international investors start buying the stocks and bonds of a particular currency, its currency will appreciate. This section examines the links between the exchange rate and international financial transactions.

1.   International Portfolios

A large volume of international financial transactions occurs daily. Wealth holders trade the financial assets of other countries. These international transactions for the most part are carried out electronically between large international banks and financial intermediaries. Wealth holders want to adjust their portfolios or asset holdings to avoid overexposure in a particular currency. Consider the position of an international bank that keeps deposits of numerous currencies. If the international bank exchanged all of its cash for one currency and that currency depreciates on the foreign exchange market, the bank loses.

International financial transactions occur because of international trade (forward exchange rate hedging), international investment spending by firms, and international portfolio diversification (wealth holders buying the stocks and bonds of another country). Banks and other financial intermediaries perform arbitrage across credit and exchange markets, looking for profitable transactions involving foreign currencies and international interest rates. Close links naturally develop between the international financial market and the foreign exchange market.

Changes in the exchange rate immediately affect the price of one nation's stocks, bonds, and other financial assets in other nations.

Suppose the nominal interest rate is 20% in a foreign nation that has pesos as its currency. The present value of a *perpetuity bond* paying 100,000 pesos per year indefinitely would be $100,000/0.20 = 500,000$ pesos. A perpetuity bond pays a yearly premium indefinitely. If you had 500,000 pesos in the bank in that country, you could earn 100,000 pesos interest every year, leaving the principal intact. Suppose the current spot exchange rate is $e = \$/peso = 0.002$, and both the dollar and peso have the same inflation rate. The dollar price of this perpetuity bond would then be $0.002 \times 500,000 = \$1,000$. An unexpected dollar appreciation to $e = 0.0015$ would decrease the price of the bond to $0.0015 \times 500,000 = \$750$ (if no more appreciation is expected). Has the bond suddenly become a bargain for an investor in the United States? The answer to this question depends on the expected future depreciation of the peso.

2. Discounting International Earnings by Expected Depreciation

The issue on an international investor's mind is what the 200,000 peso premium will be worth at the end of each year as the perpetuity bond pays off. Suppose the market expects the inflation rate in pesos to remain at its historical level of 20%, while the dollar's inflation rate is expected to be 8%. The peso, in other words, is expected to lose 12% of its value every year against the dollar.

The 100,000 peso yearly earning from the bond will be worth $200 at today's exchange rate of $e = 0.002$. One year from now the 100,000 peso premium is expected to be worth only 88% as much, or $176. Two years from now, the 100,000 peso premium is expected to be worth only 88% of that, or $176 \times 0.88 = \$154.88$. The value of the bond to an investor interested in a dollar return must be *discounted* by the additional 12% per year. The present value of the bond is thus only $100,000/(0.20 + 0.12) = 312,500$ pesos. At the current exchange rate of $\$/pesos = 0.002$, this peso bond would sell in the United States for $625. If the peso and the dollar had the same inflation rate, the peso bond would sell for $1,000. Higher discounts of the peso cause the dollar price of the foreign bond to fall.

Risk discount may also be associated with the peso bond. Suppose peso bonds have a history of defaulting 12% of the time, whereas dollar bonds default an average of only 4% of the time. An additional 8% risk discount would be placed on the value of the peso bond relative to U.S. bonds. The present value of the peso would be $100,000/(0.20 + 0.12 + 0.08) = 250,000$ pesos. At the current exchange rate, the peso bond would sell for $500.

International differences in risk premiums help investors arrange their international portfolio. While the degree of risk in international portfolios can be high when they contain foreign stocks or bonds, the returns are high. Levels of international investment have increased substantially during the past two decades.

EXAMPLE 12.7   National Credit Risk Ratings

These national credit ratings summarize the history and perception of the reliability of whether loans made to an average private investor in these countries will be repaid. These rankings are from the *Institutional Investor* (September 1990), which surveys banks worldwide. A higher ranking means a lower risk for making a loan in that nation:

Country	Rating	Rank
Japan	95	1
Switzerland	94	2
West Germany	93	3
United States	89	4
Canada	85	8
Italy	80	10
Kuwait	61	26
Russia	53	34
Israel	36	48
Venezuela	32	55
Tanzania	11	98
Nicaragua	6	109

3.   The Foreign Exchange Market and International Investment

The effect international financial markets have on the foreign exchange market is pictured in the market for Korean won in Figure 12.3. Demand for won is based in part on domestic investors who are potential buyers of Korean financial assets, stocks, and bonds.

Part of the demand for won comes from U.S. investors who are potential buyers of Korean financial assets. As the exchange rate $/won rises, the price of Korean assets in the United States rises, the quantity of Korean

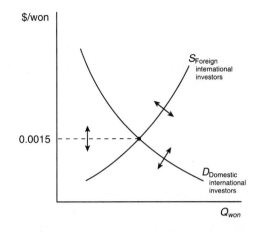

Figure 12.3. International Finance and the Foreign Exchange Market Demand for won slopes downward partly because a lower $/won exchange rate creates cheaper Korean assets in the United States. The quantity of won demanded to buy Korean assets increases. Supply of won slopes upward partly because a higher $/won exchange rate creates cheaper U.S. assets in Korea. The quantity of won supplied to buy U.S. assets increases. Changes in investment opportunities in the United States or Korea shift the supply and demand for foreign exchange, causing exchange rate adjustment.

assets demanded in the United States falls, and the quantity of won demanded falls. The demand for won thus slopes downward.

The supply of won comes from Korean investors who are potential buyers of U.S. assets. As $/won rises, the price of domestic assets in Korea falls, the quantity of U.S. assets demanded in Korea rises, and the quantity of won supplied rises. The supply of won thus slopes upward.

> International investment contributes to the structure of supply and demand in the foreign exchange market.

Suppose the expected return on Korean investments rises because of an announced policy of more liberalized trade in Korea. Investors in the United States will want to buy more Korean stocks and bonds because Korean exporting firms are expected to prosper under the new economic policy. A higher expected return on Korean stocks and bonds will increase their price because of increased demand. The demand for won also rises, causing the won to appreciate and further raising the price of Korean assets to U.S. investors.

This type of change in the exchange rate complements adjustment in the financial markets. Changes in the exchange rate work in the same direction as changes in the price of the assets, complementing the underlying forces in the international asset markets.

Suppose the expected return on U.S. investments rises because of higher investment spending on new plant and equipment by U.S. firms and forecasts of a coming expansion. Korean investors will want to buy more U.S. assets, increasing the supply of won. This depreciates the won, which in turn raises the price of U.S. assets in Korea.

The foreign exchange market works in the same direction as the underlying asset market. This is a fundamental lesson in international financial economics. Government exchange rate policy is not required to balance international financial markets and will hinder this complementary adjustment process.

International investors try to anticipate government intervention in the foreign exchange and international financial markets. Erratic behavior in international financial markets is often cited as evidence of the need for more regulation. The erratic behavior more often than not results from the market participants trying to anticipate upcoming government intervention. An old saying in foreign exchange circles is to watch what the Federal Reserve Bank is doing in the foreign exchange market and do the opposite. With central banks intervening, market participants turn their attention away from important market fundamentals.

No scheme of managed or fixed exchange rates and regulated financial markets could have handled the huge financial upheavals since the 1970s. Innovations in every industry, including banking and financial intermediation, result from competition. International competition is forcing U.S. banks and financial intermediaries to become more efficient. Banks actually favor regulation and enjoy the lack of competition brought about by a regulated industry.

4. Covered Interest Arbitrage

Asset markets are linked internationally with exchange markets through the operations of international banks and financial intermediaries. Imagine an investor with $1,000 in the United States who can earn the domestic rate of $i = 8\%$, ending the year with $1,080. Suppose the German interest rate is $i = 4\%$ and the current spot rate is $e = \$/\text{mark} = 0.26$. The $1,000 can be exchanged into $1,000/0.26 = 3,846.15$ marks, which will yield $3846.15 \times 1.04 = 4,000$ marks at the end of the year.

Suppose the investor takes this position in marks and leaves it *open*. The investor in the United States will typically want to turn the marks back into dollars at the end of the year. With an open position the investor will wait until the end of the year and sell the 4,000 marks on the *spot exchange market*, the market for foreign currency at that time. The risk of a mark depreciation during the year arises. No one knows what the value of the mark will turn out to be after a year.

This foreign exchange risk can be eliminated by covering the investment in the forward exchange market. A *forward contract* to sell 4,000 marks at the end of the year can be made in the forward exchange market. The forward exchange rate is a market rate known at the present time. Forward contracts can be signed for different time periods and for any amount.

In the example where $i = 8\%$, $i^* = 4\%$, and $e = 0.26$, this forward rate (f) will invariably be close to $f = \$/\text{mark} = 0.27$. The 4,000 marks will convert back into $1,080, the same return that could be earned in the United States. If this were not so, financial traders could make riskless arbitrage profit. In fact, thousands of such covered interest arbitrage transactions are made daily, keeping the profit on each transaction small and linking the asset and exchange markets internationally. Simultaneously, triangular arbitrage is carried out, keeping the cross rates of currencies in line.

> Fast and profitable covered interest arbitrage is carried out by large international banks, private brokers, and exchange traders, keeping international interest rates and exchange rates closely in line.

Market makers are financial intermediaries, working at banks, investment firms, and brokerage houses. The market makers are connected electronically by telephone and computer. It is a fast and fascinating market, much larger and more important to the world economy than the more publicized stock exchanges. Stock trading involves only an exchange of existing assets between wealth holders. On the other hand, international trade and investment depend on a viable exchange market. Unexpected exchange rate movements of hundredths of a cent can result in profits or losses of millions of dollars to international traders and investors. Some large international banks have gone out of business because of losses in their foreign exchange operations. Other banks have found themselves unable to compete in the international market. International financial markets are very competitive and active. Many U.S. banks are clamoring for regulation and protection, much like the U.S. auto industry since the 1970s.

EXAMPLE 12.8   Foreign Investment and the Value of the Dollar

A depreciating dollar means assets in the United States are becoming cheaper for foreign investors. Kenneth Froot and Jeremy Stein (1988) find that historically foreign direct investment (*FDI*) increases $5 billion with a 10% depreciation of the dollar. As foreign currency becomes more valuable, productive capital in the United States becomes cheaper for foreign firms. Over half of *FDI* goes into mergers and acquisitions of existing companies. In 1988 the figure was 92%. With a merger or acquisition, there would be typically little immediate change in the operation of the U.S. firm, which has simply been taken over by a foreign firm. The exchange rate is found to have little effect on international portfolio investment. Expected depreciation and nominal interest rate differentials account for portfolio investment.

EXAMPLE 12.9   National Defense Spending and the Value of the Dollar

In the eyes of many investors worldwide, the United States provides a safe haven for their funds. Political stability, lack of a military threat, and bright prospects for growth characterize the United States. When defense spending in the United States is high, the United States may appear a safer haven. Robert Ayanian (1988), as well as Vittrio Grilli and Andrea Beltratti (1989), show this is the case. Higher defense spending is associated with a higher exchange value of the dollar. When defense spending is high, U.S. assets appear safer and demand for dollars to buy U.S. financial assets increases.

5.   International Interest Rates and Exchange Rates

The link between interest rates and exchange rates in the covered interest arbitrage relation can be summarized by the equation

$$(1 + i) = (f/e)(1 + i^*).$$

The nominal interest rate at home is i; the foreign interest rate is i^*; spot and forward exchange rates are e and f.

An investor with \$1 at home can earn $(1 + i)$ buying a home bond. The alternative is to convert the \$1 to foreign currency (divide 1 by e), buy a foreign bond with return $1 + i^*$ (multiply by $1 + i^*$), and cover the earnings back into dollars (multiply by f). This involves making a spot purchase at e (dividing \$1 by e), earning $(1 + i^*)$ on each unit of foreign currency, and covering this amount back into dollars (multiplying by f). This equation expresses the covered interest arbitrage relation.

If one side of the covered interest arbitrage relation is larger than the other, four markets simultaneously operate to restore equilibrium. Profit makers push the four markets so covered interest arbitrage virtually always holds. Figure 12.4 shows the four markets involved in covered interest transactions. The initial equilibrium is exactly the one described in the example of the covered interest relation between marks and dollars.

Suppose the Federal Reserve Bank in the United States decides to expand the supply of domestic loanable funds and lower the U.S. interest rate i. U.S. asset holders notice that the return on covered foreign bonds has become relatively higher. The first step in buying a foreign bond is to buy foreign currency. The demand for marks rises, pushing e above 0.26 in Figure 12.4. The supply for loanable funds in Germany then rises, pushing i^* below 4%. Finally, U.S. investors will want to cover their earnings back into dollars. Marks are sold forward, increasing the forward supply of marks and pushing f below 0.27. All of these changes (a higher e, a higher i^*, and a lower f) lower the right side of the covered interest relation until the two sides of the relation are equal.

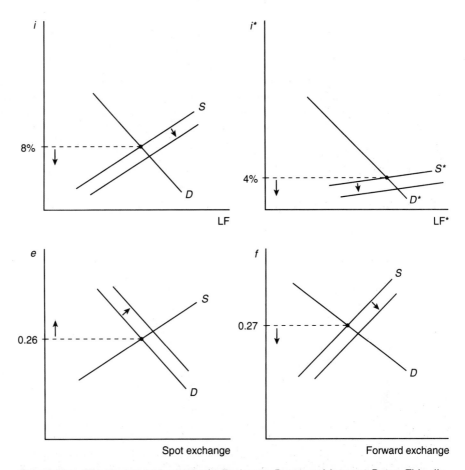

Figure 12.4. The Market Links between Exchange Rates and Interest Rates This diagram illustrates the manner in which covered interest arbitrage equates the return to riskless investments across nations. In the original equilibrium, $1 + i = (f/e)(1 + i^*)$. If i falls with a credit expansion, the demand for spot exchange rises, the supply of foreign loanable funds rises, and the supply of forward exchange falls. Every shift tends to keep the covered interest arbitrage relation in line.

Covered interest arbitrage works through the foreign exchange market and the international loanable funds market. Interest rates are linked internationally through the foreign exchange market.

EXAMPLE 12.10   International Inflation Rates and Interest Rates

These data from the IMF compare inflation rate differentials and nominal interest rate differences across five nations, as reported in *International Financial Statistics* (1986). The difference between the inflation rate and the U.S. inflation rate of 1.9% that year is reported along with the difference between each nation's interest rate and the U.S. interest rate of 6.8%. As the inflation rate difference rises, so does the difference in interest rates. Currencies that are inflating rapidly will depreciate in the foreign exchange market. Depreciating currencies will sell at a discount in the forward market, with their forward value less than their spot value. Because of covered interest arbitrage, the nominal interest rate in these depreciating currencies will be higher. These figures reflect the close link between the international loanable funds market and the foreign exchange market.

	Inflation Difference	*Interest Rate Difference*
Germany	−2.1%	−2.2%
Japan	−1.3%	−2.0%
France	0.6%	0.9%
U.K.	1.6%	3.9%
Australia	7.2%	8.9%

EXAMPLE 12.11   Interest Rate Parity (IRP) at Work During 1990

Covered interest arbitrage leads to IRP. During 1990, interest rates fell in the United States relative to Germany and Japan, and the dollar depreciated as IRP would predict. Interest rates on three-month international interbank deposits rose from 8.5% to 9.5% in Germany and from 7% to 8.2% in Japan. In the United States this interest rate fell from 8.5% to 6.5% by February 1991. The dollar depreciated 8% against the yen and 12% against the mark during 1990. From November 1990 to January 1991 the dollar appreciated because of international investors seeking safe haven during the Kuwait war. The overall dollar depreciation, if it persists, should have a positive influence on the U.S. current account during the early 1990s according to the J-curve.

Problems for Section B

B1.   With the perpetuity bond in the text paying 100,000 pesos per year, suppose the dollar is expected to have an inflation rate of 2%. Find the dollar value of the peso bond under these conditions. Do the same if the dollar inflation rate is expected to be 13%.

B2.   Diagram and explain what happens in the foreign exchange market in Figure 12.3 when

(a) the domestic interest rate falls
(b) the foreign interest rate rises
(c) news of an expected expansion in the U.S. economy comes out
(d) political unrest breaks out in Korea

B3. In the example of covered interest arbitrage in the text, find the profitable position if the forward exchange rate is $/mark = 0.26. Do the same if the forward rate is 0.28.

C. INTERNATIONAL MONEY

Money is a vital commodity for economic activity. The high degree of specialization in modern society would be impossible without a medium of exchange. This section examines the link between money and the price level. Inflation occurs when the price level (the average price of all goods) rises, causing the value of money to fall. International commerce depends on a reliable monetary system. A brief history of the international monetary system over the past 100 years is presented.

1. What Is Money?

Money is anything which performs the basic functions of money: medium of exchange, store of value, and unit of account.

Money as a *medium of exchange* makes commerce possible. Imagine how difficult it would be to *barter* or trade directly for everything you wanted. Only the most primitive societies get by completely with barter, with families trading hides for corn, meat for labor, and so on. Money allows people in an economy to specialize more and to trade with one another. International trade and finance requires an international mechanism for trading the mediums of exchange. There must be a medium of exchange across borders, some mechanism to exchange different mediums of exchange. The foreign exchange market performs this vital function.

Money as a *store of value* allows economic agents (consumers and firms) to put off purchases until a later date. If you are paid every Friday, some money must be kept through the following Thursday. During this time, money acts as a store of value, representing potential purchases through the week. If you are paid once a month, your money has to store value that much longer. A currency that is inflating quickly acts as a poor store of value. In countries suffering *hyperinflation*, tremendously high inflation rates, people scramble to spend cash before it loses value.

Money also serves as a *unit of account* or a unit for measuring the value of the vast array of goods and services. This car is worth $20,000, that shirt $25, a night on the town $50, and so on. In a particular society, people become accustomed to valuing goods and services in their currency. They are ready to make and accept payment in their currency.

Only things that can perform money's functions are able to serve as money. Bricks would be a good of value but are too heavy to act as a practical medium of exchange. Ice cream would be easier to carry but would not work well as a store of value. Paper clips would be good money if their supply could be controlled. There has to be some mechanism to limit the supply of money. If people could make their own money, they would spend little time in other pursuits and soon money would be worthless.

While money can be created by private banks and financial intermediaries, money today is universally controlled by government central banks. A government's monetary policy controls the monetary base. The banking system in market economies is made up of private commercial financial intermediaries that accept deposits and make loans. Financial intermediation facilitates lending and borrowing and effectively expands the money supply. Still, the monetary base is controlled by the central bank: the Federal Reserve Bank in the United States, the Bank of England in the United Kingdom, Bundesbank in Germany, and so on. The link between the money supply and the price level determines how well a currency can perform its basic functions. Money that does not maintain its value becomes useless for both domestic and international transactions.

2.   Money and Prices

The *demand for money* depends on its value, or the goods and services that it can potentially purchase. The price level P represents the average value of all goods and services in terms of the currency: $P = \$/\text{good}$. The inverse of P, $1/P = \text{goods}/\$$, represents the value or *purchasing power of money*.

As P rises, the purchasing power of money falls in that less goods can be exchanged for each dollar. When P rises, people want to hold less money and switch to holding other assets like stocks, bonds, gold, jewelry, and real estate. Money that is losing its value or purchasing power through inflation will not be demanded as a store of value.

The demand for money is pictured in Figure 12.5. Along the vertical axis is the value of money, $1/P$. The demand for money slopes downward. The *supply of money* is pictured as a vertical line at the current level of supply, $1 trillion. The government central bank controls the money supply and is assumed not to base supply on the price level.

A money supply of $1 trillion and price level of 1.25 are roughly the levels of M1 and the consumer price index (1982 = 1) in the United States during 1990. M1 is made up of all cash and demand deposits (bank deposits that can be withdrawn by check). The price index of 1.25 indicates that prices have risen 25% since 1982. Where supply and demand meet, the value of money $1/P = 1/1.25$ and the price level $P = 1.25$ are determined. In this example, increasing the supply of money to $1.2 trillion would lower the value of money to $1/1.5 = 0.667$ and raise P to 1.5. Lowering the supply of money to $0.8 trillion would raise the value of money to 1 and lower P to 1.

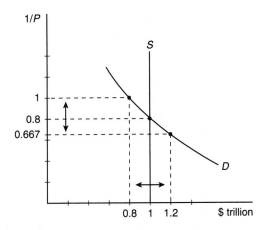

Figure 12.5. The Money Market The demand for money slopes downward because a higher price level (*P*) means a lower value of money (1/*P*) and a higher quantity of money demanded to carry out everyday transactions. For a given supply of money, the equilibrium price level of 1/1.25 = 0.8 is determined. A higher money supply lowers the value of money or raises the price level. If the money supply increases to $1.2 billion, the value of money drops to 1/1.50 = 0.667. A lower supply of money raises the value of money or lowers the price level. If the money supply falls to $80 billion, the value of money rises to 1.

The money market illustrates the quantity theory of money, based on the quantity equation

$$MV = PQ$$

M is the supply of money and *V* is its velocity (number of times on average a dollar changes hands per year). The product *MV* is the value of all transactions in the economy for the year. On the other side, *P* is the price level and *Q* is the quantity of output. The product *PQ* is the value of all output or gross national product.

If *M* increases by 20% (from $1 trillion to $1.2 trillion in Figure 12.5) and both *V* and *Q* are constant, *P* must increase by 20% (from 1.25 to 1.5). Velocity *V* is generally constant. Real output is not greatly affected by money growth as long as monetary policy is stable and reliable. If *M* falls by 20% and *Q* is unchanged, *P* would then also fall by 20%.

The quantity equation shows the strong link between the supply of money and the price level. Currencies whose supply is increasing rapidly will, *ceteris paribus*, experience more inflation than currencies whose money supply is stable or growing slowly.

Some element of the demand for a currency is typically foreign in origin. Foreign wealth holders will want to hold dollars as an asset, or at least assets in the dollar country, if they think the dollar will perform well as a store of value. If the dollar is expected to increase in value on the foreign exchange market, foreign investors will want to hold dollars.

Suppose investors over the world expect the dollar to appreciate during the next year relative to the other major currencies. The demand for dollars increases, as pictured in Figure 12.6. The increased demand drives the value of the dollar ($1/P$) from 0.8 to 0.9, lowering the price level P from 1.25 to $1/.9 = 1.11$. In the foreign exchange market, demand for dollars is simultaneously rising and the dollar is appreciating.

> The currency of a nation with a relatively low inflation rate will gain value on the foreign exchange market, while nations with relatively high inflation will have depreciating currencies.

Central banks should target a stable price level in their monetary policy. Although there is short-term and popular concern over liquidity and interest rates, a stable price level should be the goal of monetary policy. The current governor of the U.S. Federal Reserve Bank, Alan Greenspan, is an economist who realizes the crucial role of the money supply in determining the price level. Both Greenspan and Paul Volker, the previous governor, have consistently argued that stable prices are the goal of monetary policy. In 1990 a bill before the U.S. House of Representatives (House Joint Resolution 409) sought to direct the Fed to make stable prices the explicit legal goal of monetary policy.

The episodes of high inflation and international instability of the 1970s drove home the basic fact that stable prices are conducive to an efficient economy. The U.S. dollar has a particularly important role on the international scene. About 25% of international transactions are carried out in dollars. Governments and banks all over the world keep large reserves of U.S. dollars. More than 100 countries peg the value of their curren-

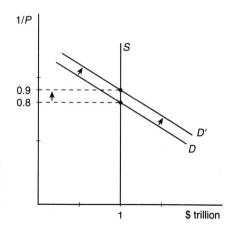

Figure 12.6. Increased Demand for Money With money supply constant, higher demand for money will increase the value of money and lower prices. In this example the increase in the demand for money from D to D' causes P to fall from 1.25 to 1.11. This increase in the demand for money can be foreign in origin.

cies to the dollar. When the dollar loses value because of oversupply, global inflation is encouraged.

EXAMPLE 12.12   Exchange Rates and Economic News

The important link between money supplies and exchange rates is illustrated in a study by Graig Hakkio and Douglas Pearce (1985). Foreign exchange traders listen to various sorts of economic news on trade deficits, national income, price indices, and so on. Only one type of news is found to have an immediate impact, and that is news about changes in the money supply growth. Exchange rates apparently adjust to the news of a change in the money supply in about 20 minutes. If the U.S. money supply increases unexpectedly, exchange traders expect a pending dollar depreciation and begin selling dollars right away. This increases the demand for foreign exchange and depreciates the dollar. There is little exchange rate movement in anticipation of money supply announcements. This illustrates the important link between money supplies and exchange rates and shows how well foreign exchange traders understand the link.

3.   Fiat Currencies and Monetary Standards

Nations take a certain amount of pride in their currency. Although a depreciating currency may help export industries, this is a less than satisfying compensation for the fact that the currency in your pocket is losing value relative to the currency in someone else's pocket. Nations have historically devised different ways to control their money supplies and price levels. The ways nations control their money supplies affect the foreign exchange market and international trade and finance. The international monetary system is an extension of all the nations' monetary systems.

Contemporary nations rely on *fiat currency,* paper money that has value simply because it is accepted as a medium of exchange. Central banks print money and create domestic credit. Some people are surprised to learn that U.S. dollars are not backed by gold or silver. The U.S. government stopped redeeming dollars for gold almost 60 years ago and stopped defining the dollar in terms of gold in 1971. Money has value only because people accept it as payment for goods and services. The U.S. dollar carries its own endorsement: "This note is legal tender for all debts, public and private."

The current international floating exchange rate system is compatible with fiat (paper) currencies. Major currencies are allowed to seek their equilibrium market exchange value, although central banks do intervene in the market. This contrasts with the *gold standard,* which lasted from the late 1800s until World War I. Governments were then willing to exchange gold for paper money and vice versa. Currency notes were equivalent to a certain amount of gold. The United States experimented with a *bimetal standard* for a period in the late 1890s, with the dollar defined in terms of both gold and silver. The *Bretton Woods* fixed exchange rate systems, which lasted from the end of World War II until the early 1970s, attempted to fix exchange rates at historically familiar levels.

4. The Gold Standard Era

During the gold standard era, which lasted from the late 1800s until World War I, the English pound was the major currency. Each pound was defined as 0.234 ounce of gold. The U.S. dollar was redeemable at 0.048 ounce of gold. This froze the dollar/pound exchange rate at $0.234/0.048 = 4.87 = \$/£$. Different currencies were widely accepted all over the world, not only in their own country, because they were redeemable into gold and regarded as completely stable in value relative to one another. There was no foreign exchange risk in international trade and investment. This created a favorable international atmosphere, resulting in high levels of international trade and investment and economic growth during the period.

The United States had little gold relative to other nations during the gold standard era. With the gold standard, growth in the money supply is limited by growth in the gold supply. Immigration and growth of output in the United States outpaced growth of the money supply during the late 1800s, and price deflation occurred. The demand for money grew faster than the supply, so the value of money $(1/P)$ rose and prices (P) fell. Falling prices created political pressure to expand the money supply.

The temporary solution was a bimetal standard, with the dollar defined in terms of both gold and silver. If the official relative price of silver in terms of gold did not exactly match the market relative price, traders could earn riskless arbitrage profit. Suppose the official price of silver was too high. Traders could buy cheap silver in the market and trade it to the government for gold. The bad money (silver) chased out the good money (gold). Gold would not circulate. Only silver circulated.

The principle that bad money chases out good money is known as *Gresham's law*, named after a British banker of the 1500s. In his day, coins actually contained the metals worth their value. It was common to see circulating coins shaved around the edges. Gresham was suspected of shaving coins himself, hence the name of the law. Anyone who found an unshaved coin (good money) would store it or shave it. Only the bad shaved money circulated, chasing out the good money.

5. The Interwar Period: Collapse of the Gold Standard

World War I made international trade and investment difficult, disrupting the foreign exchange market and destroying the international monetary system. Following the war, nations tried to return to the historical gold standard, but governments had increased their money supplies to finance the war. Inflation had pushed prices up in Europe relative to the United States.

Exchange rates from the gold standard era proved unworkable. An English pound note was worth more at the government's gold exchange window than it was worth in goods and services. The official British gold supply dwindled as traders cashed in their pound notes for gold. The pound was overvalued in terms of other currencies, which made British exports less than competitive worldwide. The United Kingdom dropped the gold standard in 1931. The U.S. dollar, still redeemable in terms of gold, was becoming the standard international currency. Investors were anxious for the apparent stability provided by gold, and they eagerly traded dollars for gold. With official U.S. gold supplies dwindling, the U.S. government stopped redeeming dollars for gold in 1933.

Governments devalued their currencies repeatedly in efforts to make their exports cheaper abroad. Inflation was high worldwide. In Germany, hyperinflation created the instability that allowed the Nazi party to take political control. In misguided efforts to save jobs, high levels of protection were imposed in the United States by the Smoot-Hawley Tariff Act and similar measures worldwide. International investment disappeared because of the high degree of exchange rate risk and political instability. The Great Depression of the 1930s was an international event.

6. The Bretton Woods System

The international monetary system fell into disarray up to the outbreak of World War II. After the war there was the desire to return to a stable international monetary system. People yearned for the stable prices associated with the gold standard. An international conference was held in Bretton Woods, New Hampshire, to create a workable international monetary system. A *gold exchange standard* evolved. Currencies were defined in terms of gold but were not generally redeemable. The U.S. dollar was defined as $0.029 = 1/35$ ounce of gold and became the international standard. At the time the United States held more than half the world's stock of gold. Other currencies were defined in terms of the dollar. The English pound was defined as $2.80; 360 Japanese yen were set equal to $1; 4.20 German marks were defined as $1; and so on. The International Monetary Fund was created to ensure that governments kept their exchange rates close to these agreed values.

The fixed exchange rates of the Bretton Woods system operated under an *adjustable peg* system. A nation with a temporary trade deficit could leave its exchange rate fixed and borrow from the IMF to meet cash shortages. If a nation had a chronic trade deficit, the IMF might eventually allow it to depreciate its currency. The decade of the 1950s was one of relative stability. International trade and investment grew at steady, if low, rates. Money supplies grew at low predictable rates, and price levels were generally stable worldwide. Europe and Japan rebuilt from the damages of war. The United States experienced BOT surpluses, which turned into deficits in the late 1950s and early 1960s. These BOT deficits suggested the dollar should depreciate. If the dollar were to lose value in terms of gold, anyone holding gold would enjoy a gain. In anticipation, the price of gold was bid up well beyond the official price of $35 an ounce. The Bretton Woods system managed to operate through the high U.S. inflation during the Vietnam War.

Economists had long debated whether floating exchange rates would operate more efficiently than the fixed exchange rate system. The dollar had not been generally redeemable for gold since 1933. The U.S. government continued to redeem foreign government holdings of dollars for gold. U.S. gold holdings steadily declined, while other nations (notably France) built up their gold holdings. As U.S. gold holdings declined, the credibility of the Bretton Woods system suffered. In 1971, President Nixon cut the dollar loose from its definition in terms of gold.

7.   The Current Floating Exchange Rate System

The OPEC oil embargoes, higher oil prices, and increased international financial activity ended the Bretton Woods system. With increased cash flows in international trade and in international loanable funds markets, fixed exchange rates proved totally unworkable. The price of gold was bid up above $600 by investors who saw it as a safe haven. Nations tried to adjust their fixed exchange rates, but by 1973 the world had moved to a floating exchange rate system. Each government was then free to determine the growth of its own money supply. Money supply growth and inflation rates generally increased. International banks greatly increased their foreign exchange operations and scrambled to establish foreign branch operations. Foreign exchange brokers and traders set up shop as speculators began to attempt to outguess the market and make profits in exchange trading. Hedging and speculating in foreign exchange slowly became institutionalized. Foreign exchange trading grew into a fast and lively worldwide electronic business.

The modern floating exchange rate system has never been characterized by entirely free markets. Governments regularly intervene to influence the value of their currency, and many impose direct controls. It is fair to call the system a *managed float*. The IMF acts much like a bank for government central banks. It makes loans to deficit nations and keeps accounts. It even supplies its own money, the *Special Drawing Right* (SDR), which is used between central banks and forms a part of each nation's monetary base.

Few analysts are completely happy with the international monetary system. Proposals for reform abound. Yet the market system has worked through periods of tremendous upheaval in international economics. Oil embargoes, debt crises, record deficits (and surpluses), emerging economic and financial powers, and increasing international investment have put strains on the international monetary system. The market system is probably superior to any sort of officially controlled coordinated system. Both economic theory and history teach us that wise governments let markets operate when they will. The positive role for government economic policy is to provide stable money supply growth so that the foreign exchange market, international trade, and international finance can operate smoothly.

Problems for Section C

C1. Explain how well each of the following, which have been used in various societies as money, would perform each of the functions of money: beaver tails, tobacco, dried buffalo chips, beads, and very large stones.

C2. If the supply of money came from competing private banks, how would the supply curve of money look? How would a private money supply system, called free banking, operate? How would the international monetary system operate?

C3. Any commodity standard of money ties the value of money to a certain quantity of some commodity. Which of these commodities would function better as money standards: gold, oil, wheat, a stock market price index?

D. MONEY AND INTERNATIONAL FINANCE

What exactly is the link among the various money supplies of different nations and international financial flows? This section concentrates on the exchange market as the international transmitter of monetary signals and on the effect of money on international finance.

1. Government Bonds and the Money Supply

A government creates debt with its deficits when it spends more than its tax revenue. Governments with deficits raise funds by selling *government bonds,* which are promises to pay the bondholder the face value of the bond at maturity. A government with debt is a demander in the loanable funds market. When the government enters the loanable funds market, demand for loanable funds rises, causing the interest rate (the price of a loan) to rise. With the increase in the supply of bonds, bond prices fall. Higher interest rates and lower bond prices attract foreign investors. Demand for the domestic currency rises, causing it to appreciate. This currency appreciation can lead to a current account deficit.

This theoretical link between the government deficit and the trade deficit has been difficult to isolate empirically. Government deficits in the

United States during the 1980s and early 1990s have been associated with current account deficits, but the dollar has both appreciated and depreciated and the current account has both risen and fallen. It should be stressed again that capital account surpluses (current account deficits) are typical for a nation with the desire and potential for growth. This potential for future prosperity most likely explains why foreign wealth holders remain willing to invest in the United States.

The U.S. government finances its deficit operations through expanding the money supply. This monetary expansion is carried out predominantly through *open market operations*. The Treasury prints new bonds, selling them to acquire cash to pay the government's payroll and bills. Meanwhile, the Federal Reserve Bank buys the new bonds, paying for them with new money, which enters the economy. The government is not compelled to limit spending to its tax revenue. The Gramm-Rudman Act is an attempt to get the U.S. government to operate with a balanced budget. Many states in the United States operate under balanced budget requirements.

2. International Money Supplies and the Price Level

In the late eighteenth century, David Hume studied the long-run relationship among national money supplies, prices, and trade. The theory of the *price specie flow mechanism* summarizes this relationship. When the money supply in one nation is increased, the price level in that nation rises and the value of that money falls. Higher prices cause the nation to export less (since exports become more expensive abroad) and import more (since imports become cheaper at home). The trade deficit creates an outflow of money to the rest of the world. The increased supply of money spills over into the rest of the world through a trade deficit. Money supplies are internationally interdependent in this way. Through the influence of price, specie (currency) flows internationally.

The close link between the supply of money and the rate of inflation is illustrated by the quantity equation, $MV = PQ$. Suppose $1 trillion is the nation's total supply of money and $4 trillion the level of real output of goods and services. This is the approximate level of money (M1) and gross national product in 1990 for the United States. On average, each dollar in the money supply changes hands four times during the year, since $4 trillion worth of transactions are made. In the quantity equation, GNP of $4 trillion is equal to PQ. Using consumer price index 1.25 as P (1982 = 1) the level of real output is $4 trillion/1.25 = 3.2 trillion. This is the real output in 1990 in terms of 1982 dollars.

If the government increases the supply of money while real output Q and money velocity V remain constant, P must rise. Suppose M rises to $1.1 trillion. By the quantity equation, $MV = 4.4$ and $PQ = 3.2P$. Then P will be $4.4/3.2 = 1.375$, a 10% increase for both M and P. Milton Friedman, a leading U.S. economist, has consistently argued since the 1950s that an indisputable empirical link exists between high money supply growth and inflation.

Evidence of a positive relationship between the growth of the money supply and inflation is overwhelming. When the money supply grows faster, inflation will be higher.

3. Purchasing Power Parity and the Real Exchange Rate

A direct link between the money supply and the foreign exchange market can be seen when it is realized that prices are linked internationally through trade. Some goods are not traded (such as haircuts in Iowa), but most goods and services can be traded. This means that *purchasing power parity* (PPP) should generally hold. PPP is stated

$$P = eP*$$

where P is the home level, $P*$ is the foreign price level, and e is the exchange rate.

There is solid empirical evidence supporting PPP, at least approximately over long periods. As more nontraded goods are excluded from the price indices P and $P*$, the PPP relationship becomes stronger. Strictly, PPP says that traded goods cost the same across nations. When all goods are freely traded, PPP is the *law of one price*, which simply says that arbitrage will equalize the price of the same good across locations.

Suppose $P = 1.25$ and $P* = 1,250$ lira. These are hypothetical price indices or average prices of all traded goods and services in the United States and Italy. The *real exchange rate* comes from the PPP relation:

$$e_r = P/P*$$

The real exchange rate in this example is e_r = \$/lira = $1.25/1,250$ = 0.001. The real exchange rate is used by currency traders in the exchange market to anticipate the fundamental direction the market exchange rate is likely to take in the future. Suppose for instance the market exchange rate is \$/lira = 0.002. The lira is then fundamentally overvalued in the market and can be expected to depreciate. Using the market exchange rate, the U.S. price level 1.25 is less than $eP* = 2.50$. Italian goods and services are overvalued by the market exchange rate. Italy will run current account deficits at the market exchange rate, and the lira should depreciate. The Italian government may try to delay this depreciation, which makes the job of predicting the time of a devaluation difficult. Being able to successfully predict exchange rate changes would result in large speculative profits in the forward exchange market.

EXAMPLE 12.13   Purchasing Power Parity in the 1930s between the United States and the United Kingdom

A unique episode occurred in 1931 when the United Kingdom gave up the gold standard. Speculation turned against the British pound, and its exchange value \$/£ dropped by 30%. The U.S. dollar remained on the gold standard and appeared a safe haven for investors. Meanwhile, P/P^* rose by 10% as described by S.N. Broadberry (1987). PPP was thus 40% out of line between the United States and the United Kingdom in 1932 and 1933. Finally, the United States dropped the gold standard, the pound appreciated, and P/P^* fell. By 1934 PPP held once again. In this instance, PPP was a reliable guide to long-run movement in the exchange rates.

4. Relative Money Supplies and the Real Exchange Rate

Figure 12.7 illustrates the theoretical relationship between the relative money supplies M/M^* of two nations and their real exchange rate P/P^*. If $M^* = 76$ billion Swiss francs and $M = \$1,000$ billion, $M/M^* = 13.2$. Corresponding to this relative money supply, $P/P^* = 1.12/1.07 = 1.05$. These are in fact the 1989 money supplies and consumer price indices (1985 = 1) for Switzerland and the United States. If M increases by 10% to $\$1.1$ trillion with all outputs and M constant, P will rise by 10% to 1.232, M/M^* will rise to 1,100/76 = 14.5, and the real exchange rate P/P^* will rise to 1.15. The Swiss franc, whose relative supply has fallen, would increase in real value.

The schedule in Figure 12.7 is upward sloping, illustrating the long-run relationship among money supplies, price levels, and the exchange

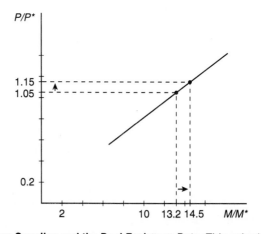

Figure 12.7. Money Supplies and the Real Exchange Rate This schedule illustrates the theoretical link between relative money supplies M/M^* and the real exchange P/P^*. Purchasing power parity ($P = eP^*$) implies that the relative price P/P^* is the real exchange rate e_r. Increasing the home money supply M relative to the foreign money supply M^* will raise M/M^* and create higher home prices relative to foreign prices. The real exchange rate rises, which causes a real depreciation of the home currency. If the exchange market value of the dollar has not fallen, it can be expected to fall in the future.

rate. Nations with relatively high growth rates in their money supply will experience higher than average inflation and currency depreciation when the growth of real output is constant. Higher inflation creates a depreciating currency.

The relationship in Figure 12.7 is empirically well established. A few of the nations with the highest inflation rates and fastest depreciating currencies in recent history have been Brazil, Mexico, and Israel. Nations that have had the lowest rates of inflation and have seen their currencies appreciating relative to others are Germany, Japan, and Switzerland.

If inflation jumps unexpectedly, as it did in the 1970s, debtors paying off fixed-term loans benefit while creditors are hurt. Unexpected deflation has exactly the opposite effect, redistributing income from debtors to creditors. If economic agents are able to anticipate the inflation rate, its level has no real effect.

> When rates of inflation are steady and predictable, exchange rate changes will be consistent and have little impact on international trade and finance.

Economic variables can be reduced to real terms, and people learn quickly to think in real terms. Businesses in Israel and along the Mexican border quote prices in U.S. dollars. This practice is common in nations where the inflation rate is so high and erratic that daily or weekly price changes are necessary just to keep up with generally rising prices.

Central banks may be able to support temporarily the value of a currency that is rapidly inflating, but they cannot do so indefinitely. Looking at the history of inflating currencies is the same as looking at the history of depreciating currencies. Inflation rates value the currency against goods, while exchange rates value the currency against other currencies.

EXAMPLE 12.14   Big Mac Purchasing Power Parity

The Economist presents a yearly comparison of Big Mac prices in various countries and uses this as a proxy measure of the real exchange rate (P/P^*). This may sound ridiculous, but Big Macs are produced and priced locally and include a wide range of labor, capital, and local intermediate inputs. In April 1989 the average price of a Big Mac in the United States was $2.02. The figures below indicate the dollar was undervalued against the won, yen, franc, mark, and pound, while it was overvalued against the Canadian dollar, Hong Kong dollar, Singapore dollar, and Yugoslavian dinar. The dollar subsequently rose in value against the won, the yen, and the European currencies, exactly as Big Mac PPP suggested it would. In Singapore and former Yugoslavia the local currencies are vastly overvalued at the official exchange rate. Black markets arise accepting dollars at close to the real exchange rate.

	P*	P/P*	Market e	Overvaluation or Undervaluation
South Korea	2,400 won	1188	666	−44%
Japan	370 yen	183	133	−27%
France	17.7 francs	8.76	6.37	−27%
Germany	4.30 marks	2.13	1.89	−11%
Britain	1.26 pounds	0.62	0.59	−5%
Canada	2.15 C$	1.06	1.19	13%
Singapore	2.80 S$	1.39	1.96	41%
Yugoslavia	7,000 dinar	3465	9001	160%

5. Controlling the Money Supply

What makes a nation choose a particular growth rate for its money supply, price level, and exchange rate? As Akira Takayama and other monetary economists consistently argue, the money supply is an *endogenous* economic variable. This means money supply growth is the result of economic processes, including central bank activity, commercial bank lending, private spending, and so on.

The primary job of the Federal Reserve Bank and other central banks is to control their nations' money supplies. This is no trivial task. The Great Depression of the 1930s has been labeled the Great Contraction by monetary experts. The money supply of the United States fell suddenly and dramatically by 25%, an unprecedented event. There was little money, as anyone who was around then would tell you. Add to this the Smoot-Hawley Tariff Act, which raised tariffs to an average of 60%, and the recipe for economic disaster is complete.

Optimal control of the money supply is one of the central and most difficult problems of economic policy. Economists at the frontier of the science wrestle with the problem of optimal money supply control using theoretical and empirical tools. Comparative studies of the different growth rates of money and economic processes influencing money supply growth across nations should help supply clues about how to control the supply of money more successfully. A strong competitive system of banking and financial intermediation is essential. The link between government deficits and an increased money supply suggests that a government wanting to control the inflation of its currency should control its spending.

Hume's price specie flow mechanism emphasizes the point that no nation's money supply and prices will be entirely independent of money growth and inflation in the rest of the world. In other words, high inflation in developing nations will influence prices in the industrial nations. A de-cline in the money supply of developed nations will be felt through a reduc-tion in prices and money supply in the developing nations. Issues of money supply and demand are among the most elusive and difficult in economics. As economists sharpen their focus and policymakers use the improving tools, the international monetary system will improve.

EXAMPLE 12.15   The Great Depression or the Great Contraction?

Many economists favor controlling the money supply by some fixed rule that everyone knows. The argument is that such a policy would provide greater price stability and smoother growth. This year's change in the money supply would be targeted at some percentage of last year's eco-nomic growth. There would be no discretionary monetary policy. Bennet McCallum (1989) builds a historical model of the U.S. economy from 1922 to 1941 and tests how such a rule would have performed. The Great Depression was precipitated by extreme protectionism (tariffs of 60%) and reactionary monetary policy (a monetary contraction of 25%). Mc-Callum finds that the U.S. economy would have grown steadily during the Depression years had there been a monetary rule. Output and em-ployment would not have collapsed as they did during the 1930s. The severe monetary contraction would not have occurred with a monetary rule.

EXAMPLE 12.16   The Undervalued and Overvalued Dollar

While purchasing power parity holds across currencies over long pe-riods, at times a currency's exchange market value is out of line with its real exchange rate. These figures illustrate that the dollar has swung around its real value relative to the mark since the late 1970s, as reported in *Economic Commentary*, Cleveland Federal Reserve Bank (1987). While the dollar has not always been at its real exchange rate, it is attracted back to the real exchange site over time. The period of rising overvalua-tion in the early 1980s is generally thought to be due to the high interest rates in the United States and the inflow of foreign investment. Prices in the United States have risen faster than those in Germany because of the higher growth rate in the U.S. money supply.

	1977	78	79	80	81	82	83	84	85	86
e	.42	.45	.55	.59	.54	.44	.39	.36	.32	.38
*P/P**	.40	.41	.41	.43	.45	.47	.48	.50	.51	.53

Problems for Section D

D1.   What difference does it make whether a Japanese or a U.S. citizen buys the U.S. bond issued to finance a government budget deficit?

D2.   If $P = \$1.25$ and $P^* = 2{,}000$ pesos, find the real exchange rate in terms of \$/peso and peso/\$. If the market rate is peso/\$ $= 1{,}500$, which currency is overvalued? Which currency can be expected to appreciate?

D3.   Suppose in Figure 12.7 the foreign money supply M^* increases to 79.8 billion Swiss francs with M at \$1 trillion. Find the relative money supply and the real exchange rate.

CONCLUSION

Issues of international money and finance are currently among the most important in economics. The nations of the world are becoming financially more dependent on one another. The gains from increased international finance are sizeable for all nations, even for developed industrial nations. The basic lesson from international economics is to reap the benefits of specialization according to comparative advantage. Free international financial markets are an important step toward the goal of increased specialization and trade and a healthy international economy.

Many of the ideas you have learned from international economics will crop up during your career and private life. As international trade and finance become more important and integrated in your everyday life, you will find yourself directly involved in business with firms and consumers in other nations. A large share of the goods and services we consume are produced in other nations. You will probably become involved in producing goods and services for export. As you go about your business, ideas from international economics will help you make sound economic decisions.

KEY TERMS

Adjustable peg	Hyperinflation
Bimetal standard	Open market operations
Covered interest arbitrage	Price specie flow mechanism
Fiat currency	Purchasing Power Parity (PPP)
Forward exchange rate	Real Exchange rate
Gold exchange standard	Real interest rate
Gold standard	Special Drawing Rights (SDRs)
Gresham's law	

REVIEW PROBLEMS

1.   Which group in a growing economy, borrowers or lenders, would favor restricting the inflow of foreign investment? How does this apply to the United States?

Is there any evidence that this group in the United States is trying to gain political influence or support?

2. Show what happens in Figure 12.2 if people in the United States start saving more because of tax reductions on income from savings. Explain the international adjustment.

3. If the home nation decides to restrict the inflow of foreign capital in Figure 12.2 with an investment quota of $2 billion, show what happens to interest rates in both nations.

4. Some of the flow of international loanable funds occurs in practice through the sale of the bonds of private firms and government bonds. What difference does it make whether the foreign investors in Figure 12.2 are buying private or government bonds? Is risk a factor?

5. The Mexican government has historically limited the foreign ownership of firms in Mexico to 49%. In other words, the government wants Mexican citizens, on paper at least, to control the firms. If this restriction were lifted, predict the effects on the peso/$ exchange rate.

6. In the example of international inflation, interest rates, and covered interest arbitrage, suppose the German interest rate is 4% and the spot exchange rate is $/mark = 0.30. Find the implied forward exchange rate. Which currency is selling at a discount?

7. Domestic automakers in the United States may not by law use as many foreign components as foreign automakers may use in their plants here. Would this influence the foreign firm's decision to build a plant in the United States? Is this an unfair advantage for the foreign firms?

8. Suppose Nissan builds a new $10 million automobile plant in the United States, raising 50% of its funds through the issue and sale of new stock in the U.S. market. How will the new plant affect the U.S. capital account? How is the U.S. balance of trade ultimately affected?

9. Suppose the supply of loanable funds in the home country decreases in the international financial markets of Figure 12.4. Explain the changes in the loanable funds market and the exchange markets.

10. Starting with the money market in Figure 12.5, show and explain what happens if foreign investors expect the dollar to depreciate over the coming year.

11. The following quote appeared in *Wachovia's Foreign Exchange Review* (January 22, 1990). Explain what is happening using concepts from this chapter:

Last week's news that the U.S. merchandise trade deficit worsened slightly in November pushed the U.S. dollar down a pfennig against the German mark. The currency later recovered in a technical correction of the mark, which was overbought in the euphoria over recent events in Eastern Europe.

12. Suppose the dollar is put on a bimetal standard again. The government defines the dollar as 0.0025 ounce of gold and 0.185 ounce of silver and stands ready to trade paper dollars for either gold or silver. In the market, the price of gold is $393.75 and the price of silver is $5.25/oz. What will arbitragers do? What will happen to the government's stocks of gold and silver? Which is good money and which is bad money: gold, silver, or cash?

13. Does a government deficit have to lead to a trade deficit? Critically examine the argument from the government deficit to the trade deficit.

14. List three reasons why PPP does not hold exactly in practice.
15. Is a nation with a relatively young population more or less likely to have unexpectedly high inflation? What about a nation with a relatively wealthy population? Which country is more likely to have monetary policy that targets a stable price level?

READINGS

Leland Yeager, *International Monetary Relations,* Harper & Row, New York, 1976. A true classic, full of insight.

Robert Baldwin and David Richardson, *International Trade and Finance: Readings,* Little, Brown & Co., Boston, 1986. A collection of good readings on exchange rates, monetary reform, and international debt and finance.

William Cline, *International Debt and the Stability of the World Economy,* Institute for International Economics, 1983. A sound analysis of international debt with a reasoned call for international banking reform.

Gary Smith, *Money, Banking, and Financial Intermediation,* Heath, Lexington, MA, 1991. An excellent introduction to monetary economics, with a lot of attention paid to international influences.

Paul Krugman, *Exchange Rate Instability,* MIT Press, Cambridge, MA, 1989. A short book about the surprising volatility of exchange rates during the 1980s.

Rudiger Dornbusch, *Exchange Rates and Inflation,* MIT Press, Cambridge, MA, 1988. A collection of Dornbusch's important work on exchange rate economics.

"Symposia: New Institutions for Developing Country Debt," *Journal of Economic Perspectives,* Winter 1990. A collection of articles by leading financial economists offering proposals for dealing with debt of the LCDs.

Paul de Graume and Theo Peeters, editors, *The ECU and European Monetary Integration,* Macmillan, New York, 1989. A collection of papers by and discussions among academics, bankers, and financial experts on the evolving European Monetary System.

Ron Jones and Peter Kenen, editors, *Handbook of International Economics, Volume II,* North-Holland, Amsterdam, 1985). Advanced surveys of important areas in international monetary and financial economics.

Central Bank Watch, the American Banker Newsletter Division. A periodical designed to keep international bankers abreast of the actions and policy of central banks around the world.

Hints and Partial Answers for Even-numbered Problems

CHAPTER 1

A2. Domestic supply rises and XD falls.

A4. When demands are identical, the country with the higher supply will be the exporter. When supplies are identical, the country with the lower demand will be the exporter.

C2. XS increases.

D2. The relative price of manufactures is $S/M = 3/2$ in the United States and $S/M = 2/3$ in Canada.

Review Problems

2. Japanese XD will rise.

4. Russian XD will rise.

6. XD^* from the rest of the world will rise.

8. XD from the United States will fall.

10. Venezuelan steel costs $22,500/50 = \$450$, which is less than the price of U.S. steel. Remember Venezuelan exports will equal U.S. imports.

12. If you favor a surplus, make certain your arguments are not mercantilistic.

14. Consider resource availability, technology, and climate.

CHAPTER 2

A2. The equation of the PPF is $220 = 4S + 5M$. The relative price is $M = 4/5S$. Half the labor force (110 workers) is employed in each sector. Outputs are $S = 27.5$ and $M = 22$.

B2. The relative price is $M/S = 5/4$ at home. The foreign country has the comparative advantage in services.

C2. If the foreign country exports good A, $3ew^* < 3w$. If the home country exports good M, $2w < 5ew^*$. The limits to the exchange rate are $0.01 > e > 0.004$.

C4. The foreign PPF connects 76 on the S axis with 57 on the M axis and 114 on the A axis.

D2. The United States has an abundance of skilled labor, which should make skilled labor a relatively cheap input. High-tech goods use a lot of skilled labor in their production and should be relatively cheap when produced in the United States.

Review Problems

2. In Delta, the relative price of services is $M/S = 5/4$. In the home country (Figure 2.1) $M/S = 2/3$. In the foreign country (Figure 2.4) $M/S = 3/2$. The home country would specialize in S, and the foreign country in M. Delta is the intermediate country and might produce both goods.

4. Autarky relative prices are $M/S = 5/6$ in the foreign country and $M/S = 5/4$ at home. The foreign country specializes producing 60 units of S, while the home country produces 65 M. In trade, 30 S exchange for 32.5 M.

6. The foreign country imports 30 M and keeps 30 S. Consumption after trade is worth 55 M. The home country imports 30 S and keeps 35 M. Consumption after trade is worth 72.5 M. In percentage terms, the home country gains more.

8. The foreign wage is $8.80. When $tt = 1.4$, $w = \$24.64$. When $tt = 0.7$, $w = \$12.32$.

10. For the home country to export M and the foreign country to export A, it must be that $(3/5)(w/w^*) > e > (1/2)(w/w^*)$.

12. The ratio of home to foreign labor input in each industry is 5 in M, 1.5 in S, and 1 in A. The foreign country will export A, and the home country will export M.

14. Since $3ew^* > 3w$ and $5w > ew^*$, $0.0267 > e > 0.0053$.

CHAPTER 3

A2. Draw the tangent price line intersecting (90,25). It intersects the M axis at about 105 and the S axis at about 135. The MRT is then $105/135 = 0.78$.

B2. The economy will specialize in M.

C2. Draw a line from the origin through the two PPFs. The slope of the PPF, the MRT, and the relative price of S increase with growth biased toward M. Producing S has a higher opportunity cost with growth biased toward M.

D2. The cost of living would be lower inside an FEZ.

Review Problems

2. The 1950 PPF contains the production point $(M,S) = (225,625)$. The 1986 PPF contains $(M,S) = (625,2200)$. The slope M/S of the PPFs is steeper at the production point in 1986.

4. Your PPF should look like Figure 3.2.

6. The terms of trade are $M/S = 1.2$. The percentage gains from trade are 21%.

8. Growth biased toward the export sector results in more trade and higher income.

10. Try to imagine the differences created by local customs, laws, input costs, and so on.

12. Agricultural output and exports would drop.

CHAPTER 4

A2. Which industry is better able to influence politicians?

B2. With a quota, price rises, quantity demanded is less than with a tariff, and quantity supplied domestically is higher.

C2. When the home relative price equals the international relative price, there is no incentive to trade.

D2. Consider the increasing geographical areas represented by congressmen, senators, and presidents.

Review Problems

2. The 50% tariff raises price inside the country to $1.5 \times \$30 = \$45$. Quantity demanded is then $D = 100 - 45 = 55$. Quantity supplied is $S = -10 + 45 = 35$.

4. The domestic autarky price is found where $D = S$: $100 - P = -10 + P \implies P = \$55$. An 83 1/3% tariff would reach this price.

6. Price with the quota is driven up to $50. Deadweight loss triangles sum to $400. The transfer loss is $100. The total loss of the quota is $500.

8. This VER of 30 units is analyzed like a quota in the shoe market. Imports equal the VER: $D - S = 30 \implies P = \$40$. Deadweight triangles sum to $50. The transfer loss is $300.

10. The economy will specialize in and export M with free trade. A tariff moves the economy away from M production.

12. Protection would probably be more difficult to pass through Congress, since each representative would be less influenced by local interests in small districts.

CHAPTER 5

A2. What happens to the offer curves if the two economies are virtually closed to international trade?

A4. The foreign offer curve falls toward its import axis.

B2. This is similar to Problem A2.

C2. The foreign country reacts to a home tariff of 4% by setting a tariff of 6%. The home country reacts to this foreign tariff by raising its tariff to 5%. The story continues on to point N.

D2. With a 6% real state of return, the price series runs $20, $21.20, $22.47, . . . , $35.82.

Review Problems

2. and **4.** The foreign offer curve falls toward its import axis.

6. A tariff on oil expands domestic extraction up along the domestic supply curve. Domestic oil owners are induced to sell their oil prematurely.

8. The foreign reaction function is vertical at 4%.

10. For two small countries the largest payoffs are in the 0% tariff bracket. Reaction functions lie along either axis. Free trade should be the result.

12. A tariff on manufactured imports will pull the OPEC offer curve in toward the M axis and could achieve the same equilibrium point B.

CHAPTER 6

A2. The MR in manufacturing is $150. The MRP of the first unit of L is $5.25. For the fifth unit of L, MRP $= $2.25.

B2. The unit value isoquant intersects the isocost line where $K = L = 0.2$.

C2. Both countries employ 60 units of K and 30 units of L in services. The home country produces more M, has a higher ratio of M to S output, and exports M if tastes are similar.

D2. If all of the labor endowment is not employed, the economy will produce less of the labor-intensive good and more of the capital-intensive good than it would with full employment.

Review Problems

2. Demand rises in the market for manufacturing capital and falls in the market for service sector capital.

4. The isocost line is $1 = $2L + $3K = $2(0.02) + 3K$, which implies $K = 0.2$. If r falls, K/L rises.

6. To find the unit labor input, $1 = $2(0.35) + 3K$, which implies $K = 0.1$.

8. The home country is labor abundant.

10. The endowment point lies between expansion paths M' and S. Use the relevant expansion paths to complete the parallelogram.

12. If the foreign endowment of labor is $L^* = 100$, the home endowment is $(K,L) = (200,50)$. Endowment differences do not affect the competitive outcome in the factor markets.

14. The home country produces $(M,S) = (400,500)$, while the foreign country produces $(M,S) = (300,600)$. The terms of trade between these points is 1:1. Both countries consume $(M,S) = (350,550)$.

16. This is a piecemeal task, but usually strong factor intensities can be recognized.

CHAPTER 7

A2. Temporary losses can be endured if positive profit is expected for the future. How would potential entrants in the market view the monopolist's loss?

A4. Buyers with higher or more inelastic demand pay a higher price. Price in the foreign market would be lower than price in the home market. Who might claim dumping?

B2. Theory is simplified with aggregation, but information is lost.

C2. If income is not spent, it can be loaned to others.

D2. Protection is not wise economic policy.

Review Problems

2. Price rises to $800. Profit will probably fall. Export revenue falls from $1,200,000 to $800,000.

4. Foreign revenue is $192, and foreign costs are $64. Home revenue is $187.50, and home costs are $75.

6. In the United States, the ratio of labor cost to capital cost is $209/$134 = 1.56. Since w/r = 1.4 in the United States the ratio of labor input to capital input is 1.56/1.4 = 1.11. In Japan the ratio of labor cost to capital cost is $97/$171 = 0.57. Since w/r = 1 in Japan, L/K = 0.57. The United States uses labor-intensive techniques even though it has relatively expensive labor.

8. Dominant firm demand (DF) runs from $10 on the P axis to the demand curve at $3. Foreign fringe supply runs from $3 on the P axis to the demand curve at $10. MC of the domestic firm originally intersects MR at the quantity where P = $7 on the DF curve.

10. The Nash equilibrium is a high output for both Saudi Arabia and Libya. Saudi Arabia can pay Libya foreign aid to remain in the cartel.

12. The PPF expands with a bias toward manufacturing.

CHAPTER 8

A2. Emigration from the foreign country is 8 million.

B2. Incoming labor raises the productivity of capital.

C2. A 5% increase in the endowment of skilled labor would lead to a $8,060 unskilled wage and a $14,940 skilled wage.

D2. Production of high-tech goods and business services, both intensive in skilled labor, will fall.

Review Problems

2. Think of the other influences on the supply and demand for each of the labor types.

4. Current immigrants are mostly unskilled Latin Americans and Asians, settling mostly in the West and Southwest. Production of labor-intensive manufactures will shift to these regions.

6. These are the activities in which U.S. firms have a comparative advantage.

8. Japan has invested in U.S. wholesale and banking industries. This lowers the return to capital and increases the wage of labor in the United States.

10. A new factor represents an increase in the stock of capital in that sector. Use the specific factors model to predict the income redistribution.

12. The answer to this question lies in the fact that Mexico is abundant in unskilled labor and scarce in capital relative to the United states. Canada and the United States have similar factor endowments.

14. Free trade zones encourage foreign investment and promote trade.

CHAPTER 9

A2. Which industry uses standard production techniques? In which industry are firm-specific inputs the most important?

B2. What happens to the pollution tax revenue?

C2. The PPF of the North should be biased toward services. Protection lessens specialization and trade. Free trade would raise wages in the labor-abundant South.

D2. Do the same groups in an economy oppose free trade and free international factor mobility?

Review Problems

2. Each plant would produce the same output.

4. Less television output and higher television prices are the outcome.

6. Any subsidy offered to a foreign MNF would induce domestic firms to ask for similar treatment.

8. The North exports services to the South in exchange for manufactures. Protection improves the terms of trade for the North.

10. An FTA would mean increased exports of manufactures from Mexico to the United States and increased exports of business services and high-tech manufactures from the United States to Mexico. A CU is difficult to envision. A CM would lead to immigration of unskilled Mexican workers to the United States and movement of capital from the United States to Mexico. An EU would force the Mexican government to lower its inflation rate.

12. Consider first the agreement between Mexico and the United States, and separately the agreement between Canada and the United States.

CHAPTER 10

A2. The import elasticity is $15/17 = 0.88$.

B2. The BOT, DI, and KA increase. In the future, *NII* falls.

B4. TS $= -\$24.6$. NII $= \$4.3$. KA $= -\$77.5$.

C2. Which country is growing? Which is stable and wealthy?

D2. PI and KA rise now. What about NII?

Review Problems

2. *XD*, the international price, our level of imports, and import expenditure all move in the same direction.

4. If $\$/M = 5$ and $\$/S = 12.50$, $S/M = (\$/M)/(\$/S) = 0.4$.

6. BOT $= -\$744$, and so on.

8. The investment flows are entered as debits for the United States and credits for Costa Rica in *DI*.

10. Some nations may be in an expansion while others are in a recession. Compare the returns on investments in single countries with diversified investments. Where would you put your money?

12. With income rising in an expansion, import expenditure would rise. Export production, however, could be rising also. No clear link between the business cycle and the BOT exists.

14. Lower tariffs would decrease production in the industry competing with imports. Higher export taxes would decrease production in the export industry.

CHAPTER 11

A2. In the market for German DM, the price of DM should be $/DM. Expectation of lower prices of German imports leads to lower prices of German imports. Will importers in the United States want to rush out and purchase German goods now?

A4. The BGS becomes positive in the contract period and turns negative as changed prices pass through the import and export markets.

B2. The idea is to limit the exchange of foreign currency for DM that occurs when Germany exports.

C2. Demand for yen is upward sloping and less steep than supply.

D2. The real return drops from $103 to $97.

Review Problems

2. The two yen prices are 495 yen and 562.50 yen. The quantities of rice demanded are 4.050 and 3.375 million. The quantities of dollars demanded are $18.225 and $15.187 million. Quantities of yen supplied are 2,004,500,000 and 1,898,437,500.

4. Demand for the export of U.S. telecommunications services falls, as does the supply of European currency.

6. The percentage change in export revenue equals the percentage change in export price plus the percentage change in export quantity. The price of home export falls 5% in the foreign country with the depreciation. The quantity of exports rises by $1.2 \times 5\% = 7\%$. The change in export revenue is thus $-5\% + 7\% = 2\%$. Do similar calculations for import expenditure. The BOT rises in the long run.

8. The central bank is selling assets (foreign currency) that should eventually rise in value.

10. Central banks were buying marks, yen, and pounds.

12. If she is exactly correct, her profit would be $320.51. If won/$ falls to 750, she would lose $512.82.

CHAPTER 12

A2. Interest payments are $160 million.

A4. Home-owned capital abroad increases to $1,543 billion, earning $92.61 billion investment income. Foreign-owned capital at home increases to $1,870.9 billion, earning $93.55 billion investment income. NII is $-$0.94 billion. Problems A3 and A4 reflect NII of the United States in 1989 and 1990.

B2. (a) $/won rises.

(b) $/won rises.

(c) The foreign exchange value of the dollar rises.

(d) $/won falls.

C2. Each bank would want its notes to maintain their value. If a particular bank's notes were overabundant, other banks would not accept them. Competing banks would be very sensitive to prices and supply would slope upward.

D2. The real exchange rate is $P/P^* = 0.000625$. The market rate is $1/1500 = \$/peso = 0.000667$.

Review Problems

2. XD for loanable funds from the United States will fall.

4. Private bonds are riskier than government bonds. Why would anyone buy a private bond?

6. Using the covered interest arbitrage relation, $f = 0.31$.

8. The KA will rise by $5 million. The BOT will ultimately rise.

10. The demand for dollars falls.

12. On the market, the relative price of gold is $\$393.75/\$5.25 = 75 = $ silver/gold. The official relative price of gold is $0.185/0.0025 = 74$. What would you do?

14. Three reasons PPP may not hold are nontraded goods, lack of free trade, and a fixed exchange rate.

References

Alavi, Jafar, & Thompson, Henry. (1988). Toward a theory of free trade zones. *The International Trade Journal, 3*, 203–217.

Amaya, Naohiro. (1988). The Japanese economy in transition: Optimistic about the short term, pessimistic about the long term. *Japan and the World Economy, 1*, 101–111.

American Association of Exporters and Importers. (1990). *US Customs House Guide.* New York: AAEI.

American Federation of Labor and Congress of Industrial Organizations. (1992). *The Pocketbook Issues.* Washington, DC: AFL-CIO.

Aw, Bee Yan, & Roberts, Mark. (1986). Estimating quality change in quota-constrained import markets: The case of US footwear. *Journal of International Economics, 16*, 45–60.

Ayanian, Robert. (1988). Political risk, national defense and the dollar. *Economic Inquiry, 26*, 345–352.

Bailey, Jessica, & Sood, James. (1987). An export strategy for banana producing countries. *The International Trade Journal, 11*, 193–206.

Baldwin, Robert. (1971). Determinants of the commodity structure of US trade. *American Economic Review, 61*, 40–48.

Barro, Robert. (1989). The Ricardian approach to budget deficits. *Journal of Economic Perspectives, 3*, 37–54.

Beeson, Patricia, & Bryan, Michael. (1986). Emerging service economy. *Economic Commentary* (June 15), Federal Reserve Bank of Cleveland.

Branson, William, & Monoyios, Nikolaos. (1977). Factor inputs in US trade. *Journal of International Economics, 7*, 111–131.

Broadberry, S. N. (1987). Purchasing power parity and the pound-dollar rate in the 1930s. *Economica, 54*, 69–78.

Brown, Lynn. (1986). Taking in each other's laundry: The service economy. *New England Economic Review* (July) Federal Reserve Bank of Boston.

Bryan, Michael, & Byrne, Susan. (1990). Don't worry: We'll grow out of it. *Economic Commentary* (October 1) Federal Reserve Bank of Cleveland.

Butcher, Kristin, & Card, David. (1990). Immigration and wages: Evidence from the 1980s. *American Economic Review,* 81, 292–296.

Card, David. (1989). The impact of the Mariel boatlift on the Miami labor market. Working Paper #3069, National Bureau of Economics Research.

Casas, Francisco, & Choi, Kwan. (1985). The Leontief paradox: Continued or Resolved? *Journal of Political Economy,* 93, 610–615.

Childs, Nathan, & Hammig, Michael. (1987). An examination of the impact of real exchange rates on US exports of agricultural commodities. *The International Trade Journal,* 2, 37–54.

Deardorff, Alan, & Stern, Robert. (1983). The economic effect of complete elimination of post-Tokyo Round tariffs. In William Cline (Ed.), *Trade Policy for the 1980s.* Washington, DC: Institute for International Economics, 673–710.

Deardorff, Alan, & Stern, Robert. (1984). *The Structure and Evolution of Recent US Trade Policy.* Chicago: University of Chicago Press.

Delong, Bradford, & Summers, Larry. (1990). Equipment, investment and economic growth. Working Paper #3513, National Bureau of Economic Research.

Dinopoulos, Elias, & Kreinin, Mordechai. (1988). Effects of the US-Japan auto VER on European prices and on US welfare. *The Review of Economics and Statistics,* 70, 484–557.

Dollar, David, & Wolff, Edward. (1988). Convergence of industry labor productivity among advanced economies, 1963–1982. *The Review of Economics and Statistics,* 70, 549–357.

Dominguez, Kathryn. (1992). The role of international organizations in the Bretton Woods system. Working Paper #3951, National Bureau of Economic Research.

Eichengreen, Barry. (1991). Historical research on international lending and debt. *Journal of Economic Perspectives,* 5, 149–169.

European Economic Community (various issues). *Annual Economic Report.* Brussels: EEC.

Federal Reserve Bank of Cleveland (various issues). *Economic Commentary.* Cleveland: FRB.

Federal Reserve Bank of Cleveland (various issues). *Economic Trends.* Cleveland: FRB.

Federal Reserve Bank of New York (various issues). *Quarterly Review.* New York: FRB.

Federal Reserve Bank of St. Louis (various issues). *International Economic Conditions.* St. Louis: FRB.

Federal Reserve Bank of St. Louis (various issues). *National Economic Trends.* St. Louis: FRB.

Federal Reserve Bank of St. Louis (various issues). *Review.* St. Louis: FRB.

Feenstra, Robert. (1988). Gains from trade in differentiated products: Japanese compact trucks. In Robert Feenstra (Ed.), *Empirical Methods for International Trade.* Cambridge: The MIT Press, 119–136.

Frenkel, Jeffrey, & Froot, Kenneth. (1990). Exchange rate forecasting techniques, survey data, and implications for the foreign exchange market. Working Paper #3470, National Bureau of Economic Research.

Froot, Kenneth, & Stein, Jeremy. (1988). Exchange rates and foreign direct investment: An imperfect capital markets approach. Working Paper #2914, National Bureau of Economic Research.

Gardner, Bruce. (1987). Causes of US farm commodity programs. *Journal of Political Economy,* 95, 290–310.

General Agreement on Tariffs and Trade (various issues). *International Trade.* Geneva: The Secretariat of the GATT.

Glesjer, Herbert, Goosens, K., & Vanden, Eede. (1982). Inter-industry versus intra-industry specialization in exports and imports: 1959–1970–1973. *Journal of International Economics,* 12, 353–369.

Griffen, James, & Teece, David. (1982). *OPEC Behavior and World Oil Prices.* London: Allen & Unwin.

Grilli, Vittrio, & Beltratti, Andrea. (1989). US military expenditure and the dollar. *Economic Inquiry,* 27, 737–744.

Grossman, Gene, & Levinshon, Jim. (1989). Import competition and the stock market return to capital. *American Economic Review,* 79, 1065–1087.

Grubel, H.G., & Lloyd, P.J. (1975). *Intraindustry Trade.* London: McMillan UK.

Hakkio, Graig, & Pearce, Douglas. (1985). The reaction of exchange rates to economic news. *Economic Inquiry,* 23, 621–636.

Hickock, Susan. (1985). The consumer cost of US trade restraints. *Quarterly Review* (Summer) Federal Reserve Bank of New York. 1–12.

Hickock, Susan, & Orr, James. (1989). Shifting patterns of US trade with selected developing Asian economies. *Quarterly Review* (Winter) Federal Reserve Bank of New York, 36–47.

Himarios, Daniel. (1989). Do devaluations improve the trade balance? The evidence revisited. *Economic Inquiry,* 27, 143–168.

Huber, Richard. (1971). Effect on prices of Japan's entry into world commerce after 1858. *Journal of Political Economy,* 79, 614–628.

Hufbauer, Gary, Berliner, Diane, & Elliott, Kimberly. (1986). *Trade Protection in the United States: 31 Case Studies.* Washington, DC: Institute for International Economics.

Hunter, Linda. (1990). US Trade Protection: Effects on the Regional Composition of Employment. *Economic Review* (January) Federal Reserve Bank of Dallas.

Hunter, Linda, & Markusen, James. (1988). Per capita income as a determinant of trade. In Robert Feenstra (Ed.) *Empirical Methods for International Trade.* Cambridge: MIT Press, 89–109.

International Monetary Fund (various issues). *Annual Report.* Washington, DC: IMF.

International Monetary Fund (various issues). *Balance of Payments Statistics Yearbook.* Washington, DC: IMF.

International Monetary Fund (various issues). *Direction of Trade Yearbook.* Washington, DC: IMF.

International Monetary Fund (various issues). *IMF Survey.* Washington, DC: IMF.

International Monetary Fund (various issues). *International Financial Statistics.* Washington, DC: IMF.

International Trade Commission. (1983). *An Assessment of US Competitiveness in High Technology Industries.* Washington, DC: U.S. Government Printing Office.

Irwin, Douglas. (1988). The welfare effects of British free trade: Debate and Evidence from the 1840s. *The Journal of Political Economy,* 96, 1142–1164.

Japanese External Trade Organization. (1988). *Handy Facts on US-Japan Economic Relations.* Atlanta: JETRO.

Karrenbrock, Jeffrey. (1990). The internationalization of the beer brewing industry. *Review,* 72 (Nov/Dec) Federal Reserve Bank of St. Louis.

Knetter, Michael. (1989). Price discrimination by US and German exporters. *American Economic Review,* 79, 198–210.

Kreinin, Mordechai. (1984). Wage competitiveness in steel and motor vehicles. *Economic Inquiry,* 22.

Kreinin, Mordechai. (1985). Internal trade and possible restrictions in high-tech products. (January) *Journal of Policy Modeling,* 7, 69–105.

Krugman, Paul. (1987). Is free trade passé? *The Journal of Economic Perspectives,* 1, 131–144.

LaLonde, Robert, & Topel, Robert. (1991). Immigrants in the American labor market: Quality, assimilation, and distributional effects. *American Economic Review,* 81, 297–302.

Leamer, Ed. (1980). The Leontief paradox reconsidered. *Journal of Political Economy,* 88, 495–503.

Leamer, Ed. (1984). *Sources of International Comparative Advantage: Theory and Evidence.* Cambridge: MIT Press.

Leontief, Wassily. (1953). Domestic production and foreign trade: The American capital position re-examined. *Proceedings of the American Philosophical Society,* September, 332–349.

McCallum, Bennet. (1989). Targets, indicators, and instruments of monetary policy. Working Paper, National Bureau of Economic Research.

McDougall, G.D.A. (1951). British and American productivity and comparative costs in international trade. *Economic Journal,* 61.

Marcus, Peter. (1982). *Comparative Circumstances of Major Steel Mills in the US, European Community, and Japan.*

Markusen, James, & Wigle, Randall. (1989). Nash equilibrium tariffs for the United States and Canada: The roles of country size, scale economies, and capital mobility. *The Journal of Political Economy,* 97, 368–386.

Marshall, Alfred. (1926). *The Official Papers of Alfred Marshall.* London: McMillan, 402.

Maskus, Keith. (1985). A test of the Heckscher-Ohlin-Vanek theorem: The Leontief commonplace. *Journal of International Economics,* 15, 201–212.

Mutti, John, & Morichi, Paul. (1983). *Changing Pattern of US Industrial Activity and Comparative Advantage.* Washington, DC: National Science Foundation.

Organization for Economic Cooperation and Development (various issues). *National Accounts.* Paris: OECD.

Organization for Economic Cooperation and Development (various issues). *OECD Outlook.* Paris: OECD.

Ott, Mack. (1989). *International Economic Conditions.* St. Louis: Federal Reserve Bank of St. Louis.

Ray, Ed. (1991). Foreign takeovers and new investments in the US. *Contemporary Policy Issues,* 9, 59–71.

Reynolds, Clark, & McClery, Robert. (1988). The political economy of immigration law: Impact of Simpson-Rodino on the United States and Mexico. *The Journal of Economic Perspectives,* 2, 117–131.

Ruffin, Roy. (1988). The missing link: The Ricardian approach to the factor endowments theory of trade. *American Economic Review,* 78, 759–772.

Ruffin, Roy, & Rassekh, Farhad. (1987). The role of foreign direct investment in US capital outflows. *American Economic Review,* 76, 1126–1130.

Shapiro, Matthew. (1987). Are cyclical fluctuations in productivity due more to supply shocks or demand shocks? Working Paper #2147, National Bureau of Economic Research.

Smith, Adam. (1776). *The Wealth of Nations.* New York: Penguin Classics.

Smith, Alasdair, & Venables, Anthony. (1988). Completing the internal market in the European community: Some industry simulations. *European Economic Review,* 32, 1501–1526.

Stern, Robert, & Maskus, Keith. (1981). Determinants of the structure of US foreign trade, 1958–76. *Journal of International Economics,* 11, 207–224.

Tarr, David, & Morker, Morris. (1987). Aggregate costs to the United States of tariffs and quotas on imports. In Dominick Salvatore (Ed.), *The New Protectionist Threat to World Welfare*. Amsterdam: North Holland, 216–229.

Thompson, Henry. (1986). Free trade and factor price polarization. *European Economic Review, 30,* 419–425.

Thompson, Henry. (1987). Do tariffs protect specific factors? *Canadian Journal of Economics,* 22, 406–412.

Thompson, Henry. (1991). Simulating a multifactor general equilibrium model of production and trade. *International Economic Journal,* 4, 21–34.

United Nations. (1987). *Foreign Direct Investment, the Service Sector, and International Banking.* New York: UN.

United Nations. (1989). *Foreign Direct Investment and Transnational Corporations in Services.* New York: UN.

United Nations (various issues). *International Trade Statistics Yearbook.* New York: UN.

United Nations (various issues). *Yearbook of Industrial Statistics.* New York: UN.

United Nations (various issues). *Yearbook of International Trade Statistics.* New York: UN.

United Nations Conference on Trade and Development (various issues). *Trade and Development Report.* New York: UNCTAD.

U.S. Congressional Budget Office. (1988). *The Economic and Budget Outlook.* Washington, DC: US Government Printing Office.

U.S. Department of Commerce (various issues). *Economic Report of the President.* Washington, DC: US Government Printing Office.

U.S. Department of Commerce. (1987). *Fixed Peproducible Wealth in the US, 1925–85.* Washington, DC: US Government Printing Office.

U.S. Department of Commerce (various issues). *Survey of Current Business.* Washington, DC: US Government Printing Office.

U.S. Department of Commerce, Bureau of the Census (various issues). *Census of Population.* Washington, DC: US Government Printing Office.

U.S. Department of Commerce, Bureau of the Census (various issues). *Statistical Abstract of the United States.* Washington, DC: US Government Printing Office.

U.S. Immigration and Naturalization Service (various issues). *Statistical Yearbook of the Immigration and Naturalization Service.* Washington, DC: US Government Printing Office.

Walter, Ingo. (1983). Structural adjustment and trade policy in the international steel industry. In William Cline (Ed.), *Trade Policy in the 1980s.* Washington, DC: Institute for International Economics, 483–525.

Weidenbaum, Murray & Munger, Tracy. (1983). Protection at any price? *Regulation* (July/August), 14–18.

Wickham, Elizabeth, & Thompson, Henry. (1989). An empirical analysis of intra-industry trade and multinational firms. In P.K.M. Tharakan & Jacob Kol (Eds.) *Intra-industry Trade: Theory, Evidence, and Extensions.* New York: Macmillan, 121–144.

Wong, Kar-Yui, (1983). International factor mobility and volume of trade: An empirical study. In Robert Feenstra (Ed.), *Empirical Methods for International Trade.* Cambridge: The MIT Press, 231–250.

World Bank. (1989). *Emerging Markets Factbook.* New York: World Bank.

World Bank (various issues). *World Development Report.* New York: World Bank.

World Competitiveness Report (various issues). Geneva: The Foundation.

Yeats, A.J. (1974). Effective tariff protection in the United States, the European Community, and Japan. *The Quarterly Review of Economics and Business,* 14, 41–50.

Author Index

Adams, John, 36
Alavi, Jafar, 104
Allen, William, 72
Amaya, Naohiro, 345
Arpan, Jeffrey, 327
Aw, Bee Yan, 125–126
Ayanian, Robert, 424

Bailey, Jessica, 241
Baldwin, Robert, 139, 204, 206, 444
Barro, Robert, 357, 363
Bastiat, Frederic, 131
Baumens, Luc, 323
Beeson, Patricia, 83
Belassa, Bela, 323
Beltrati, Andrea, 424
Bergsten, Fred, 364
Berliner, Diane, 126, 317
Bhagwati, Jagdish, 139
Blair, Roger, 253
Bourdet, Yves, 254
Broadberry, S.N., 438
Brock, William, 131, 139
Brown, Lynn, 83
Bryan, Michael, 83, 346
Buchanan, James, 328
Butcher, Kristin, 286
Byrne, Susan, 346

Card, David, 285, 286
Carrol, John, 327
Casas, Francisco, 206

Cassing, Jim, 327
Chaswick, Barry, 294
Chiang, Alpha, 173
Childs, Nathan, 392
Choi, Kwan, 206
Cline, William, 139, 364, 444
Coase, Richard, 296
Crookell, Harold, 328

Deardorff, Alan, 113, 159, 208, 216, 283
deGraume, Paul, 444
DeLong, Bradford, 99
Destler, I.M., 139
Dinopoulos, Elias, 125
Dollar, David, 213
Dominguez, Kathryn, 384
Dornbusch, Rudiger, 364, 398, 411, 444

Easton, Stephen, 328
Eichengreen, Barry, 412
Einzig, Paul, 401
Elliott, Kimberly, 126, 317

Feenstra, Robert, 91
Feldstein, Martin, 383
Fischer, Irving, 393
Frankel, Jacob, 383
Frenkel, Jeffrey, 387
Frieden, Jeffrey, 328
Friedman, Milton, 386, 436
Froot, Kenneth, 387, 423

Subject Index